W9-ARM-261

Microsoft Excel 2019
Pivot Table Data Crunching

Bill Jelen
Michael Alexander

Microsoft Excel 2019 Pivot Table Data Crunching

Published with the authorization of Microsoft Corporation by:

Pearson Education, Inc.

Copyright © 2019 by Pearson Education, Inc.

All rights reserved. Printed in the United States of America. This publication is protected by copyright, and permission must be obtained from the publisher prior to any prohibited reproduction, storage in a retrieval system, or transmission in any form or by any means, electronic, mechanical, photocopying, recording, or likewise. For information regarding permissions, request forms, and the appropriate contacts within the Pearson Education Global Rights & Permissions Department, please visit www.pearsoned.com/permissions/. No patent liability is assumed with respect to the use of the information contained herein. Although every precaution has been taken in the preparation of this book, the publisher and author assume no responsibility for errors or omissions. Nor is any liability assumed for damages resulting from the use of the information contained herein.

ISBN-13: 978-1-5093-0724-1

ISBN-10: 1-5093-0724-9

Library of Congress Control Number: 2018963618

Printed in the United States of America

1 18

Trademarks

Microsoft and the trademarks listed at http://www.microsoft.com on the "Trademarks" webpage are trademarks of the Microsoft group of companies. All other marks are property of their respective owners.

Warning and Disclaimer

Every effort has been made to make this book as complete and as accurate as possible, but no warranty or fitness is implied. The information provided is on an "as is" basis. The authors and the publisher shall have neither liability nor responsibility to any person or entity with respect to any loss or damages arising from the information contained in this book.

Special Sales

For information about buying this title in bulk quantities, or for special sales opportunities (which may include electronic versions; custom cover designs; and content particular to your business, training goals, marketing focus, or branding interests), please contact our corporate sales department at corpsales@pearsoned.com or (800) 382-3419.

For government sales inquiries, please contact governmentsales@pearsoned.com.

For questions about sales outside the U.S., please contact intlcs@pearson.com.

Editor-in-Chief: Brett Bartow

Executive Editor: Loretta Yates

Sponsoring Editor: Charvi Arora

Managing Editor: Sandra Schroeder

Senior Project Editor: Tracey Croom

Project Editor: Charlotte Kughen

Copy Editor: Kitty Wilson

Indexer: Ken Johnson

Proofreader: Paula Lowell

Technical Editor: Bob Umlas

Publishing Coordinator: Cindy Teeters

Cover Designer: Twist Creative, Seattle

Compositor: Bronkella Publishing LLC

Graphics: TJ Graham Art

To Ashvina Sharma and his team at Microsoft. Thanks for Pivot Table Defaults!

—Bill Jelen

To my 12 fans at datapigtechnologies.com.

—Mike Alexander

Contents at a Glance

Contents

Chapter 4   Grouping, sorting, and filtering pivot data   75

Chapter 10   Unlocking features with the Data Model and Power Pivot

Chapter 14 Advanced pivot table tips and techniques 387

Acknowledgments

Thanks to Mike Alexander for being my coauthor on the five previous editions of this book. At Microsoft, thanks to the Excel team for always being willing to answer questions about various features. At MrExcel.com, thanks to an entire community of people who are passionate about Excel. Finally, thanks to my wife, Mary Ellen, for her support during the writing process.

—Bill Jelen

Thanks to Bill Jelen for deciding to coauthor this book with me many editions ago. His knowledge of Excel still blows me away to this day. My deepest thanks to the professionals at Pearson Education for all the hours of work put into bringing this book to life. Thanks also to Bob Umlas, whose technical editing has helped us make numerous improvements to the examples and text in this book. Finally, a special thank you goes to the wife and kids for putting up with all the time I spent locked away on this project.

—Mike Alexander

About the Authors

Bill Jelen, Excel MVP and the host of MrExcel.com, has been using spreadsheets since 1985, and he launched the MrExcel.com website in 1998. Bill was a regular guest on *Call for Help* with Leo Laporte and has produced more than 2,200 episodes of his daily video podcast, Learn Excel from MrExcel. He is the author of 57 books about Microsoft Excel and writes the monthly Excel column for *Strategic Finance* magazine. Before founding MrExcel.com, Bill spent 12 years in the trenches, working as a financial analyst for the finance, marketing, accounting, and operations departments of a $500 million public company. He lives in Merritt Island, Florida, with his wife, Mary Ellen.

Mike Alexander is a Microsoft Certified Application Developer (MCAD) and author of several books on advanced business analysis with Microsoft Access and Excel. He has more than 15 years of experience consulting and developing Office solutions. Mike has been named a Microsoft MVP for his ongoing contributions to the Excel community.

Introduction

The pivot table is the single most powerful tool in all of Excel. Pivot tables came along during the 1990s, when Microsoft and Lotus were locked in a bitter battle for dominance of the spreadsheet market. The race to continually add enhanced features to their respective products during the mid-1990s led to many incredible features, but none as powerful as the pivot table.

With a pivot table, you can transform one million rows of transactional data into a summary report in seconds. If you can drag a mouse, you can create a pivot table. In addition to quickly summarizing and calculating data, pivot tables enable you to change your analysis on the fly by simply moving fields from one area of a report to another.

No other tool in Excel gives you the flexibility and analytical power of a pivot table.

What you will learn from this book

It is widely agreed that close to 60 percent of Excel customers leave 80 percent of Excel untouched—that is, most people do not tap into the full potential of Excel's built-in utilities. Of these utilities, the most prolific by far is the pivot table. Despite the fact that pivot tables have been a cornerstone of Excel for almost 20 years, they remain one of the most underutilized tools in the entire Microsoft Office suite.

Having picked up this book, you are savvy enough to have heard of pivot tables—and you have perhaps even used them on occasion. You have a sense that pivot tables provide a power that you are not using, and you want to learn how to leverage that power to increase your productivity quickly.

Within the first two chapters, you will be able to create basic pivot tables, increase your productivity, and produce reports in minutes instead of hours. Within the first seven chapters, you will be able to output complex pivot reports with drill-down capabilities and accompanying charts. By the end of the book, you will be able to build a dynamic pivot table reporting system.

What is new in Excel 2019's pivot tables

Luckily, Microsoft continues to invest heavily in business intelligence (BI), and pivot tables are the front end that let you access the new features. Some of the features added to Excel 2019 pivot tables include the following:

- You can specify default settings for all future pivot tables. If you want all pivot tables to start in Tabular layout instead of Compact layout, you can specify this. Do you prefer Classic layout or do you always replace empty cells with zero? Visit File, Options, Data, Pivot Table Defaults to change the settings for all future pivot tables.

- The automatic date grouping introduced in Excel 2016 pivot tables can now be turned off. The setting is found in File, Options, Data. The feature became unpopular after the release of Excel 2016.

- Pivot tables will be doing more summing and less counting. Previously, if you had a column with revenue and a few empty cells, the pivot table would choose to Count instead of Sum. In Excel 2019, a mix of empty cells and numeric cells will be treated like a numeric column and will default to Sum instead of Count.

- Power Pivot is now included in all Windows versions of Excel 2019 and Office 365. During the tenure of Office 2013–2016, only parts of Power Pivot were available. Although some of the Power Pivot functionality was available if you chose Add This Data To The Data Model while creating a pivot table, you can now access the Power Pivot tab in the ribbon. This allows you to create and view relationships in a diagram view. You can choose to sort one column by another column.

- With Power Pivot in Excel 2019, your pivot tables benefit from any new functions added to the DAX formula language. If you ever wanted to do Median in a pivot table or even report Text fields in the Values area, the new DAX functions such as MEDIAN and CONCATENATEX allow this to happen.

- Power View is being de-emphasized. Microsoft is replacing Power View with Power BI Desktop. You will find it difficult to locate the Power View icons in Excel 2019.

- If you are using Office 365, you will have access to the Insights command on the Insert tab. This command uses artificial intelligence to suggest 30 interesting charts or pivot tables that can be created from your data.

Case Study: Life Before Pivot Tables

Say that your manager asks you to create a one-page summary of a sales database. He would like to see total revenue by region and product. Suppose you do not know how to use pivot tables. You will have to use dozens of keystrokes or mouse clicks to complete this task.

First, you have to build the outline of the report:

1. Copy the Product column to a blank section of the worksheet.

2. Select Data, Remove Duplicates to eliminate the duplicates.

3. Delete the Product heading.

4. Copy the unique list of products and then use Paste Special Transpose to turn the list sideways.

5. Delete the vertical list of products.

6. Copy the Region column to a blank section of the worksheet.

7. Select Data, Remove Duplicates to remove the duplicates.

8. Delete the Region heading.

9. Cut and paste the products so they appear to the left of and below the regions.

At this point, with 27 mouse clicks or keystrokes, you've built the shell of the final report, but there are no numbers inside yet (see Figure I-1).

	B	C	D	E	F	G	H	I	J	K	L	M	N	O
1	Region	Product	Date	Customer	Quantity	Revenue	COGS	Profit			Gizmo	Gadget	Widget	Doodads
2	Midwest	Gizmo	1/1/2023	Ford	1000	22810	10220	12590		Midwest				
3	Northeast	Gadget	1/2/2023	Verizon	100	2257	984	1273		Northeast				
4	South	Gizmo	1/4/2023	Valero Energy	400	9152	4088	5064		South				
5	Midwest	Gadget	1/4/2023	Cardinal Health	800	18552	7872	10680		West				
6	West	Gadget	1/7/2023	Wells Fargo	1000	21730	9840	11890		Total				
7	Midwest	Widget	1/7/2023	General Motors	400	8456	3388	5068						

FIGURE I-1 It took 27 clicks to get to this point.

Next, you need to build the relatively new SUMIFS function to total the revenue for the intersection of a region and product. As shown in Figure I-2, the formula =SUMIFS($G$2:$G$564,$C$2:$C$564,L$1,$B$2:$B$564,$K2) does the trick. It takes 52 characters plus the Enter key to finish the formula, but I managed to enter the formula in 36 clicks or keystrokes by using some clever navigation tricks I've learned over the years.

	K	L	M	N	O	P	Q
		Gizmo	Gadget	Widget	Doodads	Total	
	Midwest	=SUMIFS($G$2:$G$564,$C$2:$C$564,L$1,$B$2:$B$564,$K2)					
	Northeast						
	South						
	West						
	Total						

FIGURE I-2 If this were the year 2006, the SUMIFS function would have been an uglier SUMPRODUCT function.

If you are adept at using the Fill handle, you need just two more mouse drags to copy the formula to the rest of the table.

Enter the heading Total for the total row and for the total column. You can do this in nine keystrokes if you type the first heading, press Ctrl+Enter to stay in the same cell, and then use Copy, select the cell for the second heading, and use Paste.

If you select K1:P6 and press Alt+= (that is, Alt and the equal sign key), you can add the total formula in three keystrokes.

With this method, which takes 77 clicks or keystrokes, you end up with a nice summary report, as shown in Figure I-3. If you could pull this off in 5 or 10 minutes, you would probably be fairly proud of your Excel prowess; there are some good tricks among those 77 operations.

K	L	M	N	O	P
	Gizmo	Gadget	Widget	Doodads	Total
Midwest	652651	544772	537965	6036	1741424
Northeast	751724	714009	620019	38860	2124612
South	918588	839551	844186	0	2602325
West	70057	65382	75349	28663	239451
Total	2393020	2163714	2077519	73559	6707812

FIGURE I-3 A mere 77 operations later, you have a summary report.

You hand the report to your manager. Within a few minutes, he comes back with one of the following requests, which will certainly cause a lot of rework:

- Could you put products down the side and regions across the top?

- Could you show me the same report for only the manufacturing customers?

- Could you show profit instead of revenue?

- Could you copy this report for each of the customers?

Invention of the pivot table

When the actual pivot table was invented is in dispute. The Excel team coined the term *pivot table*, which appeared in Excel in 1993. However, the concept was not new. Pito Salas and his team at Lotus were working on the pivot table concept in 1986 and released Lotus Improv in 1991. Before then, Javelin offered functionality similar to that of pivot tables.

The core concept behind a pivot table is that the data, formulas, and data views are stored separately. Each column has a name, and you can group and rearrange the data by dragging field names to various positions on the report.

Case Study: Life After Pivot Tables

Say that you're tired of working so hard to remake reports every time your manager wants a change. You're in luck: You can produce the same report as in the last case study but use a pivot table instead. Excel 2019 offers you 10 thumbnails of recommended pivot tables to get you close to the goal. Follow these steps:

1. Click the Insert tab of the ribbon.

2. Click Recommended PivotTables. The first recommended item is Revenue By Region (see Figure I-4).

FIGURE I-4 The first recommended pivot table is as close as you will get to the required report.

3. Click OK to accept the first pivot table.

4. Drag the Product field from the PivotTable Fields list to the Columns area (see Figure I-5).

FIGURE I-5 To finish the report, drag the Product heading to the Columns area.

5. Clear Field Headers on the right side of the ribbon.

With just five clicks of the mouse, you have the report shown in Figure I-6.

Sum of Revenue	Product				
Region	Doodads	Gadget	Gizmo	Widget	Grand Total
West	28663	65382	70057	75349	239451
Midwest	6036	544772	652651	537965	1741424
Northeast	38860	714009	751724	620019	2124612
South	0	839551	918588	844186	2602325
Grand Total	73559	2163714	2393020	2077519	6707812

FIGURE I-6 It took five clicks to create this report.

In addition, when your manager comes back with a request like the ones near the end of the prior case study, you can easily use the pivot table to make the changes. Here's a quick overview of the changes you'll learn to make in the chapters that follow:

- Could you put products down the side and regions across the top? (This change will take you 10 seconds: Drag Product to Rows and Region to Columns.)

- Could you show me the same report for only the manufacturing customers? (15 seconds: Select Insert Slicer, Sector; click OK; click Manufacturing.)

- Could you show profit instead of revenue? (10 seconds: Clear the check box for Revenue, select the check box for Profit.)

- Could you copy this report for each of the customers? (30 seconds: Move Customer to Report Filter, open the tiny drop-down menu next to the Options button, choose Show Report Filter Pages, click OK.)

Excel 2019 versus Office 365

The title of this book says Excel 2019. In reality, no one should be buying Office 2019. Instead, it is likely that you are renting Office 365. As of May 2018, Office 2019 and Office 365 were nearly equivalent.

Here's why the authors hope that you did not purchase Office 2019: The features in Office 2019 will not change. The features in Office 365 will constantly evolve and improve. The people who have been using Office 365 have enjoyed the new features described earlier in this chapter one to two years before the people who purchased Office 2019.

Because the title of this book says Excel 2019, the screenshots show the Excel 2019 ribbon. However, anyone using Office 365 will have a new look to the ribbon.

Microsoft reduced the number of colors in the Office 365 ribbon. The selected Ribbon tab is now underlined instead of being a different color. Compare the Excel 2019 Insert tab in Figure I-7 with the Office 365 Insert tab in Figure I-8.

FIGURE I-7   The Excel 2019 ribbon is very similar to the Excel 2016 ribbon.

FIGURE I-8 The Office 365 ribbon introduced in the summer of 2018 uses a new font and fewer colors.

Microsoft is experimenting with a new ribbon that goes back to a single row like the Office 2013 menus. As of the summer of 2018, that new ribbon will debut with Outlook and Excel Online and only for Office 365 customers. It remains to be seen if that ribbon ever makes it to the desktop version of Excel.

New features in Office 365

After this book is printed, the Excel team will release new features for Excel. Anyone with an Office 365 subscription will receive the new features. People with Excel 2019 will not get the new features.

For any new features introduced to Office 365, the owners of Excel 2019 will have to purchase Office 2022 in order to access those features.

But what is even worse, some features introduced will be marked as Office 365 Exclusive features. Those features will never be available to customers who buy the perpetual versions of Office, such as Office 2016, Office 2019, or Office 2022.

One such feature introduced in early 2018 is the Insights feature. This feature will send up to 250,000 cells of your data to a Microsoft server where artificial intelligence looks for trends in your data. The first few results from Insights are very similar to the Insert Recommended PivotTable logic introduced in Excel 2013 and shown previously in Figure I-4.

However, if you click the More link, Insights often provides two to three dozen suggestions. Most suggestions will insert a pivot table and a pivot chart. In the first preview of Insights, Excel will look for: rank, evenness, trend, composite signal, attribution, outstanding top two, monotonicity (always increasing or always decreasing), and unimodality (having a single peak data point).

When I used the data set from this Introduction with Insights in Office 365, Microsoft suggested 32 different possible results. One is shown in Figure I-9.

FIGURE I-9 Excel used artificial intelligence to spot these outliers.

If you regularly purchased every new version of Office, it will cost less to rent Office 365 at $10 a month than to pay $399 for the perpetual version of Office every 36 months. Office 365 offers more features than Excel 2019. Unless your buying pattern is to only buy every second or third version of Office, upgrading to Office 365 makes sense.

Who this book is for

This book is a comprehensive-enough reference for hard-core analysts yet relevant to casual users of Excel.

We assume that you are comfortable navigating in Excel and that you have some large data sets that you need to summarize.

How this book is organized

The bulk of the book covers how to use pivot tables in the Excel user interface. Chapter 10, "Unlocking features with the Data Model and Power Pivot," delves into the Power Pivot window. Chapter 13, "Using VBA to create pivot tables," describes how to create pivot tables in Excel's powerful VBA macro language. Anyone who has a firm grasp of basics such as preparing data, copying, pasting, and entering simple formulas should not have a problem understanding the concepts in this book.

About the companion content

The download files for this book include all of the data sets used to produce the book, so you can practice the concepts in the book. You can download this book's companion content from the following page:

MicrosoftPressStore.com/Excel2019PivotTable/downloads

System requirements

You need the following software and hardware to build and run the code samples for this book:

Microsoft Excel running on a Windows computer. (Yes, Excel runs on an iPad, on an Android tablet, and in a browser, but none of those are going to support creation of pivot tables anytime soon.) For people using Excel on a Mac, some of the basic pivot table concepts will apply. Power Query and Power Pivot will not run on a Mac.

Support and feedback

The following sections provide information on errata, book support, feedback, and contact information.

Stay in touch

Let's keep the conversation going! We're on Twitter:

http://twitter.com/MicrosoftPress

http://twitter.com/MrExcel

Errata, updates, and book support

We've made every effort to ensure the accuracy of this book and its companion content. You can access updates to this book—in the form of a list of submitted errata and their related corrections—at the following page:

MicrosoftPressStore.com/Excel2019PivotTable/errata

If you discover an error that is not already listed, please submit it to us at the same page.

If you need additional support, email Microsoft Press Book Support at microsoftpresscs@pearson.com.

Please note that product support for Microsoft software and hardware is not offered through the previous addresses. For help with Microsoft software or hardware, go to http://support.microsoft.com.

CHAPTER 1

Pivot table fundamentals

In this chapter, you will:

- Learn why you should use a pivot table
- Learn when to use a pivot table
- Get to know the anatomy of a pivot table
- Peek at pivot tables behind the scenes
- Examine pivot table backward compatibility

Imagine that Excel is a large toolbox that contains different tools at your disposal. The pivot table is essentially one tool in your Excel toolbox. If a pivot table were indeed a physical tool that you could hold in your hand, a kaleidoscope would most accurately represent it.

When you look through a kaleidoscope at an object, you see that object in a different way. You can turn the kaleidoscope to move around the details of the object. The object itself doesn't change, and it's not connected to the kaleidoscope. The kaleidoscope is simply a tool you use to create a unique perspective on an ordinary object.

Think of a pivot table as a kaleidoscope that is pointed at a data set. When you look at a data set through a pivot table, you can see details in the data that you might not have noticed before. Furthermore, you can turn your pivot table to see your data from different perspectives. The data set itself doesn't change, and it's not connected to the pivot table. The pivot table is simply a tool you use to create a unique perspective on your data.

A pivot table enables you to create an interactive view of your data set, called a *pivot table report*. With a pivot table report, you can quickly and easily categorize your data into groups, summarize large amounts of data into meaningful information, and perform a variety of calculations in a fraction of the time it takes by hand. But the real power of a pivot table report is that you can use it to interactively drag and drop fields within your report, dynamically change your perspective, and recalculate totals to fit your current view.

Why you should use a pivot table

As a rule, what you do in Excel can be split into two categories:

- Calculating data
- Shaping (formatting) data

Although many built-in tools and formulas facilitate both tasks, using a pivot table is often the fastest and most efficient way to calculate and shape data. Let's look at one simple scenario that illustrates this point.

You have just given your manager some revenue information by month, and he has predictably asked for more information. He adds a note to the worksheet and emails it back to you. As you can see in Figure 1-1, he would like you to add a line that shows credits by month.

	A	B	C	D	E	F	G	H
1		Jan	Feb	Mar	Apr	May	Jun	Jul
2	Revenues	66,427,076	68,619,453	69,444,496	67,669,316	69,572,075	67,196,220	66,884,7
3	Please add a "credits" line and show the amount of credits for each month							

FIGURE 1-1 Your manager predictably changes his request after you provide the first pass of a report.

To meet this new requirement, you run a query from your legacy system that provides the needed data. As usual, the data is formatted specifically to make you suffer. Instead of data by month, the legacy system provides detailed transactional data by day, as shown in Figure 1-2.

	A	B	C
1	Document Number	In Balance Date	Credit Amount
2	D29210	01/03/12	(34.54)
3	D15775	01/03/12	(313.64)
4	D46035	01/03/12	(389.04)
5	D45826	01/03/12	(111.56)
6	D69172	01/03/12	(1,630.25)
7	D25388	01/03/12	(3,146.22)
8	D49302	01/03/12	(1,217.37)
9	D91669	01/03/12	(197.44)
10	D14289	01/03/12	(33.75)
11	D38471	01/03/12	(6,759.20)
12	D18645	01/03/12	(214.54)
13	D63807	01/03/12	(19.58)
14	D77943	01/03/12	(136.17)
15	D37446	01/03/12	(128.36)

FIGURE 1-2 The data from the legacy system is by day instead of by month.

Your challenge is to calculate the total dollar amount of credits by month and shape the results into an extract that fits the format of the original report. The final extract should look like the data shown in Figure 1-3.

Jan	Feb	Mar	Apr	May	Jun	Jul
-3,695,319	-3,698,537	-3,833,977	-3,624,967	-3,800,526	-3,603,367	-3,746,754

FIGURE 1-3 Your goal is to produce a summary by month and transpose the data to a horizontal format.

Creating the extract manually would take 18 mouse clicks and 3 keystrokes:

- **Format dates to month:** 3 clicks

- **Create subtotals:** 4 clicks

- **Extract subtotals:** 6 clicks, 3 keystrokes

- **Transpose vertical to horizontal:** 5 clicks

In contrast, creating the extract with a pivot table would take 9 mouse clicks:

- **Create the pivot table report:** 5 clicks

- **Group dates into months:** 3 clicks

- **Transpose vertical to horizontal:** 1 click

Both methods give you the same extract, which you can paste into the final report, as shown in Figure 1-4.

⊿	A	B	C	D	E	F	G	H
1		Jan	Feb	Mar	Apr	May	Jun	Jul
2	Revenues	66,427,076	68,619,453	69,444,496	67,669,316	69,572,075	67,196,220	66,884,77
3	Credits	-3,695,319	-3,698,537	-3,833,977	-3,624,967	-3,800,526	-3,603,367	-3,746,754
4	Adjusted Revenues	62,731,757	64,920,916	65,610,519	64,044,349	65,771,549	63,592,853	63,138,01

FIGURE 1-4 After adding credits to the report, you can calculate net revenue.

Using a pivot table to accomplish the task just described not only cuts down the number of actions by more than half but also reduces the possibility of human error. In addition, using a pivot table allows for the quick-and-easy shaping and formatting of the data.

This example shows that using a pivot table is not just about calculating and summarizing your data. Pivot tables can often help you do a number of tasks faster and better than conventional functions and formulas. For example, you can use pivot tables to instantly transpose large groups of data vertically or horizontally. You can use pivot tables to quickly find and count the unique values in your data. You can also use pivot tables to prepare your data to be used in charts.

The bottom line is that pivot tables can help you dramatically increase your efficiency and decrease your errors on a number of tasks you might have to accomplish with Excel. Pivot tables can't do everything for you, but knowing how to use just the basics of pivot table functionality can take your data analysis and productivity to a new level.

When to use a pivot table

Large data sets, ever-changing impromptu data requests, and multilayered reporting are absolute productivity killers if you have to tackle them by hand. Going into hand-to-hand combat with one of these not only is time-consuming, but also opens up the possibility of an untold number of errors in your analysis. So how do you recognize when to use a pivot table before it's too late?

Generally, a pivot table would serve you well in any of the following situations:

- You have a large amount of transactional data that has become increasingly difficult to analyze and summarize in a meaningful way.

- You need to find relationships and groupings within your data.

- You need to find a list of unique values for one field in your data.

- You need to find data trends using various time periods.

- You anticipate frequent requests for changes to your data analysis.

- You need to create subtotals that frequently include new additions.

- You need to organize your data into a format that's easy to chart.

Anatomy of a pivot table

Because the anatomy of a pivot table is what gives it its flexibility and, indeed, its ultimate functionality, truly understanding pivot tables would be difficult without understanding their basic structure.

A pivot table is composed of four areas:

- Values area

- Rows area

- Columns area

- Filters area

The data you place in these areas defines both the utility and appearance of the pivot table.

You will go through the process of creating a pivot table in the next chapter, and the following sections prepare you for that by taking a closer look at the four pivot table areas and the functionality around them.

Values area

The *Values area* is shown in Figure 1-5. It is a large rectangular area below and to the right of the headings. In this example, the Values area contains a sum of the Revenue field.

	A	B	C	D	E	F
1	REGION	(All)				
2						
3	Sum of REVENUE	MONTH				
4	MODEL	January	February	March	April	May
5	2500P	$33,073	$29,104	$25,612	$22,538	$19,834
6	3002C	$35,880	$31,574	$27,785	$24,451	$21,517
7	3002P	$90,258	$79,427	$69,896	$61,508	$54,127
8	4055T	$13,250	$11,660	$10,261	$9,030	$7,946
9	4500C	$100,197	$88,173	$77,593	$68,281	$60,088

FIGURE 1-5 The heart of the pivot table is the Values area. This area typically includes a total of one or more numeric fields.

The Values area is the area that calculates. This area is required to include at least one field and one calculation on that field. The data fields you drop here are those you want to measure or calculate. The Values area might include Sum Of Revenue, Count Of Units, and Average Of Price.

It is also possible to have the same field dropped in the Values area twice but with different calculations. For example, a marketing manager might want to see Minimum Of Price, Average Price, and Maximum Of Price.

Rows area

The *Rows area*, as shown in Figure 1-6, is composed of the headings that go down the left side of the pivot table.

	A	B	C	D	E	F
1	REGION	(All) ▾				
2						
3	REVENUE	MONTH ▾				
4	MODEL ▾	January	February	March	April	May
5	2500P	$33,073	$29,104	$25,612	$22,538	$19,834
6	3002C	$35,880	$31,574	$27,785	$24,451	$21,517
7	3002P	$90,258	$79,427	$69,896	$61,508	$54,127
8	4055T	$13,250	$11,660	$10,261	$9,030	$7,946
9	4500C	$100,197	$88,173	$77,593	$68,281	$60,088

FIGURE 1-6   The headings down the left side of the pivot table make up the Rows area of the pivot table.

Dropping a field into the Rows area displays the unique values from that field down the rows of the left side of the pivot table. The Rows area typically has at least one field, although it is possible to have no fields. The example earlier in the chapter where you needed to produce a one-line report of credits is an example where there are no row fields.

The types of data fields you would drop here include those you want to group and categorize—for example, Products, Names, and Locations.

Columns area

The *Columns area* is composed of headings that stretch across the top of columns in the pivot table. In the pivot table in Figure 1-7, the Month field is in the Columns area.

Dropping fields into the Columns area would display your items in column-oriented perspective. The Columns area is ideal for showing trending over time. The types of data fields you would drop here include those you want to trend or show side by side—for example, Months, Periods, and Years.

	A	B	C	D	E	F
1	REGION	(All) ▾				
2						
3	Sum of REVENUE	MONTH ▾				
4	MODEL ▾	January	February	March	April	May
5	2500P	$33,073	$29,104	$25,612	$22,538	$19,834
6	3002C	$35,880	$31,574	$27,785	$24,451	$21,517
7	3002P	$90,258	$79,427	$69,896	$61,508	$54,127
8	4055T	$13,250	$11,660	$10,261	$9,030	$7,946
9	4500C	$100,197	$88,173	$77,593	$68,281	$60,088

FIGURE 1-7 The Columns area stretches across the top of the columns. In this example, it contains the unique list of months in your data set.

Filters area

The *Filters area* is an optional set of one or more drop-downs at the top of the pivot table. In Figure 1-8, the Filters area contains the Region field, and the pivot table is set to show all regions.

	A	B	C	D	E	F
1	REGION	(All) ▾				
2						
3	Sum of REVENUE	MONTH ▾				
4	MODEL ▾	January	February	March	April	May
5	2500P	$33,073	$29,104	$25,612	$22,538	$19,834
6	3002C	$35,880	$31,574	$27,785	$24,451	$21,517
7	3002P	$90,258	$79,427	$69,896	$61,508	$54,127
8	4055T	$13,250	$11,660	$10,261	$9,030	$7,946
9	4500C	$100,197	$88,173	$77,593	$68,281	$60,088

FIGURE 1-8 Filter fields are great for quickly filtering a report. The Region drop-down menu in cell B1 enables you to print this report for one particular region manager.

Dropping fields into the Filters area would enable you to filter the data items in your fields. The Filters area is optional and comes in handy when you need to filter your results dynamically. The types of data fields you would drop here include those you want to isolate and focus on—for example, Regions, Line Of Business, and Employees.

Pivot tables behind the scenes

It's important to know that pivot tables come with a few file space and memory implications for your system. To get an idea of what this means, let's look at what happens behind the scenes when you create a pivot table.

When you initiate the creation of a pivot table report, Excel takes a snapshot of your data set and stores it in a *pivot cache*, which is a special memory subsystem where your data source is duplicated for quick access. Although the pivot cache is not a physical object you can see, you can think of it as a container that stores a snapshot of the data source.

Caution   Any changes you make to your data source are not picked up by your pivot table report until you take another snapshot of the data source or "refresh" the pivot cache. Refreshing is easy: Simply right-click the pivot table and click Refresh Data. You can also click the large Refresh button on the Options tab.

The benefit of working against the pivot cache and not your original data source is optimization. Any changes you make to the pivot table report, such as rearranging fields, adding new fields, or hiding items, are made rapidly and with minimal overhead.

Pivot table backward compatibility

Almost each new version of Excel introduces pivot table features that will not work in previous editions of Excel.

Slicers created in Excel 2010 or later will not work in Excel 2007 or earlier. Timelines created in Excel 2013 will not work in Excel 2010 or earlier.

There were major pivot table limit increases in Excel 2007. Table 1-1 illustrates the differences. If you have a pivot table with more than 256 columns or any other limit shown in the table, it cannot be used in Excel 2003.

TABLE 1-1   Pivot table limitations

Category	.xls Files	.xlsx Files
Number of row fields	Limited by available memory	1,048,576 (could be limited by available memory)
Number of column fields	256	16,384
Number of page fields	256	16,384
Number of data fields	256	16,384
Number of unique items in a single pivot field	32,500	1,048,576 (could be limited by available memory)
Number of calculated items	Limited by available memory	Limited by available memory
Number of pivot table reports on one worksheet	Limited by available memory	Limited by available memory

A word about compatibility

Excel provides a tool to identify any problems with backward compatibility. To check compatibility, select File, Info, Check For Issues, Check Compatibility, as shown in Figure 1-9.

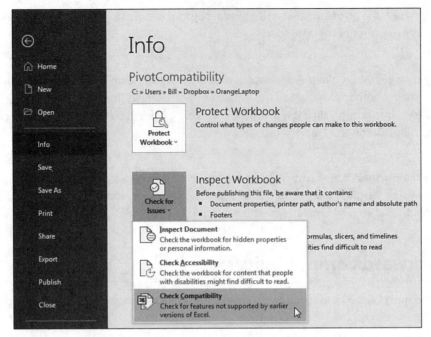

FIGURE 1-9 Open the Check For Issues drop-down menu to find the Check Compatibility tool.

In the Compatibility Checker dialog box, use the Select Versions To Show drop-down menu to choose which version of Excel your coworkers might be using. The dialog box shows issues with your pivot tables (see Figure 1-10). Anything that is labeled "Significant Loss Of Functionality" should be corrected. Anything labeled "Minor Loss Of Fidelity" refers to formatting issues.

FIGURE 1-10 The Compatibility Checker alerts you about any compatibility issues before you save to a previous version of Excel.

Next steps

In the next chapter, you'll learn how to prepare your data to be used by a pivot table. Chapter 2, "Creating a basic pivot table," also walks through creating your first pivot table report using the Create Pivot-Table dialog box.

Creating a basic pivot table

In this chapter, you will:

- Learn how to create a basic pivot table
- Understand the Recommended PivotTable and the Ideas features
- Use slicers
- Keep up with changes in the data source
- Share the pivot cache
- Save time with new PivotTable tools

When you have a family portrait taken, the photographer takes time to make sure that the lighting is right, the poses are natural, and everyone smiles his or her best smile. This preparation ensures that the resulting photo is effective in its purpose.

When you create a pivot table report, you're the photographer, taking a snapshot of your data. By taking time to make sure your data looks its best, you can ensure that your pivot table report is effective in accomplishing the task at hand.

One of the benefits of working in a spreadsheet is that you have the flexibility of laying out your data to suit your needs. Indeed, the layout you choose depends heavily on the task at hand. However, many of the data layouts used for presentations are not appropriate when used as the source data for a pivot table report.

> **Tip** As you read the following pages, which discuss preparing your data, keep in mind that pivot tables have only one hard rule pertaining to the data source: The data source must have column headings, which are labels in the first row of the data that describe the information in each column. Without column headings, you cannot create a pivot table report.

However, just because a pivot table report is created successfully does not mean that it's effective. A host of things can go wrong as a result of bad data preparation—from inaccurate reporting to problems with grouping and sorting.

Let's look at a few of the steps you can take to ensure that you end up with a viable pivot table report.

Ensuring that data is in a Tabular layout

A perfect layout for the source data in a pivot table is a Tabular layout. In Tabular layout, there are no blank rows or columns. Every column has a heading. Every field has a value in every row. Columns do not contain repeating groups of data.

Figure 2-1 shows an example of data structured properly for a pivot table. There are headings for each column. Even though the values in D2:D6 are all the same model, the model number appears in each cell. Month data is organized down the page instead of across the columns.

	A	B	C	D	E	F
1	REGION	MARKET	STORE	MODEL	MONTH	REVENUE
2	North	Great Lakes	65061011	4055T	April	$2,354
3	North	Great Lakes	65061011	4055T	February	$3,040
4	North	Great Lakes	65061011	4055T	January	$3,454
5	North	Great Lakes	65061011	4055T	March	$2,675
6	North	Great Lakes	65061011	4055T	May	$2,071
7	North	New England	2105015	2500P	April	$11,851
8	North	New England	2105015	2500P	February	$15,304
9	North	New England	2105015	2500P	January	$17,391
10	North	New England	2105015	2500P	March	$13,468
11	North	New England	2105015	2500P	May	$10,429
12	North	New England	22022012	3002C	April	$256
13	North	New England	22022012	3002C	February	$330
14	North	New England	22022012	3002C	January	$375
15	North	New England	22022012	3002C	March	$300

FIGURE 2-1 This data is structured properly for use as a pivot table source.

Tabular layouts are *database centric*, meaning you would most commonly find these types of layouts in databases. These layouts are designed to store and maintain large amounts of data in a well-structured, scalable format.

> **Tip** You might work for a manager who demands that the column labels be split into two rows. For example, he might want the heading Gross Margin to be split, with Gross in row 1 and Margin in row 2. Because pivot tables require a unique heading one row high, your manager's preference can be problematic. To overcome this problem, start typing your heading; for example, type **Gross**. Before leaving the cell, press Alt+Enter and then type **Margin**. The result is a single cell that contains two lines of data.

Avoiding storing data in section headings

Examine the data in Figure 2-2. This spreadsheet shows a report of sales by month and model for the North region of a company. Because the data in rows 2 through 24 pertains to the North region, the author of the worksheet entered the title North as a single cell in C1. This approach is effective for display of the data, but it's not effective for a pivot table data source.

Also, in Figure 2-2, the author was very creative with the model information. The data in rows 2 through 6 applies to Model 2500P, so the author entered this value once in A2 and then applied a fancy vertical format combined with Merge Cells to create an interesting look for the report. Again, although this is a cool format, it is not useful for pivot table reporting.

	A	B	C	
1			**North**	
2		January	33,073	
3		February	35,880	
4	Model 2500P	March	90,258	
5		April	13,250	
6		May	100,197	
8		January	29,104	
9		February	31,574	
10	Model 3002P	March	79,427	
11		April	11,660	
12		May	88,173	
14		January	35,880	
15		February	25,612	
16	Model 4055T	March	27,785	
17		April	69,896	
18		May	10,261	
20		January	33,073	
21		February	25,612	
22	Model 4500T	March	27,785	
23		April	69,896	
24		May	10,261	

FIGURE 2-2   Region and model data are not formatted properly in this data set.

In addition, the worksheet in Figure 2-2 is missing column headings. You can guess that column A is Model, column B is Month, and column C is Sales, but for Excel to create a pivot table, this information must be included in the first row of the data.

Avoiding repeating groups as columns

The format shown in Figure 2-3 is common. A time dimension is presented across several columns. Although it is possible to create a pivot table from this data, this format is not ideal.

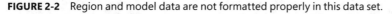

	A	B	C	D	E	F	G	H
1								
2	North	MODEL	JANUARY	FEBRUARY	MARCH	APRIL	MAY	JUNE
3		4054T	$2,789	$2,454	$2,160	$1,901	$1,673	$1,472
4		4500C	$32,605	$28,692	$25,249	$22,219	$19,553	$17,207
5		3002P	$52,437	$46,145	$40,607	$35,734	$31,446	$27,673
6		2500P	$17,391	$15,304	$13,468	$11,851	$10,429	$9,178
7		4055T	$2,468	$2,172	$1,911	$1,682	$1,480	$1,302
8		3002C	$375	$330	$290	$256	$225	$198

FIGURE 2-3   This matrix format is common but not effective for pivot tables. The Month field is spread across several columns of the report.

The problem is that the headings spread across the top of the table pull double duty as column labels and actual data values. In a pivot table, this format would force you to manage and maintain six fields, each representing a different month.

Eliminating gaps and blank cells in the data source

Delete all empty columns within your data source. An empty column in the middle of your data source causes your pivot table to fail on creation because the blank column, in most cases, does not have a column name.

Delete all empty rows within your data source. Empty rows may cause you to inadvertently leave out a large portion of your data range, making your pivot table report incomplete.

Fill in as many blank cells in your data source as possible. Although filling in cells is not required to create a workable pivot table, blank cells are generally errors waiting to happen. A good practice is to represent missing values with some logical missing value code wherever possible.

> **Note** Although eliminating gaps and blank cells might seem like a step backward for those of you who are trying to create a nicely formatted report, it pays off in the end. When you are able to create a pivot table, there will be plenty of opportunities to apply some pleasant formatting.

> **Note** In Chapter 3, "Customizing a pivot table," you'll discover how to apply styles formatting to your pivot tables.

Applying appropriate type formatting to fields

Formatting fields appropriately helps you avoid a whole host of possible issues, from inaccurate reporting to problems with grouping and sorting.

Make certain that any fields to be used in calculations are explicitly formatted as a number, currency, or any other format appropriate for use in mathematical functions. Fields containing dates should also be formatted as any one of the available date formats.

Summary of good data source design

The attributes of an effective tabular design are as follows:

- The first row of your data source is made up of field labels or headings that describe the information in each column.

- Each column in your data source represents a unique category of data.

- Each row in your data source represents individual items in each column.

- None of the column names in your data source double as data items that will be used as filters or query criteria (that is, names of months, dates, years, names of locations, or names of employees).

Case study: Cleaning up data for pivot table analysis

The worksheet shown in Figure 2-4 is a great-looking report. However, it cannot be effectively used as a data source for a pivot table. Can you identify the problems with this data set?

	A	B	C	D	E	F
1	Sector	Customer		Jan	Feb	Mar
2	Associations	IMA Houston Chapter		0	0	0
3		Association for Computers & Taxation		30094	0	0
4						
5	Consultants	Andrew Spain Consulting		89581	114596	112012
6		Data2Impact		21730	0	0
7		Cambia Factor		0	0	0
8		Fintega Financial Modelling		21015	0	0
9		Excelerator BI		0	0	0
10		Construction Intelligence & Analytics, Inc.		22104	0	2484
11						
12	Professional	Serving Brevard Realty		0	7152	24224
13		WM Squared Inc.		0	0	0
14		Juliet Babcock-Hyde CPA, PLLC		0	0	0
15						
16	Retail	Hartville MarketPlace and Flea Market		34132	40608	12427

FIGURE 2-4 Someone spent a lot of time formatting this report to look good, but what problems prevent it from being used as a data source for a pivot table?

These are the three problems with the data set and the fixes needed to get the data set pivot table ready:

- There are blank rows and columns in the data. Column C should be deleted. The blank rows between sectors (such as rows 4, 11, and 15) also should be deleted.

- Blank cells present the data in an outline format. The person reading this worksheet would probably assume that cells A6:A10 fall into the Consultants sector. These blank cells need to be filled in with the values from above.

- The worksheet presents the data for each month in several columns (one column per month). Columns D through G need to be reformatted as two columns. Place the month name in one column and the units for that month in the next column.

Cleaning this data used to require some VBA code or a bunch of manual steps in Excel. The new Get & Transform tools that debuted in Excel 2019 will make it very easy to clean this data. Follow these steps:

1. Select the entire range of data. In the sample file, it would be A1:O33.

2. Click in the Name box and type a one-word name, such as UglyData. Press Enter to name the range.

3. On the Data tab, in the Get & Transform Data group, choose From Table/Range (see Figure 2-5).

FIGURE 2-5 Originally called Power Query, but later rebranded as Get & Transform Data, these new tools that appeared on the Data tab in 2019 are amazing.

The Power Query Editor will open. Notice you have ribbon tabs for Home, Transform, Add Column, and View. Follow these steps in the Power Query Editor.

4. The formerly blank column C now has a heading of Column 3. Click that heading and choose Remove Columns from the Home tab (see Figure 2-6).

FIGURE 2-6 The Power Query Editor offers tools that are often better than their Excel equivalents.

5. Click the heading for Customer. Choose Home, Remove Rows, Remove Blank Rows (see Figure 2-7).

FIGURE 2-7 Deleting blank rows is a built-in command in Power Query.

6. Select the Sector column header. From the Transform tab, choose Fill, Down (see Figure 2-8). This amazing command will replace all the null cells with the value from above.

FIGURE 2-8 Fill Down replaces Home, Find & Select, Go To Special, Blanks, OK, =A2, and Ctrl+Enter. It is far easier to remember one command instead of many obscure commands strung together.

7. Select the headings for both Sector and Customer. Open the Unpivot Columns drop-down menu on the Transform tab. Choose Unpivot Other Columns. The result is shown in Figure 2-9. Pause for a moment to admire the sheer simplicity of steps 5 through 7. Those are three new tools that replace far more complicated tasks in Excel. Although the data could be returned to Excel at this point, there are a few simple clean-up steps left.

FIGURE 2-9 At this point, you could return the data to Excel for pivoting.

8. Right-click the Value column. Choose Rename. Type a heading of **Revenue**.

9. Open the Filter drop-down menu for Revenue. Unselect 0 to remove all the zero values.

10. Select the Attribute Column. On the Add Column tab, choose Column From Example. The first row in your data might read "Apr." If this data applies to the year 2022, type a value of **Apr 1, 2022** in the new column. Power Query fills in the remaining rows and offers a heading of Merged. Click OK (see Figure 2-10).

FIGURE 2-10 Add Column From Example is similar to Flash Fill in Excel, but it actually creates a formula that can be re-used.

11. Right-click the heading for the new Merged column. Choose Rename. Type a heading of **Date**.

12. With the Date column selected, click the Transform tab. Open the Date Type drop-down menu and choose Date. The text dates are converted to real dates.

13. You no longer need the month abbreviations shown in the Attribute column. Choose the Attribute column and then Home, Remove Columns. Before you return to Excel, look at the right side of the Power Query window for the list of Applied Steps. This is the world's greatest Undo stack. You can click any step and see what the data looked like at that point. If you made a mistake several steps ago, you can click that step and make a correction. If you want to be more impressed, select the View tab and choose Advanced Editor. All that code is a programming language called "M." By doing steps 4 through 13, you successfully wrote a program that can be reused the next time you download similar data from the I.T. department.

14. Select Home, Close, and Load. Your original data stays on Sheet1. A new Sheet2 is added to the workbook (see Figure 2-11). The cleaned data is narrow and tall. In general, narrow and tall data sets are better for pivoting.

	A	B	C	D
1	Sector	Customer	Revenue	Date
2	Associations	IMA Houston Chapter	14004	4/1/2022
3	Associations	IMA Houston Chapter	4060	6/1/2022
4	Associations	IMA Houston Chapter	18072	9/1/2022
5	Associations	IMA Houston Chapter	15104	11/1/2022
6	Associations	Association for Computers & Taxation	30094	1/1/2022
7	Associations	Association for Computers & Taxation	4270	8/1/2022
8	Consultants	Andrew Spain Consulting	89581	1/1/2022
9	Consultants	Andrew Spain Consulting	114596	2/1/2022
10	Consultants	Andrew Spain Consulting	112012	3/1/2022
11	Consultants	Andrew Spain Consulting	67408	4/1/2022
12	Consultants	Andrew Spain Consulting	84383	5/1/2022
13	Consultants	Andrew Spain Consulting	10741	6/1/2022

FIGURE 2-11 Just 11 steps in Power Query quickly cleaned the ugly data.

Not only is Power Query fast, it makes it easy to redo the data cleansing. Go back to Sheet1 and change any number in the original data. Go to Sheet2. Expand the Queries & Connections panel so you can see the Refresh icon on the far right of the UglyData query. Click Refresh. Power Query repeats all the steps and updates the result.

How to create a basic pivot table

Now that you have a good understanding of the importance of a well-structured data source, let's walk through creating a basic pivot table.

Note The sample data set used throughout this book is available for download at www.microsoftpressstore.com/Excel2019PivotTable/downloads.

To ensure that the pivot table captures the range of your data source by default, click any single cell in your data source. Next, select the Insert tab and find the Tables group. In the Tables group, select PivotTable and then choose PivotTable from the drop-down menu. Figure 2-12 demonstrates how to start a pivot table.

FIGURE 2-12 Start a pivot table by selecting PivotTable from the Insert tab.

Choosing these options activates the Create PivotTable dialog box, shown in Figure 2-13.

FIGURE 2-13 The Create PivotTable dialog box.

Tip You can also press the shortcut to start a pivot table: Press and release Alt, press and release N, and then press and release V.

As you can see in Figure 2-13, the Create PivotTable dialog box asks you only two fundamental questions:

- Where's the data that you want to analyze?

- Where do you want to put the pivot table?

Here's how you handle these two sections of the dialog box:

- **Choose The Data That You Want To Analyze**—In this section, you tell Excel where your data set is. You can specify a data set that is located within your workbook, or you can tell Excel to look for an external data set. As you can see in Figure 2-13, Excel is smart enough to read your data set and fill in the range for you. However, you always should take note of the range Excel selects to ensure that you are capturing all your data.

- **Choose Where You Want The PivotTable Report To Be Placed**—In this section, you tell Excel where you want your pivot table to be placed. This is set to New Worksheet by default, meaning that your pivot table will be placed in a new worksheet within the current workbook. You will rarely change this setting because there are relatively few times you'll need your pivot table to be placed in a specific location.

Note Note the presence of another option in the Create PivotTable dialog box shown in Figure 2-13: the Add This Data To The Data Model option. You would select this option if you were trying to consolidate multiple data sources into a single pivot table.

The Add This Data To The Data Model option is covered in detail in Chapter 7, "Analyzing disparate data sources with pivot tables," and in Chapter 10, "Unlocking features with the Data Model and Power Pivot."

In this chapter, we'll keep it basic by covering the steps to create a pivot table from using a single source, which means you can ignore this particular option.

After you have answered the two questions in the Create PivotTable dialog box, simply click the OK button. At this point, Excel adds a new worksheet that contains an empty pivot table report. Next to that is the PivotTable Fields list, shown in Figure 2-14. This pane helps you build your pivot table.

FIGURE 2-14 You use the PivotTable Fields list to build a pivot table.

Caution The icons for Columns and Rows in Figure 2-14 are reversed. A summer intern at Microsoft inadvertently reversed the icons several versions ago and no one noticed. After Bill pointed this out to the correct project manager, they pledged to restore the icons to the correct location. The dark gray portion of the icon is supposed to show where the data will be displayed when you drop a field here. Any data dropped in the Columns area will display across the top of the report (as illustrated in the icon currently in the Rows area). It feels sort of goofy to show the wrong icons in this book on pivot tables, but that's the way it is appearing to us at press time.

Finding the PivotTable Fields List

The PivotTable Fields list is your main work area in Excel 2019. This is the place where you add fields and make changes to a pivot table report. By default, this pane pops up when you place your cursor anywhere inside a pivot table. However, if you explicitly close this pane, you override the default and essentially tell the pane not to activate when you are in the pivot table.

If clicking on the pivot table does not activate the PivotTable Fields list, you can manually activate it by right-clicking anywhere inside the pivot table and selecting Show Fields list. You can also click anywhere inside the pivot table and then choose the large Fields List icon on the Analyze tab under PivotTable Tools in the ribbon.

Adding fields to a report

You can add the fields you need to a pivot table by using the four "areas" found in the PivotTable Fields list: Filters, Columns, Rows, and Values. These areas, which correspond to the four areas of the pivot table, are used to populate your pivot table with data:

Note   Review Chapter 1, "Pivot table fundamentals," for a refresher on the four areas of a pivot table.

- **Filters**—Adding a field to the Filters area enables you to filter on its unique data items. In previous versions of Excel, this area was known as the Report Filters area.

- **Columns**—Adding a field into the Columns area displays the unique values from that field across the top of the pivot table.

- **Rows**—Adding a field into the Rows area displays the unique values from that field down the left side of the pivot table.

- **Values**—Adding a field into the Values area includes that field in the Values area of your pivot table, allowing you to perform a specified calculation using the values in the field.

Fundamentals of laying out a pivot table report

Now let's pause a moment and go over some fundamentals of laying out a pivot table report. This is generally the point where most new Excel customers get stuck. How do you know which field goes where?

Before you start dropping fields into the various areas, answer two questions:

- "What am I measuring?"

- "How do I want to see it?"

The answer to the first question tells you which fields in your data source you need to work with, and the answer to the second question tells you where to place the fields.

Say that in this case, you want to measure the dollar sales by region. This automatically tells you that you need to work with the Sale Amount field and the Region field. How do you want to see it? You want regions to go down the left side of the report and the sales amount to be calculated next to each region.

To achieve this effect, you need to add the Region field to the Rows area and add the Sale Amount field to the Values area.

Find the Region field in the PivotTable Fields list, and select the check box next to it. As you can see in Figure 2-15, not only is the field automatically added to the Rows area, but your pivot table is updated to show the unique region names.

FIGURE 2-15   Select the check box next to the Region field to automatically add that field to your pivot table.

Now that you have regions in your pivot table, it's time to add in the dollar sales. To do that, simply find the Sale Amount field and select the check box next to it. As Figure 2-16 illustrates, the Sale Amount field is automatically added to the Values area, and your pivot table report now shows the total dollar sales for each region.

Row Labels	Sum of Sale Amount
CANADA	3748101.15
Midwest	7232896.2
North	2377761.45
Northeast	7639710
South	101671133.8
Southeast	21599862.2
Southwest	8441594.5
West	11853624
Grand Total	164564683.3

PivotTable Fields

Choose fields to add to report:

Search

- ☐ Product Name
- ☐ Quantity
- ☑ Sale Amount
- ☐ Equipment Cost

MORE TABLES...

Drag fields between areas below:

▼ FILTERS

▥ COLUMNS

☰ ROWS
Region ▼

Σ VALUES
Sum of Sale Amount ▼

☐ Defer Layout Update   UPDATE

FIGURE 2-16 Select the check box next to the Sale Amount field to add data to your pivot table report.

At this point, you have already created your first pivot table report!

How Does Excel Know Where Your Fields Go?

As you've just experienced, the PivotTable Fields list interface enables you to add fields to your pivot table by simply selecting the check box next to each field name. Excel automatically adds the selected fields to the pivot table. But how does Excel know which area to use for a field you select? The answer is that Excel doesn't really know which area to use, but it makes a decision based on data type. Here's how it works: When you select a check box next to a field, Excel evaluates the data type for that field. If the data type is numeric, Excel places the field into the Values area; otherwise, Excel places the field into the Rows area. This placement obviously underlines the importance of correctly assigning the data types for your fields.

Note   Blank cells in your numeric columns previously caused the column to be treated as text. A change in early 2018 for Office 365 subscribers changed this behavior. Now, a column with a mix of numbers and empty cells will be treated as values and the field will go to the Values area with a default calculation of Sum.

If you have someone who clears out cells by mashing down the spacebar several times instead of using the Delete key, Excel will treat those spaces as text. A mix of numbers and text in a column will cause Excel to default to counting the column instead of summing.

Adding layers to a pivot table

Now you can add another layer of analysis to your report. Say that now you want to measure the amount of dollar sales each region earned by product category. Because your pivot table already contains the Region and Sales Amount fields, all you have to do is select the check box next to the Product Category field. As you can see in Figure 2-17, your pivot table automatically added a layer for Product Category and refreshed the calculations to include subtotals for each region. Because the data is stored efficiently in the pivot cache, this change took less than a second.

Row Labels	Sum of Sale Amount
⊟ CANADA	3748101.15
Bar Equipment	35975.25
Commercial Appliances	71272.1
Concession Equipment	205874.6
Fryers	129636.2
Ovens and Ranges	1183772.75
Refrigerators and Coolers	1728600.95
Warmers	392969.3
⊟ Midwest	7232896.2
Bar Equipment	63713
Commercial Appliances	199187.5
Concession Equipment	197173.7
Fryers	164789
Ovens and Ranges	2428904.45
Refrigerators and Coolers	3259003.9
Warmers	920124.65
⊟ North	2377761.45
Bar Equipment	20184.9
Commercial Appliances	43965.15
Concession Equipment	102245
Fryers	69059.25
Ovens and Ranges	932126.4

PivotTable Fields

Choose fields to add to report:

Search

✓ Product Category
☐ Product Name
☐ Quantity
✓ Sale Amount
☐ Equipment Cost

Drag fields between areas below:

▼ FILTERS   ▦ COLUMNS

▦ ROWS   Σ VALUES
Region   Sum of Sale Amount
Product Category

☐ Defer Layout Update   UPDATE

FIGURE 2-17 Without pivot tables, adding layers to analyses requires hours of work and complex formulas.

Rearranging a pivot table

Suppose that the view you've created doesn't work for your manager. He wants to see Product Categories across the top of the pivot table report. To make this change, simply drag the Product Category field from the Rows area to the Columns area, as illustrated in Figure 2-18.

> **Note**   You don't have to move your fields into an area to be able to drag them around. You can actually drag fields directly from the list of fields in the PivotTable Fields list to the desired area. You can also move a field into an area by using that field's context menu: Click the black triangle next to the field name and then select the desired area.

FIGURE 2-18 Rearranging a pivot table is as simple as dragging fields from one area to another.

The report is instantly restructured, as shown in Figure 2-19.

Sum of Sale Amount	Column Labels			
Row Labels	Bar Equipment	Commercial Appliances	Concession Equipment	Fryers
CANADA	35975.25	71272.1	205874.6	129636.2
Midwest	63713	199187.5	197173.7	164789
North	20184.9	43965.15	102245	69059.25
Northeast	68407.1	285103.35	258557.4	190152.4
South	1191742.35	5923096.6	6971902.45	2420745
Southeast	283902.15	1525894.3	1569948.6	452579.35
Southwest	73528.5	289526.5	355845.45	268554.85
West	68684.65	296291.55	422201.2	276443.05
Grand Total	1806137.9	8634337.05	10083748.4	3971959.1

FIGURE 2-19 Your product categories are now column oriented.

Longing for Drag-and-Drop Functionality?

In Excel 2003 and previous versions, you had the ability to drag and drop fields directly onto the pivot table layout. This functionality is allowed only within the PivotTable Fields list (dragging into areas). However, Microsoft has provided the option of working with a classic pivot table layout, which enables the drag-and-drop functionality.

To activate the classic pivot table layout, right-click anywhere inside the pivot table and select Table Options. In the Table Options dialog box, select the Display tab and select the check box next to Classic PivotTable Layout, as demonstrated in Figure 2-20. Click the OK button to apply the change.

FIGURE 2-20 Select the check box next to Classic PivotTable Layout.

At this point, you can drag and drop fields directly onto your pivot table layout.

If you always want your pivot tables to be in Classic layout, follow these steps:

1. Select File, Options. A new Data category is added along the left panel starting in 2017 for Office 365 subscribers.

2. In the Data category, the first setting is Make Changes To The Default Layout Of Pivot-Tables. Click Edit Default Layout.

3. The Edit Default Layout dialog box offers a few common choices. Apparently, Classic layout did not make it to the top few choices. Click the PivotTable Options button in the Edit Default Layout dialog box. You will see a dialog box similar to Figure 2-20. Choose the Display tab and the Classic PivotTable Layout. Click OK three times to close each of the open dialog boxes. All future pivot tables can be built in Classic mode.

Creating a report filter

You might be asked to produce different reports for particular regions, markets, or products. Instead of building separate pivot table reports for every possible analysis scenario, you can use the Filter field to create a report filter. For example, you can create a region-filtered report by simply dragging the Region field to the Filters area and the Product Category field to the Rows area. This way, you can analyze one particular region at a time. Figure 2-21 shows the totals for just the North region.

FIGURE 2-21 With this setup, you not only can see revenues by product clearly, but also can click the Region drop-down menu to focus on one region.

Understanding the Recommended PivotTable and the Ideas features

With Excel 2013, Microsoft introduced a feature called Recommended PivotTables. You can find this feature next to the PivotTable icon on the Insert tab (refer to Figure 2-12).

This feature is Microsoft's way of getting you up and running with pivot tables by simply creating one for you. The idea is simple: Place your cursor in a tabular range of data and then click the Recommended PivotTables icon. Excel shows you a menu of pivot tables it thinks it can create for you, based on the data in your range (see Figure 2-22). When you find one that looks good to you, click it and then click OK to have Excel create it.

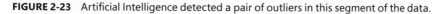

Recommended PivotTables

Sum of Sale Amount by R...

Row Labels	Sum of Sale Amount
CANADA	213571.55
Midwest	374606.05
North	155956.45
Northeast	490494.5
South	5533150.3
Southeast	903569.55
Southwest	414911.85
West	529474.75
Grand Total	8615735

Sum of Equipment Cost b...

Row Labels	Sum of Equipment Cost
AL	67302.5537
AR	6838.3701
AZ	101991.0822
CA	435126.7119
CO	24919.1515
FL	421407.4.77
GA	2032003.374
IA	19676.0494

Sum of Sale Amount by S...

Row Labels	Sum of Sale Amount
CANADA	213571.55
NB	71005.2
NS	18037
ON	63623.35
PE	119
PQ	60707
Midwest	374606.05
AR	13923

Sum of Equipment Cost, ...

Row Labels	Sum of Equipment Cost	Sum c
CANADA	120250.5643	

Sum of Sale Amount by Region

⚠ The preview was generated based on a sample of the source data and may not match the end result.

Row Labels	Sum of Sale Amount
CANADA	213571.55
Midwest	374606.05
North	155956.45
Northeast	490494.5
South	5533150.3
Southeast	903569.55
Southwest	414911.85
West	529474.75
Grand Total	**8615735**

Blank PivotTable   Change Source Data...   OK   Cancel

FIGURE 2-22 Choose from the menu of recommended pivot tables to have Excel automatically create a pivot table for you.

New Ideas feature uses artificial intelligence

The Recommended PivotTable algorithm is looking for columns with headings of Revenue, Profit, or Sales. If it cannot find any of those, it will use the last numeric column in the data set.

The new Ideas feature uses artificial intelligence to analyze up to 250,000 cells of your data. Ideas initially offers descriptive pivot tables like those produced in Recommended PivotTables, but then it offers far more advanced analyses. While the Recommended PivotTables produces 10 choices, the Ideas feature often produces over 30 choices. Figures 2-23 and 2-24 show some results available from Ideas.

For 'Internet Order: True', 'Sale Amount' has outliers at 'Order Date': 03/01/25 and 06/28/25.

(Thousands)

300
250
200
150
100
50
0

Order Date

+ Insert PivotChart   Is this helpful?

FIGURE 2-23 Artificial Intelligence detected a pair of outliers in this segment of the data.

FIGURE 2-24 Ideas detected a repeating pattern. This might indicate some weekly or monthly seasonality.

When the Ideas feature debuted in the summer of 2018, it was called Insights and was found on the Insert tab. By the end of 2018, Office 365 customers would see the feature on the right side of the Home tab, and it was rebranded as Ideas.

Unfortunately, customers who purchased a perpetual license to Excel 2019 will not have the feature in either location. Microsoft's stance is that if you are not continuing to pay a monthly subscription fee, you cannot make use of the Office intelligent services.

The reviews on the Insert Recommended PivotTables feature are mixed. On one hand, it does provide a quick and easy way to start a pivot table, especially for those of us who are not that experienced. On the other hand, Excel's recommendations are rudimentary at best. You will often find that you need to rearrange, add, or manipulate fields in the created pivot table to suit your needs. Although Excel *might* get it right the first time, it's unlikely that you will be able to leave the pivot table as is.

There is also a chance that Excel will simply not like the data range you pointed to. For example, the data in Figure 2-25 is a valid range, but Excel doesn't like the repeating dates. So, it pops up a message to indicate that there are too many duplicates to recommend a pivot table; however, it will gladly create a blank one.

FIGURE 2-25 When Excel can't recommend a pivot table based on your data, it throws an error and gives you the option of starting with a blank pivot.

All in all, the Recommended PivotTables feature can be a nice shortcut for getting a rudimentary pivot table started, but it's not a replacement for knowing how to create and manipulate pivot tables on your own.

Using slicers

With Excel 2010, Microsoft introduced a feature called *slicers*. Slicers enable you to filter your pivot table in much the same way as Filter fields filter a pivot table. The difference is that slicers offer a user-friendly interface that enables you to easily see the current filter state.

Creating a standard slicer

To understand the concept behind slicers, place your cursor anywhere inside your pivot table and then select the Insert tab on the ribbon. Click the Slicer icon (see Figure 2-26).

FIGURE 2-26   Inserting a slicer.

The Insert Slicers dialog box, shown in Figure 2-27, opens. The idea is to select the dimensions you want to filter. In this example, the Region and Market slicers are selected.

FIGURE 2-27   Select the dimensions for which you want to create slicers.

After the slicers are created, you can simply click the filter values to filter your pivot table. As you can see in Figure 2-28, clicking Midwest in the Region slicer filters your pivot table, and also the Market slicer responds by highlighting the markets that belong to the Midwest region.

FIGURE 2-28 Select the dimensions you want to filter using slicers.

> **Tip** You can select multiple values by holding down the Ctrl key on your keyboard while selecting the needed filters. Alternatively, you can enable the Multi-Select toggle next to the filter icon at the top of the slicer.

In Figure 2-29, the Multi-Select toggle was enabled and then Baltimore, California, Charlotte, and Chicago were selected. Note that Excel highlights the selected markets in the Market slicer and also highlights their associated regions in the Region slicer.

Another advantage you gain with slicers is that you can tie each slicer to more than one pivot table. In other words, any filter you apply to your slicer can be applied to multiple pivot tables.

To connect a slicer to more than one pivot table, simply right-click the slicer and select Report Connections. The Report Connections dialog box, shown in Figure 2-30, opens. Select the check box next to any pivot table that you want to filter using the current slicer.

The Multi-Select Toggle

Sum of Sale Amount	Column Labels			
Row Labels	Bar Equipment	Commercial Appliances	Concession Equipment	Fryers
Baltimore	80			352
California	66356.65	294155.55	416379.2	261042.05
Charlotte	283682.15	1525742.3	1569948.6	450972.35
Chicago	3168	9081	18218	9846.8
Grand Total	353286.8	1828978.85	2004545.8	722213.2

Region		
Midwest		
Northeast		
Southeast		
West		
CANADA		
North		
South		
Southwest		

Market		
Baltimore		
Buffalo		
California		
CANADA		
Charlotte		
Chicago		
Dakotas		
Dallas		

FIGURE 2-29 The fact that they enable you to visually see the current filter state gives slicers a unique advantage over the Filter field.

FIGURE 2-30 Choose the pivot tables you want to filter using this slicer.

At this point, any filter applied via the slicer is applied to all the connected pivot tables. Again, slicers have a unique advantage over Filter fields in that they can control the filter state of multiple pivot tables. Filter fields can control only the pivot table in which they live.

Tip Notice that in Figure 2-30, the list of pivot tables is a bit ambiguous (PivotTable1, PivotTable2). Excel automatically gives your pivot tables these generic names, which it uses to identify them. You can imagine how difficult it would be to know which pivot table is which when working with more than a handful of pivots. Therefore, you might want to consider giving your pivot tables user-friendly names, so you can recognize them in dialog boxes, such as the one you see in Figure 2-30.

You can easily change the name of a pivot table by placing your cursor anywhere inside the pivot table, selecting the Analyze tab, and entering a friendly name in the PivotTable Name input box found on the far left.

Creating a Timeline slicer

The Timeline slicer (introduced with Excel 2013) works in the same way as a standard slicer in that it lets you filter a pivot table using a visual selection mechanism instead of the old Filter fields. The difference is that the Timeline slicer is designed to work exclusively with date fields, and it provides an excellent visual method to filter and group the dates in a pivot table.

> **Note** In order to create a Timeline slicer, your pivot table must contain a field where *all* the data is formatted as dates. This means that your source data table must contain at least one column where all the values are formatted as valid dates. If even only one value in the source date column is blank or not a valid date, Excel does not create a Timeline slicer.

To create a Timeline slicer, place your cursor anywhere inside your pivot table, select the Insert tab on the ribbon, and then click the Timeline icon.

The Insert Timelines dialog box opens, showing you all the available date fields in the chosen pivot table. Here, you select the date fields for which you want to create slicers.

After your Timeline slicer is created, you can filter the data in your pivot table by using this dynamic data-selection mechanism. As you can see in Figure 2-31, clicking the April slicer filters the data in the pivot table to show only April data.

Row Labels	Sum of Sale Amount
Buffalo	42638
California	102981
CANADA	32459
Charlotte	373468.3
Chicago	4637
Dakotas	9274
Dallas	47749.4

FIGURE 2-31 Click a date selection to filter your pivot table.

Figure 2-32 demonstrates how you can expand the slicer range with the mouse to include a wider range of dates in your filtered numbers.

Row Labels	Sum of Sale Amount
Buffalo	335113
California	543023
CANADA	147187.7
Charlotte	1178225.2
Chicago	6878
Dakotas	27353.8
Dallas	469309.15
Denver	291211

FIGURE 2-32 You can expand the range on the Timeline slicer to include more data in the filtered numbers.

Want to quickly filter your pivot table by quarters? Well, you can easily do it with a Timeline slicer. Click the time period drop-down menu and select Quarters. As you can see in Figure 2-33, you also have the option of selecting Years or Days, if needed.

FIGURE 2-33   Quickly switch between filtering by years, quarters, months, and days.

> **Note**   Be aware that Timeline slicers are not backward compatible with Excel 2010 or earlier.

Case study: analyzing activity by market

Your organization has 18 markets that sell 7 types of products. You have been asked to build a report that breaks out each market and highlights the dollar sales for each product. You are starting with an intimidating transaction table that contains more than 91,000 rows of data. To start your report, do the following:

1. Place your cursor inside the data set, select the Insert tab, and click PivotTable.

2. When the Create PivotTable dialog box appears, click the OK button. At this point, you should see an empty pivot table with the PivotTable Fields list.

3. Find the Market field in the PivotTable Fields list, and select the check box next to it.

4. Find the Sale Amount field in the PivotTable Fields list, and select the check box next to it.

5. To get the product breakouts, find the Product Category field in the PivotTable Fields list and drag it into the Columns area.

In five easy steps, you have calculated and designed a report that satisfies the requirements. After a little formatting, your pivot table report should look similar to the one shown in Figure 2-34.

Sum of Sale Amount	Column Labels ▾			
Row Labels ▾	Bar Equipment	Commercial Appliances	Concession Equipment	Fryer
Baltimore	80			
Buffalo	37397.9	237297.85	187711	127
California	66356.65	294155.55	416379.2	2610
CANADA	35975.25	71272.1	205874.6	129
Charlotte	283682.15	1525742.3	1569948.6	4509
Chicago	3168	9081	18218	9
Dakotas	3386.5	7287.05	30619.2	180
Dallas	59580.3	255146	306037	151
Denver	34558.85	70068.8	75712.8	1200
Florida	1132162.05	5667950.6	6665865.45	2269
Great Lakes	16798.4	36678.1	71625.8	51
Kansas City	41891.9	61404.15	57300.7	50
Knoxville	220	153		

FIGURE 2-34 This summary can be created in less than a minute.

Lest you lose sight of the analytical power you just harnessed, keep in mind that your data source has more than 91,000 rows and 14 columns, which is a hefty set of data by Excel standards. Despite the amount of data, you produced a relatively robust analysis in a matter of minutes.

Keeping up with changes in the data source

Let's go back to the family portrait analogy. As years go by, your family will change in appearance and might even grow to include some new members. The family portrait that was taken years ago remains static and no longer represents the family today. So, another portrait needs to be taken.

As time goes by, your data might change and grow with newly added rows and columns. However, the pivot cache that feeds your pivot table report is disconnected from your data source, so it cannot represent any of the changes you make to your date source until you take another snapshot.

The action of updating your pivot cache by taking another snapshot of your data source is called *refreshing* your data. There are two reasons you might have to refresh your pivot table report:

■ Changes have been made to your existing data source.

■ Your data source's range has been expanded with the addition of rows or columns.

The following sections explain how to keep your pivot table synchronized with the changes in your data source.

Dealing with changes made to the existing data source

If a few cells in your pivot table's source data have changed due to edits or updates, you can refresh your pivot table report with a few clicks. Simply right-click inside your pivot table report and select Refresh. This selection takes another snapshot of your data set, overwriting your previous pivot cache with the latest data.

Note You can also refresh the data in a pivot table by selecting Analyze from the PivotTable Tools tab in the ribbon and then choosing Refresh.

Tip Clicking anywhere inside a pivot table activates the PivotTable Tools tabs just above the main ribbon.

Dealing with an expanded data source range due to the addition of rows or columns

When changes have been made to your data source that affect its range (for example, if you've added rows or columns), you have to update the range being captured by the pivot cache.

To do this, click anywhere inside the pivot table and then select Analyze from the PivotTable Tools tab in the ribbon. From here, select Change Data Source. This selection triggers the dialog box shown in Figure 2-35.

FIGURE 2-35 The Change PivotTable Data Source dialog box enables you to redefine the source data for your pivot table.

All you have to do here is update the range to include new rows and columns. After you have specified the appropriate range, click the OK button.

Note that if you format your pivot table source data as a table using Home, Format As Table or Ctrl+T, the Pivot Table Source range will automatically expand as the data grows. You will still have to click Refresh to pick up the new rows.

Sharing the pivot cache

You quite often need to analyze the same data set in multiple ways. In most cases, this process requires you to create separate pivot tables from the same data source. Keep in mind that every time you create a pivot table, you are storing a snapshot of the entire data set in a pivot cache. Every pivot cache that is created increases your memory usage and file size. For this reason, you should consider sharing your pivot cache.

> **Note** In situations where you need to create multiple pivot tables from the same data source, you can use the same pivot cache to feed multiple pivot tables. By using the same pivot cache for multiple pivot tables, you gain a certain level of efficiency when it comes to memory usage and file size.

In legacy versions of Excel, when you created a pivot table using a data set that was already being used in another pivot table, Excel actually gave you the option of using the same pivot cache. However, Excel 2019 does not give you such an option.

Instead, each time you create a new pivot table in Excel 2019, Excel automatically shares the pivot cache. Most of the time, this is beneficial: You can link as many pivot tables as you want to the same pivot cache with a negligible increase in memory and file size.

On the flip side, when you group one pivot table by month and year, all the pivot tables are grouped in a similar fashion. If you want one pivot table by month and another pivot table by week, you have to force a separate pivot cache. You can force Excel to create a separate pivot cache by taking the following steps:

1. Press Alt+D, release, and then press P to launch the PivotTable Wizard.

2. Click the Next button to get past the first screen of the wizard.

3. On the second screen, select the range for your pivot table and click the Next button.

4. Excel displays a wordy message saying that you can use less memory if you click Yes. Instead, click No.

5. On the next screen, click the Finish button.

At this point, you have a blank pivot table that pulls from its own pivot cache.

> **Tip** If you already have an existing pivot table, you can use an alternative method for creating a separate pivot cache: Copy and paste the existing table to a new workbook and then copy and paste the pivot table back to a new sheet in the original workbook.

Side effects of sharing a pivot cache

It's important to note that there are a few side effects to sharing a pivot cache. For example, suppose you have two pivot tables using the same pivot cache. Certain actions affect both pivot tables:

- **Refreshing your data**—You cannot refresh one pivot table and not the other. Refreshing affects both tables.

- **Adding a calculated field**—If you create a calculated field in one pivot table, your newly created calculated field shows up in the PivotTable Fields list of the other pivot table.

- **Adding a calculated item**—If you create a calculated item in one pivot table, it shows in the other as well.

- **Grouping or ungrouping fields**—Any grouping or ungrouping you perform affects both pivot tables. For instance, suppose you group a date field in one pivot table to show months. The same date field in the other pivot table is also grouped to show months.

Although none of these side effects are critical flaws in the concept of sharing a pivot cache, it is important to keep them in mind when determining whether using a pivot table as your data source is the best option for your situation.

Saving time with new PivotTable tools

Microsoft has invested a lot of time and effort in the overall pivot table experience. The results of these efforts are tools that make pivot table functionality more accessible and easier to use. The following sections look at a few of the tools that help you save time when managing pivot tables.

Deferring layout updates

The frustrating part of building a pivot table from a large data source is that each time you add a field to a pivot area, you are left waiting while Excel crunches through all that data. This can become a maddeningly time-consuming process if you have to add several fields to your pivot table.

Excel 2019 offers some relief for this problem by providing a way to defer layout changes until you are ready to apply them. You can activate this option by selecting the relatively inconspicuous Defer Layout Update check box in the PivotTable Fields list, as shown in Figure 2-36.

Here's how this feature works: With the Defer Layout Update check box selected, you prevent your pivot table from making real-time updates as you move your fields around without your pivot table. When you are ready to apply your changes, click the Update button on the lower-right corner of the PivotTable Fields list.

FIGURE 2-36 Select the Defer Layout Update check box to prevent your pivot table from updating while you add fields.

Note Remember to clear the check mark from the Defer Layout Update check box when you are done building your pivot table. Leaving it selected results in your pivot table remaining in a state of manual updates, preventing you from using other features of the pivot table, such as sorting, filtering, and grouping.

Tip Incidentally, the Defer Layout Update option is available through VBA. It can help improve the performance of any macro that automates the creation of pivot tables.

Note For detailed information on how to use VBA to create pivot tables, refer to Chapter 13, "Using VBA to create pivot tables."

Starting over with one click

Often you might want to start from scratch when working with your pivot table layouts. Excel 2019 provides a simple way to essentially start over without deleting your pivot cache. Select Analyze under the PivotTable Tools tab and select the Clear drop-down menu. As you can see in Figure 2-37, this command enables you to either clear your entire pivot table layout or remove any existing filters you might have applied in your pivot table.

FIGURE 2-37 The Clear command enables you to clear your pivot table fields or remove the applied filters from your pivot table.

Relocating a pivot table

You might find that, after you have created a pivot table, you need to move it to another location. It might be in the way of other analyses on the worksheet, or you might simply need to move it to another worksheet. Although there are several ways to move a pivot table, the easiest is Excel 2019's no-frills way: Select Analyze under the PivotTable Tools tab and select Move PivotTable. This icon activates the Move PivotTable dialog box, shown in Figure 2-38. All you have to do here is specify where you want your pivot table moved.

FIGURE 2-38 The Move PivotTable dialog box enables you to quickly move your pivot table to another location.

Next steps

In Chapter 3, you'll learn how to enhance your pivot table reports by customizing your fields, changing field names, changing summary calculations, applying formats to data fields, adding and removing subtotals, and using the Show As setting.

Customizing a pivot table

In this chapter, you will:

- Make common cosmetic changes
- Make report layout changes
- Customize a pivot table's appearance with styles and themes
- Change summary calculations
- Change the calculation in a value field
- Add and remove subtotals

Although pivot tables provide an extremely fast way to summarize data, sometimes the pivot table defaults are not exactly what you need. In such cases, you can use many powerful settings to tweak pivot tables. These tweaks range from making cosmetic changes to changing the underlying calculation used in the pivot table.

Many of the changes in this chapter can be customized for all future pivot tables using the new pivot table default settings. If you find yourself always making the same changes to a pivot table, consider making that change in the pivot table defaults.

In Excel 2019, you find controls to customize a pivot table in myriad places: the Analyze tab, Design tab, Field Settings dialog box, Data Field Settings dialog box, PivotTable Options dialog box, and context menus.

Rather than cover each set of controls sequentially, this chapter covers the following functional areas in making pivot table customization:

- **Minor cosmetic changes**—Change blanks to zeros, adjust the number format, and rename a field. The fact that you must correct these defaults in every pivot table that you create is annoying.

- **Layout changes**—Compare three possible layouts, show/hide subtotals and totals, and repeat row labels.

- **Major cosmetic changes**—Use pivot table styles to format a pivot table quickly.

- **Summary calculations**—Change from Sum to Count, Min, Max, and more.

- **Advanced calculations**—Use settings to show data as a running total, percent of total, rank, percent of parent item, and more.

- **Other options**—Review some of the obscure options found throughout the Excel interface.

Making common cosmetic changes

You need to make a few changes to almost every pivot table to make it easier to understand and interpret. Figure 3-1 shows a typical pivot table. To create this pivot table, open the Chapter 3 data file. Select Insert, Pivot Table, OK. Select the Sector, Customer, and Revenue fields check boxes, and drag the Region field to the Columns area.

Sum of Revenue	Column Labels				
Row Labels	Midwest	Northeast	South	West	Grand Total
Associations		51240	34364		85604
Association for Computers & Taxation			34364		34364
IMA Houston Chapter					
Consultants	89033				
Andrew Spain Consulting					
Cambia Factor					
Construction Intelligence & Analytics, Inc.	42316				
Data2Impact					
Excelerator BI	46717				
Fintega Financial Modelling					
Professional					
Juliet Babcock-Hyde CPA, PLLC					
Serving Brevard Realty					
WM Squared Inc.					
Retail	84740				
Bits of Confetti					
Hartville MarketPlace and Flea Market					
LaFrenier Sons Septic	50030				
New Hope Laundry	34710				
Software	812907				
Excel4Apps	750163				
F-Keys Ltd.					
Frontline Systems	62744				
Vertex42					
Training	754744				

FIGURE 3-1 A typical pivot table before customization.

This default pivot table contains several annoying items that you might want to change quickly:

- The default table style uses no gridlines, which makes it difficult to follow the rows and columns across and down.

- Numbers in the Values area are in a general number format. There are no commas, currency symbols, and so on.

- For sparse data sets, many blanks appear in the Values area. The blank cell in B5 indicates that there were no Associations sales in the Midwest. Most people prefer to see zeros instead of blanks.

- Excel renames fields in the Values area with the unimaginative name Sum Of Revenue. You can change this name.

You can correct each of these annoyances with just a few mouse clicks. The following sections address each issue.

Tip Excel MVP Debra Dalgleish sells a Pivot Power Premium add-in that fixes most of the issues listed here. Debra's add-in offers a few more features than the new PivotTable Defaults. This add-in is great if you will be creating pivot tables frequently. For more information, visit http://mrx.cl/pivpow16.

Applying a table style to restore gridlines

The default pivot table layout contains no gridlines and is rather plain. Fortunately, you can apply a table style. Any table style that you choose is better than the default.

Follow these steps to apply a table style:

1. Make sure that the active cell is in the pivot table.

2. From the ribbon, select the Design tab. Three arrows appear at the right side of the PivotTable Style gallery.

3. Click the bottom arrow to open the complete gallery, which is shown in Figure 3-2.

FIGURE 3-2 The gallery contains 85 styles to choose from.

4. Choose any style other than the first style from the drop-down menu. Styles toward the bottom of the gallery tend to have more formatting.

5. Select the check box for Banded Rows to the left of the PivotTable Styles gallery. This draws gridlines in light styles and adds row stripes in dark styles.

It does not matter which style you choose from the gallery; any of the 84 other styles are better than the default style.

Note For more details about customizing styles, see "Customizing a pivot table's appearance with styles and themes," later in this chapter.

Changing the number format to add thousands separators

If you have gone to the trouble of formatting your underlying data, you might expect that the pivot table will capture some of this formatting. Unfortunately, it does not. Even if your underlying data fields were formatted with a certain numeric format, the default pivot table presents values formatted with a general format. As a sign of some progress, when you create pivot tables from Power Pivot, you can specify the number format for a field before creating the pivot table. This functionality has not come to regular pivot tables yet.

Note For more about Power Pivot, read Chapter 10, "Unlocking features with the Data Model and Power Pivot."

For example, in the figures in this chapter, the numbers are in the thousands or tens of thousands. At this level of sales, you would normally have a thousands separator and probably no decimal places. Although the original data had a numeric format applied, the pivot table routinely formats your numbers in an ugly general style.

What is the fastest way to change the number format? It depends if you have a single value field or multiple value fields.

In Figure 3-3, the pivot table Values area contains Revenue. There are many columns in the pivot table because Product is in the Columns area. In this case, right-click any number and choose Number Format.

FIGURE 3-3 For a single value field, right-click any number and choose Number Format.

In contrast to Figure 3-3, the pivot table in Figure 3-4 contains three fields in the Values area: Revenue, Cost, and Profit. Rather than applying the Number Format to each individual column, you can format the entire pivot table by following these steps:

1. Select from the first numeric cell to the last numeric cell, including the Grand Total row or column if it is present.

2. Press Ctrl+1 to display the Format Cells dialog box.

3. Choose the Number tab across the top of the dialog box.

4. Select a number format.

5. Click OK.

Until a coding change in Excel 2010, the preceding steps would not change the number format in cases where the pivot table became taller. However, provided you include the Grand Total in your selection, these steps will change the number format for all the fields in the Values area.

FIGURE 3-4 With multiple fields in the Values area, select all number cells as shown here and change the format using the Format Cells dialog box.

Replacing blanks with zeros

One of the elements of good spreadsheet design is that you should never leave blank cells in a numeric section of a worksheet.

A blank tells you that there were no sales for a particular combination of labels. In the default view, an actual zero is used to indicate that there was activity, but the total sales were zero. This value might mean that a customer bought something and then returned it, resulting in net sales of zero. Although there are limited applications in which you need to differentiate between having no sales and having net zero sales, this seems rare. In 99% of the cases, you should fill in the blank cells with zeros.

Follow these steps to change this setting for the current pivot table:

1. Right-click any cell in the pivot table and choose PivotTable Options.

2. On the Layout & Format tab in the Format section, type **0** next to the field labeled For Empty Cells Show (see Figure 3-5).

FIGURE 3-5 Enter a zero in the For Empty Cells Show box to replace the blank cells with zero.

3. Click OK to accept the change.

The result is that the pivot table is filled with zeros instead of blanks, as shown in Figure 3-6.

	A	B	C	D	E	F
1						
2						
3	**Sum of Revenue**	Column Labels				
4	**Row Labels**	Midwest	Northeast	South	West	Grand Total
5	⊟Associations	$0	$51,240	$34,364	$0	$85,604
6	Association for Computers & Taxation	$0	$0	$34,364	$0	$34,364
7	IMA Houston Chapter	$0	$51,240	$0	$0	$51,240
8	⊟Consultants	$89,033	$0	$926,970	$115,132	$1,131,135
9	Andrew Spain Consulting	$0	$0	$869,454	$0	$869,454
10	Cambia Factor	$0	$0	$57,516	$0	$57,516
11	Construction Intelligence & Analytics, Inc.	$42,316	$0	$0	$0	$42,316
12	Data2Impact	$0	$0	$0	$59,881	$59,881
13	Excelerator BI	$46,717	$0	$0	$0	$46,717
14	Fintega Financial Modelling	$0	$0	$0	$55,251	$55,251
15	⊟Professional	$0	$0	$437,695	$39,250	$476,945
16	Juliet Babcock-Hyde CPA, PLLC	$0	$0	$31,369	$0	$31,369
17	Serving Brevard Realty	$0	$0	$406,326	$0	$406,326
18	WM Squared Inc.	$0	$0	$0	$39,250	$39,250
19	⊟Retail	$84,740	$0	$704,359	$31,021	$820,120

FIGURE 3-6 Your report is now a solid contiguous block of non-blank cells.

Changing a field name

Every field in a final pivot table has a name. Fields in the row, column, and filter areas inherit their names from the heading in the source data. Fields in the data section are given names such as Sum Of Revenue. In some instances, you might prefer to print a different name in the pivot table. You might prefer Total Revenue instead of the default name. In these situations, the capability to change your field names comes in quite handy.

> **Tip** Although many of the names are inherited from headings in the original data set, when your data is from an external data source, you might not have control over field names. In these cases, you might want to change the names of the fields as well.

To change a field name in the Values area, follow these steps:

1. Select a cell in the pivot table that contains the appropriate type of value. You might have a pivot table with both Sum Of Quantity and Sum Of Revenue in the Values area. Choose a cell that contains a Sum Of Revenue value.

2. Go to the Analyze tab in the ribbon. A Pivot Field Name text box appears below the heading Active Field. The box currently contains Sum Of Revenue.

3. Type a new name in the box, as shown in Figure 3-7. Click a cell in your pivot table to complete the entry and have the heading in A3 change. The name of the field title in the Values area also changes to reflect the new name.

FIGURE 3-7 The name typed in the Custom Name box appears in the pivot table. Although names should be unique, you can trick Excel into accepting a name that's similar to an existing name by adding a space to the end of it.

> **Note** One common frustration occurs when you would like to rename Sum Of Revenue to Revenue. The problem is that this name is not allowed because it is not unique; you already have a Revenue field in the source data. To work around this limitation, you can name the field and add a space to the end of the name. Excel considers "Revenue " (with a space) to be different from "Revenue" (with no space). Because this change is only cosmetic, the readers of your spreadsheet do not notice the space after the name.

Tip When you can see the value field name such as "Sum of Revenue" in the Excel work-sheet, you can directly type a new value to rename the field. For example, in Figure 3.7, you could type Sales in cell A3 to rename the field.

Making report layout changes

Excel 2019 offers three report layout styles. The Excel team continues to offer the Compact layout as the default report layout. If you prefer a different layout, change it using the default settings for pivot tables.

If you consider three report layouts, and the ability to show subtotals at the top or bottom, plus choices for blank rows and Repeat All Item Labels, you have 16 different layout possibilities available.

Layout changes are controlled in the Layout group of the Design tab, as shown in Figure 3-8. This group offers four icons:

- **Subtotals**—Moves subtotals to the top or bottom of each group or turns them off.

- **Grand Totals**—Turns the grand totals on or off for rows and columns.

- **Report Layout**—Uses the Compact, Outline, or Tabular forms. Offers an option to repeat item labels.

- **Blank Rows**—Inserts or removes blank lines after each group.

FIGURE 3-8 The Layout group on the Design tab offers different layouts and options for totals.

Note You mathematicians in the audience might think that 3 layouts × 2 repeat options × 2 subtotal location options × 2 blank row options would be 24 layouts. However, choosing Repeat All Item Labels does not work with the Compact layout, thus eliminating 4 of the combinations. In addition, Subtotals At The Top Of Each Group does not work with the Tabular layout, eliminating another 4 combinations.

Using the Compact layout

By default, all new pivot tables use the Compact layout that you saw in Figure 3-6. In this layout, multiple fields in the row area are stacked in column A. Note in the figure that the Consultants sector and the Andrew Spain Consulting customer are both in column A.

The Compact form is suited for using the Expand and Collapse icons. If you select one of the Sector value cells such as Associations in A5 and then click the Collapse Field icon on the Analyze tab, Excel hides all the customer details and shows only the sectors, as shown in Figure 3-9.

Total Revenue	Column Labels				
Row Labels	Midwest	Northeast	South	West	Grand Total
⊞ Associations	$0	$51,240	$34,364	$0	$85,604
⊞ Consultants	$89,033	$0	$926,970	$115,132	$1,131,135
⊞ Professional	$0	$0	$437,695	$39,250	$476,945
⊞ Retail	$84,740	$0	$704,359	$31,021	$820,120
⊞ Software	$812,907	$463,658	$0	$0	$1,276,565
⊞ Training	$754,744	$1,609,714	$498,937	$54,048	$2,917,443
Grand Total	$1,741,424	$2,124,612	$2,602,325	$239,451	$6,707,812

FIGURE 3-9 Click the Collapse Field icon to hide levels of detail.

After a field is collapsed, you can show detail for individual items by using the plus icons in column A, or you can click Expand Field on the Analyze tab to see the detail again.

> **Tip** If you select a cell in the innermost row field and click Expand Field on the Options tab, Excel displays the Show Detail dialog box, as shown in Figure 3-10, to enable you to add a new innermost row field.

FIGURE 3-10 When you attempt to expand the innermost field, Excel offers to add a new innermost field.

Using the Outline layout

When you select Design, Layout, Report Layout, Show In Outline Form, Excel puts each row field in a separate column. The pivot table shown in Figure 3-11 is one column wider, with revenue values starting in C instead of B. This is a small price to pay for allowing each field to occupy its own column. Soon, you will find out how to convert a pivot table to values so you can further sort or filter. When you do this, you will want each field in its own column.

FIGURE 3-11 The Outline layout puts each row field in a separate column.

The Excel team added the Repeat All Item Labels option to the Report Layout tab starting in Excel 2010. This alleviated a lot of busy work because it takes just two clicks to fill in all the blank cells along the outer row fields. Choosing to repeat the item labels causes values to appear in cells A6:A7, A9:A14, as shown in Figure 3-11.

Figure 3-11 shows the same pivot table from before, now in Outline form and with labels repeated.

> **Caution** This layout is suitable if you plan to copy the values from the pivot table to a new location for further analysis. Although the Compact layout offers a clever approach by squeezing multiple fields into one column, it is not ideal for reusing the data later.

By default, both the Compact and Outline layouts put the subtotals at the top of each group. You can use the Subtotals drop-down menu on the Design tab to move the totals to the bottom of each group, as shown in Figure 3-12. In Outline view, this causes a not-really-useful heading row to appear at the top of each group. Cell A5 contains "Associations" without any additional data in the columns to the right. Consequently, the pivot table occupies 44 rows instead of 37 rows because each of the 7 sector categories has an extra header.

FIGURE 3-12 With subtotals at the bottom of each group, the pivot table occupies several more rows.

Using the traditional Tabular layout

Figure 3-13 shows the Tabular layout. This layout is similar to the one that has been used in pivot tables since their invention through Excel 2003. In this layout, the subtotals can never appear at the top of the group. The new Repeat All Item Labels works with this layout, as shown in Figure 3-13.

	A	B	C	D	E
3	Revenue		Region		
4	Sector	Customer	Midwest	Northeast	South
5	⊟ Associations	IMA Houston Chapter	$0	$51,240	$0
6	Associations	Association for Computers & Taxation	$0	$0	$34,364
7	Associations Total		$0	$51,240	$34,364
8	⊟ Consultants	Andrew Spain Consulting	$0	$0	$869,454
9	Consultants	Data2Impact	$0	$0	$0
10	Consultants	Cambia Factor	$0	$0	$57,516
11	Consultants	Fintega Financial Modelling	$0	$0	$0
12	Consultants	Excelerator BI	$46,717	$0	$0
13	Consultants	Construction Intelligence & Analytics, Inc.	$42,316	$0	$0
14	Consultants Total		$89,033	$0	$926,970
15	⊟ Professional	Serving Brevard Realty	$0	$0	$406,326
16	Professional	WM Squared Inc.	$0	$0	$0
17	Professional	Juliet Babcock-Hyde CPA, PLLC	$0	$0	$31,369
18	Professional Total		$0	$0	$437,695
19	⊟ Retail	Hartville MarketPlace and Flea Market	$0	$0	$704,359

FIGURE 3-13 The Tabular layout is similar to pivot tables in legacy versions of Excel.

The Tabular layout is the best layout if you expect to use the resulting summary data in a subsequent analysis. If you wanted to reuse the table in Figure 3-13, you would do additional "flattening" of the pivot table by choosing Subtotals, Do Not Show Subtotals and Grand Totals, Off For Rows And Columns.

Case study: Converting a pivot table to values

Say that you want to convert the pivot table shown in Figure 3-13 to be a regular data set that you can sort, filter, chart, or export to another system. You don't need the Sectors totals in rows 7, 14, 18, and so on. You don't need the Grand Total at the bottom. And, depending on your future needs, you might want to move the Region field from the Columns area to the Rows area. This would allow you to add Cost and Profit as new columns in the final report.

Finally, you want to convert from a live pivot table to static values. To make these changes, follow these steps:

1. Select any cell in the pivot table.

2. From the Design tab, select Grand Totals, Off For Rows And Columns.

3. Select Design, Subtotals, Do Not Show Subtotals.

4. Drag the Region tile from the Columns area in the PivotTable Fields list. Drop this field between Sector and Customer in the Rows area.

5. Check Profit and Cost in the top of the PivotTable Fields list. Because both fields are numeric, they move to the Values area and appear in the pivot table as new columns. Rename both fields using the Current Field box on the Analyze tab. The report is now a contiguous solid block of data, as shown in Figure 3-14.

	A	B	C	D	E	F
1						
2						
3	Sector ▼	Region ▼	Customer ▼	Total Revenue	Total Profit	Total Cost
4	⊟Associations	⊟Northeast	IMA Houston Chapter	$51,240	22824	28416
5	Associations	⊟South	Association for Computers & Taxation	$34,364	15576	18788
6	⊟Consultants	⊟Midwest	Construction Intelligence & Analytics, Inc.	$42,316	18764	23552
7	Consultants	Midwest	Excelerator BI	$46,717	19961	26756
8	Consultants	⊟South	Andrew Spain Consulting	$869,454	382170	487284
9	Consultants	South	Cambia Factor	$57,516	26765	30751
10	Consultants	⊟West	Data2Impact	$59,881	25913	33968
11	Consultants	West	Fintega Financial Modelling	$55,251	24632	30619
12	⊟Professional	⊟South	Juliet Babcock-Hyde CPA, PLLC	$31,369	13730	17639
13	Professional	South	Serving Brevard Realty	$406,326	178585	227741

FIGURE 3-14 The pivot table now contains a solid block of data.

6. Select one cell in the pivot table. Press Ctrl+* to select all the data in the pivot table.

7. Press Ctrl+C to copy the data from the pivot table.

8. Select a blank section of a worksheet.

9. Right-click and choose Paste Values to open the flyout menu. Select Paste Values And Number Formatting, as shown in Figure 3-15. Excel pastes a static copy of the report to the worksheet.

Paste Values and Number Formatting

FIGURE 3-15 Use Paste Values And Number Formatting to create a static version of the data.

10. If you no longer need the original pivot table, select the entire pivot table and press the Delete key to clear the cells from the pivot table and free up the area of memory that was holding the pivot table cache.

The result is a solid block of summary data. These 27 rows are a summary of the 500+ rows in the original data set, but they also are suitable for exporting to other systems.

Controlling blank lines, grand totals, and other settings

Additional settings on the Design tab enable you to toggle various elements.

The Blank Rows drop-down menu offers the choice Insert Blank Row After Each Item. This setting applies only to pivot tables with two or more row fields. Blank rows are not added after each item in the inner row field. You see a blank row after each group of items in the outer row fields. As shown in Figure 3-16, the blank row after each sector makes the report easier to read. However, if you remove Sector from the report, you have only Customer in the row fields, and no blank rows appear (see Figure 3-17).

Sector	Customer	Doodads	Gadget	Gizmo	Widget
Total Revenue		Product			
Sector	**Customer**	**Doodads**	**Gadget**	**Gizmo**	**Widget**
⊟**Associations**	Association for Computers & Taxation	$0	$4,270	$22,958	$7,136
Associations	IMA Houston Chapter	$0	$18,064	$18,072	$15,104
Associations Total		$0	$22,334	$41,030	$22,240
⊟**Consultants**	Andrew Spain Consulting	$0	$304,198	$288,409	$276,847
Consultants	Cambia Factor	$0	$16,784	$35,200	$5,532

FIGURE 3-16 The Blank Rows setting makes the report easier to read.

Customer	Doodads	Gadget	Gizmo	Widget
Total Revenue	Product			
Customer	**Doodads**	**Gadget**	**Gizmo**	**Widget**
599CD.com	$0	$185,675	$245,491	$191,628
Andrew Spain Consulting	$0	$304,198	$288,409	$276,847
Association for Computers & Taxation	$0	$4,270	$22,958	$7,136
Bits of Confetti	$28,663	$2,358	$0	$0
Cambia Factor	$0	$16,784	$35,200	$5,532
Construction Intelligence & Analytics, Inc.	$6,036	$18,552	$17,728	$0
CPASelfStudy.com	$0	$190,533	$200,936	$177,382
Data2Impact	$0	$26,484	$19,544	$13,853
Excel4Apps	$0	$233,435	$235,761	$280,967

FIGURE 3-17 Blank rows will not appear when there is only one item in the row field.

> **Note** For those of you following along with the sample files, you may have noticed quite a leap from the pivot table in Figure 3-14 to the one in Figure 3-16, but it is still the same pivot table. Here is how to make the changes:
>
> 1. Clear the Sector, Customer, Profit, and Cost check boxes in the PivotTable Fields list.
>
> 2. Drag the Product field to the Columns area.
>
> 3. Recheck the Sector field to move it to the second Row field.
>
> 4. Make sure the active cell is in column A.
>
> 5. On the Design tab of the ribbon, open Subtotals and choose Show All Subtotals At Bottom Of Group.
>
> 6. As shown in Figure 3-16, open the Blank Rows drop-down menu and choose Insert Blank Line After Each Item.
>
> 7. To get to the pivot table shown in Figure 3-17, clear the Sector field check box.

Grand totals can appear at the bottom of each column and/or at the end of each row, or they can be turned off altogether. Settings for grand totals appear in the Grand Totals drop-down menu of the Layout group on the Design tab. The wording in this drop-down menu is a bit confusing, so Figure 3-18 shows what each option provides. The default is to show grand totals for rows and columns.

	A	B	C	D	E	F
1	Grand Totals On For Rows Only					
2	*Keeps the Grand Total column*					
3	Total Revenue	Product ▾				
4	Region ▾	Doodads	Gadget	Gizmo	Widget	Grand Total
5	Midwest	$6,036	$544,772	$652,651	$537,965	$1,741,424
6	Northeast	$38,860	$714,009	$751,724	$620,019	$2,124,612
7	South	$0	$839,551	$918,588	$844,186	$2,602,325
8	West	$28,663	$65,382	$70,057	$75,349	$239,451
9						
10	Grand Totals On For Columns Only					
11	*Keeps the Grand Total row*					
12	Total Revenue	Product ▾				
13	Region ▾	Doodads	Gadget	Gizmo	Widget	
14	Midwest	$6,036	$544,772	$652,651	$537,965	
15	Northeast	$38,860	$714,009	$751,724	$620,019	
16	South	$0	$839,551	$918,588	$844,186	
17	West	$28,663	$65,382	$70,057	$75,349	
18	Grand Total	$73,559	$2,163,714	$2,393,020	$2,077,519	
19						
20	Grand Totals Off For Rows and Columns					
21	Total Revenue	Product ▾				
22	Region ▾	Doodads	Gadget	Gizmo	Widget	
23	Midwest	$6,036	$544,772	$652,651	$537,965	
24	Northeast	$38,860	$714,009	$751,724	$620,019	
25	South	$0	$839,551	$918,588	$844,186	
26	West	$28,663	$65,382	$70,057	$75,349	
27						

FIGURE 3-18 The wording is confusing, but you can toggle off the grand total column, row, or both.

If you want a grand total column but no grand total at the bottom, choose On For Rows Only, as shown at the top of Figure 3-18. To me, this seems backward. To keep the grand total column, you have to choose to turn on grand totals for rows only. I guess the rationale is that each cell in F5:F8 is a grand total of the row to the left of the cell. Hence, you are showing the grand totals for all the rows but not for the columns. Perhaps someday Microsoft will ship a version of Excel in English-Midwest where this setting would be called "Keep the Grand Total Column." But for now, it remains confusing.

In a similar fashion, to show a grand total row but no grand total column, you open the Grand Totals menu and choose On For Columns Only. Again, in some twisted version of the English language, cell B18 is totaling the cells in the column above it.

The final choice, Off For Rows And Columns, is simple enough. Excel shows neither a grand total column nor a grand total row.

> **Tip** You can abandon these confusing menu choices by using the right-click menu. If you right-click on any cell that has the words "Grand Total," you can choose Remove Grand Total.

Back in Excel 2003, pivot tables were shown in Tabular layout and logical headings such as Region and Product would appear in the pivot table, as shown in the top pivot table in Figure 3-19. When the Excel team switched to Compact form, they replaced those headings with Row Labels and Column Labels. These add nothing to the report. To toggle off those headings, look on the far-right side of the Analyze tab for an icon called Field Headers and click it to remove Row Labels and Column Labels from your pivot tables in Compact form.

▲	A	B	C	D	E	F
1						
2	Tabular Form					
3	Revenue	Product	▼			
4	Region ▼	Doodads		Gadget	Gizmo	Widget	Grand Total
5	Midwest		$6,036	$544,772	$652,651	$537,965	$1,741,424
6	Northeast		$38,860	$714,009	$751,724	$620,019	$2,124,612
7	South		$0	$839,551	$918,588	$844,186	$2,602,325
8	West		$28,663	$65,382	$70,057	$75,349	$239,451
9						
10	Compact Form - "Region" becomes "Row Labels"					
11	Revenue	Column Labels	▼			
12	Row Lab ▼	Doodads		Gadget	Gizmo	Widget	Grand Total
13	Midwest		$6,036	$544,772	$652,651	$537,965	$1,741,424
14	Northeast		$38,860	$714,009	$751,724	$620,019	$2,124,612
15	South		$0	$839,551	$918,588	$844,186	$2,602,325
16	West		$28,663	$65,382	$70,057	$75,349	$239,451
17						
18	Compact Form - Toggle Off Field Headers					
19	Revenue					
20		Doodads		Gadget	Gizmo	Widget	Grand Total
21	Midwest		$6,036	$544,772	$652,651	$537,965	$1,741,424
22	Northeast		$38,860	$714,009	$751,724	$620,019	$2,124,612
23	South		$0	$839,551	$918,588	$844,186	$2,602,325
24	West		$28,663	$65,382	$70,057	$75,349	$239,451

FIGURE 3-19 The Compact form introduced in Excel 2007 replaced useful headings with Row Labels. You can turn these off.

> **Caution** When you arrange several pivot tables vertically, as in Figure 3-19, you'll notice that changes in one pivot table change the column widths for the entire column, often causing #### to appear in the other pivot tables. By default, Excel changes the column width to AutoFit the pivot table but ignores anything else in the column. To turn off this default behavior, right-click each pivot table and choose PivotTable Options. In the first tab of the Options dialog box, the second-to-last check box is AutoFit Column Widths On Update. Clear this check box.

Customizing a pivot table's appearance with styles and themes

You can quickly apply color and formatting to a pivot table report by using the 85 built-in styles in the PivotTable Styles gallery on the Design tab. These 85 styles are further modified by the four check boxes to the left of the gallery. Throw in the 48 themes on the Page Layout tab, and you have 65,280 easy ways to format a pivot table. If none of those provide what you need, you can define a new style.

Start with the four check boxes in the PivotTable Style Options group of the Design tab of the ribbon. You can choose to apply special formatting to the row headers, column headers, banded rows, or banded columns. My favorite choice here is banded rows because it makes it easier for the reader's eye to follow a row across a wide report. You should choose from these settings first because the choices here will modify the thumbnails shown in the Styles gallery.

As mentioned earlier, the PivotTable Styles gallery on the Design tab offers 85 built-in styles. Grouped into 28 styles each of Light, Medium, and Dark, the gallery offers variations on the accent colors used in the current theme. In Figure 3-20, you can see which styles in the gallery truly support banded rows and which just offer a bottom border between rows.

FIGURE 3-20 The styles are shown here with accents for row headers, column headers, and alternating colors in the columns.

Tip   Note that you can modify the thumbnails for the 85 styles shown in the gallery by using the four check boxes in the PivotTable Style Options group.

The Live Preview feature in Excel 2019 works in the Styles gallery. As you hover your mouse cursor over style thumbnails, the worksheet shows a preview of the style.

Customizing a style

You can create your own pivot table styles, and the new styles are added to the gallery for the current workbook only. To use the custom style in another workbook, copy and temporarily paste the formatted pivot table to the other workbook. After the pivot table has been pasted, apply the custom style to an existing pivot table in your workbook and then delete the temporary pivot table.

Say that you want to create a pivot table style in which the banded colors are three rows high. Follow these steps to create the new style:

1. Find an existing style in the PivotTable Styles gallery that supports banded rows. Right-click the style in the gallery and select Duplicate. Excel displays the Modify PivotTable Quick Style dialog box.

2. Choose a new name for the style. Excel initially appends a 2 to the existing style name, which means you have a name such as PivotStyleDark3 2. Type a better name, such as **Greenbar**.

3. In the Table Element list, click First Row Stripe. A new section called Stripe Size appears in the dialog box.

4. Select 3 from the Stripe Size drop-down, as shown in Figure 3-21.

5. To change the stripe color, click the Format button. The Format Cells dialog box appears. Click the Fill tab and then choose a fill color. If you want to be truly authentic, choose More Colors, Custom and use Red=200, Green=225, and Blue=204 to simulate 1980s-era greenbar paper. Click OK to accept the color and return to the Modify PivotTable Quick Style dialog box.

6. In the Table Element List, click Second Row Stripe. Select 3 from the Stripe Size drop-down. Modify the format to use a lighter color, such as white.

7. If you plan on creating more pivot tables in this workbook, choose the Set As Default PivotTable Style For This Document check box in the lower left.

8. Optionally, edit the colors for Header Row and Grand Total Row.

9. Click OK to finish building the style. Strangely, Excel doesn't automatically apply this new style to the pivot table. After you put in a few minutes of work to tweak the style, the pivot table does not change.

10. Your new style should be the first thumbnail visible in the Styles gallery. Click that style to apply it to the pivot table.

FIGURE 3-21 Customize the style in the Modify PivotTable Style dialog box.

> **Tip** If you have not added more than seven custom styles, the thumbnail should be visible in the closed gallery, so you can choose it without reopening the gallery.

Modifying styles with document themes

The formatting options for pivot tables in Excel 2019 are impressive. The 84 styles combined with 16 combinations of the Style options make for hundreds of possible format combinations.

In case you become tired of these combinations, you can visit the Themes drop-down menu on the Page Layout tab, where many built-in themes are available. Each theme has a new combination of accent colors, fonts, and shape effects.

To change a document theme, open the Themes drop-down menu on the Page Layout tab. Choose a new theme, and the colors used in the pivot table change to match the theme.

> **Caution** Changing the theme affects the entire workbook. It changes the colors and fonts and affects all charts, shapes, tables, and pivot tables on all worksheets of the active workbook. If you have several other pivot tables in the workbook, changing the theme will apply new colors to all the pivot tables.

> **Tip** Some of the themes use unusual fonts. You can apply the colors from a theme without changing the fonts in your document by using the Colors drop-down menu next to the Themes menu, as shown in Figure 3-22.

FIGURE 3-22 Choose new colors from the Colors menu.

Changing summary calculations

When you create a pivot table report, by default Excel summarizes the data by either counting or summing the items. Instead of Sum or Count, you might want to choose functions such as Min, Max, and Count Numeric. In all, 11 options are available.

The Excel team fixed the Count Of Revenue bug

In early 2018, Microsoft fixed a bug that caused many pivot tables to provide a count of revenue instead of a sum. If a data column contains all numbers, Excel will default to Sum as the calculation. If a column contains text, the pivot table will default to Count. But up until 2018, a bug appeared if you had a mix of numbers and empty cells. An empty cell would cause your pivot table to Count instead of Sum.

One Excel customer wrote a letter to the Excel team describing this bug: "Why are you treating empty cells as text? Treat them like any other formula would treat them and consider them to be zero. A mix of numbers and zeroes should not cause a Count of that field."

Without a single vote on Excel.UserVoice.com, someone on the Excel team patched the bug. If you have a mix of numbers and blank cells, you will no longer get a Count Of Revenue. This is a nice improvement.

Changing the calculation in a value field

The Value Field Settings dialog box offers 11 options on the Summarize Values As tab and 15 main options on the Show Values As tab. The options on the first tab are the basic Sum, Average, Count, Max, and Min options that are ubiquitous throughout Excel; the 15 options under Show Values As are interesting ones such as % of Total, Running Total, and Ranks.

There are several ways to open the Value Field Settings dialog box:

- If you have multiple fields in the Values area, double-click the heading for any value field.

- Choose any number in the Values area and click the Field Settings button in the Analyze tab of the ribbon.

- In the PivotTable Fields list, open the drop-down menu for any item in the Values area. The last item will be Value Field Settings.

- If you right-click any number in the Values area, you have a choice for Value Field Settings, plus two additional flyout menus offering six of the eleven choices for Summarize Values By and most of the choices for Show Values As (see Figure 3-23).

FIGURE 3-23   The right-click menu for any number in the Values area offers a flyout menu with the popular calculation options.

The following examples show how to use the various calculation options. To contrast the settings, you can build a pivot table where you drag the Revenue field to the Values area nine separate times.

Each one shows up as a new column in the pivot table. Over the next several examples, you will see the settings required for the calculations in each column.

To change the calculation for a field, select one Value cell for the field and click the Field Settings button on the Analyze tab of the ribbon. The Value Field Settings dialog box is similar to the Field Settings dialog box, but it has two tabs. The first tab, Summarize Values By, contains Sum, Count, Average, Max, Min, Product, Count Numbers, StdDev, StdDevP, Var, and VarP. You can choose 1 of these 11 calculation options to change the data in the column. In Figure 3-24, columns B through D show various settings from the Summarize Values By tab.

	A	B	C	D	E	F	G	H	I	J
2		Summarize Value By				Show Values As				
4	Rep	Total	Average	# of Orders	% of Total	% of Anne	Rank	RunTotal	% RunTot	ChgFromPrev
5	Anne Troy	$1,372,957	$11,836	116	20.47%	100.00%	2	1372957	20.47%	
6	Jade Miller	$2,124,612	$11,301	188	31.67%	154.75%	1	3497569	52.14%	54.75%
7	Jeffrey P. Coulson	$796,239	$10,760	74	11.87%	57.99%	4	4293808	64.01%	-62.52%
8	John Cockerill	$42,316	$10,579	4	0.63%	3.08%	10	4336124	64.64%	-94.69%
9	John Durran	$200,201	$12,513	16	2.98%	14.58%	7	4536325	67.63%	373.11%
10	Larry Vance	$869,454	$13,376	65	12.96%	63.33%	3	5405779	80.59%	334.29%
11	Michael Karpfen	$530,306	$12,052	44	7.91%	38.63%	5	5936085	88.50%	-39.01%
12	Mike Mann	$184,425	$15,369	12	2.75%	13.43%	8	6120510	91.24%	-65.22%
13	Richard Oldcorn	$107,016	$13,377	8	1.60%	7.79%	9	6227526	92.84%	-41.97%
14	Ryan Wilson	$406,326	$14,512	28	6.06%	29.59%	6	6633852	98.90%	279.69%
15	Sabine Hanschitz	$34,710	$8,678	4	0.52%	2.53%	12	6668562	99.41%	-91.46%
16	Todd A Lesko	$39,250	$9,813	4	0.59%	2.86%	11	6707812	100.00%	13.08%
17	Grand Total	$6,707,812	$11,914	563	100.00%					

Value Field Settings

Source Name: Revenue

Custom Name: Average

Summarize Values By | Show Values As

Summarize value field by

Choose the type of calculation that you want to use to summarize data from the selected field

Sum
Count
Average
Max
Min
Product

Number Format | OK | Cancel

FIGURE 3-24 Choose from the 11 summary calculations on this tab.

Column B is the default Sum calculation. It shows the total of all records for a given market. Column C shows the average order for each item by market. Column D shows a count of the records. You can change the heading to say # Of Orders or # Of Records or whatever is appropriate. Note that the count is the actual count of records, not the count of distinct items.

> **Note** Counting distinct items has been difficult in pivot tables but is now easier using PowerPivot. See Chapter 10 for more details.

Far more interesting options appear on the Show Values As tab of the Value Field Settings dialog box, as shown in Figure 3-25. Fifteen options appear in the drop-down. Depending on the option you choose, you might need to specify either a base field or a base field and a base item. Columns E through J in Figures 3-24 and 3-25 show some of the calculations possible using Show Values As.

Rename field as appropriate

Base Field and Base Item are selectively enabled

FIGURE 3-25   Fifteen different ways to show that data is available on this tab.

Table 3-1 summarizes the Show Values As options.

TABLE 3-1   Calculations in Show Value As

Show Value As	Additional Required Information	Description
No Calculation	None	
% of Grand Total	None	Shows percentages so all the detail cells in the pivot table total 100%.
% of Column Total	None	Shows percentages that total up and down the pivot table to 100%.
% of Row Total	None	Shows percentages that total across the pivot table to 100%.
% of Parent Row Total	None	With multiple row fields, shows a percentage of the parent item's total row.
% of Parent Column Total	None	With multiple column fields, shows percentage of the parent column's total.
Index	None	Calculates the relative importance of items. For an example, see Figure 3.31.
% of Parent Total	Base Field only	With multiple row and/or column fields, calculates a cell's percentage of the parent item's total.
Running Total In	Base Field only	Calculates a running total.
% Running Total In	Base Field only	Calculates a running total as a percentage of the total.
Rank Smallest to Largest	Base Field only	Provides a numeric rank, with 1 as the smallest item.
Rank Largest to Smallest	Base Field only	Provides a numeric rank, with 1 as the largest item.

% of	Base Field and Base Item	Expresses the values for one item as a percentage of another item.
Difference From	Base Field and Base Item	Shows the difference of one item compared to another item or to the previous item.
% Difference From	Base Field and Base Item	Shows the percentage difference of one item compared to another item or to the previous item.

The capability to create custom calculations is another example of the unique flexibility of pivot table reports. With the Show Data As setting, you can change the calculation for a particular data field to be based on other cells in the Values area.

The following sections illustrate a number of Show Values As options.

Showing percentage of total

In Figure 3-24, column E shows % Of Total. Jade Miller, with $2.1 million in revenue, represents 31.67% of the $6.7 million total revenue. Column E uses % Of Column Total on the Show Values As tab. Two other similar options are % Of Row Total and % Of Grand Total. Choose one of these based on whether your text fields are going down the report, across the report, or both down and across.

Using % Of to compare one line to another line

The % Of option enables you to compare one item to another item. For example, in the current data set, Anne was the top sales rep in the previous year. Column F shows everyone's sales as a percentage of Anne's. Cell F7 in Figure 3-26 shows that Jeff's sales were almost 58% of Anne's sales.

FIGURE 3-26   This report is created using the % Of option with Anne Troy as the Base Item.

To set up this calculation, choose Show Values As, % Of. For Base Field, choose Rep because this is the only field in the Rows area. For Base Item, choose Anne Troy. The result is shown in Figure 3-26.

Showing rank

Two ranking options are available. Column G in Figure 3-27 shows Rank Largest To Smallest. Jade Miller is ranked #1, and Sabine Hanschitz is #12. A similar option is Rank Smallest To Largest, which would be good for the pro golf tour.

	A	B	C	D	E	F	G	H	I	J	K	L
2			Summarize Value By				Show Values As					
4	Rep	Total	Average	# of Orders	Sum of Revenue4	% of Anne	Rank					
5	Anne Troy	$1,372,957	$11,836	116		20.47%	100.00%	2				
6	Jade Miller	$2,124,612	$11,301	188		31.67%	154.75%	1				
7	Jeffrey P. Coulson	$796,239	$10,760	74		11.87%	57.99%	4				
8	John Cockerill	$42,316	$10,579	4		0.63%	3.08%	10				
9	John Durran	$200,201	$12,513	16		2.98%	14.58%	7				
10	Larry Vance	$869,454	$13,376	65		12.96%	63.33%	3				
11	Michael Karpfen	$530,306	$12,052	44		7.91%	38.63%	5				
12	Mike Mann	$184,425	$15,369	12		2.75%	13.43%	8				
13	Richard Oldcorn	$107,016	$13,377	8		1.60%	7.79%	9				
14	Ryan Wilson	$406,326	$14,512	28		6.06%	29.59%	6				
15	Sabine Hanschitz	$34,710	$8,678	4		0.52%	2.53%	12				
16	Todd A Lesko	$39,250	$9,813	4		0.59%	2.86%	11				
17	Grand Total	$6,707,812	$11,914	563		100.00%						

FIGURE 3-27 The Rank options will rank ascending or descending.

To set up a rank, choose Value Field Settings, Show Values As, Rank Largest To Smallest. You are required to choose Base Field. In this example, because Rep is the only row field, it is the selection under Base Field.

These rank options show that pivot tables have a strange way of dealing with ties. I say *strange* because they do not match any of the methods already established by the Excel functions =RANK(), =RANK.AVG(), and =RANK.EQ(). For example, if the top two markets have a tie, they are both assigned a rank of 1, and the third market is assigned a rank of 2.

Tracking running total and percentage of running total

Running total calculations are common in reports where you have months running down the column or when you want to show that the top *N* customers make up *N*% of the revenue.

In Figure 3-28, cell I8 shows that the top four sales reps account for 76.97% of the total sales.

> **Note** To produce this figure, you have to use the Sort feature, which is discussed in depth in Chapter 4, "Grouping, sorting, and filtering pivot data." To create a similar analysis with the sample file, go to the drop-down menu in A4 and choose More Sort Options, Descending, By Total. Also note that the % Change From calculation shown in the next example is not compatible with sorting.

FIGURE 3-28 Show running totals or a running percentage of total.

To specify Running Total In (as shown in Column H) or % Running Total In (Column I), select Field Settings, Show Values As, Running Total In. You have to specify a Base Field, which in this case is the Row Field: Rep.

Displaying a change from a previous field

Figure 3-29 shows the % Difference From setting. This calculation requires a Base Field and Base Item. You could show how each market compares to Anne Troy by specifying Anne Troy as the Base Item. This would be similar to Figure 3-26, except each market would be shown as a percentage of Anne Troy.

FIGURE 3-29 The % Difference From options enable you to compare each row to the previous or next row.

With date fields, it would make sense to use % Difference From and choose (previous) as the base item. Note that the first cell will not have a calculation because there is no previous data in the pivot table.

Tracking the percentage of a parent item

The legacy % Of Total settings always divides the current item by the grand total. In Figure 3-30, cell E4 says that Chicago is 2.75% of the total data set. A common question at the MrExcel.com message board is how to calculate Chicago's revenue as a percentage of the Midwest region total. This was possible but difficult in older versions of Excel. Starting in Excel 2010, though, Excel added the % Of Parent Row, % Of Parent Column, and % Of Parent Total options.

FIGURE 3-30 An option in Excel enables you to calculate a percentage of the parent row.

To set up this calculation in Excel 2019, use Field Settings, Show Values As, % Of Parent Row Total. Cell D4 in Figure 3-30 shows that Chicago's $184,425 is 10.59% of the Midwest total of $1,741,424.

Although it makes sense, the calculation on the subtotal rows might seem confusing. D4:D8 shows the percentage of each market as compared to the Midwest total. The values in D9, D11, D16, and D19 compare the region total to the grand total. For example, the 31.67% in D11 says that the Northeast region's $2.1 million is a little less than a third of the $6.7 million grand total.

Tracking relative importance with the Index option

The final option, Index, creates a somewhat obscure calculation. Microsoft claims that this calculation describes the relative importance of a cell within a column. In Figure 3-31, Georgia peaches have an index of 2.55, and California peaches have an index of 0.50. This shows that if the peach crop is wiped out next year, it will be more devastating to Georgia fruit production than to California fruit production.

⏵	A	B	C	D	E	F	G	H	I
1	Sum of Sales	State						GA Peach	180
2	Crop	California	Georgia		Ohio Grand Total			/ GA Total	210
3	Apple	100	10	30	140			A = Worth of Peaches to GA	0.86
4	Banana	200	10	1	211				
5	Kiwi	200	10	1	211			Peach Total	285
6	Peach	100	180	5	285			/ Total	847
7	Grand Total	600	210	37	847			B = Worth of Peaches	0.34
8									
9								Index is A/B	2.55
10	Index	State							
11	Crop	California	Georgia		Ohio Grand Total				
12	Apple	1.01	0.29	4.91	1.00				
13	Banana	1.34	0.19	0.11	1.00				
14	Kiwi	1.34	0.19	0.11	1.00				
15	Peach	0.50	2.55	0.40	1.00				
16	Grand Total	1.00	1.00	1.00	1.00				

$$= \frac{GeorgiaPeach + GeorgiaTotal}{PeachTotal + Total}$$

FIGURE 3-31 Using the Index function, Excel shows that peach sales are more important in Georgia than in California.

Here is the exact calculation: First, divide Georgia peaches by the Georgia total. This is 180/210, or 0.857. Next, divide total peach production (285) by total fruit production (847). This shows that peaches have an importance ratio of 0.336. Now, divide the first ratio by the second ratio: 0.857/0.336.

In Ohio, apples have an index of 4.91, so an apple blight would be bad for the Ohio fruit industry.

I have to admit that, even after writing about this calculation for 10 years, there are parts that I don't quite comprehend. What if a state like Hawaii relied on productions of lychees, but lychees were nearly immaterial to U.S. fruit production? If lychees were half of Hawaii's fruit production but 0.001 of U.S. fruit production, the Index calculation would skyrocket to 500.

Adding and removing subtotals

Subtotals are an essential feature of pivot table reporting. Sometimes you might want to suppress the display of subtotals, and other times you might want to show more than one subtotal per field.

Suppressing subtotals with many row fields

When you have many row fields in a report, subtotals can obscure your view. For example, in Figure 3-32, there is no need to show subtotals for each market because there is only one sales rep for each market.

3	Region	Market	Rep	Sum of Revenue
4	⊟ Midwest	⊟ Chicago	Mike Mann	184425
5		Chicago Total		184425
6		⊟ Cincinnati	Richard Oldcorn	107016
7		Cincinnati Total		107016
8		⊟ Detroit	Anne Troy	1372957
9		Detroit Total		1372957
10		⊟ Louisville	John Cockerill	42316
11		Louisville Total		42316
12		⊟ Minneapolis	Sabine Hanschitz	34710
13		Minneapolis Total		34710
14	Midwest Total			1741424
15	⊟ Northeast	⊟ New York	Jade Miller	2124612
16		New York Total		2124612
17	Northeast Total			2124612
18	⊟ South	⊟ Arkla	Larry Vance	869454
19		Arkla Total		869454

FIGURE 3-32 Sometimes you do not need subtotals at every level.

If you used the Subtotals drop-down menu on the Design tab, you would turn off all subtotals, including the Region subtotals and the Market subtotals. The Region subtotals are still providing good information, so you want to use the Subtotals setting in the Field Settings dialog box. Choose one cell in the Market column. On the Analyze tab, choose Field Settings. Change the Subtotals setting from Automatic to None (see Figure 3-33).

FIGURE 3-33 Use the Subtotals setting in the Field list to turn off subtotals for one field.

To remove subtotals for the Market field, click the Market field in the bottom section of the Pivot-Table Fields list. Select Field Settings. In the Field Settings dialog box, select None under Subtotals, as shown in Figure 3-33. Alternatively, right-click a cell that contains a Market and remove the check mark from Subtotal Market.

Adding multiple subtotals for one field

You can add customized subtotals to a row or column label field. Select the Region field in the bottom of the PivotTable Fields list, and select Field Settings.

In the Field Settings dialog box for the Region field, select Custom and then select the types of subtotals you would like to see. The dialog box in Figure 3-34 shows five custom subtotals selected for the Region field. It is rare to see pivot tables use this setting. It is not perfect. Note that the count of 211 records in cell D25 automatically gets a currency format like the rest of the column, even though this is not a dollar figure. Also, the average of $12,333 for South is an average of the detail records, not an average of the individual market totals.

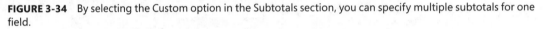

FIGURE 3-34   By selecting the Custom option in the Subtotals section, you can specify multiple subtotals for one field.

> **Tip**   If you need to calculate the average of the four regions, you can do it with the DAX formula language and Power Pivot. See Chapter 10.

Formatting one cell is new in Office 365

In the summer of 2018, a new trick appeared for Office 365 customers. You can format a cell in a pivot table, and the formatting will follow that position.

For example, in Figure 3-35, a white font on dark fill has been applied to Revenue for Doodads sales to the Software sector.

FIGURE 3-35 A new Format Cells option appears in the right-click context menu.

If you rearrange the pivot table, the dark formatting will follow the cell in the pivot table. While cell B9 was formatted in Figure 3.35, the formatting has moved to D5 in Figure 3.36.

Note that the formatting will persist if you remove the cell due to a filter. If you unselect Software from the Slicer and then reselect Software, the formatting will return.

However, if you remove Sector, Product, or Revenue from the pivot table, the individual cell formatting will be lost.

FIGURE 3-36 Rearrange the pivot table and the formatting moves so that revenue for doodads sales to the software sector stays formatted.

In Figure 3.37, a Customer field has been added as the inner-row field. The dark formatting applied to Doodads sales of Software is now expanded to C5:C8 to encompass all four customers in this group. Note that in cell C9, the subtotal for Doodads sold to the Software sector is not formatted.

⬛	A	B	C	D
2				
3	Revenue		Product ▾	
4	Sector ⌃▾	Customer ▾	Doodads	Gadget
5	⊟Software	Excel4Apps	$0	$233,43
6	Software	F-Keys Ltd.	$0	$100,78
7	Software	Vertex42	$38,860	$22,14
8	Software	Frontline Systems	$0	$14,49
9	Software Total		$38,860	$370,85
10	⊟Training	599CD.com	$0	$185,67

FIGURE 3-37 If you add an inner-row field, the formatting will expand to encompass all customers for Doodads in the Software sector.

Next steps

Note that the following pivot table customizations are covered in subsequent chapters:

- Sorting a pivot table is covered in Chapter 4, "Grouping, sorting, and filtering pivot data."

- Filtering records in a pivot table is covered in Chapter 4.

- Grouping daily dates up to months or years is covered in Chapter 4.

- Adding new calculated fields is covered in Chapter 5, "Performing calculations in pivot tables."

- Using data visualizations and conditional formatting in a pivot table is covered in Chapter 4.

Grouping, sorting, and filtering pivot data

In this chapter, you will:

- Use the PivotTable Fields list
- Sort in a pivot table
- Filter a pivot table: an overview
- Use filters for row and column fields
- Filter using the Filters area
- Group and create hierarchies in a pivot table

With Excel 2019, Microsoft has reversed the auto date grouping added to Excel 2016. Removing the feature was a good move, as the feature proved hard to predict. For anyone who loved the auto grouping and the Drill-Down and Drill-Up features, you can re-create them, although it requires a few extra steps. Grouping will be covered last in this chapter.

First, a quick overview of the PivotTable Fields. Then, a detailed look at sorting, filtering, and grouping a pivot table.

Using the PivotTable Fields list

The entry points for sorting and filtering are spread throughout the Excel interface. It is worth taking a closer look at the row header drop-downs and the PivotTable Fields list before diving in to sorting and filtering.

As you've seen in these pages, I rarely use the Compact form for a pivot table. I use Pivot Table Defaults to make sure my pivot tables start in Tabular layout instead of Compact layout. Although there are many good reasons for this, one is illustrated in Figures 4-1 and 4-2.

FIGURE 4-1 The drop-down menu in B3 for Customer is separate from the drop-down menu for Region.

FIGURE 4-2 In Compact form, one single drop-down menu tries to control sorting and filtering for all the row fields.

In Figure 4-1, a Region drop-down menu appears in A3. A Customer drop-down menu appears in B3. Each of these separate drop-downs offers great settings for sorting and filtering.

When you leave the pivot table in the Compact form, there are not separate headings for Region and Customer. Both fields are crammed into column A, with the silly heading Row Labels. This means the drop-down menu always offers sorting and filtering options for Region. Every time you go back to the A3 drop-down menu with hopes of filtering or sorting the Customer field, you have to reselect Customer from a drop-down at the top of the menu. This is an extra click. If you are making five changes to the Customer field, you are reselecting Customer over and over and over and over and over. This should be enough to convince you to abandon the Compact layout.

If you decide to keep the Compact layout and get frustrated with the consolidated Row Labels drop-down menu, you can directly access the invisible drop-down menu for the correct field by using the PivotTable Fields list, which contains a visible drop-down menu for every field in the areas at the bottom. Those visible drop-down menus do not contain the sorting and filtering options.

The good drop-down menus are actually in the top of the Fields list, but you have to hover over the field to see the drop-down menu appear. After you hover as shown in Figure 4-3, you can directly access the same customer drop-down menu shown in Figure 4-1.

FIGURE 4-3   Hover over the field in the top of the Fields list to directly access the sorting and filtering settings for that field.

Docking and undocking the PivotTable Fields list

The PivotTable Fields list starts out docked on the right side of the Excel window. Hover over the green PivotTable Fields heading in the pane, and the mouse pointer changes to a four-headed arrow. Drag to the left to enable the pane to float anywhere in your Excel window.

After you have undocked the PivotTable Fields list, you might find that it is difficult to redock it on either side of the screen. To redock the Fields list, you must grab the title bar and drag until at least 85% of the Fields list is off the edge of the window. Pretend that you are trying to remove the floating Fields list completely from the screen. Eventually, Excel gets the hint and redocks it. Note that you can dock the PivotTable Fields list on either the right side or the left side of the screen.

Rearranging the PivotTable Fields list

As shown in Figure 4-4, a small gear-wheel icon appears near the top of the PivotTable Fields list. Select this drop-down menu to see its five possible arrangements. Although the default is to have the Fields section at the top of the list and the Areas section at the bottom of the list, four other arrangements are possible. Other options let you control whether the fields in the list appear alphabetically or in the same sequence that they appeared in the original data set.

FIGURE 4-4 Use this drop-down menu to rearrange the PivotTable Fields list.

The final three arrangements offered in the drop-down menu are rather confusing. If someone changes the PivotTable Fields list to show only the Areas section, you cannot see new fields to add to the pivot table.

If you ever encounter a version of the PivotTable Fields list with only the Areas section (see Figure 4-4) or only the Fields section, remember that you can return to a less-confusing view of the data by using the arrangement drop-down menu.

Using the Areas section drop-downs

As shown in Figure 4-5, every field in the Areas section has a visible drop-down arrow. When you select this drop-down arrow, you see four categories of choices:

- The first four choices enable you to rearrange the field within the list of fields in that area of the pivot table. You can accomplish this by dragging the field up or down in the area.

- The next four choices enable you to move the field to a new area. You could also accomplish this by dragging the field to a new area.

- The next choice enables you to remove the field from the pivot table. You can also accomplish this by dragging the field outside the Fields list.

- The final choice displays the Field Settings dialog box for the field.

FIGURE 4-5 Use this drop-down menu to rearrange the fields in your pivot table.

Sorting in a pivot table

Items in the row area and column area of a pivot table are sorted in ascending order by any custom list first. This allows weekday and month names to sort into Monday, Tuesday, Wednesday, … instead of the alphabetical order Friday, Monday, Saturday, …, Wednesday.

If the items do not appear in a custom list, they will be sorted in ascending order. This is fine, but in many situations, you want the customer with the largest revenue to appear at the top of the list. When you sort in descending order using a pivot table, you are setting up a rule that controls how that field is sorted, even after new fields are added to the pivot table.

> **Tip** Excel 2019 includes four custom lists by default, but you can add your own custom list to control the sort order of future pivot tables. See the section "Using a custom list for sorting," later in this chapter.

Sorting customers into high-to-low sequence based on revenue

Three pivot tables appear in Figure 4-6. The first pivot table shows the default sort for a pivot table: Customers are arranged alphabetically, starting with Adaept, Calleia, and so on.

In the second pivot table, the report is sorted in descending sequence by Total Revenue. This pivot table was sorted by selecting cell E3 and choosing the ZA icon in the Data tab of the ribbon. Although that sounds like a regular sort, it is better. When you sort inside a pivot table, Excel sets up a rule that will be used after you make additional changes to the pivot table.

	A	B	C	D	E	F	G	H
1	Customers AZ is default			Sort descending by revenue			After adding fields, sort rule remains	
2								
3	Customer	Total $		Customer	Total $			Total $
4	Adaept Information Mana	498937		MySpreadsheetLab	869454		⊟Consulting	2555333
5	Calleia Company	406326		Surten Excel	750163		Surten Excel	750163
6	Excel Design Solutions Ltd	71651		SkyWire, Inc.	704359		NetCom Computer	613514
7	Excel Learning Zone	72680		SpringBoard	622794		Adaept Information N	498937
8	Excel4Apps	91320		NetCom Computer	613514		Calleia Company	406326
9	Excel-Translator.de	42316		St. Peter's Prep	568851		Excel Design Solution	71651
10	F-Keys Ltd.	34710		Adaept Information Mana	498937		Yesenita	62744
11	JEVS Human Services	50030		The Salem Ohio Historical	427349		Symons	55251
12	LearnExcelBooks.com	34364		Calleia Company	406326		JEVS Human Services	50030
13	MyExcelOnline.com	54048		MyOnlineTrainingHub.cor	390978		Spain Enterprises	46717
14	MyOnlineTrainingHub.com	390978		Excel4Apps	91320		⊟Museums	427349
15	MySpreadsheetLab	869454		Excel Learning Zone	72680		The Salem Ohio Histo	427349

FIGURE 4-6 When you override the default sort, Excel remembers the sort as additional fields are added.

The pivot table in columns G:H shows what happens after you add Sector as a new outer row field. Within each sector, the pivot table continues to sort the data in descending order by revenue. Within Consulting, Surten Excel appears first, with $750K, followed by NetCom, with $614K.

You could remove Customer from the pivot table, do more adjustments, and then add Customer back to the column area, and Excel would remember that the customers should be presented from high to low.

If you could see the entire pivot table in G3:H35 in Figure 4-6, you would notice that the sectors are sorted alphabetically. It might make more sense, though, to put the largest sectors at the top. The following tricks can be used for sorting an outer row field by revenue:

- You can select cell G4 and then use Collapse Field on the Analyze tab to hide the customer detail. When you have only the sectors showing, select H4 and click ZA to sort descending. Excel understands that you want to set up a sort rule for the Sector field.

- You can temporarily remove Customer from the pivot table, sort descending by revenue, and then add Customer back.

- You can use More Sort Options, as described in the following paragraphs.

To sort the Sector field, you should open the drop-down menu for the Sector field. Hover over Sector in the top of the PivotTable Fields list, and click the drop-down arrow that appears (see Figure 4-7). Or, if your pivot table is shown in Tabular layout or Outline layout, you can simply open the drop-down arrow in cell G3.

Inside the drop-down menu, choose More Sort Options to open the Sort (Sector) dialog box. In this dialog box, you can choose to sort the Sector field in Descending order by Total $ (see Figure 4-8).

FIGURE 4-7 For explicit control over sort order, open this drop-down menu.

FIGURE 4-8 Choose to sort Sector based on the Total $ field.

The Sort (Sector) dialog box shown in Figure 4-8 includes a More Options button in the lower left. If you click this button, you arrive at the More Sort Options dialog box, in which you can specify a custom list to be used for the first key sort order. You can also specify that the sorting should be based on a column other than Grand Total.

In Figure 4-10, the pivot table includes Product in the column area. If you wanted to sort the customers based on total gadget revenue instead of total revenue, for example, you could do so with the More Sort Options dialog box. Here are the steps:

1. Open the Customer heading drop-down menu in B4.

2. Choose More Sort Options.

3. In the Sort (Customer) dialog box, choose More Options.

4. In the More Sort Options (Customer) dialog box, choose the Sort By Values In Selected Column option (see Figure 4-9).

5. Click in the reference box and then click cell D5. Note that you cannot click the Gadget heading in D4; you have to choose one of the Gadget value cells.

6. Click OK twice to return to the pivot table.

FIGURE 4-9 Using More Sort Options, you can sort by a specific pivot field item.

If your pivot table has only one field in the Rows area, you can set up the "Sort by Doodads" rule by doing a simple sort using the Data tab. Select any cell in B5:B30 and choose Data, ZA. The pivot table will be sorted with the largest Doodads customers at the top (see Figure 4-10). Note that you cannot sort from the Doodads heading in B4. Sorting from there will sort the product columns by revenue.

	A	B	C	D	E
3	Total $	Product			
4	Customer	Doodads	Gadget	Gizmo	Widget
5	Excel Learning Zone	38860	22140	11680	0
6	Excel4Apps	28663	20115	30068	12474
7	Excel-Translator.de	6036	18552	17728	0
8	JEVS Human Services	0	30104	4614	15312
9	MySpreadsheetLab	0	304198	288409	276847
10	Adaept Information Management	0	182755	173770	142412

FIGURE 4-10 Sort from cell E5 to sort by Doodads.

Using a manual sort sequence

The Sort dialog box offers something called a *manual sort*. Rather than using the dialog box, you can invoke a manual sort in a surprising way.

Note that the products in Figure 4-10 are in the following order: Doodads, Gadget, Gizmo, and Widget. It appears that the Doodads product line is a minor product line and probably would not fall first in the product list.

Place the cell pointer in cell E4 and type the word **Doodads**. When you press Enter, Excel figures out that you want to move the Doodads column to be last. All the values for this product line move from column B to column E. The values for the remaining products shift to the left.

One unintended consequence is that the customers re-sort based on the product that moved to column B: Gadget. This is because the "Sort by Doodads" rule was actually a "Sort by whatever is in column B" rule.

In Figure 4-11, note the numbers in row 17 and compare them to the numbers in row 5 in Figure 4-10. The values followed the change in headings.

This behavior is completely unintuitive. You should never try this behavior with a regular (non–pivot table) data set in Excel. You would never expect Excel to change the data sequence just by moving the labels. Figure 4-11 shows the pivot table after a new column heading has been typed in cell E4.

	A	B	C	D	E	F
3	Total $	Product				
4	Customer	Gadget	Gizmo	Widget	Doodads	Grand Total
5	St. Peter's Prep	367915	200936	0	0	568851
6	MySpreadsheetLab	304198	288409	276847	0	869454
7	Surten Excel	233435	235761	280967	0	750163
8	NetCom Computer	204234	205758	203522	0	613514
9	SpringBoard	185675	245491	191628	0	622794
10	SkyWire, Inc.	185286	224935	294138	0	704359
11	Adaept Information Management	182755	173770	142412	0	498937
12	The Salem Ohio Historical Society	178254	149551	99544	0	427349
13	Calleia Company	133009	159354	113963	0	406326
14	MyOnlineTrainingHub.com	100784	165727	124467	0	390978
15	JEVS Human Services	30104	4614	15312	0	50030
16	Vertex42	26484	19544	13853	0	59881
17	Excel Learning Zone	22140	11680	0	38860	72680
18	Excel Design Solutions Ltd	20950	41066	9635	0	71651
19	MyExcelOnline.com	20610	7032	26406	0	54048
20	Excel4Apps	20115	30068	12474	28663	91320
21	Spain Enterprises	19520	25378	1819	0	46717

FIGURE 4-11 Simply type a heading in E4 to rearrange the columns.

If you prefer to use the mouse, you can drag and drop the column heading to a new location. Select a column heading. Hover over the edge of the active cell border until the mouse changes to a four-headed arrow. Drag the cell to a new location, as shown in Figure 4-12. When you release the mouse, all the value settings move to the new column.

	A	B	C	D	E	F
3	Total $	Product			D4:D31	
4	Customer	Gadget	Gizmo	Widget	Doodads	Grand Total
5	St. Peter's Prep	367915	200936	0	0	568851
6	MySpreadsheetLab	304198	288409	276847	0	869454
7	Surten Excel	233435	235761	280967	0	750163
8	NetCom Computer	204234	205758	203522	0	613514
9	SpringBoard	185675	245491	191628	0	622794
10	SkyWire, Inc.	185286	224935	294138	0	704359

FIGURE 4-12 Use drag and drop to move a column to a new position.

> **Caution** After you use a manual sort, any new products you add to the data source are automatically added to the end of the list rather than appearing alphabetically.

Using a custom list for sorting

Another way to permanently change the order of items along a dimension is to set up a custom list. All future pivot tables created on your computer will automatically respect the order of the items in a custom list.

The pivot table at the top of Figure 4-13 includes weekday names. The weekday names were added to the original data set by using =TEXT(F2,"DDD") and copying down. Excel automatically puts Sunday first and Saturday last, even though this is not the alphabetical sequence of these words. This happens because Excel ships with four custom lists to control the days of the week, months of the year, and the three-letter abbreviations for both.

FIGURE 4-13 The weekday names in B4:H4 follow the order specified in the Custom Lists dialog box.

You can define your own custom list to control the sort order of pivot tables. Follow these steps to set up a custom list:

1. In an out-of-the-way section of the worksheet, type the products in their proper sequence. Type one product per cell, going down a column.

2. Select the cells containing the list of regions in the proper sequence.

3. Click the File tab and select Options.

4. Select the Advanced category in the left navigation bar. Scroll down to the General group and click the Edit Custom Lists button. In the Custom Lists dialog box, your selection address is entered in the Import text box, as shown in Figure 4-13.

5. Click Import to bring the products in as a new list.

6. Click OK to close the Custom Lists dialog box, and then click OK to close the Excel Options dialog box.

The custom list is now stored on your computer and is available for all future Excel sessions. All future pivot tables will automatically show the product field in the order specified in the custom list. Figure 4-14 shows a new pivot table created after the custom list was set up.

	A	B	C	D	E	F
3	Sum of Profit	Product				
4	Market	Gizmo	Widget	Gadget	Doodads	Grand Total
5	New York	273896	150766	318020	16996	759678
6	Arkla	124684	123662	133824	0	382170
7	Atlanta	81760	64372	87576	0	233708
8	Charlotte	71540	49973	57072	0	178585

FIGURE 4-14 After you define a custom list, all future pivot tables will follow the order in the list.

To sort an existing pivot table by the newly defined custom list, follow these steps:

1. Open the Product header drop-down menu and choose More Sort Options.

2. In the Sort (Product) dialog box, choose More Options.

3. In the More Sort Options (Product) dialog box, clear the AutoSort check box.

4. As shown in Figure 4-15, in the More Sort Options (Product) dialog box, open the First Key Sort Order drop-down menu and select the custom list with your product names.

5. Click OK twice.

1	Total $	Weekda ▾							Gran
2	Years ▾	Sun	Mon	Tue	Wed	Thu	Fri	Sat	Gran
3	2018	467298	464146	676020	548114	407297	336666	508012	3
4	2019	500421	436751	484159	550600	498438	441651	388239	3
5	Grand Total	967719	900897	1160179	1098714	905735	778317	896251	6
6									
7								Desired Sequence	
8	Total $	Product ▾						Gizmo	
9	Years ▾	Gadget	Widget	Gizmo	Doodads	Grand Total		Widget	
10	2018	1144099	1046163	1152075	65216	3407553		Gadget	
11	2019	1196997	853974	1240945	8343	3300259		Doodads	
12	Grand Total	2341096	1900137	2393020	73559	6707812			

Custom Lists

Custom Lists

Custom lists:

NEW LIST
Sun, Mon, Tue, Wed, Thu, Fri, :
Sunday, Monday, Tuesday, We
Jan, Feb, Mar, Apr, May, Jun, Jt
January, February, March, Apri
Alabama , Alaska , Arizona , Ari

List entries:

[Add]

[Delete]

Press Enter to separate list entries.
Import list from cells: $H$8:$H$11 [Import]

FIGURE 4-15 Choose to sort by the custom list.

> ⚠ **Caution** Items in a custom list will automatically sort to the top of all future pivot tables. If you have a pivot table of people using their first names, people with names like Jan, May, and April will automatically appear before other names. Names that appear in any list, even across several custom lists will sort in the wrong sequence. To turn off this behavior for one pivot table: right-click one cell in the pivot table and choose PivotTable options. On the Totals & Filters tab, unselect Use Custom Lists When Sorting. If you want to turn this off for all pivot tables, change the Pivot Table Defaults using File, Options, Data, Edit Default Layout, PivotTable Options.

Filtering a pivot table: an overview

Excel 2019 provides dozens of ways to filter a pivot table. Figure 4-16 shows some of the filters available. These methods, and the best way to use each one, are discussed in the following sections.

FIGURE 4-16 This figure shows a fraction of the available filtering choices.

There are four ways to filter a pivot table, as shown in Figure 4-16:

- The Date Timeline filter in G4:H10 was introduced in Excel 2013.

- The Market filter in G12:H19 is an example of the slicer introduced in Excel 2010.

- A drop-down menu in B1 offers what were known as page filters in Excel 2003, report filters in Excel 2010, and now simply filters.

- Cell G4 offers the top-secret AutoFilter location.

- Drop-down menus in A4 and B3 lead to even more filters.

- You see the traditional check box filters for each pivot item.

- A Search box filter was introduced in Excel 2010.

- A flyout menu has Label filters.

- Depending on the field type, you might see a Value Filters flyout menu, including the powerful Top 10 filter, which can do Top 10, Bottom 5, Bottom 3%, Top $8 Million, and more.

- Depending on the field type, you might see a Date Filters flyout menu, with 37 virtual filters such as Next Month, Last Year, and Year to Date.

Using filters for row and column fields

If you have a field (or fields) in the row or column area of a pivot table, a drop-down menu with filtering choices appears on the header cell for that field. In Figure 4-16, a Customer drop-down menu appears in A4, and a Product drop-down menu appears in B3. The pivot table in that figure is using Tabular layout. If your pivot tables use Compact layout, you see a drop-down menu on the cell with Row Labels or Column Labels.

If you have multiple row fields, it is just as easy to sort using the invisible drop-down menus that appear when you hover over a field in the top of the PivotTable Fields list.

Filtering using the check boxes

You might have a few annoying products appear in a pivot table. In the present example, the Doodads product line is a specialty product with very little sales. It might be an old legacy product that is out of line, but it still gets an occasional order from the scrap bin. Every company seems to have these orphan sales that no one really wants to see.

The check box filter provides an easy way to hide these items. Open the Product drop-down menu and clear the Doodads check box. The product is hidden from view (see Figure 4-17) .

FIGURE 4-17   Open the Product filter and clear the Doodads check box.

What if you need to clear hundreds of items' check boxes in order to leave only a few items selected? You can toggle all items off or on by using the Select All check box at the top of the list. You can then select the few items that you want to show in the pivot table.

In Figure 4-18, Select All turned off all customers and then two clicks reselected Excel4Apps and F-Keys Ltd.

FIGURE 4-18 Use Select All to toggle all items off or on.

The check boxes work great in this tiny data set with 26 customers. In real life, with 500 customers in the list, it will not be this easy to filter your data set by using the check boxes.

Filtering using the search box

When you have hundreds of customers, the search box can be a great timesaver. In Figure 4-19, the database includes consultants, trainers, and other companies. If you want to narrow the list to companies with *Excel* or *spreadsheet* in their name, you can follow these steps:

1. Open the Customer drop-down menu.

2. Type **Excel** in the search box (see Figure 4-19).

FIGURE 4-19 Select the results of the first search.

3. By default, Select All Search Results is selected. Click OK.

4. Open the Customer drop-down menu again.

5. Type **spreadsheet** in the search box.

6. Choose Add Current Selection to Filter, as shown in Figure 4-20. Click OK.

FIGURE 4-20 For the second search, add these results to the existing filter.

You now have all customers with either *Excel* or *spreadsheet* in the name.

> **Caution**   Filters applied with the search box are single-use filters. If you add more data to the underlying data and refresh the pivot table, this filter will not be reevaluated.
>
> If you need to reapply the filter, it would be better to use the Label filters as discussed in the following section. Label filters would work to find every customer with Excel in the name. It would not work to find "Excel or spreadsheet."

Filtering using the Label Filters option

The search box isn't perfect. What if you want to find all the Lotus 1-2-3 consultants and turn those off? There is no Select Everything Except These Results choice. Nor is there a Toggle All Filter Choices choice. However, the Label Filters option enables you to handle queries such as "select all customers that do not contain 'Lotus.'"

Text fields offer a flyout menu called Label Filters. To filter out all of the Insurance customers, you can apply a Does Not Contain filter (see Figure 4-21). In the next dialog box, you can specify that you want customers that do not contain Excel, Exc, or Exc* (see Figure 4-22).

FIGURE 4-21 Choose Label Filters, Does Not Contain.

FIGURE 4-22 Specify to exclude customers containing Excel.

Note that label filters are not additive. You can only apply one label filter at a time. If you take the data in Figure 4-21 and apply a new label filter of between D and Fzzz, some Excel customers that were filtered out in Figure 4-22 come back, as shown in Figure 4-23.

FIGURE 4-23 Note that a second label filter does not get added to the previous filter. Excel is back in.

Filtering a Label column using information in a Values column

The Value Filters flyout menu enables you to filter customers based on information in the Values columns. Perhaps you want to see customers who had between $20,000 and $30,000 of revenue. You can use the Customer heading drop-down menu to control this. Here's how:

1. Open the Customer drop-down menu.

2. Choose Label Filters.

3. Choose Between (see Figure 4-24).

4. Type the values **20000** and **30000**, as shown in Figure 4-25.

FIGURE 4-24 Value Filters for the Customer column will look at values in the Revenue field.

FIGURE 4-25 Choose customers between 20000 and 30000, inclusive.

5. Click OK.

The results are inclusive; if a customer had exactly $20,000 or exactly $30,000, they are returned along with the customers between $20,000 and $30,000.

Note Choosing a Value filter clears out any previous Label filters.

Creating a top-five report using the Top 10 filter

One of the more interesting value filters is the Top 10 filter. If you are sending a report to the VP of Sales, she is not going to want to see hundreds of pages of customers. One short summary with the top customers is almost more than her attention span can handle. Here's how to create it:

1. Go to the Customer drop-down menu and choose Value Filters, Top 10.

2. In the Top 10 Filter dialog box, which enables you to choose Top or Bottom, leave the setting at the default of Top.

3. In the second field, enter any number of customers: 10, 5, 7, 12, or something else.

4. In the third drop-down menu on the dialog box, select from Items, Percent, and Sum. You could ask for the top 10 items. You could ask for the top 80% of revenue (which the theory says should be 20% of the customers). Or you could ask for enough customers to reach a sum of $5 million (see Figure 4-26).

FIGURE 4-26 Create a report of the top five customers.

The $1,758,220 total shown in cell B9 in Figure 4-26 is the revenue of only the visible customers. It does not include the revenue for the remaining customers. You might want to show the grand total of all customers at the bottom of the list. You have a few options:

- A setting on the Design tab, under the Subtotals drop-down menu, enables you to include values from filtered items in the totals. This option is available only for OLAP data sets and data sets where you choose Add This Data To The Data Model when creating the pivot table.

> **Note** See Chapter 10, "Unlocking features with the Data Model and Power Pivot," for more information on working with Power Pivot.

- You can remove the grand total from the pivot table in Figure 4-27 and build another one-row pivot table just below this data set. Hide the heading row from the second pivot table, and you will appear to have the true grand total at the bottom of the pivot table.

- If you select the blank cell to the right of the last heading (C3 in Figure 4-26), you can turn on the filter on the Data tab. This filter is not designed for pivot tables and is usually grayed out. After you've added the regular filters, open the drop-down menu in B3. Choose Top 10 Filter and ask for the top six items, as shown in Figure 4-27. This returns the top five customers and the grand total from the data set.

> **Caution** Be aware that this method is taking advantage of a bug in Excel. Normally, the Filter found on the Data tab is not allowed in a pivot table. If you use this method and later refresh the pivot table, the Excel team will not update the filter for you. As far as they know, the option to filter is grayed out when you are in a pivot table.

FIGURE 4-27 You are taking advantage of a hole in the fabric of Excel to apply a regular AutoFilter to a pivot table.

Filtering using the Date filters in the Label drop-down menu

If your label field contains all dates, Excel replaces the Label Filter flyout with a Date Filters flyout. These filters offer many virtual filters, such as Next Week, This Month, Last Quarter, and so on (see Figure 4-28).

FIGURE 4-28 The Date Filters menu offers various virtual date periods.

If you choose Equals, Before, After, or Between, you can specify a date or a range of dates.

Options for the current, past, or next day, week, month, quarter, or year occupy 15 options. Combined with Year To Date, these options change day after day. You can pivot a list of projects by due date and always see the projects that are due in the next week by using this option. When you open the workbook on another day, the report recalculates.

> **Tip** A week runs from Sunday through Saturday. If you select Next Week, the report always shows a period from the next Sunday through the following Saturday.

When you select All Dates In The Period, a new flyout menu offers options such as Each Month and Each Quarter.

Caution If your date field contains dates and times, the Date Filters might not work as expected. You might ask for dates equal to 4/15/2022, and Excel will say that no records are found. The problem is that 6:00 p.m. on 4/15/2022 is stored internally as 44666.75, with the ".75" representing the 18 hours elapsed in the day between midnight and 6:00 p.m. If you want to return all records that happened at any point on April 15, select the Whole Days check box in the Date Filter dialog box.

Filtering using the Filters area

Pivot table veterans remember the old Page area section of a pivot table. This area has been renamed the Filters area and still operates basically the same as in legacy versions of Excel. Microsoft did add the capability to select multiple items from the Filters area. Although the Filters area is not as showy as slicers, it is still useful when you need to replicate your pivot table for every customer.

Adding fields to the Filters area

The pivot table in Figure 4-29 is a perfect ad-hoc reporting tool to give to a high-level executive. He can use the drop-down menus in B1:B4 and E1:E4 to find revenue quickly for any combination of sector, region, market, rep, customer, product, date, or weekday. This is a typical use of filters.

	A	B	C	D	E
1	Sector	(All) ▾		Customer	(All) ▾
2	Region	(All) ▾		Product	Gizmo ▾
3	Market	(All) ▾		Date	(All) ▾
4	Rep	(All) ▾		Weekday	Fri ▾
5					
6	Sum of Revenue	Sum of Profit			
7	274860	122640			

FIGURE 4-29 With multiple fields in the Filters area, this pivot table can answer many ad-hoc queries.

To set up the report, drag Revenue and Cost to the Values area and then drag as many fields as desired to the Filters area.

If you add many fields to the Filters area, you might want to use one of the obscure pivot table options settings. Click Options on the Analyze tab. On the Layout & Format tab of the PivotTable Options dialog box, change Report Filter Fields per Column from 0 to a positive number. Excel rearranges the Filter fields into multiple columns. Figure 4-29 shows the filters with four fields per column. You can also change Down, Then Over to Over, Then Down to rearrange the sequence of the Filter fields.

Choosing one item from a filter

To filter the pivot table, click any drop-down menu in the Filters area of the pivot table. The drop-down menu always starts with (All) but then lists the complete unique set of items available in that field.

Choosing multiple items from a filter

At the bottom of the Filters drop-down menu is a check box labeled Select Multiple Items. If you select it, Excel adds a check box next to each item in the drop-down menu. This enables you to select multiple items from the list.

In Figure 4-30, the pivot table is filtered to show revenue from multiple sectors, but it is impossible to tell which sectors are included.

	A	B	C	D	E
1					
2					
3					
4					
5	Sector	(Multiple Items) ⫟		Region	Northeast ⫟
6	Market	(Multiple Items) ⫟		Rep	(All) ▾
7	Product	Gadget ⫟		Customer	(Multiple Items) ⫟
8	Date	(All) ▾		Weekday	(All) ▾
9					
10	Sum of Revenue	Sum of Cost			
11	713137	395117			
12					

FIGURE 4-30 You can select multiple items, but after the Filter drop-down menu closes, you cannot tell which items were selected.

> **Tip** Selecting multiple items from the filter leads to a situation where the person reading the report will not know which items are included. Slicers solve this problem.

Replicating a pivot table report for each item in a filter

Although slicers are now the darlings of the pivot table report, the good old-fashioned report filter can still do one trick that slicers cannot do. Say you have created a report that you would like to share with the industry managers. You have a report showing customers with revenue and profit. You would like each industry manager to see only the customers in their area of responsibility.

Follow these steps to quickly replicate the pivot table:

1. Make sure the formatting in the pivot table looks good before you start. You are about to make several copies of the pivot table, and you don't want to format each worksheet in the workbook, so double-check the number formatting and headings now.

2. Add the Sector field to the Filters area. Leave the Sector filter set to (All).

3. Select one cell in the pivot table so that you can see the Analyze tab in the ribbon.

4. Find the Options button in the left side of the Analyze tab. Next to the Options tab is a drop-down menu. Don't click the big Options button. Instead, open the drop-down menu (see Figure 4-31).

FIGURE 4-31 Click the tiny drop-down arrow next to the Options button.

5. Choose Show Report Filter Pages. In the Show Report Filter Pages dialog box, you see a list of all the fields in the report area. Because this pivot table has only the Sector field, this is the only choice (see Figure 4-32).

FIGURE 4-32 Select the field by which to replicate the report.

6. Click OK and stand back.

Excel inserts a new worksheet for every item in the Sector field. On the first new worksheet, Excel chooses the first sector as the filter value for that sheet. Excel renames the worksheet to match the sector. Figure 4-33 shows the new Consulting worksheet, with neighboring tabs that contain Museums, Retail, Training, and Utilities.

> **Tip** If the underlying data changes, you can refresh all of the Sector worksheets by using Refresh on one Sector pivot table. After you refresh the Consulting worksheet, all the pivot tables refresh.

FIGURE 4-33 Excel quickly adds one page per sector.

Filtering using slicers and timelines

Slicers are graphical versions of the Report Filter fields. Rather than hiding the items selected in the filter drop-down menu behind a heading such as (Multiple Items), the slicer provides a large array of buttons that show at a glance which items are included or excluded.

To add slicers, click the Insert Slicer icon on the Analyze tab. Excel displays the Insert Slicers dialog box. Choose all the fields for which you want to create graphical filters, as shown in Figure 4-34.

FIGURE 4-34 Choose fields for slicers.

Initially, Excel chooses one-column slicers of similar color in a cascade arrangement (see Figure 4-35). However, you can change these settings by selecting a slicer and using the Slicer Tools Options tab in the ribbon.

FIGURE 4-35 The slicers appear with one column each.

You can add more columns to a slicer. If you have to show 50 two-letter state abbreviations, that will look much better as 5 rows of 10 columns than as 50 rows of 1 column. Click the slicer to get access to the Slicer Tools Analyze tab. Use the Columns spin button to increase the number of columns in the slicer. Use the resize handles in the slicer to make the slicer wider or shorter. To add visual interest, choose a different color from the Slicer Styles gallery for each field.

After formatting the slicers, arrange them in a blank section of the worksheet, as shown in Figure 4-36.

FIGURE 4-36 After formatting, your slicers might fit on a single screen.

Three colors might appear in a slicer. The dark color indicates items that are selected. Gray boxes often mean the item has no records because of other slicers. White boxes indicate items that are not selected.

Note that you can control the heading for the slicer and the order of items in the slicer by using the Slicer Settings icon on the Slicer Tools Options tab of the ribbon. Just as you can define a new pivot table style, you can also right-click an existing slicer style and choose Duplicate. You can change the font, colors, and so on.

A new icon debuted in Excel 2016, in the top bar of the slicer. The icon appears as three check marks. When you select this icon, you can select multiple items from the slicer without having to hold down the Ctrl key.

Using timelines to filter by date

After slicers were introduced in Excel 2010, there was some feedback that using slicers was not an ideal way to deal with date fields. You might end up adding some fields to your original data set to show (perhaps) a decade and then use the group feature for year, quarter, and month. You would end up with a whole bunch of slicers all trying to select a time period, as shown in Figure 4-37.

FIGURE 4-37   Four different slicers are necessary to filter by date.

For Excel 2013, Microsoft introduced a new kind of filter called a *Timeline slicer*. To use one, select one cell in your pivot table and choose Insert Timeline from the Analyze tab. Timeline slicers can only apply to fields that contain dates. Excel gives you a list of date fields to choose from, although in most cases, there is only one date field from which to choose.

Figure 4-38 shows a Timeline slicer. Perhaps the best part of a Timeline slicer is the drop-down menu that lets you repurpose the timeline for days, months, quarters, or years. This works even if you have not grouped your daily dates up to months, quarters, or years.

FIGURE 4-38   A single Timeline slicer can filter your pivot table by month, quarter, year, or day.

Driving multiple pivot tables from one set of slicers

Chapter 12, "Enhancing pivot table reports with macros," includes a tiny macro that lets you drive two pivot tables with one set of filters. This has historically been difficult to do unless you used a macro.

Now, one set of slicers or timelines can be used to drive multiple pivot tables or pivot charts. In Figure 4-39, the Market slicer is driving three elements. It drives the pivot table in the top left with revenue by sector and product. It drives two pivot tables created for the top-right and lower-left charts.

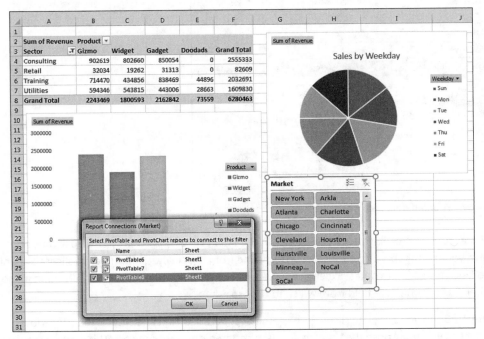

FIGURE 4-39   Three pivot elements controlled by the same slicer.

Note For more information about how to create pivot charts, refer to Chapter 6, "Using pivot charts and other visualizations."

The following steps show you how to create three pivot tables that are tied to a single slicer:

1. Create your first pivot table.

2. Select a cell in the first pivot table. Choose Insert Slicer. Choose one or more fields to be used as a slicer. Alternatively, insert a Timeline slicer for a date field.

3. Select the entire pivot table.

4. Copy with Ctrl+C or the Copy command.

5. Select a new blank area of the worksheet.

6. Paste. Excel creates a second pivot table that shares the pivot cache with the first pivot table. In order for one slicer to run multiple pivot tables, they must share the same pivot cache.

7. Change the fields in the second pivot table to show some other interesting analysis.

8. Repeat steps 3–7 to create a third copy of the pivot table.

The preceding steps require you to create the slicer after you create the first pivot table but before you make copies of the pivot table.

If you already have several existing pivot tables and need to hook them up to the same slicer, follow these steps:

1. Click the slicer to select it. When the slicer is selected, the Slicer Tools Design tab of the ribbon appears.

2. Select the Slicer Tools Design tab and choose Report Connections. Excel displays the Report Connections (Market) dialog box. Initially, only the first pivot table is selected.

3. As shown in Figure 4-40, choose the other pivot tables in the dialog box and click OK.

FIGURE 4-40 Choose to hook this slicer up to the other pivot tables.

4. If you created multiple slicers and/or timelines, repeat steps 1 through 3 for the other slicers.

The result is a dashboard in which all of the pivot tables and pivot charts update in response to selections made in the slicer (see Figure 4-41).

FIGURE 4-41 All of the pivot charts and pivot tables update when you choose from the slicer.

> **Tip** The worksheet in Figure 4-41 would be a perfect worksheet to publish to SharePoint or to your OneDrive. You can share the workbook with coworkers and allow them to interact with the slicers. They won't need to worry about the underlying data or enter any numbers; they can just click on the slicer to see the reports update.

Grouping and creating hierarchies in a pivot table

Pivot tables have the ability to do roll-ups in memory. You can roll daily dates up to weeks, months, quarters, or years. Time can roll up to minutes or hours. Numbers can be grouped into equal-size buckets. Text entries can be grouped into territories.

You can use the Power Pivot grid to define a hierarchy so you can quickly drill down on a pivot table or chart.

Grouping numeric fields

The Grouping dialog box for numeric fields enables you to group items into equal ranges. This can be useful for creating frequency distributions. The pivot table in Figure 4-42 is quite the opposite of anything you've seen so far in this book. The numeric field—Revenue—is in the Rows area. A text field—

Customer—is in the Values area. When you put a text field in the Values area, you get a count of how many records match the criteria. In its present state, this pivot table is not that fascinating; it is telling you that exactly one record in the database has a total revenue of $23,990.

FIGURE 4-42   Nothing interesting here—just lots of order totals that appear exactly one time in the database.

Select one number in column A of the pivot table. Select Group Field from the Analyze tab of the ribbon. Because this field is not a date field, the Grouping dialog box offers fields for Starting At, Ending At, and By. As shown in Figure 4-43, you can choose to show amounts from 0 to 30,000 in groups of 5,000.

FIGURE 4-43   Create a frequency distribution by grouping the order size into $5,000 buckets.

After grouping the order size into buckets, you might want to add additional fields, such as Revenue and % Of Revenue shown as a percentage of the total.

Note   The grouping dialog box requires all groups to be the same size. I have heard questions where people want to group into 0–100K, 200K–500K, but this is not possible using the Grouping feature. You would have to add a new column to the source data in order to create these groupings.

Case Study: Grouping text fields for redistricting

Say that you get a call from the VP of Sales. The Sales Department is secretly considering a massive reorganization of the sales regions. The VP would like to see a report showing revenue after redistricting. You have been around long enough to know that the proposed regions will change several times before the reorganization happens, so you are not willing to change the Region field in your source data quite yet.

First, build a report showing revenue by market. The VP of Sales is proposing eliminating two regional managers and redistricting the country into three super-regions. While holding down the Ctrl key, highlight the five regions that will make up the new West region. Figure 4-44 shows the pivot table before the first group is created.

FIGURE 4-44 Use the Ctrl key to select the noncontiguous cells that make up the new region.

From the Analyze tab, click Group Selection. Excel adds a new field called Market2. The five selected regions are arbitrarily rolled up to a new territory called Group1. In Figure 4.45, the Group1 label in A4 is the first item in the new Market2 virtual field. The other items in the Market2 field includee Atlanta in A10, Charlotte in A12 and so on. The similar items in A11 and A13 are items in the original Market field. Use care while holding down the Ctrl key to select the unbolded markets for the South region: Atlanta in row 11, Charlotte in row 13, Huntsville in row 11, and Louisville in row 23...

Click Group Selection to group the markets in the proposed Southeast region. Repeat to group the remaining regions into the proposed Northeast region. Figure 4-46 shows what it looks like when you have grouped the markets into new regions. Five things need further adjustment: the names of Group1, Group2, Group3, and Market2, and the lack of subtotals for the outer row field.

Row Labels	Sum of Revenue
⊟ Group1	
Arkla	869454
Houston	796239
Minneapolis	34710
NoCal	200201
SoCal	39250
⊟ Atlanta	
Atlanta	530306
⊟ Charlotte	
Charlotte	406326
⊟ Chicago	
Chicago	184425
⊟ Cincinnati	
Cincinnati	60299
⊟ Cleveland	
Cleveland	1800306
⊟ Hunstville	
Hunstville	46717
⊟ Louisville	
Louisville	42316
⊟ New York	
New York	1697263
Grand Total	6707812

FIGURE 4-45 The first super-region is arbitrarily called Group1.

Row Labels	Sum of Revenue
⊟ Group1	
Arkla	869454
Houston	796239
Minneapolis	34710
NoCal	200201
SoCal	39250
⊟ Group2	
Atlanta	530306
Charlotte	406326
Hunstville	46717
Louisville	42316
⊟ Group3	
Chicago	184425
Cincinnati	60299
Cleveland	1800306
New York	1697263
Grand Total	6707812

FIGURE 4-46 The markets are grouped, but you have to do some cleanup.

Cleaning up the report takes only a few moments:

1. Select cell A4. Type **West** to replace the arbitrary name Group1.

2. Select cell A10. Type **Southeast** to replace the arbitrary name Group2.

3. Select A15. Type **Northeast** to replace Group3.

4. Select any outer heading in A4, A10, or A15. Click Field Settings on the Analyze tab.

5. In the Field Settings dialog box, replace the Custom Name of Market2 with Proposed Region. Also, in the Field Settings dialog box, change the Subtotals setting from None to Automatic.

Figure 4-47 shows the pivot table that results, which is ready for the VP of Sales.

3	Row Labels	Sum of Revenue
4	⊟West	**1939854**
5	Arkla	869454
6	Houston	796239
7	Minneapolis	34710
8	NoCal	200201
9	SoCal	39250
10	⊟Southeast	**1025665**
11	Atlanta	530306
12	Charlotte	406326
13	Hunstville	46717
14	Louisville	42316
15	⊟Northeast	**3742293**
16	Chicago	184425
17	Cincinnati	60299
18	Cleveland	1800306
19	New York	1697263
20	Grand Total	**6707812**

FIGURE 4-47 It is now easy to see that these regions are heavily unbalanced.

You can probably predict that the Sales Department needs to shuffle markets to balance the regions. To go back to the original regions, select any Proposed Region cell in A4, A10, or A15 and choose Ungroup. You can then start over, grouping regions in new combinations.

Grouping date fields manually

Excel provides a straightforward way to group date fields. Select any date cell in your pivot table. On the Analyze tab, click Group Field in the Group option.

When your field contains date information, the date version of the Grouping dialog box appears. By default, the Months option is selected. You have choices to group by Seconds, Minutes, Hours, Days, Months, Quarters, and Years. It is possible—and usually advisable—to select more than one field in the Grouping dialog box. In this case, select Months and Years, as shown in Figure 4-48.

There are several interesting points to note about the resulting pivot table. First, notice that the Years field has been added to the PivotTable Fields list. Don't let this fool you. Your source data is not changed to include the new field. Instead, this field is now part of your pivot cache in memory.

FIGURE 4-48 Business users of Excel usually group by months (or quarters) and years.

Another interesting point is that, by default, the Years field is automatically added to the same area as the original date field in the pivot table layout, as shown in Figure 4-49. Although this happens automatically, you are free to pivot months and years onto the opposite axis of the report. This is a quick way to create a year-over-year sales report.

FIGURE 4-49 By default, Excel adds the new grouped date field to your pivot table layout.

Including years when grouping by months

Although this point is not immediately obvious, it is important to understand that if you group a date field by month, you also need to include the year in the grouping. If your data set includes January 2024 and January 2025, selecting only months in the Grouping dialog box will result in both January 2024 and January 2025 being combined into a single row called January (see Figure 4-50).

FIGURE 4-50 If you fail to include the Year field in the grouping, the report mixes sales from last January and this January into a single row called January.

Grouping date fields by week

The Grouping dialog box offers choices to group by second, minute, hour, day, month, quarter, and year. It is also possible to group on a weekly or biweekly basis.

The first step is to find either a paper calendar or an electronic calendar, such as the Calendar feature in Outlook, for the year in question. If your data starts on January 1, 2024, it is helpful to know that January 1 is a Monday that year. You need to decide if weeks should start on Sunday or Monday or any other day. For example, you can check the paper or electronic calendar to learn that the nearest starting Sunday is December 31, 2023.

Select any date heading in your pivot table. Then select Group Field from the Analyze tab. In the Grouping dialog box, clear all the By options and select only the Days field. This enables the spin button for Number of Days. To produce a report by week, increase the number of days from 1 to 7.

Next, you need to set up the Starting At date. If you were to accept the default of starting at January 1, 2024, all your weekly periods would run from Monday through Sunday. By checking a calendar before you begin, you know that you want the first group to start on December 31, 2023, to have weeks that run Sunday through Monday. Figure 4-51 shows the settings in the Grouping dialog box and the resulting report.

Sum of Revenue	Sector				
Date	Consulting	Retail	Training	Utilities	Grand Total
12/31/2023 - 1/6/2024	0				52771
1/7/2024 - 1/13/2024	24872				68040
1/14/2024 - 1/20/2024	14029				25416
1/21/2024 - 1/27/2024	35362				53354
1/28/2024 - 2/3/2024	32790				69332
2/4/2024 - 2/10/2024	6974				28682
2/11/2024 - 2/17/2024	30803				42233
2/18/2024 - 2/24/2024	0				82794
2/25/2024 - 3/2/2024	21456				15774
3/3/2024 - 3/9/2024	0				60866
3/10/2024 - 3/16/2024	43213				62264
3/17/2024 - 3/23/2024	6765				44488
3/24/2024 - 3/30/2024	46805				85911
3/31/2024 - 4/6/2024	34504				78484
4/7/2024 - 4/13/2024	8016				37772
4/14/2024 - 4/20/2024	0				26828
4/21/2024 - 4/27/2024	22530	0	27269	32956	82755

Grouping dialog box:

Auto

- Starting at: 12/31/2023 — Start date
- Ending at: 12/29/2025

By

Seconds
Minutes
Hours
Days — Choose only Days
Months
Quarters
Years

Number of days: 7 — Number of days

OK   Cancel

FIGURE 4-51 Group dates up to weekly periods.

> **Caution** If you choose to group by week, none of the other grouping options can be selected. You cannot group this or any field by month, quarter, or year. You cannot add calculated items to the pivot table.

AutoGrouping pivot table dates

Excel 2016 introduced an AutoGroup feature for dates. If you dragged a date field to a pivot table, Excel would quickly add date rollups and define a hierarchy for the dates.

The feature was turned on by default, and the only way to turn it off was a change in the Registry.

I love the concept of teaching people that daily dates can easily be rolled up. But for the people who needed to report daily dates, the AutoGroup was inconsistent and confusing. The logic used to choose which rollups would be present would sometimes leave out daily dates from the hierarchy.

Today, Excel 2019 will not automatically AutoGroup. You can choose to allow the AutoGroup if you loved this feature. Go To File, Options, Data, and deselect Disable Automatic Grouping Of Date/Time Columns In Pivot Tables.

Understanding how Excel decides what to AutoGroup

If you have daily dates that include an entire year or that fall in two or more years, Excel 2019 groups the daily dates to include years, quarters, and months. If you need to report by daily dates, you will have to select any date cell, choose Group Field, and add Days. Note that the rules change if your data is in the Data Model. In that case, AutoGroup would include daily dates as well.

If you have daily dates that fall within one calendar year and span more than one month, Excel groups the daily dates to month and includes daily dates.

 Caution If your company is closed on New Year's Day and you have no sales on January 1, a data set that stretches from January 2 to December 31 will fit the "less than a full year" case and will include months and daily dates.

If your data contains times that do not cross over midnight, you get hours, minutes, and seconds. If the times span more than one day, you get days, hours, minutes, and seconds.

Using AutoGroup

Say that you have a column in your data set with daily dates that span two years. When you add this Date field to the Rows area of your pivot table, you will see rows for each year instead of hundreds of daily dates. If your pivot table is in Tabular layout, you will see extra columns for Quarter and Date that appear to have no data (see Figure 4-52).

When you look in the Pivot Table Fields list, you see that the Rows area automatically includes three fields: Years, Quarter, and Date. All three of these are virtual fields created by grouping the daily dates up to months, quarters, and years.

The three fields are added to either the Rows area or the Columns area. However, only the highest level of the date field will be showing. To see the quarters and years, click one cell that contains a year and then click the Expand button in the Analyze tab of the ribbon (see Figure 4-53). To see months, select a cell containing a quarter and click the Expand button again (see Figure 4-54).

	A	B	C	D	E	F	G	H
1								
2								
3	Sum of Revenue			Region ▼				
4	Years ▼	Quarter ▼	Date ▼	West	Midwest	Northeast	South	Grand Total
5	⊞ 2024			127340	972790	897378	1410045	3407553
6	⊞ 2025			112111	1149266	799885	1238997	3300259
7	Grand Total			239451	2122056	1697263	2649042	6707812
8								

FIGURE 4-52 Excel can automatically groups two years' worth of daily dates up to months, quarters, and years

	A	B	C	D	E	F	G	H
1								
2								
3	Sum of Revenue			Region				
4	Years	Quar	Date	West	Midwest	Northeast	South	Grand Total
5	⊟2024	⊞Qtr1		50456	305554	200651	298422	855083
6	2024	⊞Qtr2		14548	255161	164685	339891	774285
7	2024	⊞Qtr3		35696	240744	252185	425327	953952
8	2024	⊞Qtr4		26640	171331	279857	346405	824233
9	2024 Total			127340	972790	897378	1410045	3407553
10	⊟2025	⊞Qtr1		26874	236872	241157	223159	728062
11	2025	⊞Qtr2		22917	312764	195775	289873	821329
12	2025	⊞Qtr3		34220	277681	111477	376440	799818
13	2025	⊞Qtr4		28100	321949	251476	349525	951050
14	2025 Total			112111	1149266	799885	1238997	3300259
15	Grand Total			239451	2122056	1697263	2649042	6707812
16								

FIGURE 4-53 Use Expand Field to show the quarters.

	A	B	C	D	E	F	G	H
1								
2								
3	Sum of Revenue			Region				
4	Years	Quar	Date	West	Midwest	Northeast	South	Grand Total
5	⊟2024	⊟Qtr1	Jan	21730	144169	60482	46841	273222
6	2024	Qtr1	Feb	20610	98554	54552	138349	312065
7	2024	Qtr1	Mar	8116	62831	85617	113232	269796
8	2024	Qtr1 Total		50456	305554	200651	298422	855083
9	2024	⊟Qtr2	Apr	4948	93796	55909	121987	276640
10	2024	Qtr2	May	4846	103775	43518	179937	332076

FIGURE 4-54 Expand Field again to show the monthly data.

Creating an easy year-over-year report

You can use date grouping to easily create a year-over-year report. You can either manually group the dates to years or use the AutoGroup.

Follow these steps:

1. Create a pivot table with Years in the Columns area and Months in the Rows area. Drag Revenue to the Values area. By default, the pivot table will offer a Grand Total column, as shown in Figure 4-55.

2. Right-click the Grand Total heading and choose Remove Grand Total.

3. Drag Revenue a second time to the Values area.

4. In the Columns area, drag Years so it is below Values. You will have the pivot table shown in Figure 4-56.

	A	B	C	D	E
1					
2					
3	Sum of Revenue	Years			
4	Date	2024	2025	Grand Total	
5	Jan	273222	274936	548158	
6	Feb	312065	236565	548630	
7	Mar	269796	216561	486357	
8	Apr	276640	292003	568643	
9	May	332076	287443	619519	
10	Jun	165569	241883	407452	
11	Jul	385767	295851	681618	
12	Aug	311745	286891	598636	
13	Sep	256440	217076	473516	
14	Oct	304246	308986	613232	
15	Nov	231872	301880	533752	
16	Dec	288115	340184	628299	
17	Grand Total	3407553	3300259	6707812	
18					

FIGURE 4-55 Group daily dates to months and years. Drag Years to go across the report.

	A	B	C	D	E
1					
2					
3		Values	Years		
4		Sum of Revenue		Sum of Revenue2	
5	Date	2024	2025	2024	2025
6	Jan	273222	274936	273222	274936
7	Feb	312065	236565	312065	236565
8	Mar	269796	216561	269796	216561
9	Apr	276640	292003	276640	292003
10	May	332076	287443	332076	287443
11	Jun	165569	241883	165569	241883
12	Jul	385767	295851	385767	295851
13	Aug	311745	286891	311745	286891
14	Sep	256440	217076	256440	217076
15	Oct	304246	308986	304246	308986
16	Nov	231872	301880	231872	301880
17	Dec	288115	340184	288115	340184
18	Grand Total	3407553	3300259	3407553	3300259
19					

FIGURE 4-56 This year and last year appear twice across the top of the report.

5. Double-click the Sum of Revenue2 heading in cell D4 to display the Value Field Settings dialog box.

6. In the Value Field Settings dialog box, select the Show Values As tab. In the Show Values As drop-down menu, choose % Difference From. In the Base Field list, choose Years. In the Base Item, choose (Previous), as shown in Figure 4-57.

	A	B	C	D	E	F
1						
2						
3		**Values**	**Years**			
4		Sum of Revenue		**Sum of Revenue2**		
5	**Date**	**2024**	**2025**	**2024**	**2025**	
6	Jan	273222	274936		0.63%	
7	Feb	312065	236565		-24.19%	
8	Mar	269796				
9	Apr	276640				
10	May	332076				
11	Jun	165569				
12	Jul	385767				
13	Aug	311745				
14	Sep	256440				
15	Oct	304246				
16	Nov	231872				
17	Dec	288115				
18	**Grand Total**	3407553				
19						
20						
21						
22						
23						
24						
25						

Value Field Settings

Source Name: Revenue

Custom Name: Sum of Revenue2

Summarize Values By | **Show Values As**

Show values as

% Difference From

Base field:	Base item:
Quantity	(previous)
Revenue	(next)
Profit	<1/1/2024
Cost	2024
Quarters	2025
Years	>12/29/2025

Number Format | OK | Cancel

FIGURE 4-57 Change the second Revenue columns to percentage difference from the previous year.

7. Close the Value Field Settings dialog box. Column E will show the percentage change from the first year to the last year. Column D will be blank because the pivot table has no data from 2023 to use to compare to 2024.

8. Hide column D.

9. Select the 2025 heading in E5. Press Ctrl+1 for Format Cells. On the Number tab, choose Custom. Type a format of `;;;"% Change"`.

You have a report showing year 1 versus year 2 and a percentage change. You can easily remove the Months from column A and insert Region, Market, or Product to see the year-over-year change. Figure 4-58 shows a year-over-year report for Regions.

	A	B	C	E
1				
2				
3		**Values**	**Years**	
4		Sum of Revenue		
5	**Region**	**2024**	**2025**	**% Change**
6	West	127340	112111	-11.96%
7	Midwest	972790	1149266	18.14%
8	Northeast	897378	799885	-10.86%
9	South	1410045	1238997	-12.13%
10	**Grand Total**	3407553	3300259	-3.15%
11				

FIGURE 4-58 Once you have the year-over-year report set up, you can swap any field in to column A.

Creating hierarchies

Back in Figures 4-53 through 4-55, you used the Expand Field to drill in to different date levels. If you build your pivot table using the Data Model, you can use the Diagram View in Power Pivot to create a formal hierarchy. Once you have a hierarchy in your pivot table, you can use the Drill Down and Drill Up buttons that are perpetually grayed out in the ribbon.

Consider the pivot table and pivot chart shown in Figure 4-59. The pivot table is built using the Data Model; when you choose Insert Pivot Table, make sure to choose Add This Data To The Data Model. The pivot table has regions in the Rows area and Products in the Columns area. The pivot chart is showing a stacked column chart.

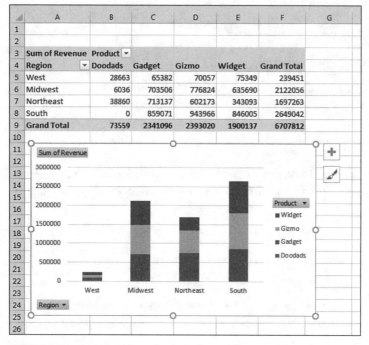

FIGURE 4-59   A pivot table and a pivot chart without any hierarchy.

Follow these steps to add a hierarchy below Region:

1. Click the Manage icon in the Power Pivot tab of the ribbon.

2. On the Home tab of the Power Pivot for Excel window, click Diagram View.

3. Resize the Range table so you can see all the fields.

4. Click on the top field for the hierarchy: Region. Ctrl+click the remaining members of the hierarchy: Market and Rep.

5. Right-click on Region and choose Create Hierarchy (see Figure 4-60).

FIGURE 4-60 Select Region, Market, and Rep. Right-click and choose Create Hierarchy.

6. Hierarchy1 will appear at the bottom of the table. Right-click the name and choose Rename. Type a meaningful name such as Geography (see Figure 4-61).

FIGURE 4-61 The hierarchy is shown at the bottom of the table.

7. Carefully review the sequence of the hierarchy. In Figure 4-61, Rep is appearing before Market. This is incorrect. Right-click on Market and choose Move Up.

8. Close the Power Pivot window and return to Excel. After a brief pause, the PivotTable Fields list will show the table name (Range), the hierarchy name (Geography), and something called More Fields.

9. Remove Region from the Rows area. Choose the Geography hierarchy from the PivotTable Fields list. As shown in Figure 4-62, you have something very similar to Figure 4-59. However, note that Drill Down is now enabled in the ribbon.

FIGURE 4-62 Plus signs appear next to each region. The Drill Down icon is enabled.

10. Select cell A7 for South. Click on Drill Down. The pivot table and pivot chart will change to show the markets in the South region (see Figure 4-63).

You can keep using Drill Down or Drill Up to travel through the hierarchy.

FIGURE 4-63 After drilling down on the South region, the markets in the South appear. The Drill Up icon is now enabled.

Next steps

In Chapter 5, "Performing calculations in pivot tables," you'll learn how to use pivot table formulas to add new virtual fields to a pivot table.

Performing calculations in pivot tables

In this chapter, you will:

- Introduce calculated fields and calculated items
- Create a calculated field
- Create a calculated item
- Understand the rules and shortcomings of pivot table calculations
- Manage and maintain pivot table calculations

Introducing calculated fields and calculated items

When analyzing data with pivot tables, you will often need to expand your analysis to include data based on calculations that are not in your original data set. Excel provides a way to perform calculations within a pivot table through calculated fields, measures, and calculated items.

A *calculated field* is a data field you create by executing a calculation against existing fields in the pivot table. Think of a calculated field as a virtual column added to your data set. This column takes up no space in your source data, contains the data you define with a formula, and interacts with your pivot data as a field—just like all the other fields in your pivot table.

A *measure* is a calculated field created in a Data Model pivot table using the Data Analysis Expressions (DAX) formula language. In many cases, measures run circles around calculated fields. In order to create a measure, you have to choose "Add This Data To The Data Model" when creating the pivot table. Measures are discussed in length in Chapter 10, "Unlocking features with the Data Model and Power Pivot." Refer to "Creating Median in a pivot table using DAX measures," "Reporting text in the Values area," and "Using time intelligence," in Chapter 10. Measures are also used in the case study at the end of this chapter: "Case study: Using DAX measures instead of calculated fields."

A *calculated item* is a data item you create by executing a calculation against existing items within a data field. Think of a calculated item as a virtual row of data added to your data set. This virtual row takes up no space in your source data and contains summarized values based on calculations performed on other rows in the same field. Calculated items interact with your pivot data as data items—just like all the other items in your pivot table.

With calculated fields and calculated items, you can insert a formula into a pivot table to create your own custom field or data item. Your newly created data becomes a part of your pivot table, interacting with other pivot data, recalculating when you refresh, and supplying you with a calculated metric that does not exist in your source data.

The example in Figure 5-1 demonstrates how a basic calculated field can add another perspective on your data. Your pivot table shows total sales amount and contracted hours for each market. A calculated field that shows your average dollar per hour enhances this analysis and adds another dimension to your data.

	A	B	C	D
1				
2	Row Labels	Sales_Amount	Contracted Hours	Avg Dollar Per Hour
3	BUFFALO	$450,478	6,864	$65.63
4	CALIFORNIA	$2,254,735	33,014	$68.30
5	CANADA	$776,245	12,103	$64.14
6	CHARLOTTE	$890,522	14,525	$61.31
7	DALLAS	$467,089	6,393	$73.06
8	DENVER	$645,583	8,641	$74.71
9	FLORIDA	$1,450,392	22,640	$64.06
10	KANSASCITY	$574,899	8,547	$67.26
11	MICHIGAN	$678,705	10,744	$63.17
12	NEWORLEANS	$333,454	5,057	$65.94
13	NEWYORK	$873,581	14,213	$61.46
14	PHOENIX	$570,255	10,167	$56.09
15	SEATTLE	$179,827	2,889	$62.25
16	TULSA	$628,405	9,583	$65.57
17	Grand Total	$10,774,172	165,380	$65.15

FIGURE 5-1 Avg Dollar per Hour is a calculated field that adds another perspective to your data analysis.

Now, you might look at Figure 5-1 and ask, "Why go through all the trouble of creating calculated fields or calculated items? Why not just use formulas in surrounding cells or even add the calculation directly into the source table to get the information needed?"

To answer these questions, in the next sections, we will look at the three different methods you can use to create the calculated field in Figure 5-1:

■ Manually add the calculated field to your data source.

■ Use a formula outside your pivot table to create the calculated field.

■ Insert a calculated field directly into your pivot table.

Method 1: Manually add a calculated field to the data source

If you manually add a calculated field to your data source, the pivot table can pick up the field as a regular data field (see Figure 5-2). On the surface, this option looks simple, but this method of precalculating metrics and incorporating them into your data source is impractical on several levels.

▲	N	O	P	Q	R
1	Sales_Amount	Contracted Hours	Sales_Period	Sales_Rep	Avg Dollar Per Hour
2	$197.95	2	P08	5060	$98.98
3	$197.95	2	P08	5060	$98.98
4	$191.28	3	P08	5060	$63.76
5	$240.07	4	P11	44651	$60.02
6	$147.22	2	P08	160410	$73.61
7	$163.51	2	P02	243	$81.76
8	$134.01	3	P02	243	$44.67
9	$134.01	3	P02	243	$44.67
10	$134.01	3	P02	243	$44.67
11	$239.00	3	P01	4244	$79.67
12	$215.87	4	P02	5030	$53.97
13	$180.57	4	P02	64610	$45.14
14	$240.07	4	P02	213	$60.02

FIGURE 5-2 Precalculating calculated fields in your data source is both cumbersome and impractical.

If the definitions of your calculated fields change, you have to go back to the data source, recalculate the metric for each row, and refresh your pivot table. If you have to add a metric, you have to go back to the data source, add a new calculated field, and then change the range of your pivot table to capture the new field.

Method 2: Use a formula outside a pivot table to create a calculated field

You can add a calculated field by performing the calculation in an external cell with a formula. In the example shown in Figure 5-3, the Avg Dollar per Hour column was created with formulas referencing the pivot table.

| D3 | ▼ | : | × | ✓ | fx | =B3/C3 |

▲	A	B	C	D
1				
2	Row Labels ▼	Sales_Amount	Contracted Hours	Avg Dollar Per Hour
3	BUFFALO	$450,478	6,864	$65.63
4	CALIFORNIA	$2,254,735	33,014	$68.30
5	CANADA	$776,245	12,103	$64.14
6	CHARLOTTE	$890,522	14,525	$61.31
7	DALLAS	$467,089	6,393	$73.06
8	DENVER	$645,583	8,641	$74.71
9	FLORIDA	$1,450,392	22,640	$64.06
10	KANSASCITY	$574,899	8,547	$67.26
11	MICHIGAN	$678,705	10,744	$63.17
12	NEWORLEANS	$333,454	5,057	$65.94
13	NEWYORK	$873,581	14,213	$61.46
14	PHOENIX	$570,255	10,167	$56.09
15	SEATTLE	$179,827	2,889	$62.25
16	TULSA	$628,405	9,583	$65.57
17	Grand Total	$10,774,172	165,380	$65.15

FIGURE 5-3 Typing a formula next to your pivot table essentially gives you a calculated field that refreshes when your pivot table is refreshed.

Although this method gives you a calculated field that updates when your pivot table is refreshed, any changes in the structure of your pivot table have the potential of rendering your formula useless.

As you can see in Figure 5-4, moving the Market field to the Filters area changes the structure of your pivot table—and exposes the weakness of makeshift calculated fields that use external formulas.

	A	B	C	D
1	Market	(All)		
2				Avg Dollar Per Hour
3	Sales_Amount	Contracted Hours		#VALUE!
4	$10,774,172	165,380		#DIV/0!
5				#DIV/0!
6				#DIV/0!
7				#DIV/0!
8				#DIV/0!
9				#DIV/0!
10				#DIV/0!
11				#DIV/0!
12				#DIV/0!
13				#DIV/0!
14				#DIV/0!
15				#DIV/0!
16				#DIV/0!
17				#DIV/0!

FIGURE 5-4 External formulas can cause errors when the pivot table structure is changed.

Method 3: Insert a calculated field directly into a pivot table

Inserting a calculated field directly into a pivot table is the best option. Going this route eliminates the need to manage formulas, provides for scalability when your data source grows or changes, and allows for flexibility in the event that your metric definitions change.

Another huge advantage of this method is that you can alter your pivot table's structure and even measure different data fields against your calculated field without worrying about errors in your formulas or losing cell references.

The pivot table report shown in Figure 5-5 is the same one you see in Figure 5-1, except it has been restructured to show the average dollar per hour by market and product.

	A	B	C	D	E
1					
2	Market	Product_Description	Sales_Amount	Contracted Hours	Avg Dollar Per Hour
3	⊟BUFFALO	Cleaning & Housekeeping Services	$66,845	982	$68.07
4		Facility Maintenance and Repair	$69,570	821	$84.74
5		Fleet Maintenance	$86,460	1,439	$60.08
6		Green Plants and Foliage Care	$34,831	490	$71.08
7		Landscaping/Grounds Care	$65,465	1,172	$55.86
8		Predictive Maintenance/Preventative Maintenance	$127,307	1,960	$64.95
9	BUFFALO Total		$450,478	6,864	$65.63
10	⊟CALIFORNIA	Cleaning & Housekeeping Services	$37,401	531	$70.44
11		Facility Maintenance and Repair	$281,198	3,103	$90.62
12		Fleet Maintenance	$337,225	5,737	$58.78
13		Green Plants and Foliage Care	$830,413	11,900	$69.78
14		Landscaping/Grounds Care	$248,343	3,421	$72.59
15		Predictive Maintenance/Preventative Maintenance	$520,156	8,322	$62.50
16	CALIFORNIA Total		$2,254,735	33,014	$68.30

FIGURE 5-5 Your calculated field remains viable even when your pivot table's structure changes to accommodate new dimensions.

The bottom line is that there are significant benefits to integrating your custom calculations into a pivot table, including the following:

- Elimination of potential formula and cell reference errors.

- Ability to add or remove data from your pivot table without affecting your calculations.

- Ability to auto-recalculate when your pivot table is changed or refreshed.

- Flexibility to change calculations easily when your metric definitions change.

- Ability to manage and maintain your calculations effectively.

> **Note** If you move your data to PowerPivot, you can use the DAX formula language to create more powerful calculations. See Chapter 10, "Unlocking features with the Data Model and Power Pivot," to get a concise look at the DAX formula language.

Creating a calculated field

Before you create a calculated field, you must first have a pivot table, so build the pivot table shown in Figure 5-6.

Once you have a pivot table, it's time to create your first calculated field. To do this, you must activate the Insert Calculated Field dialog box. Select Analyze under the PivotTable Tools tab and then select Fields, Items, & Sets from the Calculations group. Selecting this option activates a drop-down menu from which you can select Calculated Field, as demonstrated in Figure 5-7.

	A	B	C
1			
2	Market	Sales_Amount	Contracted Hours
3	BUFFALO	$450,478	6,864
4	CALIFORNIA	$2,254,735	33,014
5	CANADA	$776,245	12,103
6	CHARLOTTE	$890,522	14,525
7	DALLAS	$467,089	6,393
8	DENVER	$645,583	8,641
9	FLORIDA	$1,450,392	22,640
10	KANSASCITY	$574,899	8,547
11	MICHIGAN	$678,705	10,744
12	NEWORLEANS	$333,454	5,057
13	NEWYORK	$873,581	14,213
14	PHOENIX	$570,255	10,167
15	SEATTLE	$179,827	2,889
16	TULSA	$628,405	9,583
17	Grand Total	$10,774,172	165,380

FIGURE 5-6 Create the pivot table shown here.

Note Normally, the fields in the Values area of Figure 5-6 would be called Sum Of Sales_ Amount and Sum Of Contracted Hours. After creating the default pivot table, click in cell B2 and type a new name of **Sales_Amount** followed by a space. In a similar fashion, rename C2 from Sum Of Contracted Hours to **Contracted Hours** followed by a space.

FIGURE 5-7 Start the creation of your calculated field by selecting Calculated Field.

After you select Calculated Field, Excel activates the Insert Calculated Field dialog box, as shown in Figure 5-8.

FIGURE 5-8 The Insert Calculated Field dialog box assists you in creating a calculated field in a pivot table.

Notice the two input boxes, Name and Formula, at the top of the dialog box. The objective here is to give your calculated field a name and then build the formula by selecting the combination of data fields and mathematical operators that provide the metric you are looking for.

As you can see in Figure 5-9, you first give your calculated field a descriptive name—that is, a name that describes the utility of the mathematical operation. In this case, enter **Avg Dollar Per Hour** in the Name input box.

FIGURE 5-9 Give your calculated field a descriptive name.

Next, go to the Fields list and double-click the Sales_Amount field. Enter / to let Excel know you plan to divide the Sales_Amount field by something.

> ⚠️ **Caution**   By default, the Formula input box in the Insert Calculated Field dialog box contains = 0. Ensure that you delete the zero before continuing with your formula.

At this point, your dialog box should look similar to the one shown in Figure 5-10.

FIGURE 5-10 Start your formula with = `Sales_Amount/`.

Next, double-click the Contracted Hours field to finish your formula, as illustrated in Figure 5-11.

Finally, select Add and then click OK to create the new calculated field.

As you can see in Figure 5-12, the pivot table creates a new field called Sum Of Avg Dollar Per Hour. Note that in addition to adding your calculated field to the pivot table, Excel also adds your new field to the PivotTable Fields list.

FIGURE 5-11 The full formula, =Sales_Amount/'Contracted Hours', gives you the calculated field you need.

	A	B	C	D
1				
2	**Market**	Sales_Amount	Contracted Hours	Sum of Avg Dollar Per Hour
3	BUFFALO	$450,478	6,864	65.62911859
4	CALIFORNIA	$2,254,735	33,014	68.29634034
5	CANADA	$776,245	12,103	64.13660002
6	CHARLOTTE	$890,522	14,525	61.30963787
7	DALLAS	$467,089	6,393	73.06264195
8	DENVER	$645,583	8,641	74.71164101
9	FLORIDA	$1,450,392	22,640	64.06325088
10	KANSASCITY	$574,899	8,547	67.26324675
11	MICHIGAN	$678,705	10,744	63.1706022
12	NEWORLEANS	$333,454	5,057	65.93902511
13	NEWYORK	$873,581	14,213	61.46351298
14	PHOENIX	$570,255	10,167	56.08882561
15	SEATTLE	$179,827	2,889	62.24548633
16	TULSA	$628,405	9,583	65.57495878
17	**Grand Total**	$10,774,172	165,380	65.14797303

FIGURE 5-12 You can change the settings on your new calculated field—for example, field name, number format, color—just as you would on any other field.

> **Note** The resulting values from a calculated field are not formatted. You can easily apply any desired formatting by using some of the techniques from Chapter 3, "Customizing a pivot table."

Does this mean you have just added a column to your data source? The answer is no.

Calculated fields are similar to the pivot table's default subtotal and grand total calculations in that they are all mathematical functions that recalculate when the pivot table changes or is refreshed. Calculated fields merely mimic the hard fields in your data source; you can drag them, change field settings, and use them with other calculated fields.

Take a moment and take another close look at Figure 5-11. Notice that the formula entered there is in a format similar to the one used in the standard Excel formula bar. The obvious difference is that instead of using hard numbers or cell references, you are referencing pivot data fields to define the arguments used in this calculation. If you have worked with formulas in Excel before, you will quickly grasp the concept of creating calculated fields.

Case study: Summarizing next year's forecast

All the branch managers in your company have submitted their initial revenue forecasts for next year. Your task is to take the first-pass numbers they submitted and create a summary report that shows the following:

- Total revenue forecast by market

- Total percentage growth over last year

- Total contribution margin by market

Because these numbers are first-pass submissions and you know they will change over the course of the next two weeks, you decide to use a pivot table to create the requested forecast summary.

Start by building the initial pivot table, shown in Figure 5-13, to include Revenue Last Year and Forecast Next Year for each market. After creating the pivot table, you will see that by virtue of adding the Forecast Next Year field in the data area, you have met your first requirement: to show total revenue forecast by market.

	A	B	C
1			
2			
3	MARKET ▾	Revenue Last Year	Forecast Next Year
4	BUFFALO	$450,478	$411,246
5	CALIFORNIA	$2,254,735	$2,423,007
6	CANADA	$776,245	$746,384
7	CHARLOTTE	$890,522	$965,361
8	DALLAS	$467,089	$510,635
9	DENVER	$645,583	$722,695
10	FLORIDA	$1,450,392	$1,421,507
11	KANSASCITY	$574,899	$607,226
12	MICHIGAN	$678,705	$870,447
13	NEWORLEANS	$333,454	$366,174
14	NEWYORK	$873,581	$953,010
15	PHOENIX	$570,255	$746,721
16	SEATTLE	$179,827	$214,621
17	TULSA	$628,405	$661,726
18	Grand Total	$10,774,172	$11,620,760

FIGURE 5-13   The initial pivot table is basic, but it provides the data for your first requirement: show total revenue forecast by market.

The next metric you need is percentage growth over last year. To get this data, you need to add a calculated field that calculates the following formula:

```
(Forecast Next Year / Revenue Last Year) - 1
```

To achieve this, do the following:

1. Activate the Insert Calculated Field dialog box, and name your new field **Percent Growth** (see Figure 5-14).

2. Delete the 0 in the Formula input box.

3. Enter **(** (an opening parenthesis).

FIGURE 5-14 Name your new field Percent Growth.

4. Double-click the Forecast Next Year field.

5. Enter **/** (a division sign).

6. Double-click the Revenue Last Year field.

7. Enter **)** (a closing parenthesis).

8. Enter **-** (a minus sign).

9. Enter the number **1**.

At this point, the formula is `= ( 'Forecast Next Year'/'Revenue Last Year')-1`.

> **Tip** You can use any constant in your pivot table calculations. Constants are static values that do not change. In this example, the number 1 is a constant. While the value of Revenue Last Year or Forecast Next Year will almost certainly change based on the available data, the number 1 will always have the same value.

After you have entered the full formula, your dialog box should look like the one shown in Figure 5-15.

With your formula typed in, you can now click OK to add your new field. After changing the format of the resulting values to percentages, you have a nicely formatted Percent Growth calculation in your pivot table. At this point, your pivot table should look like the one shown in Figure 5-16.

FIGURE 5-15 With just a few clicks, you have created a variance formula!

MARKET	Revenue Last Year	Forecast Next Year	Sum of Percent Growth
BUFFALO	$450,478	$411,246	-8.7%
CALIFORNIA	$2,254,735	$2,423,007	7.5%
CANADA	$776,245	$746,384	-3.8%
CHARLOTTE	$890,522	$965,361	8.4%
DALLAS	$467,089	$510,635	9.3%
DENVER	$645,583	$722,695	11.9%
FLORIDA	$1,450,392	$1,421,507	-2.0%
KANSASCITY	$574,899	$607,226	5.6%
MICHIGAN	$678,705	$870,447	28.3%
NEWORLEANS	$333,454	$366,174	9.8%
NEWYORK	$873,581	$953,010	9.1%
PHOENIX	$570,255	$746,721	30.9%
SEATTLE	$179,827	$214,621	19.3%
TULSA	$628,405	$661,726	5.3%
Grand Total	$10,774,172	$11,620,760	7.9%

FIGURE 5-16 You have added a Percent Growth calculation to your pivot table.

With this newly created view into your data, you can easily see that three markets need to resubmit their forecasts to reflect positive growth over last year (see Figure 5-17).

▲	A	B	C	D
1				
2				
3	**MARKET** ▼	**Revenue Last Year**	**Forecast Next Year**	**Sum of Percent Growth**
4	BUFFALO	$450,478	$411,246	-8.7%
5	CALIFORNIA	$2,254,735	$2,423,007	7.5%
6	CANADA	$776,245	$746,384	-3.8%
7	CHARLOTTE	$890,522	$965,361	8.4%
8	DALLAS	$467,089	$510,635	9.3%
9	DENVER	$645,583	$722,695	11.9%
10	FLORIDA	$1,450,392	$1,421,507	-2.0%
11	KANSASCITY	$574,899	$607,226	5.6%
12	MICHIGAN	$678,705	$870,447	28.3%
13	NEWORLEANS	$333,454	$366,174	9.8%
14	NEWYORK	$873,581	$953,010	9.1%
15	PHOENIX	$570,255	$746,721	30.9%
16	SEATTLE	$179,827	$214,621	19.3%
17	TULSA	$628,405	$661,726	5.3%
18	Grand Total	$10,774,172	$11,620,760	7.9%

FIGURE 5-17   You can already discern some information from the calculated field, which identifies three problematic markets.

Now it's time to focus on your last requirement, which is to find total contribution margin by market. The original data set includes a column for Variable Cost Next Year where the values are stored as negative values. To get this data, you need to add a calculated field that calculates the following formula:

```
Forecast Next Year + Variable Cost Next Year
```

> **Note**   A quick look at Figure 5-17 confirms that the Variable Cost Next Year field is not displayed in the pivot table report. Can you build pivot table formulas with fields that are currently *not even in* the pivot table? The answer is yes; you can use any field that is available to you in the PivotTable Fields list, even if the field is not shown in the pivot table.

To create this field, do the following:

1.   Activate the Insert Calculated Field dialog box and name your new field `Contribution Margin`.

2.   Delete the 0 in the Formula input box.

3.   Double-click the Forecast Next Year field.

4.   Enter + (a plus sign).

5.   Double-click the Variable Cost Next Year field.

After you have entered the full formula, your dialog box should look like the one shown in Figure 5-18.

FIGURE 5-18 With just a few clicks, you have created a formula that calculates contribution margin.

Now that you have created the Contribution Margin calculation, this report is ready to be formatted and delivered (see Figure 5-19).

	A	B	C	D	E
1					
2					
3	**MARKET** ▼	**Revenue Last Year**	**Forecast Next Year**	**Sum of Percent Growth**	**Sum of Contribution Margin**
4	BUFFALO	$450,478	$411,246	-8.7%	($169,546)
5	CALIFORNIA	$2,254,735	$2,423,007	7.5%	$1,152,641
6	CANADA	$776,245	$746,384	-3.8%	$118,415
7	CHARLOTTE	$890,522	$965,361	8.4%	$360,343
8	DALLAS	$467,089	$510,635	9.3%	($908,021)
9	DENVER	$645,583	$722,695	11.9%	($697,393)
10	FLORIDA	$1,450,392	$1,421,507	-2.0%	$865,700
11	KANSASCITY	$574,899	$607,226	5.6%	($328,773)
12	MICHIGAN	$678,705	$870,447	28.3%	($92,813)
13	NEWORLEANS	$333,454	$366,174	9.8%	($586,405)
14	NEWYORK	$873,581	$953,010	9.1%	$506,335
15	PHOENIX	$570,255	$746,721	30.9%	$318,496
16	SEATTLE	$179,827	$214,621	19.3%	($163,738)
17	TULSA	$628,405	$661,726	5.3%	($1,193,984)
18	**Grand Total**	**$10,774,172**	**$11,620,760**	**7.9%**	**($818,743)**

FIGURE 5-19 Contribution Margin is now a data field in your pivot table report, thanks to your calculated field.

With this pivot table report, you can easily analyze any new forecast submissions by refreshing your report with the new updates.

Creating a calculated item

As you learned at the beginning of this chapter, a calculated item is a virtual data item you create by executing a calculation against existing items within a data field. Calculated items come in especially handy when you need to group and aggregate a set of data items.

For example, the pivot table in Figure 5-20 gives you sales amount by sales period. Imagine that you need to compare the average performance of the most recent six sales periods to the average of the prior seven periods. That is, you want to take the average of P01–P07 and compare it to the average of P08–P13.

> **Note** Watch the Grand Total amount through the next several examples. The $10.77 million shown in Figure 5-20 is the correct amount.

	M	N
3	Sales_Period ▼	Sum of Sales_Amount
4	P01	$681,865
5	P02	$1,116,916
6	P03	$657,611
7	P04	$865,498
8	P05	$925,802
9	P06	$868,930
10	P07	$640,587
11	P08	$1,170,262
12	P09	$604,552
13	P10	$891,253
14	P11	$949,605
15	P12	$887,665
16	P13	$513,625
17	Grand Total	$10,774,172
18		

FIGURE 5-20 You want to compare the most recent six sales periods to the average of the prior seven periods.

> **Caution** Calculated Items are always added to one specific field in the pivot table. In this case, you are calculating new totals along the Sales_Period field. Thus, you must select one of the Sales_Period cells before selecting Calculated Item from the Fields Items and Sets drop-down menu.

Place your cursor on any data item in the Sales_Period field, and then select Fields, Items, & Sets from the Calculations group. Next, select Calculated Item, as shown in Figure 5-21.

Selecting this option opens the Insert Calculated Item dialog box. A quick glance at Figure 5-22 shows you that the top of the dialog box identifies which field you are working with. In this case, it is the Sales_Period field. In addition, notice that the Items list box is automatically filled with all the items in the Sales_Period field.

FIGURE 5-21 Start the creation of your calculated item by selecting one cell that represents a sales period and then selecting Calculated Item.

FIGURE 5-22 The Insert Calculated Item dialog box is automatically populated to reflect the field with which you are working.

You need to give your calculated item a name and then build its formula by selecting the combination of data items and operators that provide the metric you are looking for.

In this example, name your first calculated item **Avg P1-P7 Sales**, as shown in Figure 5-23.

Next, you can build your formula in the Formula input box by selecting the appropriate data items from the Items list. In this scenario, you want to create the following formula:

```
=Average(P01, P02, P03, P04, P05, P06, P07)
```

Enter the formula shown in Figure 5-23 into the Formula input box.

Click OK to activate your new calculated item. As you can see in Figure 5-24, you now have a data item called Avg P1-P7 Sales.

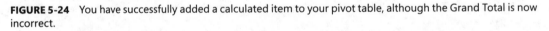

FIGURE 5-23 Enter a formula that gives you the average of P01–P07.

	A	B
1		
2		
3	**Row Labels** ▼	**Sum of Sales_Amount**
4	P01	$681,865
5	P02	$1,116,916
6	P03	$657,611
7	P04	$865,498
8	P05	$925,802
9	P06	$868,930
10	P07	$640,587
11	P08	$1,170,262
12	P09	$604,552
13	P10	$891,253
14	P11	$949,605
15	P12	$887,665
16	P13	$513,625
17	Avg P1-P7 Sales	$822,458
18	**Grand Total**	**$11,596,630**

FIGURE 5-24 You have successfully added a calculated item to your pivot table, although the Grand Total is now incorrect.

You can use any worksheet function in both a calculated field and a calculated item. The only restriction is that the function you use cannot reference external cells or named ranges. In effect, this means you can use any worksheet function that does not require cell references or defined names to work (such as COUNT, AVERAGE, IF, and OR).

Create a calculated item to represent the average sales for P08–P13, as shown in Figure 5-25.

FIGURE 5-25   Create a second calculated item.

Now you can hide the individual sales periods so that the report shows only the two calculated items. As shown in Figure 5-26, after a little formatting, your calculated items allow you to compare the average performance of the six most recent sales periods to the average of the prior seven periods.

FIGURE 5-26   You can now compare the six most recent sales periods to the average of the prior seven periods.

> **Caution**   It is often prudent to hide the data items you used to create your calculated item. In Figure 5-26, notice that all periods have been hidden. This prevents any grand totals and subtotals from showing incorrect aggregations. One could argue that the sum of two averages shown in the Grand Total row is meaningless. Remove the Grand Total by using PivotTable Tools | Design, Grand Totals, Off For Rows And Columns.

Understanding the rules and shortcomings of pivot table calculations

There is no better way to integrate your calculations into a pivot table than by using calculated fields and calculated items. However, calculated fields and calculated items do come with their own set of drawbacks. It's important you understand what goes on behind the scenes when you use pivot table calculations, and it's even more important to be aware of the boundaries and limitations of calculated fields and calculated items to avoid potential errors in your data analysis.

The following sections highlight the rules related to calculated fields and calculated items that you will most likely encounter when working with pivot table calculations.

Remembering the order of operator precedence

Just as in a spreadsheet, you can use any operator in your calculation formulas—meaning any symbol that represents a calculation to perform (+, −, *, /, %, ^). Moreover, just as in a spreadsheet, calculations in a pivot table follow the order of operator precedence. In other words, when you perform a calculation that combines several operators, as in (2+3) * 4/50%, Excel evaluates and performs the calculation in a specific order. The order of operations for Excel is as follows:

- Evaluate items in parentheses.

- Evaluate ranges (:).

- Evaluate intersections (spaces).

- Evaluate unions (,).

- Perform negation (−).

- Convert percentages (%).

- Perform exponentiation (^).

- Perform multiplication (*) and division (/), which are of equal precedence.

- Perform addition (+) and subtraction (−), which are of equal precedence.

- Evaluate text operators (&).

- Perform comparisons (=, <>, <=, >=).

> **Note** Operations that are equal in precedence are performed left to right.

Consider this basic example. The correct answer to (2+3)*4 is 20. However, if you leave off the parentheses, so that you have 2+3*4, Excel performs the calculation like this: 3*4 = 12 + 2 = 14. The order of operator precedence mandates that Excel perform multiplication before addition. Entering 2+3*4 gives you the wrong answer. Because Excel evaluates and performs all calculations in parentheses first, placing 2+3 inside parentheses ensures the correct answer.

Here is another widely demonstrated example. If you enter 10^2, which represents the exponent 10 to the second power as a formula, Excel returns 100 as the answer. If you enter −10^2, you expect −100 to be the result, but instead Excel returns 100 yet again. The reason is that Excel performs negation before exponentiation, which means Excel converts 10 to −10 before doing the exponentiation, effectively calculating −10*−10, which indeed equals 100. When you use parentheses in the formula, −(10^2), Excel calculates the exponent before negating the answer, giving you −100.

Understanding the order of operations helps you avoid miscalculating your data.

Using cell references and named ranges

When you create calculations in a pivot table, you are essentially working in a vacuum. The only data available to you is the data that exists in the pivot cache. Therefore, you cannot reach outside the confines of the pivot cache to reference cells or named ranges in your formula.

Using worksheet functions

When you build calculated fields or calculated items, Excel enables you to use any worksheet function that accepts numeric values as arguments and returns numeric values as the result. Some of the many functions that fall into this category are COUNT, AVERAGE, IF, AND, NOT, and OR.

Some examples of functions you cannot use are VLOOKUP, INDEX, SUMIF, COUNTIF, LEFT, and RIGHT. Again, these are all impossible to use because they either require cell array references or return textual values as the result.

Using constants

You can use any constant in your pivot table calculations. Constants are static values that do not change. For example, in the formula [Units Sold]*5, 5 is a constant. Though the value of Units Sold might change based on the available data, 5 always has the same value.

Referencing totals

Your calculation formulas cannot reference a pivot table's subtotals or grand total. This means that you cannot use the result of a subtotal or grand total as a variable or an argument in a calculated field. Measures created using the DAX formula language can overcome this limitation.

Rules specific to calculated fields

Calculated fields will not work in all cases. There are times when it is better to add the intermediate calculation to the original data set.

Consider the very simple data set shown in Figure 5-27. You had two sales of apples in Q1. The first was five cases at $20 and then five cases at $25. The total Q1 sales should be $225 derived by calculating =SUM(5*20,5*25).

	A	B	C	D	E	F	G
1	Qtr	Product	Units	Price		Total Q1 Apple	
2	1	Apple	5	20		100	
3	1	Apple	5	25		125	
4	1	Banana	3	28		225	
5	1	Banana	2	33			
6	1	Cherry	3	42			

FIGURE 5-27   The total sales for apples in Q1 should be $225.

The pivot table will get this calculation wrong on several levels. Cell L2 in Figure 5-28 adds the two unit prices together, producing a meaningless answer of $45. The calculated field in M2 then takes the correct total of 10 cases of apples times the incorrect price of $45 to arrive at $450 as the total Q1 revenue for apples. Recall that the correct answer from Figure 5-27 should have been $225. The problem gets worse at the Q1 total of $9,424 versus a correct answer of $1,192. At the Grand Total level, the pivot table is showing $137,372 versus a correct answer of $4,257.

Based on the example in Figure 5-28, you would think that the rule is that pivot tables are summing first and then the calculated field is multiplying the summary numbers. But this is not always true.

	I	J	K	L	M	N
1	Qtr	Product	Total Units	Total Price	Calc: Units Times Price	
2	⊟1 Apple		10	45	450	
3	1 Banana		5	61	305	
4	1 Cherry		5	89	445	
5	1 Dill		11	109	1199	
6	1 Total		31	304	9424	
7	⊟2 Apple		7	39	273	

FIGURE 5-28   This pivot table was wrong before it got to the calculated field in column M.

Based on Figure 5-28, the rule seems to be that the pivot table will perform the aggregation first and then use the formulas in the Calculated Field. However, look at a different example from the same data set. Your manager wants to know the lowest price for apples, the highest price for apples, and the difference between those.

Drag Price to the Values area two more times. Double-click the heading in N1 and change the calculation to Minimum. Double-click the heading in O1 and change the calculation to Maximum. The numbers in columns N and O are correct.

But then add a calculated field with MAX(Price) - MIN(Price), as shown in Figure 5-29. If Excel is doing the aggregation first, the answer to this formula should be 25–20 or 5. But the answer is zero. This indicates that Excel is reaching back and doing this math: =SUM(MAX(D2)-MIN(D2),MAX(D3)-MIN(D3)). Why does the calculation engine change methods? If you worked in Redmond on the Excel team, you could do some Excel archeology in the code base to figure it out, but the easier method is to switch from calculated fields to measures, as described in the following case study.

	I	J	N	O	P	Q
	Qtr	Product	Min Price	Max Price	Calc: Max minus Min	
	⊟1 Apple		20	25	0	
	1 Banana		28	33	0	
	1 Cherry		42	47	0	
	1 Dill		52	57	0	

Insert Calculated Field

Name: Max Minus Min   Modify

Formula: = MAX(Price) - MIN(Price)   Delete

FIGURE 5-29   Min and Max work fine, but the Max Minus Min fails as a calculated field.

Case study: Using DAX measures instead of calculated fields

You can correctly solve this using a combination of Power Query, the Data Model, and a DAX measure:

1. Select one cell in your data and use Home, Format As Table.

2. On the Table Tools Design tab, change the name of your table from Table1 to Original-Data.

3. From the Data tab, choose From Table/Range in the Get & Transform Data group.

4. In the Power Query editor, select Add Column, Custom Column. Define Revenue as =[Units]*[Price] (see Figure 5-30).

FIGURE 5-30 Add a virtual calculation at the row level using Power Query.

5. Select your new Revenue column in Power Query. On the Transform tab, open the Data Type drop-down menu and choose Currency.

6. In the top right of the Power Query Editor, change the Name from OriginalData to Da-taWithRevenue.

7. In Power Query, open the Close & Load drop-down menu on the Home tab. Choose Close and Load To.

8. In the Import Data dialog box, choose Only Create Connection. Choose the box for Add This Data To The Data Model and click OK (see Figure 5-31).

FIGURE 5-31 Load the query to the Data Model as a Connection.

9. Insert a new blank worksheet in the workbook.

10. From the blank worksheet, select Insert, PivotTable.

11. In the Create PivotTable dialog box, the choice for Use This Workbook's Data Model will
    already be selected (see Figure 5-32). Click OK.

FIGURE 5-32 When Power Query added your data to the Data Model and you start from a blank worksheet, Excel defaults to using the data in the Data Model.

12. In the PivotTable Fields list, you will see two tables: OriginalData and DataWithRevenue.
    Expand the DataWithRevenue table. Drag Qtr and Product to the Rows area. Drag Units
    and Revenue to the Values area. At this point, the Revenue in Column D is correct. The
    next steps will attempt to show the Min, Max, and Delta of the unit prices.

13. Drag Price to the Values area twice.

14. Double-click the heading for the first price and change the calculation to Min. Change the field name to Min Price.

15. Double-click the heading for the second price. Change the calculation to Max. Change the field name to `Max Price`.

> **Caution** If you listen to the Power Pivot pros, such as my good friend Rob Collie at PowerPivotPro.com, he will tell you that steps 14 and 15 have created a pair of evil "implicit measures." Rob will ominously warn you to never use implicit measures. I generally believe in my head that Rob must have really had a bad experience with implicit measures in his adolescent years on the Power Pivot team. I am sure Rob has a reason for saying they are evil that is way above my head. But here is my confession: I've now heard Rob say this for nine years. For nine years, I have ignored Rob and used implicit measures all the time. No evil has befallen me in those nine years. None. My hair is a bit grayer, but it is not because of these implicit measures.
>
> Now, I know that Rob is super busy running around the country doing Power Pivot seminars, and I know he will never have time to read this book and will never read this page.
>
> But do me a favor: If you ever run into Rob Collie in a dark alley, please don't tell him that I am encouraging you to use implicit measures. Let's keep that between us.

16. In the PivotTable Fields list, right-click the DataWithRevenue heading and choose Add Measure....

17. In the Measure dialog box, type a Measure Name of Max Minus Min.

18. Move to the Formula box. Type an equal sign and then the left square bracket. This will bring up a list of all fields. Choose [Max of Price] from the list. Type a minus sign and another left square bracket. Choose [Min of Price] (see Figure 5-33). Optionally, use the Category list box to classify the calculation as currency with 0 decimal places.

FIGURE 5-33 Create a measure using DAX.

Click OK to finish adding the measure. Wait. Wait some more. Nothing happens to your pivot table. I get tripped up by this every single time. You would think that Excel would add the new measure to the pivot table automatically. But it doesn't. Instead, the new Max Minus Min appears with an *fx* logo in the PivotTable Fields list (see Figure 5-34). This makes me think, "Why did I go to the trouble of adding this measure if I didn't want to add it to the pivot table?" But look, I appreciate the Excel team and the Pivot Table team, and I would never say those thoughts out loud.

FIGURE 5-34 You've defined the measure, but Excel does not automatically add it to the pivot table.

19. Choose the Max Minus Min field in the PivotTable Fields list. It will automatically move to the Values area.

The result is shown in Figure 5-35. The calculation for Max Minus Min is correct at all levels. Examine the Q1 total line in row 6. The Min price for the quarter is Apples at $20. The Max price is Dill at $57. The Max Minus Min in G6 is $37.

	Qtr	Product	Units	Revenue	Min Price	Max Price	Max Minus Min	
1								
2	⊟1	Apple	10	225	20	25	$5	
3	1	Banana	5	150	28	33	$5	
4	1	Cherry	5	220	42	47	$5	
5	1	Dill	11	597	52	57	$5	
6	1 Total		31	1192	20	57	$37	
7	⊟2	Apple	7	134	17	22	$5	
8	2	Banana	12	306	23	28	$5	
9	2	Cherry	9	353	37	42	$5	
10	2	Dill	5	260	50	55	$5	
11	2 Total		33	1053	17	55	$38	
12	⊟3	Apple	6	105	15	20	$5	
13	3	Banana	8	172	19	24	$5	
14	3	Cherry	6	243	38	43	$5	
15	3	Dill	7	386	53	58	$5	
16	3 Total		27	906	15	58	$43	
17	⊟4	Apple	8	180	20	25	$5	
18	4	Banana	7	218	29	34	$5	
19	4	Cherry	6	213	33	38	$5	
20	4	Dill	10	495	47	52	$5	
21	4 Total		31	1106	20	52	$32	
22	Grand Total		122	4257	15	58	$43	
23								

FIGURE 5-35 Using a DAX measure, the Max Minus Min calculation works.

I don't want to disparage the regular pivot table calculated fields, but every time I run into something that a pivot table cannot do, I find that a few DAX measures can solve the problem.

> **Note** The real reason that Excel does not add your new measure to the pivot table is simple: Many people will build complex calculations in steps. Only the final measure is used in the pivot table.

To learn more about DAX, check out Rob Collie's book *Power Pivot and Power BI* (ISBN 978-1-61547-062-4) or Matt Allington's *Supercharge Excel* (ISBN 978-1-61547-053-2).

Rules specific to calculated items

To use calculated items effectively, it is important that you understand a few ground rules:

- You cannot use calculated items in a pivot table that uses averages, standard deviations, or variances. Conversely, you cannot use averages, standard deviations, or variances in a pivot table that contains a calculated item.

- You cannot use a page field to create a calculated item, nor can you move any calculated item to the report filter area.

- You cannot add a calculated item to a report that has a grouped field, nor can you group any field in a pivot table that contains a calculated item.

- When building your calculated item formula, you cannot reference items from a field other than the one you are working with.

As you think about the pages you have just read, don't be put off by these shortcomings of pivot tables. Despite the clear limitations highlighted, the capability to create custom calculations directly into your pivot table remains a powerful and practical feature that can enhance your data analysis.

Now that you are aware of the inner workings of pivot table calculations and understand the limitations of calculated fields and items, you can avoid the pitfalls and use these features with confidence.

Managing and maintaining pivot table calculations

In your dealings with pivot tables, you will find that sometimes you don't keep a pivot table for more than the time it takes to say, "Copy, Paste Values." Other times, however, it will be more cost-effective to keep a pivot table and all its functionality intact.

When you find yourself maintaining and managing pivot tables through changing requirements and growing data, you might find the need to maintain and manage your calculated fields and calculated items as well.

Editing and deleting pivot table calculations

When a calculation's parameters change, or you no longer need a calculated field or calculated item, you can activate the appropriate dialog box to edit or remove the calculation.

Simply activate the Insert Calculated Field or Insert Calculated Item dialog box, and select the Name drop-down menu, as demonstrated in Figure 5-36.

FIGURE 5-36 Opening the drop-down menu under Name reveals all the calculated fields or items in the pivot table.

As you can see in Figure 5-37, after you select a calculated field or item, you have the option of deleting the calculation or modifying the formula.

FIGURE 5-37 After you select the appropriate calculated field or item, you can either delete or modify the calculation.

Changing the solve order of calculated items

If the value of a cell in your pivot table is dependent on the results of two or more calculated items, you have the option of changing the solve order of the calculated items. That is, you can specify the order in which the individual calculations are performed.

To specify the order of calculations, you need the Solve Order dialog box. To get there, place your cursor anywhere in the pivot table, select Fields, Items, & Sets from the Calculations group, and then select Solve Order.

The Solve Order dialog box, shown in Figure 5-38, lists all the calculated items that currently exist in the pivot table. The order in which the formulas are listed here is the order in which the pivot table will perform the operations. To make changes to this order, select any of the calculated items you see and then click Move Up, Move Down, or Delete, as appropriate.

FIGURE 5-38 After you identify the calculated item you are working with, simply move the item up or down to change the solve order. You also have the option of deleting items in this dialog box.

Documenting formulas

Excel provides a nice little function that lists the calculated fields and calculated items used in a pivot table, along with details on the solve order and formulas. This feature comes in especially handy if you need to quickly determine what calculations are being applied in a pivot table and which fields or items those calculations affect.

To list your pivot table calculations, simply place your cursor anywhere in the pivot table and select Fields, Items, & Sets and then select List Formulas. Excel creates a new tab in your workbook that lists the calculated fields and calculated items in the current pivot table. Figure 5-39 shows an example of a tab created by the List Formulas command.

Calculated Field		
Solve Order	**Field**	**Formula**
Calculated Item		
Solve Order	**Item**	**Formula**
1	'Avg P1-P7 Sales'	= AVERAGE(P01,P02,P03,P04,P05,P06,P07)
2	'Avg P8-P13 Sales'	= AVERAGE(P08,P09,P10,P11,P12,P13)
3	'Baseline Average'	=(P01+P02 +P03)/3
Note:	When a cell is updated by more than one formula,	
	the value is set by the formula with the last solve order.	
	To change formula solve orders,	
	use the Solve Order command on the Pivot Formulas drop down menu.	

FIGURE 5-39   The List Formulas command documents the details of your pivot table calculations quickly and easily.

Next steps

In Chapter 6, "Using pivot charts and other visualizations," you will discover the fundamentals of pivot charts and the basics of representing your pivot data graphically. You'll also get a firm understanding of the limitations of pivot charts and alternatives to using pivot charts.

Using pivot charts and other visualizations

In this chapter, you will:

- Learn about pivot charts
- Create a pivot chart
- Keep pivot chart rules in mind
- Examine alternatives to using pivot charts
- Use conditional formatting with pivot tables
- Create custom conditional formatting rules

What is a pivot chart...really?

When sharing your analyses with others, you will quickly find that there is no getting around the fact that people want charts. Pivot tables are nice, but they show a lot of pesky numbers that take time to absorb. Charts, on the other hand, enable users to make split-second determinations about what the data is actually revealing. Charts offer instant gratification, allowing users to immediately see relationships, point out differences, and observe trends. The bottom line is that managers today want to absorb data as fast as possible, and nothing delivers that capability faster than a chart. This is where pivot charts come into play. Whereas pivot tables offer the analytical, pivot charts offer the visual.

A common definition of a pivot chart is a graphical representation of the data in a pivot table. Although this definition is technically correct, it somehow misses the mark on what a pivot chart truly does.

When you create a standard chart from data that is not in a pivot table, you feed the chart a range made up of individual cells holding individual pieces of data. Each cell is an individual object with its own piece of data, so your chart treats each cell as an individual data point and thus charts each one separately.

However, the data in a pivot table is part of a larger object. The pieces of data you see inside a pivot table are not individual pieces of data that occupy individual cells. Rather, they are items inside a larger pivot table object that is occupying space on your worksheet.

When you create a chart from a pivot table, you are not feeding it individual pieces of data inside individual cells; you are feeding it the entire pivot table layout. Indeed, a *pivot chart* is a chart that uses a PivotLayout object to view and control the data in a pivot table.

Using the PivotLayout object allows you to interactively add, remove, filter, and refresh data fields inside a pivot chart just like in a pivot table. The result of all this action is a graphical representation of the data you see in a pivot table.

Creating a pivot chart

Based on the rather complicated definition just provided, you might get the impression that creating a pivot chart is difficult. The reality is that it's quite a simple task, as you'll see in this section.

The pivot table in Figure 6-1 provides for a simple view of revenue by market. The Business_Segment field in the report filter area lets you parse out revenue by line of business.

Note: The pivot table in Figure 6-1 is shown in Tabular layout. The Sum Of Sales_Amount heading in B3 has been replaced by typing Sales Amount in B3.

	A	B	C
1	Business_Segment (All)		
2			
3	Market	Sales Amount	
4	CALIFORNIA	$2,254,735	
5	FLORIDA	$1,450,392	
6	MICHIGAN	$678,705	
7	BUFFALO	$450,478	
8	CANADA	$776,245	
9	CHARLOTTE	$890,522	
10	DALLAS	$467,089	
11	DENVER	$645,583	
12	KANSASCITY	$574,899	
13	NEWORLEANS	$333,454	
14	NEWYORK	$873,581	
15	PHOENIX	$570,255	
16	SEATTLE	$179,827	
17	TULSA	$628,405	
18	Grand Total	$10,774,172	
19			

FIGURE 6-1 This basic pivot table shows revenue by market and allows for filtering by line of business.

Creating a pivot chart from this data would not only allow for an instant view of the performance of each market but would also permit you to retain the ability to filter by line of business.

To start the process, place your cursor anywhere inside the pivot table and click the Insert tab on the ribbon. On the Insert tab, you can see the Charts group displaying the various types of charts you can create. Here, you can choose the chart type you would like to use for your pivot chart. For this example, click the Column chart icon and select the first 2-D column chart, as shown in Figure 6-2.

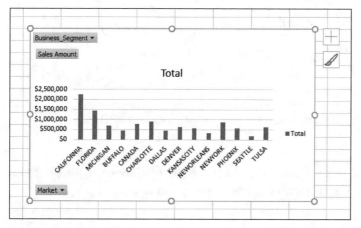

FIGURE 6-2 Select the chart type you want to use.

Figure 6-3 shows the chart Excel creates after you choose a chart type.

FIGURE 6-3 Excel creates your pivot chart on the same sheet as your pivot table.

Tip Notice that pivot charts are now, by default, placed on the same sheet as the source pivot table. If you long for the days when pivot charts were located on their own chart sheets, you are in luck. All you have to do is place your cursor inside a pivot table and then press F11 to create a pivot chart on its own sheet.

You can easily change the location of a pivot chart by right-clicking the chart (outside the plot area) and selecting Move Chart. This activates the Move Chart dialog box, in which you can specify the new location.

You now have a chart that is a visual representation of your pivot table. More than that, because the pivot chart is tied to the underlying pivot table, changing the pivot table in any way changes the chart. For example, as Figure 6-4 illustrates, adding the Region field to the pivot table adds a region dimension to your chart.

FIGURE 6-4 The pivot chart displays the same fields that the underlying pivot table displays.

> **Note** The pivot chart in Figure 6-4 does not display the subtotals shown in the pivot table. When creating a pivot chart, Excel ignores subtotals and grand totals.

In addition, filtering a business segment not only filters the pivot table, but also the pivot chart. All this behavior comes from the fact that pivot charts use the same pivot cache and pivot layout as their corresponding pivot tables. This means that if you add or remove data from the data source and refresh the pivot table, the pivot chart updates to reflect the changes.

Take a moment to think about the possibilities. You can essentially create a fairly robust interactive reporting tool on the power of one pivot table and one pivot chart—no programming necessary.

Understanding pivot field buttons

In Figure 6-4, notice the gray buttons and drop-downs on the pivot chart. These are called pivot field buttons. By using these buttons, you can dynamically rearrange the chart and apply filters to the underlying pivot table.

An Expand Entire Field (+) and Collapse Entire Field (-) buttons are automatically added to any pivot chart that contains nested fields. Figure 6-4 shows these buttons in the lower-right corner of the chart.

Clicking Collapse Entire Field (-) on the chart collapses the data series and aggregates the data points. For example, Figure 6-5 shows the same chart collapsed to the Region level. You can click

Expand Entire Field (+) to drill back down to the Market level. These new buttons enable customers to interactively drill down or roll up the data shown in pivot charts.

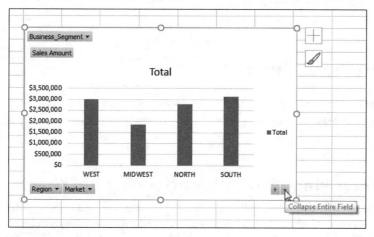

FIGURE 6-5 The new Expand Entire Field (+) and Collapse Entire Field (-) buttons allow for dynamic drill down and grouping of chart series.

Tip Keep in mind that pivot field buttons are visible when you print a pivot table. If you aren't too keen on showing the pivot field buttons directly on your pivot charts, you can remove them by clicking your chart and then selecting the Analyze tab. On the Analyze tab, you can use the Field Buttons drop-down menu to hide some or all of the pivot field buttons.

Tip Did you know you can also use slicers with pivot charts? Simply click a pivot chart, select the Analyze tab, and then click the Insert Slicer icon to take advantage of all the benefits of slicers with your pivot chart!

Note See "Using slicers" in Chapter 2, "Creating a basic pivot table," to get a quick refresher on slicers.

Creating a Pivot Chart from Scratch

You don't have to build a pivot table before creating a pivot chart. You can go straight from raw data to a pivot chart. Simply click any single cell in your data source and select the Insert tab. Look on the far-right side of the Charts group. Select the PivotChart drop-down menu and then choose PivotChart. This activates the Create PivotChart dialog box. At this point, you go through the same steps you would take if you were building a pivot table.

> **Note** In Chapter 9, "Using cube formulas with the Data Model or OLAP data," you will find out how to create pivot charts that are completely decoupled from any pivot table.

Keeping pivot chart rules in mind

As with other aspects of pivot table technology, pivot charts come with their own set of rules and limitations. The following sections give you a better understanding of the boundaries and restrictions of pivot charts.

Changes in the underlying pivot table affect a pivot chart

The primary rule you should always be cognizant of is that a pivot chart that is based on a pivot table is merely an extension of the pivot table. If you refresh, move a field, add a field, remove a field, hide a data item, show a data item, or apply a filter, the pivot chart reflects your changes.

Placement of data fields in a pivot table might not be best suited for a pivot chart

One common mistake people make when using pivot charts is assuming that Excel places the values in the column area of the pivot table in the x-axis of the pivot chart.

For instance, the pivot table in Figure 6-6 is in a format that is easy to read and comprehend. The structure chosen shows Sales_Period in the column area and Region in the row area. This structure works fine in the pivot table view.

	A	B	C	D	E	F
1	Business_Segment	(All)				
2						
3	Sales Amount	Sales_Period				
4	Region	P01	P02	P03	P04	P05
5	MIDWEST	$109K	$207K	$102K	$155K	$159K
6	NORTH	$181K	$261K	$183K	$215K	$235K
7	SOUTH	$198K	$334K	$189K	$256K	$283K
8	WEST	$193K	$315K	$183K	$240K	$248K
9	Grand Total	$682K	$1,117K	$658K	$865K	$926K
10						

FIGURE 6-6   The placement of the data fields works for a pivot table view.

Suppose you decide to create a pivot chart from this pivot table. You would instinctively expect to see fiscal periods across the x-axis and lines of business along the y-axis. However, as you can see in Figure 6-7, the pivot chart comes out with Region on the x-axis and Sales_Period on the y-axis.

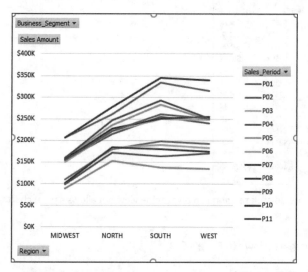

FIGURE 6-7   Creating a pivot chart from your nicely structured pivot table does not yield the results you were expecting.

So why does the structure in the pivot table not translate to a clean pivot chart? The answer has to do with the way pivot charts handle the different areas of a pivot table.

In a pivot chart, both the x-axis and y-axis correspond to specific areas in your pivot table:

- **y-axis**—Corresponds to the column area in a pivot table and makes up the y-axis of a pivot chart.

- **x-axis**—Corresponds to the row area in a pivot table and makes up the x-axis of a pivot chart.

Given this information, look again at the pivot table in Figure 6-6. This structure says that the Sales_Period field will be treated as the y-axis because it is in the column area. Meanwhile, the Region field will be treated as the x-axis because it is in the row area.

Now suppose you were to rearrange the pivot table to show fiscal periods in the row area and lines of business in the column area, as shown in Figure 6-8.

	A	B	C	D	E	F
1	Business_Segment (All) ▾					
2						
3	Sales Amount	Region ▾				
4	Sales_Period ▾	MIDWEST	NORTH	SOUTH	WEST	Grand Total
5	P01	$109K	$181K	$198K	$193K	$682K
6	P02	$207K	$261K	$334K	$315K	$1,117K
7	P03	$119K	$207K	$215K	$209K	$750K
8	P04	$170K	$242K	$274K	$266K	$953K
9	P05	$166K	$234K	$302K	$261K	$962K
10	P06	$152K	$241K	$248K	$250K	$891K
11	P07	$158K	$238K	$271K	$262K	$929K
12	P08	$170K	$248K	$289K	$281K	$988K
13	P09	$147K	$226K	$226K	$242K	$841K
14	P10	$160K	$241K	$294K	$264K	$959K
15	P11	$171K	$249K	$292K	$271K	$982K
16	P12	$121K	$211K	$197K	$192K	$720K
17	Grand Total	$1,849K	$2,779K	$3,141K	$3,005K	$10,774K
18						

FIGURE 6-8 This format makes for slightly more difficult reading in a pivot table view but allows a pivot chart to give you the effect you are looking for.

This arrangement generates the pivot chart shown in Figure 6-9.

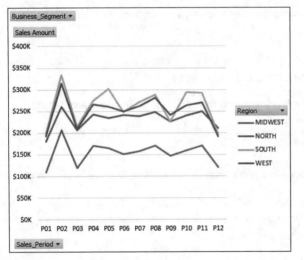

FIGURE 6-9 With the new arrangement in your pivot table, you get a pivot chart that makes sense.

A few formatting limitations still exist in Excel 2019

With versions of Excel prior to Excel 2007, many users avoided using pivot charts because of their many formatting limitations. These limitations included the inability to resize or move key components of the pivot chart, the loss of formatting when underlying pivot tables were changed, and the inability to use certain chart types. Because of these limitations, most users viewed pivot charts as being too clunky and impractical to use.

Over the last few versions of Excel, Microsoft introduced substantial improvements to the pivot chart functionality. Today, the pivot charts in Excel 2019 look and behave very much like standard charts. However, a few limitations persist in this version of Excel that you should keep in mind:

- You still cannot use XY (scatter) charts, bubble charts, stock charts, and custom visuals when creating a pivot chart. This includes the new sunburst and waterfall chart types introduced in Excel 2016.

- Applied trend lines can be lost when you add or remove fields in the underlying pivot table.

- The chart titles in the pivot chart cannot be resized.

Tip Although you cannot resize the chart titles in a pivot chart, you can make the font bigger or smaller to indirectly resize a chart title. Alternatively, you can opt to create your own chart title by simply adding a text box that will serve as the title for your chart. To add a text box, select the Text Box command on the Insert tab and then click on your pivot chart. The resulting text box will be fully customizable to suit your needs.

Case study: Creating an interactive report showing revenue by product and time period

You have been asked to provide both region and market managers with an interactive reporting tool that will allow them to easily see revenues across products for a variety of time periods. Your solution needs to give managers the flexibility to filter out a region or market if needed, as well as give managers the ability to dynamically filter the chart for specific periods.

Given the amount of data in your source table and the possibility that this will be a recurring exercise, you decide to use a pivot chart. Start by building the pivot table shown in Figure 6-10.

	A	B
1	Region	(All)
2	Market	(All)
3		
4	**Product_Description**	**Sales Amount**
5	Cleaning & Housekeeping Services	$1,139K
6	Facility Maintenance and Repair	$2,361K
7	Fleet Maintenance	$2,628K
8	Green Plants and Foliage Care	$1,277K
9	Landscaping/Grounds Care	$1,191K
10	Predictive Maintenance/Preventative Maintenance	$2,179K
11	**Grand Total**	**$10,774K**
12		

FIGURE 6-10 The initial pivot table meets all the data requirements.

Next, place your cursor anywhere inside the pivot table and click Insert. On the Insert tab, you can see the Charts menu displaying the various types of charts you can create. Choose the Column chart icon and select the first 2-D column chart. You immediately see a chart like the one in Figure 6-11.

FIGURE 6-11 Your raw pivot chart needs some formatting to meet requirements.

Notice that the legend along the right side of the chart with the word Total is pointless in this chart. Regular Excel charts stopped adding single-entry legends in Excel 2013, yet they persist in pivot charts. Click the Legend to select it and press the Delete key.

Next, click the newly created chart and select Insert Timeline from the Analyze tab under PivotChart Tools (see Figure 6-12).

FIGURE 6-12 Insert a Timeline slicer.

Excel opens the Insert Timelines dialog box, shown in Figure 6-13, which lists the available date fields in the pivot table. From the list, select Invoice_Date.

FIGURE 6-13 Insert a Timeline slicer for Invoice_Date.

You have created a slicer that aggregates and filters the pivot chart by time-specific periods (see Figure 6-14).

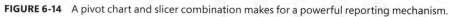

FIGURE 6-14 A pivot chart and slicer combination makes for a powerful reporting mechanism.

Note See "Using slicers" in Chapter 2 to get a quick refresher on Timeline slicers.

At this point, you can remove any superfluous pivot field buttons from the chart. In this case, the only buttons you need are the Region and Market drop-downs, which give your users an interactive way to filter the pivot chart. The other gray buttons you see on the chart are not necessary.

You can remove superfluous pivot field buttons by clicking the chart and selecting the Analyze tab in the ribbon. You can then use the Field Buttons drop-down menu to choose the field buttons you want to be visible in the chart. In this case, you want only the Report filter field buttons to be visible, so select only that option (see Figure 6-15).

FIGURE 6-15 Use the Field Buttons drop-down menu to hide any unwanted pivot field buttons on the chart.

Your final pivot chart should look like the one in Figure 6-16.

FIGURE 6-16 Your final report meets all the requirements of content and interactivity.

You now have a pivot chart that enables a manager to interactively review revenue by product and time period. This pivot chart also gives anyone using this report the ability to filter by region and market.

Examining alternatives to using pivot charts

There are generally two reasons you would need an alternative to using pivot charts:

- You do not want the overhead that comes with a pivot chart.

- You want to avoid some of the formatting limitations of pivot charts.

In fact, sometimes you might create a pivot table simply to summarize and shape data in preparation for charting. In these situations, you don't plan on keeping the source data, and you definitely don't want a pivot cache taking up memory and file space.

The example in Figure 6-17 shows a pivot table that summarizes revenue by quarter for each product.

	A	B	C	D	E	F
1						
2	Sum of Sales_Amount	Invoice_Date				
3	Product_Description	Qtr1	Qtr2	Qtr3	Qtr4	Grand Total
4	Cleaning & Housekeeping Services	$257,218	$290,074	$297,251	$294,049	$1,138,593
5	Facility Maintenance and Repair	$563,799	$621,715	$600,810	$574,834	$2,361,158
6	Fleet Maintenance	$612,496	$691,440	$674,592	$649,269	$2,627,798
7	Green Plants and Foliage Care	$293,194	$325,276	$329,787	$328,527	$1,276,783
8	Landscaping/Grounds Care	$288,797	$310,670	$303,086	$288,363	$1,190,915
9	Predictive Maintenance/Preventative Maintenance	$533,127	$567,391	$552,380	$526,027	$2,178,925
10	Grand Total	$2,548,631	$2,806,566	$2,757,906	$2,661,069	$10,774,172

FIGURE 6-17 This pivot table was created to summarize and chart revenue by quarter for each product.

Keep in mind that you need this pivot table only to summarize and shape data for charting. You don't want to keep the source data, nor do you want to keep the pivot table, with all its overhead.

Caution If you try to create a chart using the data in the pivot table, you'll inevitably create a pivot chart. This effectively means you have all the overhead of the pivot table looming in the background. Of course, this could be problematic if you do not want to share your source data with end users or if you don't want to inundate them with unnecessarily large files.

The good news is you can use a few simple techniques to create a chart from a pivot table but not end up with a pivot chart. Any one of the following four methods does the trick:

- Turn the pivot table into hard values.

- Delete the underlying pivot table.

- Distribute a picture of the pivot table.

- Use cells linked back to the pivot table as the source data for the chart.

Details about how to use each of these methods are discussed in the next sections.

Method 1: Turn the pivot table into hard values

After you have created and structured a pivot table appropriately, select the entire pivot table and copy it. Then select Paste Values from the Insert tab, as demonstrated in Figure 6-18. This action essentially deletes your pivot table, leaving you with the last values that were displayed in the pivot table. You can subsequently use these values to create a standard chart.

> **Note** This technique effectively disables the dynamic functionality of your pivot chart—that is, the pivot chart becomes a standard chart that cannot be interactively filtered or refreshed. This is also true with method 2 and method 3, which are outlined in the following sections.

FIGURE 6-18 The Paste Values functionality is useful when you want to create hard-coded values from pivot tables.

Method 2: Delete the underlying pivot table

If you have already created a pivot chart, you can turn it into a standard chart by simply deleting the underlying pivot table. To do this, select the entire pivot table and press the Delete key on the keyboard. Keep in mind that with this method, unlike with method 1, you are left with none of the values that made up the source data for the chart. In other words, if anyone asks for the data that feeds the chart, you will not have it.

> **Tip** Here is a handy tip to keep in the back of your mind: If you ever find yourself in a situation where you have a chart, but the data source is not available, activate the chart's data table. One quick way is to select the chart, click the Plus icon at the top-right corner of the chart, and select Data Table. The data table lets you see the data values that feed each series in the chart.

Method 3: Distribute a picture of the pivot chart

Now, it might seem strange to distribute pictures of a pivot chart, but this is an entirely viable method of distributing your analysis without a lot of overhead. In addition to very small file sizes, you also get the added benefit of controlling what your clients can see.

To use this method, simply copy a pivot chart by right-clicking the chart itself (outside the plot area) and selecting Copy. Then open a new workbook. Right-click anywhere in the new workbook, select Paste Special, and then select the picture format you prefer. A picture of your pivot chart is placed in the new workbook.

> **Caution**   If you have pivot field buttons on your chart, they will also show up in the copied picture. This will not only be unsightly but might leave your audience confused because the buttons don't work. Be sure to hide all pivot field buttons before copying a pivot chart as a picture. You can remove them by clicking on your chart and then selecting the Analyze tab. On the Analyze tab, you can use the Field Buttons drop-down menu and choose Hide All.

Method 4: Use cells linked back to the pivot table as the source data for the chart

Many Excel users shy away from using pivot charts solely based on the formatting restrictions and issues they encounter when working with them. Often these users give up the functionality of a pivot table to avoid the limitations of pivot charts.

However, if you want to retain key functionality in your pivot table, such as report filters and top 10 ranking, you can link a standard chart to your pivot table without creating a pivot chart.

In the example in Figure 6-19, a pivot table shows the top 10 markets by contracted hours, along with their total revenue. Notice that the report filter area allows you to filter by business segment so you can see the top 10 markets segment.

	A	B	C
1	Business_Segment (All)		
2			
3	**Market**	Contracted Hours	Sales_Amount
4	CALIFORNIA	33,014	$2,254,735
5	FLORIDA	22,640	$1,450,392
6	CHARLOTTE	14,525	$890,522
7	NEWYORK	14,213	$873,581
8	CANADA	12,103	$776,245
9	MICHIGAN	10,744	$678,705
10	PHOENIX	10,167	$570,255
11	TULSA	9,583	$628,405
12	DENVER	8,641	$645,583
13	KANSASCITY	8,547	$574,899
14	**Grand Total**	144,177	$9,343,323

FIGURE 6-19   This pivot table allows you to filter by business segment to see the top 10 markets by total contracted hours and revenue.

Suppose you want to turn this view into an XY scatter chart to be able to point out the relationship between the contracted hours and revenues.

Well, a pivot chart is definitely out because you can't build pivot charts with XY scatter charts. The techniques outlined in methods 1, 2, and 3 are also out because those methods disable the interactivity you need.

So what's the solution? Use the cells around the pivot table to link back to the data you need, and then chart those cells. In other words, you can build a mini data set that feeds your standard chart. This data set links back to the data items in your pivot table, so when your pivot table changes, so does your data set.

Click your cursor in a cell next to your pivot table, as demonstrated in Figure 6-20, and reference the first data item that you need to create the range you will feed to your standard chart.

When you build the formula in E4, make sure to type =**B4** without using the mouse or arrow keys to point to B4. If you use the mouse or arrow keys, Excel will insert the GETPIVOTDATA function instead of your formula.

Now copy the formula you just entered and paste that formula down and across to create your complete data set. At this point, you should have a data set that looks like the one shown in Figure 6-21.

	A	B	C	D	E
1	Business_Segment (All)				
2					
3	Market	Contracted Hours	Sales_Amount		
4	CALIFORNIA	33,014	$2,254,735		=B4
5	FLORIDA	22,640	$1,450,392		
6	CHARLOTTE	14,525	$890,522		
7	NEWYORK	14,213	$873,581		
8	CANADA	12,103	$776,245		
9	MICHIGAN	10,744	$678,705		
10	PHOENIX	10,167	$570,255		
11	TULSA	9,583	$628,405		
12	DENVER	8,641	$645,583		
13	KANSASCITY	8,547	$574,899		
14	Grand Total	144,177	$9,343,323		

FIGURE 6-20 Start your linked data set by referencing the first data item you need to capture.

	A	B	C	D	E	F
1	Business_Segment (All)					
2						
3	Market	Contracted Hours	Sales_Amount		Contracted Hours	Sales_Amount
4	CALIFORNIA	33,014	$2,254,735		33,014	2,254,735
5	FLORIDA	22,640	$1,450,392		22,640	1,450,392
6	CHARLOTTE	14,525	$890,522		14,525	890,522
7	NEWYORK	14,213	$873,581		14,213	873,581
8	CANADA	12,103	$776,245		12,103	776,245
9	MICHIGAN	10,744	$678,705		10,744	678,705
10	PHOENIX	10,167	$570,255		10,167	570,255
11	TULSA	9,583	$628,405		9,583	628,405
12	DENVER	8,641	$645,583		8,641	645,583
13	KANSASCITY	8,547	$574,899		8,547	574,899
14	Grand Total	144,177	$9,343,323			

FIGURE 6-21 Copy the formula and paste it down and across to create your complete data set.

When your linked data set is complete, you can use it to create a standard chart. In this example, you are creating an XY scatter chart with this data. You could never do this with a pivot chart.

Figure 6-22 demonstrates how this solution offers the best of both worlds. You can filter out a particular business segment using the page field, and you also have all the formatting freedom of a standard chart without any of the issues related to using a pivot chart.

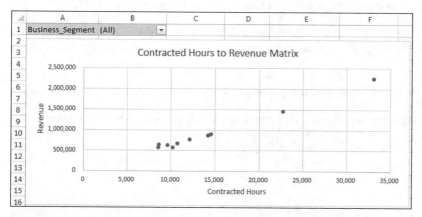

FIGURE 6-22   This solution allows you to continue using the functionality of your pivot table without any of the formatting limitations you would have with a pivot chart.

Using conditional formatting with pivot tables

In the next sections, you'll learn how to leverage the magic combination of pivot tables and conditional formatting to create interactive visualizations that serve as an alternative to pivot charts.

An example of using conditional formatting

To start the first example, create the pivot table shown in Figure 6-23.

	A	B	C
1			
2	**Market**	Sum of Sales_Amount	Sum of Sales_Amount2
3	BUFFALO	$450,478	450,478
4	CALIFORNIA	$2,254,735	2,254,735
5	CANADA	$776,245	776,245
6	CHARLOTTE	$890,522	890,522
7	DALLAS	$467,089	467,089
8	DENVER	$645,583	645,583
9	FLORIDA	$1,450,392	1,450,392
10	KANSASCITY	$574,899	574,899
11	MICHIGAN	$678,705	678,705
12	NEWORLEANS	$333,454	333,454
13	NEWYORK	$873,581	873,581
14	PHOENIX	$570,255	570,255
15	SEATTLE	$179,827	179,827
16	TULSA	$628,405	628,405
17	**Grand Total**	$10,774,172	10,774,172

FIGURE 6-23   Create this pivot table.

Suppose you want to create a report that enables your managers to see the performance of each sales period graphically. You could build a pivot chart, but you decide to use conditional formatting. In this example, you'll go the easy route and quickly apply some data bars.

Select all the Sum Of Sales_Amount2 values in the Values area. After you have highlighted the revenue for each Sales_Period, click the Home tab and select Conditional Formatting in the Styles group. Then select Data Bars and select one of the Solid Fill options, as shown in Figure 6-24.

You immediately see data bars in your pivot table, along with the values in the Sum Of Sales_Amount2 field. You want to hide the actual value and show only the data bar. To do this, follow these steps:

1. Click the Conditional Formatting drop-down menu on the Home tab and select Manage Rules.

2. In the Rules Manager dialog box, select the data bar rule you just created and select Edit Rule.

3. Select the Show Bar Only check box (see Figure 6-25).

FIGURE 6-24 Apply data bars to the values in your pivot table.

As you can see in Figure 6-26, you now have a set of bars that correspond to the values in your pivot table. This visualization looks like a sideways chart, doesn't it? What's more impressive is that as you filter the markets in the report filter area, the data bars dynamically update to correspond with the data for the selected market.

FIGURE 6-25 Check the Show Bar Only option to get a clean view of just the data bars.

◢	A	B	C
1			
2	**Market** ▼	**Sum of Sales_Amount**	**Sum of Sales_Amount2**
3	BUFFALO	$450,478	
4	CALIFORNIA	$2,254,735	
5	CANADA	$776,245	
6	CHARLOTTE	$890,522	
7	DALLAS	$467,089	
8	DENVER	$645,583	
9	FLORIDA	$1,450,392	
10	KANSASCITY	$574,899	
11	MICHIGAN	$678,705	
12	NEWORLEANS	$333,454	
13	NEWYORK	$873,581	
14	PHOENIX	$570,255	
15	SEATTLE	$179,827	
16	TULSA	$628,405	
17	**Grand Total**	$10,774,172	10,774,172

FIGURE 6-26 You have applied conditional data bars with just three easy clicks!

Preprogrammed scenarios for condition levels

In the previous example, you did not have to trudge through a dialog box to define the condition levels. How can that be? Excel 2019 has a handful of preprogrammed scenarios that you can leverage when you want to spend less time configuring your conditional formatting and more time analyzing your data.

For example, to create the data bars you've just employed, Excel uses a predefined algorithm that takes the largest and smallest values in the selected range and calculates the condition level for each bar.

Other examples of preprogrammed scenarios include the following:

- Top Nth Items

- Top Nth %

- Bottom Nth Items

- Bottom Nth %

- Above Average

- Below Average

As you can see, Excel 2019 makes an effort to offer the conditions that are most commonly used in data analysis.

> **Note** To remove the applied conditional formatting, place your cursor inside the pivot table, click the Home tab, and select Conditional Formatting in the Styles group. From there, select Clear Rules and then select Clear Rules From This PivotTable.

Creating custom conditional formatting rules

It's important to note that you are by no means limited to the preprogrammed scenarios mentioned in the previous section. You can still create your own custom conditions.

To see how this works, you need to begin by creating the pivot table shown in Figure 6-27.

◢	A	B	C	D
1	Product_Description (All)			
2				
3	Market	Sales_Amount	Contracted Hours	Dollars Per Hour
4	BUFFALO	$450,478	6,864	$65.63
5	CALIFORNIA	$2,254,735	33,014	$68.30
6	CANADA	$776,245	12,103	$64.14
7	CHARLOTTE	$890,522	14,525	$61.31
8	DALLAS	$467,089	6,393	$73.06
9	DENVER	$645,583	8,641	$74.71
10	FLORIDA	$1,450,392	22,640	$64.06
11	KANSASCITY	$574,899	8,547	$67.26
12	MICHIGAN	$678,705	10,744	$63.17
13	NEWORLEANS	$333,454	5,057	$65.94
14	NEWYORK	$873,581	14,213	$61.46
15	PHOENIX	$570,255	10,167	$56.09
16	SEATTLE	$179,827	2,889	$62.25
17	TULSA	$628,405	9,583	$65.57
18	Grand Total	$10,774,172	165,380	$65.15

FIGURE 6-27 This pivot table shows Sales_Amount, Contracted_Hours, and a calculated field that calculates Dollars Per Hour.

In this scenario, you want to evaluate the relationship between total revenue and dollars per hour. The idea is that some strategically applied conditional formatting helps identify opportunities for improvement.

Place your cursor in the Sales_Amount column. Click the Home tab and select Conditional Formatting, and then select New Rule. This activates the New Formatting Rule dialog box, shown in Figure 6-28. In this dialog box, you need to identify the cells where the conditional formatting will be applied, specify the rule type to use, and define the details of the conditional formatting.

First, you must identify the cells where your conditional formatting will be applied. You have three choices:

- **Selected Cells**—This selection applies conditional formatting to only the selected cells.

- **All Cells Showing "Sales_Amount" Values**—This selection applies conditional formatting to all values in the Sales_Amount column, including all subtotals and grand totals. This selection is ideal for use in analyses using averages, percentages, or other calculations where a single conditional formatting rule makes sense for all levels of analysis.

- **All Cells Showing "Sales_Amount" Values for "Market"**—This selection applies conditional formatting to all values in the Sales_Amount column at the Market level only. (It excludes subtotals and grand totals.) This selection is ideal for use in analyses using calculations that make sense only within the context of the level being measured.

FIGURE 6-28   The New Formatting Rule dialog box.

Note The words *Sales_Amount* and *Market* are not permanent fixtures of the New Formatting Rule dialog box. These words change to reflect the fields in your pivot table. Sales_Amount is used here because the cursor is in that column. Market is used because the active data items in the pivot table are in the Market field.

In this example, the third selection (All Cells Showing "Sales_Amount" Values for "Market") makes the most sense, so click that radio button, as shown in Figure 6-29.

Next, in the Select A Rule Type section, you must specify the rule type you want to use for the conditional format. You can select one of five rule types:

- **Format All Cells Based On Their Values**—This selection enables you to apply conditional formatting based on some comparison of the actual values of the selected range; that is, the values in the selected range are measured against each other. This selection is ideal when you want to identify general anomalies in your data set.

- **Format Only Cells That Contain**—This selection enables you to apply conditional formatting to cells that meet specific criteria you define. Keep in mind that the values in your range are not measured against each other when you use this rule type. This selection is useful when you are comparing your values against a predefined benchmark.

- **Format Only Top Or Bottom Ranked Values**—This selection enables you to apply conditional formatting to cells that are ranked in the top or bottom *N*th number or percentage of all the values in the range.

FIGURE 6-29 Click the radio button next to All Cells Showing "Sales_Amount" Values for "Market."

- **Format Only Values That Are Above Or Below Average**—This selection enables you to apply conditional formatting to values that are mathematically above or below the average of all values in the selected range.

- **Use A Formula To Determine Which Cells To Format**—This selection enables you to specify your own formula and evaluate each value in the selected range against that formula. If the values evaluate to true, the conditional formatting is applied. This selection comes in handy when you are applying conditions based on the results of an advanced formula or mathematical operation.

> **Note** You can use data bars, color scales, and icon sets only when the selected cells are formatted based on their values. This means that if you want to use data bars, color scales, and icon sets, you must select the Format All Cells Based On Their Values rule type.

In this scenario, you want to identify problem areas using icon sets; therefore, you want to format the cells based on their values, so select Format All Cells Based On Their Values.

Finally, you need to define the details of the conditional formatting in the Edit The Rule Description section. Again, you want to identify problem areas using the slick icon sets that are offered by Excel 2019. Therefore, select Icon Sets from the Format Style drop-down box.

After selecting Icon Sets, select a style appropriate to your analysis. The style selected in Figure 6-30 is ideal in situations in which your pivot tables cannot always be viewed in color.

FIGURE 6-30   Select Icon Sets from the Format Style drop-down box.

With this configuration, Excel applies the sign icons based on the percentile bands >=67, >=33, and <33. Keep in mind that you can change the actual percentile bands based on your needs. In this scenario, the default percentile bands are sufficient.

Click the OK button to apply the conditional formatting. As you can see in Figure 6-31, you now have icons that enable you to quickly determine where each market falls in relation to other markets in terms of revenue.

Now apply the same conditional formatting to the Dollars Per Hour field. When you are done, your pivot table should look like the one shown in Figure 6-32.

Take a moment to analyze what you have here. With this view, a manager can analyze the relationship between total revenue and dollars per hour. For example, the Dallas market manager can see that he is in the bottom percentile for revenue but in the top percentile for dollars per hour. With this information, he immediately sees that his dollars per hour rates might be too high for his market. Conversely, the New York market manager can see that she is in the top percentile for revenue but in the bottom percentile for dollars per hour. This tells her that her dollars per hour rates might be too low for her market.

Remember that this in an interactive report. Each manager can view the same analysis by product by simply filtering the report filter area!

	A	B	C	D
1	Product_Description	(All)		
2				
3	Market	Sales_Amount	Contracted Hours	Dollars Per Hour
4	BUFFALO	◆ $450,478	6,864	$65.63
5	CALIFORNIA	● $2,254,735	33,014	$68.30
6	CANADA	◆ $776,245	12,103	$64.14
7	CHARLOTTE	△ $890,522	14,525	$61.31
8	DALLAS	◆ $467,089	6,393	$73.06
9	DENVER	◆ $645,583	8,641	$74.71
10	FLORIDA	△ $1,450,392	22,640	$64.06
11	KANSASCITY	◆ $574,899	8,547	$67.26
12	MICHIGAN	◆ $678,705	10,744	$63.17
13	NEWORLEANS	◆ $333,454	5,057	$65.94
14	NEWYORK	△ $873,581	14,213	$61.46
15	PHOENIX	◆ $570,255	10,167	$56.09
16	SEATTLE	◆ $179,827	2,889	$62.25
17	TULSA	◆ $628,405	9,583	$65.57
18	Grand Total	$10,774,172	165,380	$65.15

FIGURE 6-31 You have applied your first custom conditional formatting!

⊿	A	B	C	D
1	Product_Description (All)			
2				
3	Market	Sales_Amount	Contracted Hours	Dollars Per Hour
4	BUFFALO	◇ $450,478	6,864 △	$65.63
5	CALIFORNIA	⬤ $2,254,735	33,014 △	$68.30
6	CANADA	◇ $776,245	12,103 △	$64.14
7	CHARLOTTE	△ $890,522	14,525 ◇	$61.31
8	DALLAS	◇ $467,089	6,393 ⬤	$73.06
9	DENVER	◇ $645,583	8,641 ⬤	$74.71
10	FLORIDA	△ $1,450,392	22,640 △	$64.06
11	KANSASCITY	◇ $574,899	8,547 △	$67.26
12	MICHIGAN	◇ $678,705	10,744 △	$63.17
13	NEWORLEANS	◇ $333,454	5,057 △	$65.94
14	NEWYORK	△ $873,581	14,213 ◇	$61.46
15	PHOENIX	◇ $570,255	10,167 ◇	$56.09
16	SEATTLE	◇ $179,827	2,889 △	$62.25
17	TULSA	◇ $628,405	9,583 △	$65.57
18	Grand Total	$10,774,172	165,380	$65.15

FIGURE 6-32 You have successfully created an interactive visualization.

Using Power BI Custom Visuals in Excel

Office 365 customers will soon have the chance to add Power BI Custom Visuals to Excel. These visual will not support data in a pivot table. To use a custom visual such as the Word Cloud shown in Figure 6-33, you will have to copy the data outside of a pivot table.

The process of installing a custom visualization has not been defined yet. Currently, while the feature is in development, you have to use a sidecar method described at http://mrx.cl/trycustomvisuals.

After installing the Word Cloud add-in, you can follow these steps:

1. Copy some text to Excel.

2. Use Data, Text to Columns, Delimited By A Space to break the phrases into words.

3. Copy all of the words into a single column.

4. Use a pivot table to count the number of occurrences of each word. The pivot table should have Word in the first column and Volume in the second column.

5. Use formulas to copy the data from the pivot table to a regular Excel range.

6. Select this data.

7. Use the Plus icon in the Charts group and select More Custom Visuals....

8. Select the Word Cloud visualization.

9. When the visualization appears, select Chart Tools Design, Format. A Charts panel will appear on the right side of the screen.

10. Clear the check box for Stop Words.

11. Under Rotate Text, choose from -70 to 70. Choose up to seven orientations.

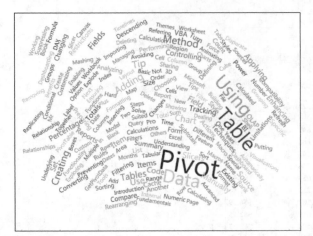

FIGURE 6-33 The word cloud shows hundreds of words, but frequently used words appear larger: Pivot, Data, Using, and Table.

> **Caution**   As this book goes to print, the Custom Visuals feature is available only to those using the Insiders channel of Office 365.

Next steps

In Chapter 7, "Analyzing disparate data sources with pivot tables," you will find out how to bring to-gether disparate data sources into one pivot table. You will create a pivot table from multiple data sets and learn the basics of creating pivot tables from other pivot tables.

Analyzing disparate data sources with pivot tables

In this chapter, you will:

- Use the Data Model
- Build a pivot table using external data sources
- Leverage Power Query to extract and transform data

U p to this point, you have been working with one local table located in the worksheet within which you are operating. Indeed, it would be wonderful if every data set you came across was neatly packed in one easy-to-use Excel table. Unfortunately, the business of data analysis does not always work out that way.

The reality is that some of the data you encounter will come from disparate data sources—sets of data that are from separate systems, stored in different locations, or saved in a variety of formats. In an Excel environment, disparate data sources generally fall into one of two categories:

- **External data**—External data is exactly what it sounds like—data that is not located in the Excel workbook in which you are operating. Some examples of external data sources are text files, access tables, SQL Server tables, and other Excel workbooks.

- **Multiple ranges**—Multiple ranges are separate data sets located in the same workbook but separated either by blank cells or by different worksheets. For example, if your workbook has three tables on three different worksheets, each of your data sets covers a range of cells. You are therefore working with multiple ranges.

A pivot table can be an effective tool when you need to summarize data that is not neatly packed into one table. With a pivot table, you can quickly bring together either data found in an external source or data found in multiple tables within your workbook. In this chapter, you'll discover various techniques for working with external data sources and data sets located in multiple ranges within a workbook.

Using the Data Model

Excel 2013 introduced a new in-memory analytics engine called the Data Model that is based on the Power Pivot engine. Every workbook has one Data Model that enables you to work with and analyze disparate data sources like never before.

The idea behind the Data Model is simple. Let's say you have two tables: a Customers table and an Orders table. The Orders table contains basic information about invoices (customer number, invoice date, and revenue). The Customers table contains information such as customer number, customer name, and state. If you want to analyze revenue by state, you have to join the two tables and aggregate the Revenue field in the Orders table by the State field in the Customers table.

In the past, in order to do this, you would have had to go through a series of gyrations involving using VLOOKUP, SUMIF, or other functions. With the new Data Model, however, you can simply tell Excel how the two tables are related (they both have customer number) and then pull them into the Data Model. The Excel Data Model then builds an analytical cube based on that customer number relationship and exposes the data through a pivot table. With the pivot table, you can create the aggregation by state with a few mouse clicks.

> **Note** The Data Model is using the Power Pivot data engine. Starting with Excel 2019, every Windows version of Excel includes full access to the Power Pivot tools. See Chapter 10, "Unlocking features with the Data Model and Power Pivot."

Building out your first Data Model

Imagine that you have the Transactions table shown in Figure 7-1. On another worksheet, you have the Employees table shown in Figure 7-2. Both of these tables have been formatted as a table using Home, Format As Table.

Using Format As Table creates names like Table1 and Table2. After formatting as a table, visit the Table Tools, Design tab and assign new names such as Transactions and Employees.

	A	B	C	D
1	Sales_Rep	Invoice_Date	Sales_Amount	Contracted Hours
2	4416	1/5/2022	111.79	2
3	4416	1/5/2022	111.79	2
4	160006	1/5/2022	112.13	2
5	6444	1/5/2022	112.13	2
6	160006	1/5/2022	145.02	3
7	52661	1/5/2022	196.58	4
8	6444	1/5/2022	204.20	4
9	51552	1/5/2022	225.24	3
10	55662	1/6/2022	86.31	2

FIGURE 7-1 This table shows transactions by sales rep number.

	A	B	C	D
1	Employee_Number	Last_Name	First_Name	Job_Title
2	21	SIOCAT	ROBERT	SERVICE REPRESENTATIVE 3
3	42	BREWN	DONNA	SERVICE REPRESENTATIVE 3
4	45	VAN HUILE	KENNETH	SERVICE REPRESENTATIVE 2
5	104	WIBB	MAURICE	SERVICE REPRESENTATIVE 2
6	106	CESTENGIAY	LUC	SERVICE REPRESENTATIVE 2
7	113	TRIDIL	ROCH	SERVICE REPRESENTATIVE 2
8	142	CETE	GUY	SERVICE REPRESENTATIVE 3
9	145	ERSINEILT	MIKE	SERVICE REPRESENTATIVE 2
10	162	GEBLE	MICHAEL	SERVICE REPRESENTATIVE 2
11	165	CERDANAL	ALAIN	SERVICE REPRESENTATIVE 3
12	201	GEIDRIOU	DOMINIC	TEAMLEAD 1

FIGURE 7-2   This table provides information on employees: first name, last name, and job title.

You need to create an analysis that shows sales by job title. This would normally be difficult, given the fact that sales and job title are in two separate tables. But with the new Data Model, you can follow these simple steps:

1. Go to the Data tab of the ribbon and click Relationships.

2. In the Relationships dialog box, click New....

3. In the Create Relationships dialog box, the primary table is the Transactions table. The Column (Foreign) is Sales_Rep. On the next row of the dialog box, specify Employees as the Related Table and Employee Number as the Related Column (Primary Key) (see Figure 7-3).

FIGURE 7-3   Define a relationship between the two tables.

The importance of primary keys

In Figure 7-3, the lower-right drop-down menu is called Related Column (Primary). The term *Primary* in this case means that the Data Model uses this field from the associated table as the primary key.

A *primary key* is a field that contains only unique non-null values (no duplicates or blanks). Primary key fields are necessary in the Data Model to prevent aggregation errors and duplications. Every relationship you create must have a field designated as the primary key.

In the scenario in Figure 7-2, the Employees table must have all unique values in the Employee_Number field, with no blanks or null values. This is the only way Excel can ensure data integrity when joining multiple tables.

4. Click OK to create the relationship. This process might take a bit of time because this is the point where the two tables are added to the Data Model.

5. Click OK to close the Relationships dialog box.

6. Insert a new blank worksheet in the workbook.

7. From the blank worksheet, select Insert, PivotTable. Excel will default to Use This Workbook's Data Model, as shown in Figure 7-4.

FIGURE 7-4 Because you've defined a relationship, Excel assumes you want to use the Data Model.

Notice the PivotTable Fields list in Figure 7-5. This is the Data Model version. You have two tabs at the top for Active and All. Each table appears in the Field Well, and both are initially collapsed so you cannot see the fields inside.

FIGURE 7-5 Each table appears in the PivotTable Fields panel.

8. Use the Greater-Than icon next to each table to expand the table. Drag Job_Title from the Employees table to Rows. Drag Sales_Amount from the Transactions table to Values.

After you create the relationship, you have a single pivot table that effectively uses data from both tables to create the analysis you need. Figure 7-6 illustrates that using the Excel Data Model, you have achieved the goal of showing sales by job title.

FIGURE 7-6 You have achieved your goal of showing sales by job title.

Managing relationships in the Data Model

After you assign tables to the Data Model, you might need to adjust the relationships between the tables. To make changes to the relationships in a Data Model, activate the Manage Relationships dialog box.

Click the Data tab in the ribbon and select the Relationships command. The dialog box shown in Figure 7-7 appears.

FIGURE 7-7 The Manage Relationships dialog box enables you to make changes to the relationships in the Data Model.

The Manage Relationships dialog box offers the following buttons:

- **New**—Create a new relationship between two tables in the Data Model.

- **Edit**—Alter the selected relationship.

- **Activate**—Enforce the selected relationship; that is, tell Excel to consider the relationship when aggregating and analyzing the data in the Data Model.

- **Deactivate**—Turn off the selected relationship; that is, tell Excel to ignore the relationship when aggregating and analyzing the data in the Data Model.

- **Delete**—Remove the selected relationship.

Adding a new table to the Data Model

You can add a new table to the Data Model by using Home, Format As Table. Until you define a relationship to the table, it might be shown in the All tab of the PivotTable Fields list instead of the Active tab.

Although you can hunt down the new table on the All tab, it is best to define a new relationship using Data, Relationships before adding the field to the pivot table. Defining a relationship will move the table to the Active tab.

Limitations of the Data Model

As with everything else in Excel, the Data Model does have limitations. Table 7-1 highlights the maximum and configurable limits for the Excel Data Model.

TABLE 7-1 Data model limitations

Object	Specification
Data Model size	In 32-bit environments, Excel workbooks are subject to a 2GB limit. This includes the in-memory space shared by Excel, the Data Model, and add-ins that run in the same process. In 64-bit environments, there are no hard limits on file size. Workbook size is limited only by available memory and system resources.
Characters in a table or column name	100 characters
Number of tables in the Data Model	2,147,483,647
Number of rows in each table in the Data Model	The limit is 1,999,999,997 rows.
Number of columns and calculated columns in each table in the Data Model	2,147,483,647
Number of distinct values in a column	The limit is 1,999,999,997 values.
String length in each field	The limit is 536,870,912 bytes (512MB), which is equivalent to 268,435,456 Unicode characters (256 mega-characters).

Building a pivot table using external data sources

Excel is certainly good at processing and analyzing data. In fact, pivot tables themselves are a testament to the analytical power of Excel. However, despite all its strengths, Excel makes for a poor relational data management platform, primarily for three reasons:

- A data set's size has a significant effect on performance, making for less efficient data crunching. The reason for this is the fundamental way Excel handles memory. When you open an Excel file, the entire file is loaded into RAM to ensure quick data processing and access. The drawback to this behavior is that Excel requires a great deal of RAM to process even the smallest change in a spreadsheet (and typically gives you a "Calculating" indicator in the status bar). Although Excel 2019 offers more than 1 million rows and more than 16,000 columns, creating and managing large data sets causes Excel to slow down considerably, making data analysis a painful endeavor.

- The lack of a relational data structure forces the use of flat tables that promote redundant data. This also increases the chance for errors.

- There is no way to index data fields in Excel to optimize performance when you're attempting to retrieve large amounts of data.

In smart organizations, the task of data management is not performed by Excel; rather, it is primarily performed by relational database systems such as Microsoft Access and SQL Server. These databases are used to store millions of records that can be rapidly searched and retrieved. The effect of this separation in tasks is that you have a data management layer (your database) and a presentation layer (Excel). The trick is to find the best way to get information from your data management layer to your presentation layer for use by your pivot table.

Managing your data is the general idea behind building a pivot table using an external data source. Building pivot tables from external systems enables you to leverage environments that are better suited to data management. This means you can let Excel do what it does best: analyze and create a presentation layer for your data. The following sections walk you through several techniques for building pivot tables using external data.

Building a pivot table with Microsoft Access data

Often Access is used to manage a series of tables that interact with each other, such as a Customers table, an Orders table, and an Invoices table. Managing data in Access provides the benefit of a relational database where you can ensure data integrity, prevent redundancy, and easily generate data sets via queries.

Most Excel customers use an Access query to create a subset of data and then import that data into Excel. From there, the data can be analyzed with pivot tables. The problem with this method is that it forces the Excel workbook to hold two copies of the imported data sets: one on the spreadsheet and one in the pivot cache. Holding two copies obviously causes the workbook to be twice as big as it needs to be, and it introduces the possibility of performance issues.

In Excel 2019 and Office 365, Microsoft is encouraging everyone to use Power Query instead of the legacy Get External Data tools. For this chapter, you will use the legacy tools. Before you can do that, you need to bring the icons back to the ribbon.

Choose File, Options, Data. At the bottom of the Excel Options dialog box, choose From Access (Legacy). Click OK. Close your workbook and reopen. You can now find the From Access (Legacy) has been revealed under Data, Get Data, Legacy Wizards (see Figure 7-8).

FIGURE 7-8 You have to use Excel Options to bring the legacy wizards back.

To try out this functionality, create a blank workbook in Excel.

1. Choose Data, Get Data, Legacy Wizards, From Access (Legacy).

2. Clicking the From Access button activates a dialog box, asking you to select the database you want to work with. Select your database.

3. After your database has been selected, the dialog box shown in Figure 7-9 appears. This dialog box lists all the tables and queries available. In this example, select the query called Sales_By_ Employee and click the OK button.

FIGURE 7-9 Select the table or query you want to analyze.

> **Note** In Figure 7-9, notice that the Select Table dialog box contains a column called Type. There are two types of Access objects you can work with: views and tables. View indicates that the data set listed is an Access query, and Table indicates that the data set is an Access table.
>
> In this example, notice that Sales_By_Employee is actually an Access query. This means that you import the results of the query. This is true interaction at work: Access does all the back-end data management and aggregation, and Excel handles the analysis and presentation!

4. Next, you see the Import Data dialog box, where you select the format in which you want to import the data. As you can see in Figure 7-10, you have the option of importing the data as a table, as a pivot table, or as a pivot table with an accompanying pivot chart. You also have the option to tell Excel where to place the data.

5. Select the radio button next to PivotTable Report, and click the OK button.

FIGURE 7-10 Select the radio button next to PivotTable Report.

At this point, you should see the PivotTable Fields list shown in Figure 7-11. From here, you can use this pivot table just as you normally would.

The wonderful thing about this technique is that you can refresh the data simply by refreshing the pivot table. When you refresh, Excel takes a new snapshot of the data source and updates the pivot cache.

FIGURE 7-11 Your pivot table is ready to use.

> **Caution** If you create a pivot table that uses an Access database as its source, you can refresh that pivot table only if the table or view is available. That is to say, deleting, moving, or renaming the database used to create the pivot table destroys the link to the external data set, thus destroying your ability to refresh the data. Deleting or renaming the source table or query has the same effect.
>
> Following that reasoning, any clients using your linked pivot table cannot refresh the pivot table unless the source is available to them. If you need your clients to be able to refresh, you might want to make the data source available via a shared network directory.

Building a pivot table with SQL Server data

In the spirit of collaboration, Excel 2019 vastly improves your ability to connect to transactional databases such as SQL Server. With the connection functionality found in Excel, creating a pivot table from SQL Server data is as easy as ever.

Before you can use the legacy SQL Server tools, go to File, Options, Data. At the bottom of the panel, choose From SQL Server (Legacy). Create a new Excel workbook and you will find the command has been added to the Data tab, as described next.

Start on the Data tab and select Get Data, Legacy Wizards, From SQL Server (Legacy), as shown in Figure 7-12.

Selecting this option activates the Data Connection Wizard, as shown in Figure 7-13. The idea here is to configure your connection settings so Excel can establish a link to the server.

FIGURE 7-12 From the drop-down menu, select From SQL Server (Legacy).

Note There is no sample file for this example. The essence of this demonstration is the interaction between Excel and a SQL server data source. The actions you take to connect to your particular database are the same as demonstrated here.

You need to provide Excel with some authentication information. As you can see in Figure 7-13, you enter the name of your server as well as your username and password.

FIGURE 7-13 Enter your authentication information and click the Next button.

> **Note** If you are typically authenticated via Windows Authentication, you simply select the Use Windows Authentication option.

Next, you select the database with which you are working from a drop-down menu containing all available databases on the specified server. As you can see in Figure 7-14, a database called Adventure-Works2012 has been selected in the drop-down box. Selecting this database causes all the tables and views in it to be exposed in the list of objects below the drop-down menu. All that is left to do in this dialog box is to choose the table or view you want to analyze and then click the Next button.

FIGURE 7-14 Specify your database and then choose the table or view you want to analyze.

The next screen in the wizard, shown in Figure 7-15, enables you to enter some descriptive information about the connection you've just created.

FIGURE 7-15 Enter descriptive information for your connection.

> **Note** All the fields in the dialog box shown in Figure 7-15 are optional edits only. That is, if you bypass this screen without editing anything, your connection works fine.

Here are the fields you'll use most often:

- **File Name**—In the File Name input box, you can change the file name of the .odc (Office Data Connection) file generated to store the configuration information for the link you just created.

- **Save Password in File**—Under the File Name input box, you have the option of saving the password for your external data in the file itself (via the Save Password In File check box). Selecting this check box actually enters your password in the file. Keep in mind that this password is not encrypted, so anyone interested enough could potentially get the password for your data source simply by viewing your file with a text editor.

- **Description**—In the Description field, you can enter a plain description of what this particular data connection does.

- **Friendly Name**—The Friendly Name field enables you to specify your own name for the external source. You typically enter a name that is descriptive and easy to read.

When you are satisfied with your descriptive edits, click the Finish button to finalize your connection settings. You immediately see the Import Data dialog box, shown in Figure 7-16. In it you select a pivot table and then click the OK button to start building your pivot table.

FIGURE 7-16 When your connection is finalized, you can start building your pivot table.

Leveraging Power Query to extract and transform data

Every day, millions of Excellers manually pull data from some source location, manipulate that data, and integrate it into their pivot table reporting.

This process of extracting, manipulating, and integrating data is called ETL. ETL refers to the three separate functions typically required to integrate disparate data sources: extraction, transformation, and loading. The extraction function involves reading data from a specified source and extracting a desired subset of data. The transformation function involves cleaning, shaping, and aggregating data to convert it to the desired structure. The loading function involves actually importing or using the resulting data.

In an attempt to empower Excel analysts to develop robust and reusable ETL processes, Microsoft created Power Query. Power Query enhances the ETL experience by offering an intuitive mechanism to extract data from a wide variety of sources, perform complex transformations on that data, and then load the data into a workbook or the Data Model.

In the following sections, you'll see how Power Query works and discover some of the innovative ways you can use it to help save time and automate the steps for importing clean data into your pivot table reporting models.

Power Query: No longer an add-in

Starting in Excel 2016, Power Query is not an add-in. It's a native feature of Excel, just like charts and pivot tables are native features. In an odd branding misstep, Microsoft scrapped the Power Query name in the Excel ribbon. The tools are located in the Get & Transform Data group of the Data tab in the ribbon.

You may have previously installed the Power Query add-in when you were working with Excel 2010 or Excel 2013. Indeed, Microsoft still offers the Power Query add-in for previous versions of Excel. Simply enter the search term "Excel Power Query Add-in" into your favorite search engine to find the free Excel 2010 and 2013 installation packages.

Again, don't expect to find an Excel 2016 or Excel 2019 version of the Power Query add-in, as it's already built into Excel.

Power Query basics

Although Power Query is relatively intuitive, it's worth taking the time to walk through a basic scenario to understand its high-level features. To start this basic look at Power Query, you need to import Microsoft Corporation stock prices from the past 30 days by using Yahoo Finance. For this scenario, you need to perform a web query to pull the data needed from Yahoo Finance. As shown in the following example, the Get & Transform group of the Data tab contains all the commands you need to start this query.

To start your query, follow these steps:

1. Select the From Web icon in the Get & Transform Data group of the Data tab of the ribbon (see Figure 7-17).

FIGURE 7-17 Starting a Power Query web query.

2. In the dialog box that appears (see Figure 7-18), enter in the URL for the data you need—in this case, `https://finance.yahoo.com/quote/history?p=MSFT&tsrc=fin-srch`.

FIGURE 7-18 Enter the target URL containing the data you need.

3. After a bit of gyrating, the Navigator pane shown in Figure 7-19 appears. Here, you select the data source you want extracted. You can click on each table to see a preview of the data. In this case, Table 2 holds the historical stock data you need, so click on Table 2 and then click the Transform Data button.

FIGURE 7-19 Select the correct data source and then click the Edit button.

Note You may have noticed that the Navigator pane shown in Figure 7-19 offers a Load button (to the left of the Transform Data button). The Load button allows you to skip any editing and import your targeted data as is. If you are sure you will not need to transform or shape your data in any way, you can opt to click the Load button to import the data directly into the Data Model or a spreadsheet in your workbook.

Note Excel used to offer a web scraping tool that was also called From Web. This has been removed from the ribbon. You can add it back using File, Options, Data and then choosing From Web (Legacy). After reopening your workbook, the command will be found under Data, Get Data, Legacy Wizards.

When you click the Transform Data button, Power Query activates a new Power Query Editor window, which contains its own ribbon and a preview pane that shows a preview of the data (see Figure 7-20). Here, you can apply certain actions to shape, clean, and transform the data before importing.

FIGURE 7-20 The Query Editor window allows you to shape, clean, and transform data.

The idea is to work with each column shown in the Power Query Editor, applying the necessary actions that will give you the data and structure you need. You'll dive deeper into column actions later in this chapter. For now, you need to continue toward the goal of getting the last 30 days of stock prices for Microsoft Corporation.

Scrolling through the data, you notice that there are some dividend records mixed in with the data (see Figure 7-21). Those records contain text along with a number, and those are the reason that Power Query is treating the columns as text. (Notice the ABC icon next to the column heading. This indicates Text.)

FIGURE 7-21 The Dividend record on row 22 is causing the column to be reported as Text.

4. There are several ways to eliminate the dividend rows. You could use the Filter drop-down menu. But here is a fast way. Click on the column heading for Open. Ctrl+click on the column heading for Adjusted Close. On the Transform tab, open the Data Type drop-down menu and choose Currency. This will cause the dividend rows to report as an error.

5. Right-click the Open heading and choose Remove Errors (see Figure 7-22). You will be left with only the rows that have stock prices.

FIGURE 7-22 After converting to Currency, the dividend rows are reporting an error and can be removed.

6. Remove all the columns you do not need by right-clicking each one and clicking Remove. (Besides the Date field, the only other columns you need are the High, Low, and Adjusted Close fields.) Alternatively, you can hold down the Ctrl key on your keyboard, select the columns you want to keep, right-click any of the selected columns, and then choose Remove Other Columns.

7. Once all the errors are removed, add a Week Of field that displays the week each date in the table belongs to. To do this, right-click the Date field and select the Duplicate Column option. A new column is added to the preview. Right-click the newly added column, select the Rename option, and then rename the column Week Of.

8. Select the Transform tab on the Power Query ribbon and then choose Date, Week, Start Of The Week, as shown in Figure 7-23. Excel transforms the date to display the start of the week for a given date.

FIGURE 7-23 The Power Query ribbon can be used to apply transformation actions such as displaying the start of the week for a given date.

9. To limit the results to the last 30 days, open the Filter drop-down menu for the Date field. Choose In The Previous..., as shown in Figure 7-24.

FIGURE 7-24 Choose to filter the Date field using In The Previous....

10. Specify that you want data for the last 30 days, as shown in Figure 7-25. Choosing the last 30 days instead of a specific date will allow the report to be refreshed on any day in the future.

FIGURE 7-25 The Power Query ribbon can be used to apply transformation actions such as displaying the start of the week for a given date.

11. When you've finished configuring your Power Query feed, save, and output the results. To do this, click Home, Close & Load.

Note Alternatively, you can open the Close & Load drop-down menu and choose Load To. You can choose to output the results to the Data Model. Or, you can choose to save the query as a query connection only, which means you will be able to use the query in various in-memory processes without needing to actually output the results anywhere.

At this point, you will have a table similar to the one shown in Figure 7-26, which can be used to produce the pivot table you need.

	A	B	C	D	E	F	G
1	Date	Open	High	Low	Adj Close**	Week Of	
2	9/12/2018	111.43	111.85	110.51	111.71	9/9/2018	
3	9/11/2018	108.9	111.59	108.89	111.24	9/9/2018	
4	9/10/2018	108.84	109.64	108.36	109.38	9/9/2018	
5	9/7/2018	108.23	108.72	107.23	108.21	9/2/2018	
6	9/6/2018	108.25	108.99	107.51	108.74	9/2/2018	
7	9/5/2018	111.01	111.42	108.1	108.49	9/2/2018	
8	9/4/2018	110.85	111.96	110.22	111.71	9/2/2018	
9	8/31/2018	111.69	112.78	111.52	112.33	8/26/2018	
10	8/30/2018	111.67	112.61	111.44	111.95	8/26/2018	

FIGURE 7-26 Your final query pulled from the Internet—transformed, put into an Excel table, and ready to use in a pivot table.

Take a moment to appreciate what Power Query allowed you to do just now. With a few clicks, you searched the Internet, found some data, shaped the data to keep only the columns you needed, and even manipulated that data to add an extra Week Of dimension to the base data. This is what Power Query is about: enabling you to easily extract, filter, and reshape data without the need for any programmatic coding skills.

Understanding applied steps

Power Query uses its own formula language (known as the "M" language) to codify your queries. As with macro recording, each action you take when working with Power Query results in a line of code being written into the Applied Steps list box. Query steps are embedded M code that allow your actions to be repeated each time you refresh your Power Query data.

To get back into your query, right-click the Query name in the Queries & Connections pane. Choose Edit.

The applied steps appear along the right side of the screen (see Figure 7-27). Click any applied step to see how the data looked at that point in the process. The formula bar shows what action happened at that step.

FIGURE 7-27   Query steps can be viewed and managed in the Applied Steps section of the Query Settings pane.

Each query step represents an action you took to get to a data table. You can click on any step to see the underlying M code in the Power Query formula bar. For example, clicking the step called Removed Errors reveals the code for that step in the formula bar.

You can right-click on any step to see a menu of options for managing your query steps. Figure 7-28 illustrates the following options:

- **Edit Settings**—Edit the arguments or parameters that defines the selected step.

- **Rename**—Give the selected step a meaningful name.

- **Delete**—Remove the selected step. Be aware that removing a step can cause errors if subsequent steps depend on the deleted step.

- **Delete Until End**—Remove the selected step and all following steps.

- **Insert Step After**—Insert a new step after this step.

- **Move Up**—Move the selected step up in the order of steps.

- **Move Down**—Move the selected step down in the order of steps.

- **Extract Previous**—Extracts the steps before the selected step into a new query. You will be asked to give the new query a name.

- **View Native Query**—Show the underlying SQL behind a Source step.

- **Properties**—Add a description to any step. The description will be added as a comment in your M code. View the full M code using View, Advanced Editor.

FIGURE 7-28   Right-click on any query step to edit, rename, delete, or move the step.

Viewing the Advanced Query Editor

Power Query gives you the option of viewing and editing a query's embedded M code directly. While in the Power Query Editor window, click the View tab of the ribbon and select Advanced Editor. You will see the M code created as you performed various steps (see Figure 7-29).

If you read Ken Puls book on Power Query, *M Is for Data Monkey* (ISBN 978-1-61547-034-1), you might occasionally be told to type some code directly into the advanced editor. For example, I was doing training for a client. They had a large CSV file where the first three rows contained metadata such as Run Date and other fields. The actual headings for the file started in Row 4. There is no way to deal with this in the Power Query Editor, but one line of code typed into the Advanced Editor solved the problem.

I personally know one person who starts with a blank Advanced Editor and types his code from scratch. But for the vast majority of people reading this book, building the M code using the Power Query Editor will be the usual workflow.

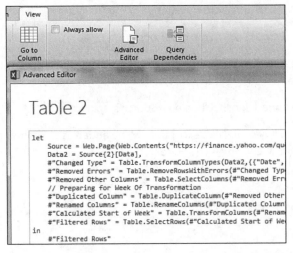

FIGURE 7-29 View the M code created by your steps of cleaning the data.

Refreshing Power Query data

The best part of Power Query comes on the second day that you have to run your report. After using the Power Query Editor to clean your data on the first day, the next time you need to run the report, you simply open your workbook and refresh the data. Power Query will go back to the original source and reperform all the steps.

If you chose to load your Power Query results to an Excel table in the existing workbook, you can manually refresh by right-clicking on the table and selecting the Refresh option.

For queries that are loaded directly to the Data Model, open the Queries & Connections pane by using Data, Queries & Connections. Right-click any query and choose Refresh.

Managing existing queries

As you add various queries to a workbook, you will need a way to manage them. Excel accommodates this need by offering the Queries and Connections pane, which enables you to edit, duplicate, refresh, and generally manage all the existing queries in the workbook. Activate the Workbook Queries pane by selecting the Queries & Connections command on the Data tab of the Excel ribbon.

You need to find the query you want to work with and then right-click it to take any one of these actions (see Figure 7-30):

FIGURE 7-30 Right-click any query in the Queries and Connections pane to see the available management options.

- **Copy**—Copy an existing query. You can paste a copy into this workbook (perhaps changing a filter step for a different region).

- **Paste**—Paste a copied query.

- **Edit**—Open the Power Query Editor, where you can modify the query steps.

- **Delete**—Delete the selected query.

- **Rename**—Rename the name of a query.

- **Refresh**—Refresh the data in the selected query.

- **Load To**—Activate the Load To dialog box, where you can redefine where the selected query's results are used.

- **Duplicate**—Create a copy of the query.

- **Reference**—Create a new query that references the output of the original query.

- **Merge**—Merge the selected query with another query in the workbook by matching specified columns.

- **Append**—Append the results of another query in the workbook to the selected query.

- **Send To Data Catalog**—Publish and share the selected query via a Power BI server that your IT department sets up and manages.

- **Export Connection File**—Saves the connection information in an Office Data Connection (.odc) file. You can then import the .odc file to other workbooks or on other computers. To consume an .odc file in another workbook, use Data, Existing Connections and browse for the *.odc file.

- **Move To Group**—Move the selected query into a logical group you create for better organization.

- **Move Up**—Move the selected query up in the Workbook Queries pane.

- **Move Down**—Move the selected query down in the Workbook Queries pane.

- **Show The Peek**—Show a preview of the query results for the selected query.

- **Properties**—Rename the query and add a friendly description.

The Workbook Queries pane is especially useful when your workbook contains several queries. Think of it as a kind of table of contents that allows you to easily find and interact with the queries in your workbook.

Understanding column-level actions

Right-clicking a column in the Power Query Editor activates a context menu that shows a full list of the actions you can take. You can also apply certain actions to multiple columns at one time by selecting two or more columns before right-clicking. Figure 7-31 shows the available column-level actions, and Table 7-2 explains them, as well as a few other actions that are available only in the Power Query Editor ribbon.

FIGURE 7-31 Right-click any column to see the column-level actions you can use to transform the data.

Note Note that all of the column-level actions available in Power Query are also available in the Power Query Editor ribbon. So, you can either opt for the convenience of right-clicking to quickly select an action or choose to utilize the more visual ribbon menu. There are a few useful column-level actions found only in the ribbon (see Table 7-2).

TABLE 7-2 Column-level actions

Action	Purpose	Available When Selecting Multiple Columns?
Copy	Copies the column to the clipboard.	Yes
Remove	Removes the selected column from the Power Query data.	Yes
Remove Other Columns	Removes all non-selected columns from the Power Query data.	Yes
Duplicate Column	Creates a duplicate of the selected column as a new column placed at the far right of the table. The name given to the new column is Copy of *X*, where *X* is the name of the original column.	No
Add Column From Examples	Creates a new column based on an example that you type. This is similar to Flash Fill in Excel but better because the result will show you the formula needed to achieve the result.	
Remove Duplicates	Removes all rows from the selected column where the values duplicate earlier values. The row with the first occurrence of a value is not removed.	Yes
Remove Errors	Removes rows containing errors in the selected column.	Yes
Change Type	Changes the data type of the selected column to any of these types: Binary, Date, Date/Time, Date/Time/Timezone, Duration, Logical, Number, Text, Time, or Using Locale (which localizes data types to the country you specify).	Yes
Transform	Changes the way values in the column are rendered. You can choose from the following options: Lowercase, Uppercase, Capitalize Each Word, Trim, Clean, Length, JSON, and XML. If the values in the column are date/time values, the options are Date, Time, Day, Month, Year, and Day Of Week. If the values in the column are number values, the options are Round, Absolute Value, Factorial, Base-10 Logarithm, Natural Logarithm, Power, and Square Root.	Yes
Replace Values	Replaces one value in the selected column with another specified value.	Yes
Replace Errors	Replaces unsightly error values with your own friendlier text.	Yes
Group By	Aggregates data by row values. For example, you can group by state and either count the number of cities in each state or sum the population of each state.	Yes
Fill	Fills empty cells in the column with the value of the first non-empty cell. You have the option of filling up or filling down.	Yes
Unpivot Columns	Transposes the selected columns from column oriented to row oriented or vice versa.	Yes
Unpivot Other Columns	Transposes the unselected columns.	Yes
Unpivot Only Selected Columns	Transposes the selected columns from column oriented to row oriented or vice versa.	Yes

Rename	Renames the selected column to a name you specify.	No
Move	Moves the selected column to a different location in the table. You have these choices for moving the column: Left, Right, To Beginning, and To End.	Yes
Drill Down	Navigates to the contents of the column. This is used with tables that contain metadata representing embedded information.	No
Add As New Query	Creates a new query with the contents of the column. This is done by referencing the original query in the new one. The name of the new query is the same as the column header of the selected column.	No
Split Column (Ribbon Only)	Splits the value of a single column into two or more columns or rows, based on a number of characters or a given delimiter, such as a comma, semicolon, or tab.	No
Merge Column (Ribbon Only)	Merges the values of two or more columns into a single column that contains a specified delimiter, such as a comma, semicolon, or tab.	Yes
Date & Time Transformation (Ribbon Only)	Allows for mathematical operations for a column formatted as Date or Time. You have the option of returning values such as Age or Duration. Or you can choose to return dates that represent time dimensions such as End Of Month, Start Of Week, End Of Quarter, or Day Of Year.	No

Understanding table actions

While you're in the Power Query Editor, Power Query allows you to apply certain actions to an entire data table. You can see the available table-level actions by clicking the Table Actions icon shown in Figure 7-32.

FIGURE 7-32 Click the Table Actions icon in the upper-left corner of the Power Query Editor Preview pane to see the table-level actions you can use to transform the data.

Table 7-3 lists the table-level actions and describes the primary purpose of each one.

TABLE 7-3 Table-level actions

Action	Purpose
Copy Entire Table	Copies the table to the clipboard.
Use First Row As Headers	Replaces each table header name with the values in the first row of each column.
Add Custom Column	Inserts a new column after the last column of the table. The values in the new column are determined by the value or formula you define.
Add Column From Examples	Similar to using Flash Fill in Excel.
Invoke Custom Function	Reuses a custom function that you have previously written. If you have to routinely apply a transformation to many tables in your workbook, you can write the transformation once in a blank query and then reuse it in each table using Invoke Custom Function.
Add Conditional Column	Helps you to build a new column with If-Then-Else logic. You fill out a simple dialog box, and Excel writes the correct formula.
Add Index Column	Adds a new column with row numbers such as 1, 2, 3. Alternatively, you can specify any starting number and increment to create an index column such as 5, 10, 15, and so on.
Add Index Column	Inserts a new column containing a sequential list of numbers starting from 1, 0, or another specified value you define.
Choose Columns	Choose the columns you want to keep in the query results.
Keep Top Rows	Keeps the top N rows.
Keep Bottom Rows	Keeps the bottom N rows.
Keep Range Of Rows	Keeps from rows N through NN.
Keep Duplicates	Keeps the items that appear more than once in the table.
Keep Errors	Keeps only the error rows and discards everything else.
Remove Top Rows	Removes the top N rows from the table.
Remove Bottom Rows	Removes the bottom N rows from the table.
Remove Alternate Rows	Removes alternate rows from the table, starting at the first row to remove and specifying the number of rows to remove and the number of rows to keep.
Remove Duplicates	Removes all rows where the values in the selected columns duplicate earlier values. The row with the first occurrence of a value set is not removed.
Remove Errors	Removes rows containing errors in the currently selected columns.
Merge Queries	Creates a new query that merges the current table with another query in the workbook by matching specified columns.
Append Queries	Creates a new query that appends the results of another query in the workbook to the current table.

Note All of the table-level actions available in Power Query are also available in the Power Query Editor ribbon. You can either opt for the convenience of right-clicking to quickly select an action or choose to utilize the more visual ribbon menu.

Power Query connection types

Microsoft has invested a great deal of time and resources in ensuring that Power Query can connect to a wide array of data sources. Whether you need to pull data from an external website, a text file, a database system, Facebook, or a web service, Power Query can accommodate most, if not all, your source data needs.

You can see all the available connection types by clicking on the New Query drop-down menu on the Data tab. Power Query offers the ability to pull from a wide array of data sources:

- **From File**—Pull data from a specified Excel file, text file, CSV file, XML file, JSON folder, or SharePoint folder.

- **From Database**—Pull data from SQL Server, Microsoft Access, Analysis Services, Oracle, IBM DB2, MySQL, PostgreSQL, Sybase, Teradata, or SAP HANA.

- **From Azure**—Pull data from Azure SQL Database, Data Warehouse, HD Insights, Blog Storage, Table Storage, or Data Lake Store.

- **From Online Services**—Pull data from SharePoint Online List, Microsoft Exchange Online, Dynamics 365 Online, Facebook, Salesforce Objects, or Salesforce Reports.

- **From Other Sources**—Pull data from a wide variety of sources, such as Table/Range, Web, Microsoft Query, SharePoint List, OData Feed, Hadoop File, Active Directory, Microsoft Exchange, ODBC, and OLEDB.

- **From Table**—Query data from a defined Excel table within the current workbook.

- **Combine Queries**—Lets you append two queries of similar data (perhaps last year and this year) or merge two queries, essentially doing a VLOOKUP between two queries.

Case study: Transposing a data set with Power Query

In Chapter 2, "Creating a basic pivot table," you learned that the perfect layout for the source data in a pivot table is Tabular layout. Tabular layout is a particular table structure where there are no blank rows or columns, every column has a heading, every field has a value in every row, and columns do not contain repeating groups of data.

Unfortunately, you often encounter data sets like the one shown in Figure 7-33. The problem here is that the month headings are spread across the top of the table, doing double duty as column labels and actual data values. In a pivot table, this format would force you to manage and maintain 12 fields, each representing a different month.

	A	B	C	D	E	F
1	Market	Product_Description	Jan	Feb	Mar	Apr
2	BUFFALO	Cleaning & Housekeeping Se	6,220	4,264	5,386	6,444
3	BUFFALO	Facility Maintenance and Re	3,256	9,490	4,409	4,958
4	BUFFALO	Fleet Maintenance	5,350	8,925	6,394	6,522
5	BUFFALO	Green Plants and Foliage Car	2,415	2,580	2,402	2,981
6	BUFFALO	Landscaping/Grounds Care	5,474	4,501	5,324	5,706

FIGURE 7-33 You need to convert this matrix-style table to a Tabular data set so it can be used in a pivot table.

You can leverage Power Query to easily transform this matrix-style data set to one that is appropriate for use with a pivot table. Follow these steps:

1. Select one cell inside your data. Select Data, From Table/Range. Excel will ask you to confirm that your data has headers. Click OK. The Power Query Editor appears.

2. In the Power Query Editor, hold down the Ctrl key as you select the Market and Product_Description fields (which are the fields you do not want to transpose).

3. Go to the Transform tab on the Power Query Editor ribbon, select the Unpivot Columns drop-down menu, and then select Unpivot Other Columns (see Figure 7-34). All of the month names now fall under a column called Attributes.

FIGURE 7-34 Power Query's Unpivot transformation makes quick work of tricky transpose operations.

4. Rename the Attributes column Month. Rename the Values column to Revenue.

5. Click the Home tab on the Power Query Editor ribbon and select the Close & Load command to send the results to a new worksheet in the current workbook.

Amazingly, that is it! If all went well, you should now have a table similar to the one shown in Figure 7-35.

	A	B	C	D
1	Market	Product_Description	Month	Revenue
2	BUFFALO	Cleaning & Housekeeping Services	Jan	6219.66
3	BUFFALO	Cleaning & Housekeeping Services	Feb	4263.92
4	BUFFALO	Cleaning & Housekeeping Services	Mar	5386.12
5	BUFFALO	Cleaning & Housekeeping Services	Apr	6443.99
6	BUFFALO	Cleaning & Housekeeping Services	May	4360.14
7	BUFFALO	Cleaning & Housekeeping Services	Jun	5097.46
8	BUFFALO	Cleaning & Housekeeping Services	Jul	7566.19
9	BUFFALO	Cleaning & Housekeeping Services	Aug	4263.92
10	BUFFALO	Cleaning & Housekeeping Services	Sep	7245.64
11	BUFFALO	Cleaning & Housekeeping Services	Oct	3847.15
12	BUFFALO	Cleaning & Housekeeping Services	Nov	6540.21
13	BUFFALO	Cleaning & Housekeeping Services	Dec	5610.45
14	BUFFALO	Facility Maintenance and Repair	Jan	3255.82
15	BUFFALO	Facility Maintenance and Repair	Feb	9490
16	BUFFALO	Facility Maintenance and Repair	Mar	4409.23

FIGURE 7-35 Your data is now ready for use in a pivot table.

In just a few clicks, you were able to transpose your data set in preparation for use in a pivot table. Even better, this query can be refreshed! As new month columns or rows are added to the source table, Power Query will rerun your steps and automatically include any new data in the resulting table.

The new Power Query functionality is an exciting addition to Excel. In the past, it was a chore to import and clean external data in preparation for pivot table reporting. Now with Power Query, you can create automated extraction and transformation procedures that traditionally would require personnel and skillsets found only in the IT department.

One more Power Query example

I (Bill) do 35 live seminars a year, traveling around the country, showing off Excel tips and tricks. I always walk around the room beforehand, looking for Excel questions. Recently, I ran into a beleaguered accountant who had a manager who kept sending workbooks that looked like Figure 7-36. Each project occupied one row. The expenses were entered in a single cell, using Alt+Enter to separate each line.

Obviously, this is not how you should set up data in Excel. But the manager won't change. He has been doing it this way for 38 years and only has 12 more years until retirement and wants the total to appear in column B. Impossible, right?

FIGURE 7-36   Each cell in B4:B7 is about as useful as putting the data in Microsoft Word.

Power Query is improving every month. Luckily, just a month before I ran into this data set, Microsoft added Split By Delimiter, To Rows.

Take the data into Power Query. Select the Expenses Column. On the Home tab, choose Split Column, By Delimiter. In the Split Column By Delimiter dialog box, choose Advanced Options. Change the

Split Into from Columns to Rows. Clear out the dash that was entered in the Custom Delimiter box. At the bottom, use Insert Special Character and Line Feed. Figure 7-37 shows the dialog box.

FIGURE 7-37 Split each line feed into a new row.

Look at Figure 7-38. The Apple, Banana, Cherry was split to three rows. For the two new rows, the Project was copied to the new rows. If you have more data in columns C through J, all that data would be replicated for the new rows.

Initially, the data in Figure 7-38 had Apple – $218 in one column. Selecting Split Column, By Delimiter, and clicking OK easily splits the data at the dash.

Right now, you would likely be thrilled to take this data back to Excel. But let's go even further.

	AB꜀ Project	AB꜀ Expenses.1	$ Expenses.2
1	A87	Apple	218
2	A87	Banana	857
3	A87	Cherry	693
4	B35	Date	428
5	B35	Elderberry	696
6	B35	Fig	265
7	B35	Guava	213

FIGURE 7-38 Using Split Column twice solves the problem of the bad data.

Delete the products in the Expenses.1 column. Select the Project column and choose Group By. In the Group By dialog box, choose to Group By Project and create a new column called TotalExpense that is a Sum Of Expense.2. This will produce a table with one row per project. Each row will list the total expense for that project.

When you Close and Load, Excel will insert a new worksheet with a new table. Each project occurs once, with the total expense. A simple VLOOKUP from the original table brings the totals back next to the horrible data (see Figure 7-39).

The only tricky part left was to teach the manager to click Data, Refresh All after making any edits.

FIGURE 7-39 A VLOOKUP returns the Power Query answer back to the original data set.

Every time that I think that I am going to have to reach for VBA, I am amazed that Power Query saves the day.

Next steps

Chapter 8, "Sharing dashboards with Power BI," covers the ins and outs of sharing pivot tables with the world. In that chapter, you will find out how you can distribute your pivot tables through the web.

Sharing dashboards with Power BI

In this chapter, you will:

- Get started with Power BI Desktop
- Build interactive reports
- Publish to Power BI
- Design a workbook as an interactive web page

Power BI Desktop is a new application that lets you share interactive dashboards based on your Excel data. Authoring of dashboards is quick—you are basically building pivot charts by dragging fields to a PivotTable Fields list.

Charts are automatically interactive—if you select something in one chart, all the other charts will filter to the selected item. You can create hierarchies to allow people to drill down into the data.

With a monthly subscription, you can publish your dashboards to the Power BI servers. You can invite others in your company to consume your reports on their computers or mobile devices.

Getting started with Power BI Desktop

Getting started with Power BI Desktop is free. You will need a work email account—Hotmail or Gmail will not qualify. Start at PowerBI.Microsoft.com. Sign up and download Power BI Desktop for free.

When you first open Power BI, you will sign in with the account credentials that you created. You are then presented with a start screen with a number of tutorials, as shown in Figure 8-1.

FIGURE 8-1 Power BI Desktop is the authoring tool for Power BI.

Preparing data in Excel

Before you can use Power BI, you need to prepare the data you want to use in it. To do this, build an Excel workbook with each of your data sets formatted as a table. Using the sample files for this book, you would perform the following steps to create a data model in PowerBIData.xlsx:

1. Select each of the three data sets and format as tables using Ctrl+T.

2. Name the tables Sales, Geography, and Calendar.

Caution It is tempting to do a lot of pre-work in Excel, such as defining relationships, marking data categories, creating synonyms, and defining hierarchies. It is best to do this work in Power BI Desktop, since many of these settings are lost when using Home, Get Data, From Excel.

Tip If you do already have queries and relationships defined in your Excel file, you should use File, Import, Excel Workbook Contents as described next instead of Get Data, Excel.

Importing data to Power BI

The most obvious way to get Excel data into Power BI is not the best. If you choose Home, Get Data, From Excel, you can import the data but any queries, relationships, KPIs, and synonyms will be lost.

First, Power BI Desktop has an icon where the File menu should be. It is good to see the Power BI team learned nothing from the mistakes in Office 2007. Click on the File icon to the left of the Home tab. Choose Import, Excel Workbook Contents. Browse to and select your Excel workbook.

An oddly old message appears saying "We don't work directly with Excel workbooks, but we know how to extract the useful content from them." Click Start.

At the end, a message will show you the migration is complete and report what has been imported (see Figure 8-2).

Note Power BI Desktop offers a full version of Power Query. Use the Home, Edit button to launch Power Query.

Import Excel workbook contents   ✕

✓ Migration completed

Queries (3 items)
  ✓ Sales
  ✓ Geography
  ✓ Calendar

Data model tables (3 items)
  ✓ Sales
  ✓ Geography
  ✓ Calendar

Close

FIGURE 8-2   Power BI can import queries and tables from Excel.

Getting oriented to Power BI

Welcome to a new, unfamiliar world. Power BI opens with a vast expanse of white nothing covering the middle 80% of your screen. A common reaction is: "What do I do now?"

Let's take a look at various elements in the Power BI screen.

In the top right are two panels called Visualizations and Fields (see Figure 8-3).

The Fields panel is essentially like the top part of the PivotTable Field list. While you start out seeing table names Calendar1, Geography, and Sales, you can use the triangle icon to expand any table and see the fields in that table.

The Visualizations panel starts with about 30 built-in data visualizations. You can add more visualizations using the icon with three dots. Below the panel of visualizations is the Values area. This is like the bottom half of the PivotTable Fields list. You will drag fields here to create a visualization. The Paint Roller icon leads to various formatting choices that are available for a visualization.

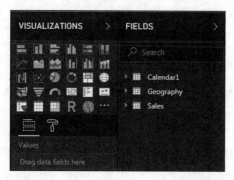

FIGURE 8-3   Create new visualizations using these tools in the top right.

In the lower left of the Power BI Desktop screen is a tab labeled Page 1 and a plus sign to add more pages (see Figure 8-4). These are like worksheet tabs in Excel. You can build a report with multiple pages of dashboards.

FIGURE 8-4 Add more pages in the lower left.

In the top left of the screen, there are three icons labeled Report, Data, and Relationships (see Figure 8-5). The Report view is where you will build your dashboard. The Data view shows you the data loaded in Power BI and is very similar to the Manage Data Model screen in Power Pivot. The Relationships view is similar to the Diagram view in Power Pivot.

FIGURE 8-5 Where is your data? Click the second icon along the left.

Preparing data in Power BI

To create effective reports in Power BI, you want to create some relationships and further customize your data.

Click on the Relationships icon (see the bottom icon on the left in Figure 8-6).

In the Relationships view, you will see that Power BI Desktop automatically detected a relationship between the Sales table and the Geography table. Hover over the line between the tables and Power BI Desktop will show you that the Customer field is used to create the relationship in both tables.

You will also note that Power BI could not figure out that the Calendar1 table should be related to the Sales table.

And, if you resize the tables, you will see the Sigma icon next to Quantity, Revenue, COGS, and Profit. This is correct and means that Power BI will summarize those fields. However, Power BI is also planning on totaling the MonthNo and Year fields in the Calendar table. This is not correct.

FIGURE 8-6 Power BI Desktop detected the relationship between Sales and Geography.

You need to define a relationship between the Sales and Calendar1 table. Click on Date in the Sales table. Drag and drop that field on the Date field in Calendar1 to create the relationship.

To prevent the Year field from showing up as a Sum Of Year, follow these steps:

1. Click on the Data icon. It is the second of three icons along the left side of the screen. In the Data view, you will see the values from one of your tables. To switch to another table, select the table from the Fields panel on the right side of the screen. As an Excel pro, looking on the right side of the screen seems foreign. You would think that there should be tabs at the bottom of the screen for the three data tables.

2. Click on the heading for MonthNo to select that column.

3. Go to the Modeling tab in Power BI. Change the Default Summarization from Sum to Don't Summarize (see Figure 8-7).

4. Repeat Steps 2 and 3 for any other numeric columns that should not be summarized. In the current data, it is the Year field. In other data, you might find numeric account numbers, cost centers, or item numbers.

FIGURE 8-7 By default, Power BI Desktop wants to sum any field that is completely numeric. Override this behavior for years, months, account numbers, and so on.

Assign categories to any geography or image URL fields. Power BI Desktop can plot your data on a map if you have fields like city, zip code, or state. Using the Data view, display the Geography table. Click on each heading for City, State, and Country and choose the appropriate data type using the Data Category drop-down menuon the Modeling tab (see Figure 8-8).

If you want to display images in your report, include a column with the URL for each image. Choose the Image URL category for that column. When you display the field in a table, the image from that URL will appear.

FIGURE 8-8 Categorize any geographic fields.

Defining synonyms in Power BI Desktop

Your company might have specific terms that are used. As an example, I worked in accounting for a company that made handheld computers. While I had a field in the database called COGS (for Cost Of Goods Sold), everyone in this company called this "MLO" (which stood for Material Labor and Overhead).

One of the cool features of Power BI is the ability to type natural language queries. If you define synonyms, Power BI will recognize that MLO is referring to the COGS field in the data.

Select the Relationships icon (it is the third icon in along the left side of the screen). In the Modeling tab of the ribbon, choose Synonyms. Click on the appropriate table in the Diagram view. A panel along the right side lists all of the fields. By default, each field starts with a synonym equal to the field name. Type more synonyms, each separated by a comma (see Figure 8-9).

FIGURE 8-9   Define synonyms to improve natural language queries.

Building an interactive report with Power BI Desktop

Now that your data has been set up in Power BI Desktop, it is time to begin creating charts and tables that will appear in the dashboard.

Building your first visualization

Click the Report icon (this is the top of the three icons along the left side of Power BI Desktop). The large empty white canvas appears in the center of your screen.

Look in the Visualizations panel. There are many built-in tools available. To get your feet wet, choose the first item—a stacked bar chart (see Figure 8-10).

Notice that the field areas changes from Values to Axis, Legend, and Value. Every time that you choose a visualization type, the list of field types will change.

FIGURE 8-10 To start, choose any visualization from the Visualizations panel.

When you choose a bar chart from the Visualizations panel, a tile placeholder appears on the canvas, as shown in Figure 8-11. You can resize this tile using any of the eight resize handles. Or, drag by the Title Bar area (it is in the vicinity of the two horizontal bars near the top center) to move it to a different location.

FIGURE 8-11 Before you add fields to a visualization, it starts as a blank tile.

To add fields to the visualization, choose Revenue from the Sales table. Choose Region from the Geography table. Region will move to the Axis drop zone. Revenue will move to the Values drop zone (see Figure 8-12).

FIGURE 8-12 Choose fields for the chart.

At the top of the drop zones, there is a paint roller icon. Click that to find formatting options for the chart. These options will be different depending on the type of visualization.

In Figure 8-13, the Data Labels have been turned on. The remaining options in the figure let you customize the appearance of the data labels.

FIGURE 8-13 Use the Paint Roller section to format your chart.

You might experiment with the Show Background options. You can color the tile with any theme color and set the transparency for the color.

The third icon is the Analysis icon. This looks like a search box with a chart trend line in the magnifying glass. For the Bar Chart visualization, the only choice is to add a Constant Line. Some companies might have the need to show a line at an arbitrary position. In Figure 8-14, the settings to draw a dotted line at $1.5 Million is shown.

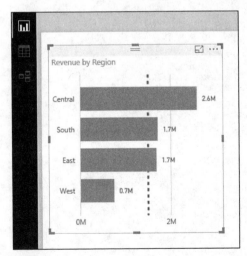

FIGURE 8-14   Set up a constant line.

With the settings in Figures 8-12 through 8-14, you will get the chart shown in Figure 8-15.

FIGURE 8-15   A bar chart with data labels and a constant line at $1.5 Million.

There are two different ways to sort this chart. Use the Three Dots icon in the top right of the chart to choose if regions should be sorted alphabetically or by revenue (see Figure 8-16).

The other icon to the left of the Ellipsis icon is a Full Screen icon. Instead, you can use the Spotlight selection in the menu. This causes all other charts to fade in the background and keeps the current chart as the focus.

FIGURE 8-16 Settings for the chart are in a menu accessed through the ellipsis.

Building your second visualization

This will seem very simple, but it trips me up every time. In order to create a second tile in your report, you must click away from the first tile. It is easy...click anywhere into the white nothingness of the report canvas.

But if you forget to click away and click the Column Chart visualization, you will change the current chart from a bar chart to a column chart. I don't know why I constantly forget this step, but I constantly forget this step.

Click into the white space of the report. Choose a Column chart from the Visualization panel. Drag Revenue to the Values area. Drag Customer to the Axis area. Drag Product to the Legend area.

The result shown in Figure 8-17 is a column chart with customers along the bottom. The three product lines are stacked for each column. In this particular data set, there 10 big customers and a whole bunch of tiny customers. You could resize the column chart to be very wide and show the long tail of small customers. But you can also drag the right edge of the chart in to show only ten largest customers. A scrollbar would let someone drag over to see the small customers.

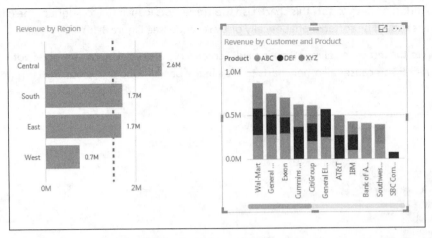

FIGURE 8-17   A second visualization is a column chart showing customer and product.

Cross-filtering charts

Here is where the magic of Power BI starts to kick in. Let's face it, you could have created both previous charts in Excel. The Constant Line would have required some Andy Pope–style charting tricks, but it could have been done. The magic is how every chart in Power BI can filter the other charts.

Click on the bar for Central region in the first chart. The second chart will update. Central region customers will stay bright. Other customers will fade to a lighter color (see Figure 8-18).

FIGURE 8-18   By choosing the Central region from the bar chart, the customer chart reacts.

Creating a drill-down hierarchy

Interactive hierarchies are very easy to set up in Power BI Desktop. Click the first bar chart to select it. Display the Fields section in the Visualizations panel. The Axis contains the Region field. Drag three more fields from the geography table and drop them beneath Region: State, City, and Customer (see Figure 8-19).

Nothing appears to change in the chart, but you have set up a cool drill-down feature.

FIGURE 8-19   Stack four fields in the Axis area to create a drill-down.

Once the hierarchy has been created, a new Drill Down icon appears in the top right of the chart. Click the icon shown in Figure 8-20 to enable drill-down mode.

FIGURE 8-20   Click to turn on drill-down mode.

Once drill-down mode is active, click on Central in the bar chart to see a new chart of all the states in the Central region.

Notice how the column chart updates to show only customers in the Central region (see Figure 8-21).

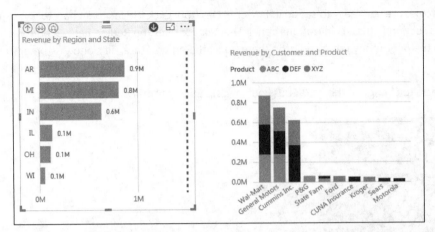

FIGURE 8-21 Click the Central bar in the bar chart and the chart drills down to show states in the Central region.

From Figure 8-21, you could continue to click on Arkansas and drill down to Bentonville. Click on Bentonville and drill down to Wal-Mart. But, since that is not very interesting, click the Drill Up icon in the top left of the chart to return to all regions.

Click on South, and click on Texas. The results in Figure 8-22 show the city level: Dallas, Irving, and Houston.

The choices from the point shown in Figure 8-22 are very subtle. You could click on one of the three cities to show the customers in that city. Or, you could decide you want to see all the customers in any of the three cities. The second icon in the top left is two down-arrows. Click that icon to move one level down the hierarchy without any further filtering. You will see Exxon, AT&T, Southwest, SBC, and Compaq.

FIGURE 8-22 Drill down to the city level.

To return to the region level, click the Drill Up icon several times.

Importing a custom visualization

You can add new visualizations to Power BI Desktop. The last icon in the Visualizations area is three dots. Click those dots and choose Import From Marketplace.

You can browse a variety of free visualizations. In Figure 8-23, click the Add button next to Enlighten Aquarium.

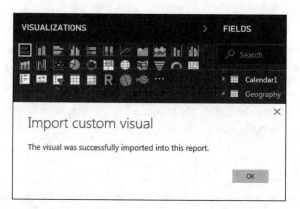

FIGURE 8-23 Power BI visualizations are open source, so you will find a wide array of useful and not-so-useful visualizations.

After adding the Enlighten Aquarium visualization, you will see a new fish icon in the Visualizations panel (see Figure 8-24).

FIGURE 8-24 Installing new visualizations from the Marketplace is a hassle-free experience.

Click in a blank area of your report canvas. Add a new visualization by clicking the Fish icon in the Visualizations panel.

The field drop zones are now labeled Fish and Fish Size. Drag Customer to the Fish area and Revenue to the Fish Size.

An aquarium appears in your report with various-size fish swimming back and forth (see Figure 8-25). Click on the biggest fish—it will stop swimming, and an information panel appears with Wal-Mart and 869,454.

The aquarium will respond to cross-filtering. If you filter the bar chart to just South, only the five fish from the South region will be swimming.

FIGURE 8-25 A fish chart in Power BI.

> **Note** In May 2018, Microsoft announced that you would soon be able to add the Power BI Custom Visuals to Office 365 versions of Excel. I cannot wait for the day when all my column charts will be replaced with aquarium charts.

Publishing to Power BI

Now that your data has been set up in Power BI Desktop, you can share it with others by publishing to Power BI.

Power BI runs in any modern browser. There are dedicated apps for the iPad, iPhone, and Android phones. The default report is designed for a computer screen.

Designing for the mobile phone

If your report will be consumed by people on mobile phones, you can specify how the tiles should be arranged on the phone.

In Power BI Desktop, go to View, Phone Layout. You can rearrange and resize the visualization tiles, as shown in Figure 8-26.

FIGURE 8-26   Optionally, decide on the layout for a mobile phone.

Publishing to a workspace

On the Home tab in Power BI, choose Publish. The Publish to Power BI dialog box will ask you which workspace to use (see Figure 8-27).

FIGURE 8-27   A report must be published to a workspace.

After publishing, you can choose to view in Power BI or to see Insights. Figure 8-28 shows your report running in the Chrome browser.

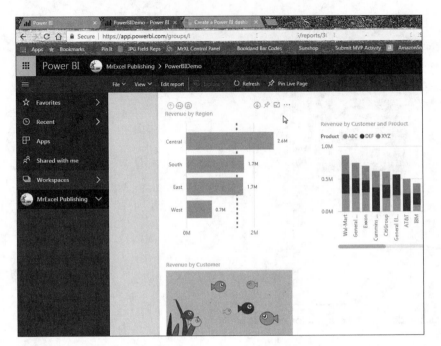

FIGURE 8-28   View the report in a browser.

Using artificial intelligence for Insights

In the summer of 2018, the Office 365 version of Excel offered an artificial intelligence feature called Insights. It works great and uses artificial intelligence to look for patterns in your data.

Power BI also has an Insights feature, as shown in Figure 8-29.

In Excel, the feature would offer 30+ different charts. In Power BI, you get four charts. I supposed there is a much better chance for finding something interesting in 30 charts instead of four charts. So far, the Insights in Excel seem better than those in Power BI, but this is one of those features that might improve over time.

For example, the top-left chart detected that more cities tends to mean more geography. This is a trivial discovery and not useful at all. In the lower-right chart, there were many more dates with invoices in the Manufacturing sector than other sectors. Again, this is because manufacturing is the largest sector and is a trivial discovery.

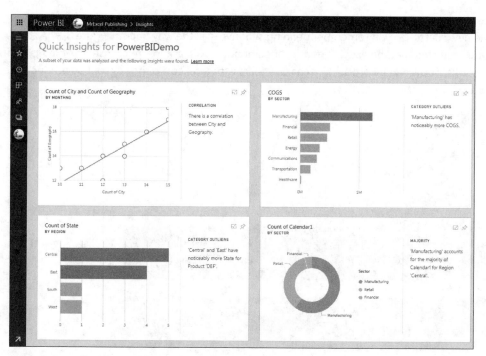

FIGURE 8-29 Power BI offers four charts with insights.

Using Q&A to query data

One of the best features to demo in Power BI is the Q&A feature. Unfortunately, this feature only works with dashboards, not reports. And the things you build with Power BI Desktop are reports. You cannot currently build a dashboard using Power BI.

To try out the Q&A feature, choose one chart and select the Pin Visual icon on the top right of the chart. Create a new dashboard, as shown in Figure 8-30.

FIGURE 8-30 Pin any visualization from a report to create a dashboard.

Once you have a dashboard, you can type natural language queries. As you type, Power BI will generate new charts. Do you remember defining synonyms all the way back in Figure 8-9? At that point, you predicted that the executives at your company would ask for "mlo" instead of "cogs." When someone asks "Show mlo by product," a chart renders with total cost of goods sold by product (see Figure 8-31).

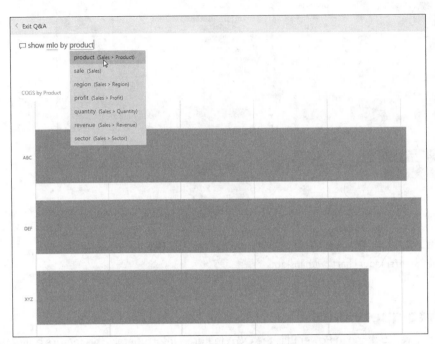

FIGURE 8-31 The Q&A feature lets someone create new charts by simply typing queries.

Designing a workbook as an interactive web page

You can use the Excel client to design a workbook for use as a web page. Imagine a set of slicers at the top, then a pivot table and a few pivot charts, all on one screen of data. A person who visits your workbook in a browser can interact with the slicers and see the results. And here is the best part: You can protect your intellectual property. You can choose to publish Sheet1 in the browser and not show other worksheets. The pivot tables on Sheet1 reach back to use information on Sheet2, but no one is able to hack in and unhide Sheet2. They can't see your formulas.

Figure 8-32 shows a top customers report with several slicers. The source data and the source pivot table are located on back worksheets.

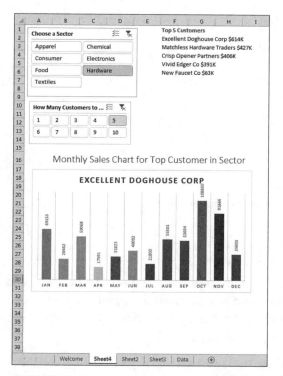

FIGURE 8-32 You can make and share a worksheet that does not look like Excel.

Adapting the workbook to create a web page might involve these tasks:

- Isolate the visible parts of the report on a single worksheet. Cut anything that does not need to be seen from the first worksheet and paste it to the hidden worksheet. In this example, you could cut the formula for first-year interest and put it on the hidden worksheet.

- Consider whether any input cells can be changed to slicers. Slicers are excellent for selecting values in a web page. The How Many Customers To Show slicer in Figure 8-32 is tied to a simple 10-row data set and pivot table on the hidden worksheet. The formulas in F2:F11 pulls the top values from the pivot table. When someone chooses from the slicer, the proper number of top customers are shown.

- Take a few steps to make your worksheet not look like Excel: On the View tab, clear the check boxes Formula Bar, Gridlines, and Headings.

Figure 8-33 shows the workbook in the Excel client. The first worksheet is visible, but most of the data is on the hidden worksheet.

You need to control what is shown in the browser, so choose File, Info, Browser View Options. In the Show tab, open the drop-down menu, and change Entire Workbook to Sheets. You can then clear the check box for the hidden worksheet (see Figure 8-33).

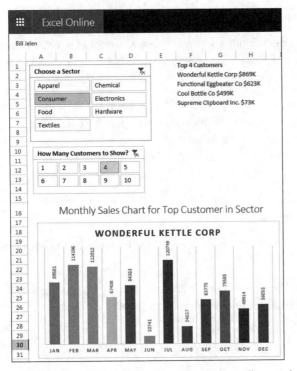

FIGURE 8-33 Choose which worksheet will be visible and which ones will be hidden.

Save the workbook to your OneDrive account.

> **Tip** You should test the workbook before sharing it. Make sure that the parameters work and that everything looks correct. When you are signed in to OneDrive and open your own workbook, it might automatically open in Edit mode. Go to the View tab and choose Reading View.

Figure 8-34 shows the workbook in the browser. If you click a slicer, the filters change and the pivot tables and pivot charts update.

FIGURE 8-34 This is a cool interactive web page, all created using Excel skills.

> **Tip** If you are reading this book, I bet that you know a lot about Microsoft Excel. You can probably knock out amazing formulas that do all sorts of calculations. Now, with just that knowledge, you can create amazing interactive web pages.

Sharing a link to a web workbook

The easiest way to share a web workbook is to use the Share With People command in OneDrive. This enables other people to interact with your workbook, but it also lets them download the whole workbook to their computers.

While you are viewing the workbook, use Share, Share With People, as shown in Figure 8-35.

FIGURE 8-35 While viewing the workbook in the Excel Web App, click Share, Share With People.

The Share dialog box offers two categories:

- You can send an email inviting others to use the workbook.

- You can get a link that you can distribute.

When someone receives your URL and follows the link, she arrives at a read-only copy of the application shown previously in Figure 8-34. Any changes that she makes to the slicer or the parameters are not saved to the workbook. The next person gets a fresh copy of the workbook.

Next steps

Chapter 9, "Using cube formulas with the Data Model or OLAP data," returns to Excel and shows you how you can analyze external data in Excel pivot tables. Check out the section at the end of Chapter 9 on using Cube functions to break out of the traditional format of pivot tables.

Using cube formulas with the Data Model or OLAP data

In this chapter, you will:

- Be introduced to OLAP
- Connect to an OLAP cube
- Understand the structure of an OLAP cube
- Understand the limitations of OLAP pivot tables
- Create an offline cube
- Break out of the pivot table mold with cube functions
- Add calculations to OLAP pivot tables

There is a great technique with pivot tables where you convert the pivot table to a series of cube formulas. Originally, this technique was only relevant for someone who had SQL Service Analysis Services installed. But today, one click on Add This Data To The Data Model moves your data set to the Power Pivot engine, and Power Pivot stores data in an OLAP engine. Thus, you can use cube formulas simply by moving your data to the Data Model.

I have some non-scientific rationale: If I am doing one of my Power Excel seminars and there are 100 people in the room who use pivot tables, only three to five of those people have ever heard of SQL Server Analysis Services. I have been the co-author of this book for 15 years and six editions. When this chapter was about OLAP tools, I skipped over it every time because I knew that I did not have SQL Server Analysis Services installed.

So, I am changing the focus of the chapter to start with the cube formulas that everyone can use if you simply select the check box for Add This Data To The Data Model.

If you have Excel 2013 or newer on a Windows computer, you can use the examples in the first section of this chapter. After seeing how cool cube formulas are, you are free to skip to Chapter 10 once you get to the OLAP material

Converting your pivot table to cube formulas

You might have encountered the GETPIVOTDATA function as a way to extract cells from a pivot table based on a pivot cache. Cube formulas are a more powerful function that only work when the pivot table is based on an OLAP cube. When you select the check box to Add This Data To The Data Model, Excel is converting your data to a cube. Thus, the cube formulas will work.

Why are cube formulas more powerful? The GETPIVOTDATA function refers to an existing pivot table and extracts cells that already exist in the pivot table to another location. In contrast, cube formulas can completely replace a pivot table. Cube formulas reach into the data store and pull summary data into Excel even if you don't have that data in a pivot table yet.

The easiest way to get started with cube formulas is to let Excel convert an existing pivot table to cube formulas.

Before you get started with your pivot table, format the underlying data with Ctrl+T. Excel uses a name such as Table1. It is important to edit that name before you begin. You will be typing this name frequently, so make the name meaningful but short. For this example, I will use the name CustData.

Select one cell in your data. Insert, PivotTable. Choose Add This Data To The Data Model and click OK. Build a pivot table with Customers in the Rows, Revenue in the Values, and Sector as a Slicer (see Figure 9-1).

FIGURE 9-1   Start with a pivot table based on the Data Model.

With one cell in the pivot table selected, go to the Analysis tab in the ribbon. Select OLAP Tools, Convert To Formulas, as shown in Figure 9-2.

Your entire pivot table is replaced with a series of stand-alone formulas. The pivot table no longer exists. The CUBEVALUE and CUBEMEMBER formulas are reaching into the Data Model to retrieve summary results (see Figure 9-3).

FIGURE 9-2 Excel offers to convert your pivot table to cube formulas.

FIGURE 9-3 The former pivot table is converted to a series of formulas.

These formulas are stand-alone formulas. You can rearrange them. If you ever wanted to insert blank rows in your pivot table, you can do it now; there are no pivot table limitations on this report because it is no longer a pivot table.

If you need to grab just the Boeing revenue and put it in a dashboard, you can use one single CUBEVALUE formula to do that.

The primary cube function is CUBEVALUE. The syntax requires the name of the connection and then a series of member_expressions. For pivot tables based on the Data Model, the connection name is always "ThisWorkbookDataModel."

For the member_expressions, the formula in B4 is pointing to ABC Stores in A4, the words "Sum Of Revenue" in B3 and the name of the slicer: Slicer_Sector. Had there been more slicers associated with the pivot table, there would have been additional member_expressions for each slicer.

The formula in B4 is as follows:

```
=CUBEVALUE("ThisWorkbookDataModel",$A4,B$3,Slicer_Sector)
```

You need to be particularly careful with this point: The formula is pointing to A4, which appears to contain the words "ABC Stores." But it is not using the text that we can see in cell A4. In fact, if you would change the formula to the following:

```
=CUBEVALUE("ThisWorkbookDataModel","ABC Stores",B$3,Slicer_Sector)
```

it would stop working. The CUBEVALUE formula is making use of the actual formula text in A4 and B3. Those cells contain CUBEMEMBER functions.

The syntax is:

```
CUBEMEMBER(Connection, Member_Expression, [Caption])
```

The formula to return the words "Sum Of Revenue" to cell B3 is the following:

```
=CUBEMEMBER("ThisWorkbookDataModel","[Measures].[Sum of Revenue]")
```

The optional caption argument allows you to display something different in the cell other than the words "Sum Of Revenue." For example, if you wanted to put the word "Revenue" in the cell, you could use a caption of "Revenue." Regular pivot tables would not let you reuse the word revenue, but it is not a problem here.

So far, everything is great. But the next part of the results of Convert To Cube Formulas is going to be a problem down the road. For the customer name cells in A4 to A30, Excel created formulas like this:

```
=CUBEMEMBER("ThisWorkbookDataModel","[CustData].[Customer].&[ABC Stores]")
```

Hard-coding the customer name in the formula is not efficient. Customers are going to come and go. Next year, ABC Stores might not even be a customer. And other customers will appear.

You don't have to wait for the underlying data to change in order to be disappointed. If you choose Manufacturing from the Slicer, the CUBEVALUE formulas in column B update to show only manufacturing results. But the list of customers in column A does not change, leaving a bunch of empty cells in column B (see Figure 9-4).

FIGURE 9-4   Choose from the slicer. The formulas in B4:B30 update correctly, but the list of customers in A4:A30 does not update.

We are going to pull out some tricks to make these cube formulas more robust. The first is from Rob Collie at PowerPivotPro.com. As Rob explains the CUBESET function:

The CUBESET function is useless by itself. It can return a list of all the customers in the underlying data set. It won't display those customers for you, but it forms the basis that allow later formulas to list those customers. Here is the syntax:

```
CUBESET(connection, set_expression, [caption], [sort_order], [sort_by])
```

- **Connection** will always be "ThisWorkbookDataModel" for pivot tables based on the Data Model.

- **Set_expression**—Rather than return a single member like CUBEMEMBER, CUBESET returns a whole set of values. There are many different ways to represent a set, but the most common way is <ColumnName>.children, which returns all unique values of that column. For our current example, the table name is [CustData]. The field name is [Customer]. You would use "[Cust-Data].[Customer].children" in quotations marks as the second argument.

- **Caption** is optional. Excel won't display the members of the cube set in this cell, so specifying a caption allows you to visually see that there is something in the cell. Power Pivot Pros love to put "" here, but I hate that because then I can't ever find the cell that contains the formula. You could put a caption of "Hey Bill, the CUBESET function is here," but "All Customers" might be less geeky and actually serve to help you remember what is going on when you revisit this workbook months or years from now.

- **Sort_order** (optional)—An integer from 0 to 7, representing "No Sorting," "Sort Ascending," "Sort Descending," "Alpha Ascending," "Alpha Descending," "DB order ascending," and "DB order descending."

- **Sort_by** (optional)—The measure you want to sort by. You would use [Measures].[Customer] instead of [Range].[Customer]. This argument is ignored unless you specify 1 or 2 for sort_order (ascending or descending).

Figure 9-5 shows the formula returning a caption of "All Customers." The formula is as follows:

```
=CUBESET("ThisWorkbookDataModel",
        "[CustData].[Customer].children",
        "All Customers",
        2,
        "[Measures].[Sum of Revenue]")
```

FIGURE 9-5 The cell reads "All Customers," but it actually contains a pointer to the complete set of customers.

At this point, cell E3 contains a list of all customers, but you can't see them. You can use CUBERANKEDMEMBER to extract those customers to cells in the worksheet.

To get the first customer, you would use the following:

```
=CUBERANKEDMEMBER("ThisWorkbookDataModel",$E$3,1)
```

The 1 as the third argument says that you want the first customer from the set stored in E3. Writing 1 is very clear, but it will be inefficient to copy the formula for the other customers. Switch the 1 to ROW(1:1). This reference will automatically change to ROW(2:2), ROW(3:3) as you copy the formula down the worksheet.

Use this formula in E5:

```
=CUBERANKEDMEMBER("ThisWorkbookDataModel",$E$3,ROW(1:1))
```

You have 27 customers today, so copy the formula down to more than 27 rows. That way, if someone adds a new customer, the formulas will pick up that customer.

To save space in the figure, rows 11 through 30 have been hidden in Figure 9-6. You will see that after the final customer, the remaining cells show up as #N/A. You can correct this later with the IFNA function.

	E	F	G	H	I	J
3	All Customers					
4						
5	=CUBERANKEDMEMBER("ThisWorkbookDataModel",$E$3,ROW(1:1))					
6	General Motors					
7	Exxon					
8	Cummins Inc.					
9	CitiGroup					
10	General Electric					
31	Motorola					
32	#N/A					
33	#N/A					
34	#N/A					
35	#N/A					
36						
37						
38						

FIGURE 9-6 The CUBERANKEDMEMBER retrieves the customers from the set in E3.

It is time to return to the CUBEVALUE function from Figure 9-3. But this time, instead of referring to the customer names in column A, refer to the customer names in column E. Use this formula in F5 and copy down:

```
=CUBEVALUE("ThisWorkbookDataModel",$E5,B$3,Slicer_Sector)
```

The result is a series of formulas that retrieve data from the Data Model as shown in Figure 9-7.

f_x	=CUBEVALUE("ThisWorkbookDataModel",$E5,B$3,Slicer_Sector)						

	E	F	G	H	I	J
	All Customers					
	Wal-Mart	869,454				
	General Motors	750,163				
	Exxon	704,359				
	Cummins Inc.	622,794				
	CitiGroup	613,514				
	General Electric	568,851				
	Motorola	31,021				
	#N/A	#N/A				
	#N/A	#N/A				
	#N/A	#N/A				
	#N/A	#N/A				

FIGURE 9-7   This solution is more robust than the original formulas created by Excel.

There is some cleanup to do.

The CUBEVALUE formula in Figure 9-7 is still referring to the Sum Of Revenue cell back in B$3. Cut that cell and paste to F1. Add an extra argument to change the caption to "Revenue."

Wrap all of the formulas in the =IFNA(, "") function so that #N/A errors do not appear.

I am performing the following steps to demonstrate how this is all working:

1. I am adding $150,000 to Cummins Inc. to move them into the #2 position.

2. I inserted a new row in the original data table with a $575,000 sale to a new company Venkman Industries.

3. Click Refresh All on the Data tab of the ribbon.

As shown in Figure 9-8, the Cube formulas update and you have a new report.

	E	F
3	All Customers	Revenue
4		
5	Wal-Mart	869,454
6	Cummins Inc.	772,794
7	General Motors	750,163
8	Exxon	704,359
9	CitiGroup	613,514
10	Venkman Industries	575,000
31	Lowe's	31,369
32	Motorola	31,021
33		

FIGURE 9-8   Use Refresh All on the Data tab to pick up any changes in the underlying data.

Before you think everything is perfect, go back to your slicer and choose Manufacturing. The numbers update, but the CUBESET is still returning all customers whether they are manufacturing or not as shown in Figure 9-9.

FIGURE 9-9 The formulas update, but the non-manufacturing customers remain.

There are three paths at this point. First, you could use the new SORTBY and FILTER modern array functions to extract only the customers with revenue as shown in Figure 9-10. This is easy, provided everyone who will use the workbook has Office 365. But, it is currently wonky, in that the array formulas don't see the change in the Data Model. After every Refresh All, you have to edit the array formula and press Enter. I've reported this bug to Joe McDaid, but I really expect Joe to report back that this is by design and that it will take a while before it is fixed.

The second path is to dive into MDX. Former Excel PM Dany Hoter is the world's expert on this and provided an example that I will include with the downloads for this book. It is ugly, complicated, and requires a bunch of helper cells.

I have massive respect for both Dany and Joe. But I am hoping for Joe to correct the issue and then the modern array formulas will save the day.

FIGURE 9-10 The new FILTER function prevents you from having to dive into the MDX.

The cube functions in collaboration with a Data Model pivot table open an interesting set of possibilities for reusing pivot table data in dashboards and other reports.

The rest of this chapter dives into OLAP and SQL Server Analysis Services.

Introduction to OLAP

Online analytical processing (OLAP) is a category of data warehousing that enables you to mine and analyze vast amounts of data with ease and efficiency. Unlike other types of databases, OLAP databases are designed specifically for reporting and data mining. In fact, there are several key differences between standard transactional databases, such as Access and SQL Server, and OLAP databases.

Records within a transactional database are routinely added, deleted, and updated. OLAP databases, on the other hand, contain only snapshots of data. The data in an OLAP database is typically archived data, stored solely for reporting purposes. Although new data may be appended on a regular basis, existing data is rarely edited or deleted.

Another difference between transactional databases and OLAP databases is structure. Transactional databases typically contain many tables; each table usually contains multiple relationships with other tables. Indeed, some transactional databases contain so many tables that it can be difficult to determine how each table relates to another.

In an OLAP database, however, all the relationships between the various data points have been predefined and stored in *OLAP cubes*. These cubes already contain the relationships and hierarchies you need to easily navigate the data within. Consequently, you can build reports without needing to know how the data tables relate to one another.

The biggest difference between OLAP and transactional databases is the way the data is stored. The data in an OLAP cube is rarely stored in raw form. OLAP cubes typically store data in views that are already organized and aggregated; that is, grouping, sorting, and aggregations are predefined and ready to use. This makes querying and browsing for data far more efficient than in a transactional database, where you have to group, aggregate, and sort records on the fly.

> **Note** An OLAP database is typically set up and maintained by the database administrator in your IT department. If your organization does not utilize OLAP databases, you might want to speak with your database administrator about the possibility of using some OLAP reporting solutions.

Connecting to an OLAP cube

Before you can browse OLAP data, you must establish a connection to an OLAP cube. Start on the Data tab and select Get Data, From Database, From Analysis Services (see Figure 9-11).

FIGURE 9-11 Select the Data Connection Wizard.

Selecting this option activates the Data Connection Wizard, shown in Figure 9-12. The idea here is that you configure your connection settings so Excel can establish a link to the server. Here are the steps to follow:

> **Note** The examples in this chapter have been created using the Analysis Services Tutorial cube that comes with SQL Server Analysis Services 2017. The actions you take to connect to and work with *your* OLAP database are the same as demonstrated here because the concepts are applicable to any OLAP cube you are using.

1. Provide Excel with authentication information. Enter the name of your server as well as your username and password, as demonstrated in Figure 9-12. Click Next.

FIGURE 9-12 Enter your authentication information and click Next.

> **Note** If you are typically authenticated via Windows Authentication, you simply select the Use Windows Authentication option.

2. Select the database with which you are working from the drop-down menu. As Figure 9-13 illustrates, the Analysis Services Tutorial database is selected for this scenario. Selecting this database causes all the available OLAP cubes to be exposed in the list of objects below the drop-down menu. Choose the cube you want to analyze and then click Next.

FIGURE 9-13 Specify your database and then choose the OLAP cube you want to analyze.

3. On the next screen, shown in Figure 9-14, enter some descriptive information about the connection you've just created.

> **Note** All the fields in the screen shown in Figure 9-14 are optional. That is, you can bypass this screen without editing anything, and your connection will work fine.

4. Click the Finish button to finalize your connection settings. You immediately see the Import Data dialog box, as shown in Figure 9-15.

5. In the Import Data dialog box, select PivotTable Report and then click the OK button to start building your pivot table.

FIGURE 9-14 Edit descriptive information for your connection.

FIGURE 9-15 When your connection is finalized, you can start building your pivot table.

Understanding the structure of an OLAP cube

When a pivot table is created, you might notice that the PivotTable Fields list looks somewhat different from that of a standard pivot table. The reason is that the PivotTable Fields list for an OLAP pivot table is arranged to represent the structure of the OLAP cube you are connected to.

To effectively browse an OLAP cube, you need to understand the component parts of OLAP cubes and the way they interact with one another. Figure 9-16 illustrates the basic structure of a typical OLAP cube.

FIGURE 9-16 The basic structure of an OLAP cube.

As you can see, the main components of an OLAP cube are dimensions, hierarchies, levels, members, and measures:

- **Dimensions**—Major classifications of data that contain the data items that are analyzed. Some common examples of dimensions are the Products dimension, Customer dimension, and Employee dimension. The structure shown in Figure 9-16 is the Products dimension.

- **Hierarchies**—Predefined aggregations of levels within a particular dimension. A hierarchy enables you to pivot and analyze multiple levels at one time without having any knowledge of the relationships between the levels. In the example in Figure 9-16, the Products dimension has three levels that are aggregated into one hierarchy called Product Categories.

- **Levels**—Categories of data that are aggregated within a hierarchy. You can think of levels as data fields that can be queried and analyzed individually. In Figure 9-16, note that there are three levels: Category, Subcategory, and Product Name.

- **Members**—The individual data items within a dimension. Members are typically accessed via the OLAP structure of dimension, hierarchy, level, and member. In the example shown in Figure 9-16, the members you see belong to the Product Name level. The other levels have their own members and are not shown here.

- **Measures**—The data values within the OLAP cube. Measures are stored within their own dimension, appropriately called the *Measures dimension*. The idea is that you can use any combination of dimension, hierarchy, level, and member to query the measures. This is called *slicing the measures*.

Now that you understand how the data in an OLAP cube is structured, take a look at the PivotTable Fields list in Figure 9-17, and the arrangement of the available fields should begin to make sense.

FIGURE 9-17 The PivotTable Fields list for an OLAP pivot table.

As you can see, the measures are listed first under the Sigma icon. These are the only items you can drop in the Values area of the pivot table. Next, you see dimensions represented next to the table icon. In this example, you see the Product dimension. Under the Product dimension, you see the Product Categories hierarchy that can be drilled into. Drilling into the Product Categories hierarchy enables you to see the individual levels.

The cool thing is that you can browse the entire cube structure by simply navigating through your PivotTable Fields list! From here, you can build your OLAP pivot table report just as you would build a standard pivot table.

Understanding the limitations of OLAP pivot tables

When working with OLAP pivot tables, you must remember that the source data is maintained and controlled in the Analysis Services OLAP environment. This means that every aspect of the cube's behavior—from the dimensions and measures included in the cube to the ability to drill into the details of a dimension—is controlled via Analysis Services. This reality translates into some limitations on the actions you can take with your OLAP pivot tables.

When your pivot table report is based on an OLAP data source, keep in mind the following:

- You cannot place any field other than measures into the Values area of the pivot table.

- You cannot change the function used to summarize a data field.

- The Show Report Filter Pages command is disabled.

- The Show Items With No Data option is disabled.

- The Subtotal Hidden Page Items setting is disabled.

- The Background Query option is not available.

- Double-clicking in the Values field returns only the first 1,000 records of the pivot cache.

- The Optimize Memory check box in the PivotTable Options dialog box is disabled.

Creating an offline cube

With a standard pivot table, the source data is typically stored on your local drive. This way, you can work with and analyze your data while you're disconnected from the network. However, this is not the case with OLAP pivot tables. With an OLAP pivot table, the pivot cache is never brought to your local drive. This means that while you are disconnected from the network, your pivot table is out of commission. You can't even move a field while disconnected.

If you need to analyze your OLAP data while disconnected from your network, you need to create an offline cube. An *offline cube* is essentially a file that acts as a pivot cache, locally storing OLAP data so that you can browse that data while disconnected from the network.

To create an offline cube, start with an OLAP-based pivot table. Place your cursor anywhere inside the pivot table and click the OLAP Tools drop-down menu button on the PivotTable Tools Analyze tab. Then select Offline OLAP, as shown in Figure 9-18.

Selecting this option activates the Offline OLAP Settings dialog box (see Figure 9-19), where you click the Create Offline Data File button. The Create Cube File wizard shown in Figure 9-19 appears. Click Next to start the process.

FIGURE 9-18   Select the Offline OLAP option to start the creation of an offline cube.

FIGURE 9-19 Start the Create Cube File wizard.

As you can see in Figure 9-20, you first select the dimensions and levels you want included in your offline cube. Your selections tell Excel which data you want to import from the OLAP database. The idea is to select only the dimensions that you need available to you while you're disconnected from the server. The more dimensions you select, the more disk space your offline cube file takes up.

FIGURE 9-20 Select the dimensions and level you want included in your offline cube.

Clicking Next moves you to the next dialog box, shown in Figure 9-21. Here, you are given the opportunity to filter out any members or data items you do not want included. For instance, the Extended Amount measure is not needed, so its check box has been cleared. Clearing this box ensures that this measure will not be imported and therefore will not take up unnecessary disk space.

The final step is to specify a name and location for your cube file. In Figure 9-22, the cube file is named MyOfflineCube.cub, and it will be placed in a directory called c:\aaa\.

Note The file name extension for all offline cubes is .cub.

FIGURE 9-21 Clear the check boxes for any members you do not need to see offline.

FIGURE 9-22 Specify a name and location for your cube file.

After a few moments of crunching, Excel outputs your offline cube file to your chosen directory. To test it, simply double-click the file to automatically generate an Excel workbook that is linked to the offline cube via a pivot table.

After your offline cube file has been created, you can distribute it to others and use it while disconnected from the network.

> **Tip** When you're connected to the network, you can open your offline cube file and refresh the pivot table within. This automatically refreshes the data in the cube file. The idea is that you can use the data within the cube file while you are disconnected from the network and can refresh the cube file while a data connection is available. Any attempt to refresh an offline cube while disconnected causes an error.

Breaking out of the pivot table mold with cube functions

Cube functions are Excel functions that can be used to access OLAP data outside a pivot table object. In pre-2010 versions of Excel, you could find cube functions only if you installed the Analysis Services add-in. In Excel 2010, cube functions were brought into the native Excel environment. To fully understand the benefit of cube functions, take a moment to walk through an example.

Exploring cube functions

One of the easiest ways to start exploring cube functions is to allow Excel to convert your OLAP-based pivot table into cube formulas. Converting a pivot table to cube formulas is a delightfully easy way to create a few cube formulas without doing any of the work yourself. The idea is to tell Excel to replace all cells in the pivot table with a formula that connects to the OLAP database. Figure 9-23 shows a pivot table connected to an OLAP database.

Gender	F .T				
Sales Amount	Calendar Year ⌄				
Model Name ⌄	2011	2012	2013	2014	Grand Total
All-Purpose Bike Stand			$21,147	$1,113	$22,260
Bike Wash			$3,244	$239	$3,482
Classic Vest			$15,939	$1,524	$17,463
Cycling Cap			$9,341	$476	$9,817
Fender Set - Mountain			$21,518	$1,429	$22,947
Half-Finger Gloves			$15,967	$980	$16,947
Hitch Rack - 4-Bike			$17,040	$1,440	$18,480
HL Mountain Tire			$22,750	$1,540	$24,290
HL Road Tire			$13,496	$880	$14,377
Hydration Pack			$19,137	$1,045	$20,181
LL Mountain Tire			$9,121	$1,000	$10,121
LL Road Tire			$10,466	$838	$11,304
Long-Sleeve Logo Jersey			$41,042	$2,849	$43,891
ML Mountain Tire			$15,205	$1,410	$16,614
ML Road Tire			$10,871	$650	$11,520
Mountain Bottle Cage			$9,481	$549	$10,030

FIGURE 9-23   A normal OLAP pivot table.

With just a few clicks, you can convert any OLAP pivot table into a series of cube formulas. Place the cursor anywhere inside the pivot table and click the OLAP Tools drop-down menu button on the Pivot-Table Tools Analyze tab. Select Convert To Formulas, as shown in Figure 9-24.

If your pivot table contains a report filter field, the dialog box shown in Figure 9-25 appears. This dialog box gives you the option of converting your filter drop-down selectors to cube formulas. If you select this option, the drop-down selectors are removed, leaving a static formula. If you need to have your filter drop-down selectors intact so that you can continue to interactively change the selections in the filter field, leave the Convert Report Filters check box cleared.

FIGURE 9-24 Select the Convert To Formulas option to convert your pivot table to cube formulas.

Convert to Formulas

By default, conversion permanently replaces PivotTable data values, row labels, and column labels by substituting formulas for them. If report filters exist, they remain so that you can still filter data.

Selecting Convert Report Filters also permanently replaces existing report filters by substituting formulas for them, removing the ability to filter data.

☐ Convert Report Filters

[Convert]   [Cancel]

FIGURE 9-25 Excel gives you the option of converting your report filter fields.

> **Note** If you are working with a pivot table in Compatibility mode, Excel automatically converts the filter fields to formulas.

After a second or two, the cells that used to house a pivot table are now homes for cube formulas. Note that, as shown in Figure 9-26, any styles you have applied are removed.

So why is this capability useful? Well, now that the values you see are no longer part of a pivot table object, you can insert rows and columns, you can add your own calculations, you can combine the data with other external data, and you can modify the report in all sorts of ways by simply moving the formulas around.

	A	B	C	D	E	F	G	H	I
1	Gender	F	▼						
2									
3	Sales Amount	Calendar Year							
4	Model Name	2011	2012	2013	2014	Grand Total			
5	All-Purpose Bike Stand			21147	1113	22260			
6	Bike Wash			3243.6	238.5	3482.1			
7	Classic Vest			15938.5	1524	17462.5			
8	Cycling Cap			9340.61	476.47	9817.08			
9	Fender Set - Mountain			21518.42	1428.7	22947.12			
10	Half-Finger Gloves			15967.48	979.6	16947.08			
11	Hitch Rack - 4-Bike			17040	1440	18480			
12	HL Mountain Tire			22750	1540	24290			
13	HL Road Tire			13496.4	880.2	14376.6			
14	Hydration Pack			19136.52	1044.81	20181.33			
15	LL Mountain Tire			9121.35	999.6	10120.95			
16	LL Road Tire			10465.63	838.11	11303.74			
17	Long-Sleeve Logo Jersey			41041.79	2849.43	43891.22			
18	ML Mountain Tire			15204.93	1409.53	16614.46			
19	ML Road Tire			10870.65	649.74	11520.39			
20	Mountain Bottle Cage			9480.51	549.45	10029.96			

D5 formula bar: =CUBEVALUE("LAPTOP-U21M363N_SQLMREXCEL Analysis Services Tutorial",$B$1,$A$3,$A5,D$4)

FIGURE 9-26 Note in the formula bar that these cells are now a series of cube formulas!

Adding calculations to OLAP pivot tables

In Excel 2010 and earlier, OLAP pivot tables were limited in that you could not build your own calculations within OLAP pivot tables. This means you could not add the extra layer of analysis provided by the calculated fields and calculated items functionality in standard pivot tables.

> **Note** Calculated fields and calculated items are covered in Chapter 5, "Performing calculations in pivot tables." If you haven't read it already, you might find it helpful to read that chapter first in order to build the foundation for this section.

Excel 2013 changed that with the introduction of the new OLAP tools—calculated measures and calculated members. With these two tools, you are no longer limited to just using the measures and members provided through the OLAP cube by the database administrator. You can add your own analysis by building your own calculations.

In this section, you'll explore how to build your own calculated measures and calculated members.

> ### A Word About MDX
>
> When you are using a pivot table with an OLAP cube, you are sending MDX (multidimensional expressions) queries to the OLAP database. MDX is an expression language that is used to return data from multidimensional data sources (that is, OLAP cubes).
>
> As your OLAP pivot table is refreshed or changed, subsequent MDX queries are passed to the OLAP database. The results of the query are sent back to Excel and displayed through the pivot

table. This is how you are able to work with OLAP data without having a local copy of a pivot cache.

When building calculated measures and calculated members, you need to utilize MDX syntax. This is the only way the pivot table can communicate your calculation to the back-end OLAP database.

The examples in this book use basic MDX constructs in order to demonstrate the calculated measures and calculated members functionality. If you need to create complex calculated measures and calculated members, you will want to invest some time learning more about MDX.

That being said, the topic of MDX is robust and beyond the scope of this book. If, after reading this section, you have a desire to learn more about MDX, consider picking up *MDX Solutions* (by George Spofford et al), an excellent guide to MDX that is both easy to understand and comprehensive.

Creating calculated measures

A *calculated measure* is essentially the OLAP version of a calculated field. When you create a calculated measure, you basically create a new data field based on some mathematical operation that uses the existing OLAP fields.

In the example shown in Figure 9-27, an OLAP pivot table contains products along with their respective quantities and revenues. Say that you want to add a new measure that calculates average sales price per unit.

	A	B	C
1	Model Name	Order Quantity	Sales Amount
2	All-Purpose Bike Stand	249	$39,591
3	Bike Wash	908	$7,219
4	Classic Vest	562	$35,687
5	Cycling Cap	2,190	$19,688
6	Fender Set - Mountain	2,121	$46,620
7	Half-Finger Gloves	1,430	$35,021
8	Hitch Rack - 4-Bike	328	$39,360
9	HL Mountain Tire	1,396	$48,860
10	HL Road Tire	858	$27,971
11	Hydration Pack	733	$40,308
12	LL Mountain Tire	862	$21,541
13	LL Road Tire	1,044	$22,436
14	Long-Sleeve Logo Jersey	1,736	$86,783
15	ML Mountain Tire	1,161	$34,818

FIGURE 9-27   You want to add a calculation to this OLAP pivot table to show average sales price per unit.

Place your cursor anywhere in the pivot table and select the PivotTable Tools Analyze tab. Then select MDX Calculated Measure, as shown in Figure 9-28. This activates the New Calculated Measure dialog box, shown in Figure 9-29.

FIGURE 9-28 Choose the MDX Calculated Measure command.

FIGURE 9-29 Use the New Calculated Measure dialog box to build your calculated measure.

In the New Calculated Measure dialog box, take the following actions:

1. Give your calculated measure a name by entering it in the Name input box.

2. Choose a measure group where Excel should place your calculated measure. If you don't choose one, Excel automatically places your measure in the first available measure group.

3. Enter the MDX syntax for your calculation in the MDX input box. To save a little time, you can use the list on the left to choose the existing measures you need for your calculation. Simply

double-click the measures needed, and Excel pops them into the MDX input box. In this example, the calculation for the average sales price is:

```
IIF([Measures].[Order Quantity] = 0,NULL,[Measures].[Sales Amount]/[Measures].
[Order Quantity]).
```

4. Click OK.

> **Tip** In the New Calculated Measure dialog box, shown in Figure 9-29, notice the Test MDX button. You can click this to ensure that the MDX you entered is well formed. Excel lets you know via a message box if your syntax contains any errors.

After you have built your calculated measure, you can go to the PivotTable Fields list and select your newly created calculation (see Figure 9-30).

FIGURE 9-30 Add your newly created calculation to your pivot table via the PivotTable Fields list.

As you can see in Figure 9-31, your calculated measure adds a meaningful layer of analysis to the pivot table.

	A	B	C	D
1	Model Name ▾	Order Quantity	Sales Amount	Avg Sales Price
2	All-Purpose Bike Stand	249	$39,591	$159.00
3	Bike Wash	908	$7,219	$7.95
4	Classic Vest	562	$35,687	$63.50
5	Cycling Cap	2,190	$19,688	$8.99
6	Fender Set - Mountain	2,121	$46,620	$21.98
7	Half-Finger Gloves	1,430	$35,021	$24.49
8	Hitch Rack - 4-Bike	328	$39,360	$120.00
9	HL Mountain Tire	1,396	$48,860	$35.00
10	HL Road Tire	858	$27,971	$32.60
11	Hydration Pack	733	$40,308	$54.99
12	LL Mountain Tire	862	$21,541	$24.99
13	LL Road Tire	1,044	$22,436	$21.49
14	Long-Sleeve Logo Jersey	1,736	$86,783	$49.99
15	ML Mountain Tire	1,161	$34,818	$29.99

FIGURE 9-31 Your pivot table now contains your calculated measure!

Note It's important to note that when you create a calculated measure, it exists in your workbook only. In other words, you are not building your calculation directly in the OLAP cube on the server. This means no one else connected to the OLAP cube will be able to see your calculations unless you share or distribute your workbook.

Creating calculated members

A *calculated member* is essentially the OLAP version of a calculated item. When you create a calculated member, you basically create a new data item based on some mathematical operation that uses the existing OLAP members.

In the example shown in Figure 9-32, an OLAP pivot table contains sales information for each quarter in the year. Let's say you want to aggregate quarters 1 and 2 into a new data item called First Half of Year. You also want to aggregate quarters 3 and 4 into a new data item called Second Half of Year.

	A	B	C	D
1	Calendar Quarter ▾	Order Quantity	Sales Amount	Avg Sales Price
2	1	12,601	$5,749,853	$456.30
3	2	14,441	$6,840,488	$473.69
4	3	15,557	$7,670,590	$493.06
5	4	17,799	$9,097,746	$511.14
6	Grand Total	60,398	$29,358,677	$486.09

FIGURE 9-32 You want to add new calculated members to aggregate the four quarters into First Half of Year and Second Half of Year.

Place your cursor anywhere in the pivot table and select the PivotTable Tools Analyze tab. Then select MDX Calculated Member, as shown in Figure 9-33. The New Calculated Member dialog box opens (see Figure 9-34).

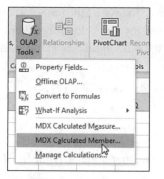

FIGURE 9-33 Choose the MDX Calculated Member command.

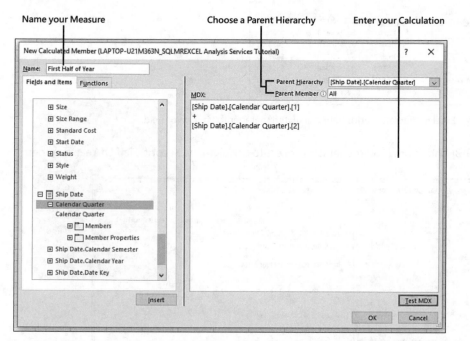

FIGURE 9-34 Use the New Calculated Member dialog box to build your calculated member.

In the New Calculated Member dialog box, take the following actions:

1. Give your calculated member a name by entering it in the Name input box.

2. Choose the parent hierarchy for which you are creating new members. Be sure to leave Parent Member set to All. This ensures that Excel takes into account all members in the parent hierarchy when evaluating your calculation.

3. Enter the MDX syntax for your calculation in the MDX input box. To save a little time, you can use the list on the left to choose the existing members you need for your calculation. Simply double-click the member needed, and Excel pops them into the MDX input box. In the example in Figure 9-34, you are adding quarter 1 and quarter 2:

```
[Ship Date].[Calendar Quarter].[1] + [Ship Date].[Calendar Quarter].[2].
```

4. Click OK.

As soon as you click OK, Excel shows your newly created calculated member in the pivot table. As you can see in Figure 9-35, your calculated member is included with the other original members of the pivot field.

	A	B	C	D
1	Calendar Quarter	Order Quantity	Sales Amount	Avg Sales Price
2	1	12,601	$5,749,853	$456.30
3	2	14,441	$6,840,488	$473.69
4	3	15,557	$7,670,590	$493.06
5	4	17,799	$9,097,746	$511.14
6	First Half of Year	27,042	$12,590,341	$465.58
7	Grand Total	60,398	$29,358,677	$486.09

FIGURE 9-35 Excel immediately adds your calculated member to your pivot field.

Figure 9-36 shows how you repeat the process to calculate the Second Half Of Year member.

FIGURE 9-36 Repeat the process for any additional calculated members.

Notice in Figure 9-37 that Excel makes no attempt to remove any of the original members. In this case, you see that quarters 1 through 4 are still in the pivot table. This might be fine for your situation, but in most scenarios, you will likely hide these members to avoid confusion.

Calendar Quarter	Order Quantity	Sales Amount	Avg Sales Price
1	12,601	$5,749,853	$456.30
2	14,441	$6,840,488	$473.69
3	15,557	$7,670,590	$493.06
4	17,799	$9,097,746	$511.14
First Half of Year	27,042	$12,590,341	$465.58
Second Half of Year	33,356	$16,768,337	$502.71
Grand Total	60,398	$29,358,677	$486.09

FIGURE 9-37   Excel shows your final calculated members along with the original members. It is a best practice to remove the original members to avoid confusion.

Note   Remember that your calculated member exists in your workbook only. No one else connected to the OLAP cube is able to see your calculations unless you share or distribute your workbook.

Caution   If the parent hierarchy or parent member is changed in the OLAP cube, your calculated member ceases to function. You must re-create the calculated member.

Managing OLAP calculations

Excel provides an interface for managing the calculated measures and calculated members in an OLAP pivot table. Simply place your cursor anywhere in the pivot table and select the PivotTable Tools Analyze tab. Then select Manage Calculations, as shown in Figure 9-38.

FIGURE 9-38   Activate the Manage Calculations dialog box.

The Manage Calculations dialog box, shown in Figure 9-39, appears, offering three commands:

- **New**—Create a new calculated measure or calculated member.

- **Edit**—Edit the selected calculation.

- **Delete**—Permanently delete the selected calculation.

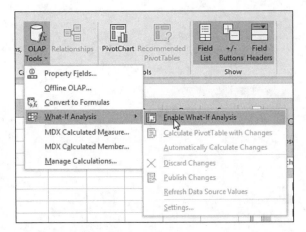

FIGURE 9-39 The Manage Calculations dialog box enables you to create a new calculation, edit an existing calculation, or delete an existing calculation.

Performing what-if analysis with OLAP data

Another piece of functionality that Microsoft introduced in Excel 2013 is the ability to perform what-if analysis with the data in OLAP pivot tables. With this functionality, you can actually edit the values in a pivot table and recalculate your measures and members based on your changes. You even have the ability to publish your changes back to the OLAP cube.

To make use of the what-if analysis functionality, create an OLAP pivot table and then go to the PivotTable Tools Analyze tab. Once there, select What-If Analysis, Enable What-If Analysis, as shown in Figure 9-40.

FIGURE 9-40 Enabling what-if analysis allows you to change the values in a pivot table.

At this point, you can edit the values in your pivot table. After you have made changes, you can right-click any of the changed values and choose Calculate PivotTable With Change (see Figure 9-41). This forces Excel to reevaluate all the calculations in the pivot table based on your edits—including your calculated members and measures.

	A	B	C	D
1	Model Name ▼	Order Quantity	Sales Amount	Avg Sales Price
2	All-Purpose Bike Stand	249	$39,591	$159.00
3	Bike Wash	908	$7,219	$7.95
4	Classic Vest	562	$35,687	$63.50
5	Cycling Cap	2,190	$19,688	$8.99
6	Fender Set - Mountain	4,432	$46,620	$21.98
7	Half-Finge		$35,021	$24.49
8	Hitch Rack	Value has been changed	$39,360	$120.00
9	HL Mounta	Data source value: (click to retrieve)	$48,860	$35.00
10	HL Road Ti	Calculate PivotTable with Change	$27,971	$32.60
11	Hydration	Discard Change	$40,308	$54.99
12	LL Mounta	What-If Analysis Settings	$21,541	$24.99

FIGURE 9-41 Choose Calculate PivotTable With Change to reevaluate all your calculations.

The edits you make to your pivot table while using what-if analysis are, by default, local edits only. If you are committed to your changes and would like to actually make the changes on the OLAP server, you can tell Excel to publish your changes. To do this, in the PivotTable Tools Analyze tab, select What-If Analysis, Publish Changes (see Figure 9-42). This triggers a "write-back" to the OLAP server, meaning the edited values are sent to the source OLAP cube.

> **Note**   You need adequate server permissions to publish changes to the OLAP server. Your database administrator can guide you through the process of getting write access to your OLAP database.

FIGURE 9-42 Excel lets you publish your changes to the source OLAP cube!

Next steps

In Chapter 10, "Unlocking features with the Data Model and Power Pivot," you'll find out how to use Power Pivot to create powerful reporting models that are able to process and analyze millions of rows of data in a single pivot table.

Unlocking features with the Data Model and Power Pivot

In this chapter, you will:

- Replace VLOOKUP with the Data Model
- Unlock hidden features with the Data Model
- Process big data with Power Query
- Use advanced Power Pivot techniques
- Overcome limitations of the Data Model

When I first saw the Power Pivot add-in in 2008, I thought the big news was the ability to handle 100 million rows in Excel. As time passes, and I realize that I frequently have anywhere near a million rows of data, I have started to appreciate the other powerful features that become available when you choose the box Add This Data To The Data Model.

The phrase "Add this data to the Data Model" is a very boring phrase. During the era of Excel 2013 and Excel 2016, Microsoft was slowly incorporating more of the Power Pivot tools into the core Excel.

At the same time, they were trying to convince customers to pay an extra two dollars every month for Power Pivot. You can see where the goal in Excel 2013 was to make the phrase "Add this data to the Data Model" sound pretty boring. If no one selected the box, then people might think they had to pay the extra two dollars a month.

But today, with Excel 2019 including the full Power Pivot feature set, there is no reason for Microsoft to be so cagey. When you see "Data Model," you should think "Power Pivot."

Replacing VLOOKUP with the Data Model

Some people describe Power Pivot as being able to do Access in Excel. This is true to a point: Power Pivot and the Data Model let you create a relationship between two tables.

Consider the two tables shown in Figures 10-1 and 10-2. The first data set, located on Sheet1, is a transactional data set. There are columns for Date, Invoice Number, Product, Quantity, Revenue, and Profit.

Note the formatting in Figure 10-1. Use either Home, Format As Table or press Ctrl+T to format the data as a table. The formatting is not the important part. Making the data into a table is important if you will be joining two data sets in Excel.

When you press Ctrl+T, Excel will give the data set a name of Table1. Press Ctrl+T on another data set and that table will be called Table2. These are horrible names. Take the time to go to the Table Tools Design tab of the ribbon and type a new name. In Figure 10-1, the table is called "Data." The SQL Server pro would call this table "Fact." I prefer "Data" just to differentiate myself from the SQL Server people.

FIGURE 10-1   Press Ctrl+T to format your data as a table. Give the table a meaningful name.

While there are hundreds or thousands of invoices in the Data table, the second table is much smaller. It contains one row for each customer and maps the customer name to a sector and a region.

In most legacy situations, if you needed to create revenue by region, you would knock out a column or two of VLOOKUP functions and bring the Region data in to the first table.

But with the Data Model, you do not have to do the VLOOKUP. Simply leave the two data sets on Sheet1 and Sheet2. You do want to take the extra step of defining the lookup table as a table using Ctrl+T. As Figure 10-2 shows, you can rename the table to be Lookup or CustomerLookup or anything that is meaningful to you.

FIGURE 10-2   Define the lookup data as a table using Ctrl+T. Rename the table.

Later in this chapter, you will see how to use the Relationships icon to define a relationship. But in this first example, you can create a pivot table without defining a relationship first.

Select one cell in the original data set. Choose Insert, PivotTable. Excel will assume you want to create the pivot table from the table called Data.

In the lower-left corner of the Create PivotTable dialog box, select the check box for Add This Data To The Data Model (see Figure 10-3).

FIGURE 10-3   Choose to add your data to the Data Model.

The first thing you might notice: It will take 8–16 seconds for the Pivot Table Fields list to appear. This delay is caused by Excel loading the Power Pivot engine in the background.

The next two items are very subtle. First, the table name appears at the top of the fields in the PivotTable Fields list. You could use the triangle to collapse those field names. Second, the words "Active" and "All" appear at the top of the PivotTable Fields list. The choice for "All" is the groundbreaking feature (see Figure 10-4).

When you click All, a confusing series of things happens, as shown in Figure 10-5. The data table collapses to a single line. The Lookup table appears in the field list. The data table is bold, indicating that you have chosen fields from that table. The Lookup table is not bold, meaning that it is not yet part of the Data Model.

FIGURE 10-4 Notice the choices for Active and All at the top of the Fields list.

FIGURE 10-5 Choose All and any other tables in the workbook are listed in the PivotTable Fields list.

Click the Lookup table name to reveal the fields Customer, Sector, and Region. Drag the Sector field to the Columns area. Drag the Region to the Rows area.

As shown in Figure 10-6, every non-zero number in the pivot table is reporting the Grand Total of 6,707,812. This is clearly wrong. A large yellow box in the top of the PivotTable Fields list warns you Relationships Between Tables May Be Needed. You have choices of Auto-Detect or Create.

FIGURE 10-6 Choose fields from the second workbook and the results in the pivot table will be wrong. This is because you have not created relationships.

Click the Auto-Detect button. This is a simple relationship: One table has many occurrences of each customer, and it is mapped as a lookup table with one occurrence of each customer. Excel figures out the relationship and updates the numbers in the pivot table (see Figure 10-7).

> **Tip** In Excel 2019, you can use Relationships on the Data tab to explicitly define a relationship to avoid this awkward state of having wrong numbers in the pivot table. This is discussed later in this chapter.

FIGURE 10-7 Excel joined the data and lookup tables in memory and reported the results using fields in both tables.

The results in Figure 10-7 are fairly groundbreaking. You just had Excel do a database join between data on two worksheets. You did not have to know how to do a VLOOKUP.

Even if you know and love VLOOKUP, when you get to a data set with 100,000 records and lookup table with 12 columns, you don't want to build 1,200,000 VLOOKUP formulas to join those data sets together. Power Pivot and the Data Model scales perfectly.

For me, joining two tables in a single pivot table is the number-one benefit of Power Pivot and the Data Model. But there are many more powerful features unlocked when you select the Data Model check box while creating a pivot table.

Unlocking hidden features with the Data Model

I do 35 live Excel seminars every year. I hear a variety of Excel questions in those seminars. Some questions are common enough that they pop up a couple times a year. When my answer starts with "Have you ever noticed the box called 'Add This Data To The Data Model'?," people can't believe that the answer has been right there, hiding in Excel. A typical reaction from the audience member: "How was anyone supposed to know that "Add This Data To The Data Model" means that I can create a median in a pivot table?"

Counting Distinct in a pivot table

Consider the three pivot tables shown in Figure 10-8. The question is: "How many unique customers are in each sector?" The pivot table in columns A and B allow you to figure out the answer. You can mentally count that there are two customers (B4 and B5) in the Associations sector. There are six customers listed in the Consultants sector.

But how would you present the top-left pivot table to your manager? You would have to grab some paper and jot down Associations: 2, Consultants: 6, Professional: 3, and so on.

When you try to build a pivot table to answer the question, you might get the wrong results shown in D3:E10. This pivot table says it is calculating a "Count Of Customer," but this is actually the number of invoices in each sector.

The trick to solving the problem is to add your data to the Data Model.

The pivot table in D13:E20 in Figure 10-8 is somehow reporting the correct number of unique customers in each sector.

A regular pivot table offers 11 calculations: Sum, Count, Average, Max, Min, Product, Count Numbers, StdDev, StdDevP, Var, and VarP. These calculations have not changed in 33 years.

But if you create your pivot table and select the check box for Add This Data To The Data Model, a new calculation option appears at the end of the Value Field Settings dialog: Distinct Count.

FIGURE 10-8 When you try to figure out the number of customers in a sector, it does not work.

Drag customer to the Values area. Double-click the Count Of Customer heading. Choose Distinct Count. Change the title, and you have the solution shown in Figure 10-8. Figure 10-9 shows the Value Field Settings dialog box.

FIGURE 10-9 Distinct Count appears in Data Model pivot tables.

One oddity: The Product calculation is missing from the Value Field Settings for the Data Model. I've never met anyone who actually used the Product calculation. But if you were a person who loved Product, then having Excel swap out Product to make room for Distinct Count will not be popular. You can add a new measure with =PRODUCT([Revenue]) to replicate the product calculation. See the example about creating median later in this chapter.

Including filtered items in totals

Excel pivot tables offer an excellent filtering feature called Top 10. This feature is very flexible: It can be Top 10 Items, Bottom 5 Items, Top 80%, or Top Records To Get To $4 Million In Revenue.

Shortening a long report to show only the top 5 items is great for a dashboard or a summary report.

But there is an annoyance when you use any of the filters.

In Figure 10-10, the top pivot table occupies rows 3 through row 31. Revenue is shown both as Revenue and as a % of Total. The largest customer is Andrew Spain Consulting with 869K. In the top pivot table, the Grand Total is $6.7 Million, and Andrew Spain is 12.96% of that total.

In the same figure, rows 34:40 show the same pivot table with the Top 5 selected in the Top 10 filter. The Grand Total now shows only $3.56 Million. Andrew Spain is 24% of the smaller total number.

This is wrong. Andrew should be 12.96% of the total—not 24%.

	A	B	C
3	Customer	Sum of Revenue	% of Total
25	CPASelfStudy.com	568851	8.48%
26	MySpreadsheetLab	613514	9.15%
27	599CD.com	622794	9.28%
28	Hartville MarketPlace and Flea Market	704359	10.50%
29	Excel4Apps	750163	11.18%
30	Andrew Spain Consulting	869454	12.96%
31	Grand Total	6707812	100.00%
32			
33	Values Filters, Top 10, Top 5 Items		
34	Customer	Sum of Revenue	% of Total
35	MySpreadsheetLab	613514	17.23%
36	599CD.com	622794	17.49%
37	Hartville MarketPlace and Flea Market	704359	19.78%
38	Excel4Apps	750163	21.07%
39	Andrew Spain Consulting	869454	24.42%
40	Grand Total	3560284	100.00%
41			

FIGURE 10-10 Using the Top 10 Filter can change the Percentage Of Total calculation.

On January 30, 2007, Microsoft released Excel 2007. A new feature was added to Excel called Include Filtered Items In Subtotals. This feature would solve the problem in Figure 10-10. But as you can see, the feature is grayed out (see Figure 10-11). It has been grayed every day since January 30, 2007. I can attest to that, because I check every day to see if it is enabled.

To solve the problem? Choose Add This Data To The Data Model as you create the pivot table. This enables the choice. The asterisk on the Grand Total in cell A49 means that there are rows hidden from the pivot table that are included in the totals.

FIGURE 10-11 Include Filtered Items In Totals is grayed out.

More importantly, the % of Column calculation is still reporting the correct 12.96% for Andrew Spain Consulting (see Figure 10-12).

	B	C	D
Customer			
	Sum of Revenue	% of Total	
	704359	19.78%	
	750163	21.07%	
	869454	24.42%	
	3560284	100.00%	

42	Data Model and Include Filtered Items in Subtotals		
43	Customer	Sum of Revenue	% of Total
44	MySpreadsheetLab	613514	9.15%
45	599CD.com	622794	9.28%
46	Hartville MarketPlace and Flea Market	704359	10.50%
47	Excel4Apps	750163	11.18%
48	Andrew Spain Consulting	869454	12.96%
49	Grand Total *	6707812	100.00%

FIGURE 10-12 By choosing the Data Model, the calculation is correct.

Creating median in a pivot table using DAX measures

Pivot tables still do not support the median calculation. But when you add the data to the Data Model, you can build any calculation supported by the DAX formula language. Between Excel 2016 and Excel 2019, the DAX formula language was expanded to include a median calculation.

Calculations made with DAX are called *measures*. Figure 10-13 shows different ways to start a DAX calculation. You can right-click the table name in the PivotTable Fields list and choose Add Measure, or you can use the Measures drop-down menu on the PowerPivot tab in Excel. Using the Measures drop-down menu is slightly better because any new measures are automatically added to the Values area of a pivot table.

FIGURE 10-13 Build a pivot table using the Data Model and then add a measure.

Figure 10-14 shows the Measure dialog box. There are several fields:

- The Table Name will be filled in automatically for you.

- Type a meaningful name for the new calculation in the Measure Name box.

- You can leave the Description box empty.

- The *fx* button lets you choose a function from a list.

- The Check Formula button will look for syntax errors.

- Type `=Median(Range[Revenue])` as the formula.

- In the lower-left, choose a number format.

As you type the formula, something that feels like AutoComplete will offer tool tips on how to build the formula. When you finish typing the formula, click the Check formula button. You want to see the result No Errors In Formula, as shown in Figure 10-14.

FIGURE 10-14 Build a measure to calculate median.

Click OK. Median Revenue will appear in the Fields list. Choose the field in the Fields list and it will get added to your pivot table.

Column E in Figure 10-15 shows the median for each sector.

FIGURE 10-15 A pivot table with medians.

Calculations created by measures are easy to reuse. Change the pivot table from Figure 10-15 to show Regions in A instead of Sector. The measure is reused and starts calculating median by Region (see Figure 10-16).

	A	D	E	F
3	**Region** ▾	**Average of Revenue**	**Median Revenue**	
4	Midwest	12093.22222	$12,642	
5	Northeast	11301.12766	$10,624	
6	South	12333.29384	$12,360	
7	West	11972.55	$10,307	
8	**Grand Total ***	**11914.40853**	**$11,858**	
9				

FIGURE 10-16 The measure keeps working if you change the shape of the pivot table.

Reporting text in the Values area

Pivot tables are great at reporting numbers. But you've never really been able to display text answers in the Values area of a pivot table.

The new DAX calculation for CONCATENATEX will return a text value to each value in the pivot table.

In Figure 10-17, the original data is shown in columns A:C. Each customer is assigned a team of three staff members: a Sales Rep, a Manager, and a Customer Service Rep.

You would like to build a report with Customers down the side and Roles across the top. In each Values area, list the name of the people assigned.

The pivot table shown in Figure 10-17 uses the CONCATENATEX function to product the report.

	A	B	C	D	E	F	G	H
1	**Customer**	**Role**	**Name**					
2	599CD.com	Rep	Andy					
3	599CD.com	Manager	Jared		**Names**	**Role** ▾		
4	599CD.com	Service	Xavier		**Customer** ▾	**Manager**	**Rep**	**Service**
5	Andrew Spain Consulting	Rep	Ike		599CD.com	Jared	Andy	Xavier
6	Andrew Spain Consulting	Manager	Nan		Andrew Spain Consulting	Nan	Ike	Yazmin
7	Andrew Spain Consulting	Service	Yazmin		Association for Computers & Taxation	Nan	Hank	Xavier
8	Association for Computers &	Rep	Hank		Bits of Confetti	Okie	Matt	Xavier
9	Association for Computers &	Manager	Nan		Cambia Factor	Nan	Duke	Zeke
10	Association for Computers &	Service	Xavier					
11	Bits of Confetti	Rep	Matt					
12	Bits of Confetti	Manager	Okie					
13	Bits of Confetti	Service	Xavier					
14	Cambia Factor	Rep	Duke					
15	Cambia Factor	Manager	Nan					
16	Cambia Factor	Service	Zeke					
17	Construction Intelligence &	Rep	Barb					
18	Construction Intelligence &	Manager	Jared					
19	Construction Intelligence &	Service	Yazmin					

Measure

Table Name: Range

Measure Name: Names

Value Description:

Formula: *fx* Check DAX Formula

=CONCATENATEX(Range,[Name],", ")

FIGURE 10-17 This narrow data set is pivoted to show text going across.

Processing big data with Power Query

You might have been excited when Excel moved from 65,536 rows in Excel 2003 to 1,048,576 rows in Excel 2007. But what if you have more than a million rows of data?

The 10-BigData.txt file included with the sample files has 1.8 million rows of data. How can you analyze this data in Excel?

You can use the Power Query tools in the Get & Transform group of the Data tab of the ribbon. There are several different strategies:

- Edit the file using Power Query. Try to remove the unnecessary records. You might not need sales from the outlet store or anything before 2005. If you can get the 1.8 million rows below 1,048,576 records, you can load directly to the Excel grid.

- Group the file using Power Query. Maybe you know that you will not ever care about daily data. You can add a formula in Power Query to calculate monthly dates from the daily dates. Group the data by Store, Category, and Month, summing the quantity and revenue. If that data is under 1,048,576 rows, you can load to the Excel grid.

- Skip the Excel grid and load directly to the Data Model using Power Pivot. You can still add calculated columns in the Power Pivot grid.

- Use a hybrid approach: Use Power Query to remove sales through the outlet store, but then load to the Data Model.

When you load directly to the Data Model, you lose the ability to do any analysis other than a pivot table. But, you will have a much smaller file size. 65 MB of data in a text file will often become 4 MB of data in the Data Model.

The following paragraphs will outline the hybrid approach.

To load a text file using Power Query, choose From Text/CSV in the Data tab's Get & Transform Data group (see Figure 10-18).

FIGURE 10-18 The Get & Transform Data group makes up the Power Query tools.

In the next dialog box, browse to and locate your text file. This dialog box is not shown. After you click OK, the preview in Figure 10-19 appears. If the file is under 1048575 rows and if you don't have to edit the query at all, you can click Load. I've never been able to click Load. I always choose Transform Data.

After you choose Transform Data, the first 1000 rows from the file will appear in the Power Query editor. Tools are spread over the Home, Transform, and Add Column tabs.

In the current example, you want to remove four store IDs. If you open the Filter drop-down menu for StoreID, the choices are based on the first 1000 rows. The outlet stores that you need to remove are deep in the file and not in the filter drop-down menu. Instead, choose Value Filters, Does Not Equal.

FIGURE 10-19 Make sure the preview is pointing to the correct file and then click Transform Data.

The dialog box shown in Figure 10-20 appears. Type the first store number to remove. Click OK. Repeat for the other three stores.

FIGURE 10-20 Choose a store to remove during import. This particular store is an outlet mall and not usually included in the report.

Looking at Figure 10-20, there is an Advanced version of the Filter. There is the option to specify a second store using the And or Or option. Each pass through this dialog box gets recorded as a different row in the Applied Steps pane. You might want the filters to be four separate lines so you can easily duplicate one later when a new outlet store is added.

If you have four stores to remove, repeat the steps in Figure 10-20 three more times.

Adding a new column using Power Query

The text file includes a date field. You want to add new columns for Year, Month Name, and Month Number. The function language in Power Query is annoyingly different from the functions in Excel. Plus, the language is case sensitive. In Excel, you could use =YEAR(A2), =year(a2), =Year(A2), or =yEaR(A2). But in Power Query, you would have to type =Date.Year([Date]) to do the same calculation. It had to be typed exactly that way. =date.year([date]) would return an error.

In the summer of 2018, Microsoft introduced a new icon called Column From Examples. This feature is similar to Flash Fill in Excel with one massive improvement: Column From Examples will insert the correct formula in the query so that step can be reused on a newer version of the text file.

I am a big fan of Column From Examples. Every time that I used to build a formula in Power Query, I knew that the process would involve the following:

1. Find the online Power Query function reference.

2. Search to try to find the syntax.

3. Copy the syntax without really learning anything.

4. Make a resolution to learn these new functions as well as I know Excel one day.

5. Never follow up with step #4.

Today, with Column From Examples, I know that I will never need to learn the Power Query functions.

Here are the steps to add a calculated Year field to your text file as it is imported.

1. In the Power Query editor, click on the Date heading to select that column.

2. On the Add Column tab, open the Column From Examples drop-down menu and choose From Selection, as shown in Figure 10-21.

A new cell will appear on the right edge of the query window. Type the correct value for this year. In this case, you would type **2000**.

In response to your typing 2000, a menu appears with the choices shown in Figure 10-22. Look at that list. I just wanted a year. But they are offering all sorts of amazing things such as End Of Quarter From Date or End Of Year From Date. Those might come in handy someday, but today, you just want the year, so choose 2000 (Year From Date).

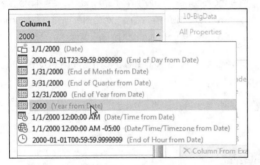

FIGURE 10-21 Select the column that contains the source data.

By clicking this option, Power Query adds a new column with a heading of Year and the correct formula. You can look in the formula bar and see `Date.Year([Date])`, so there is an opportunity to learn the function language.

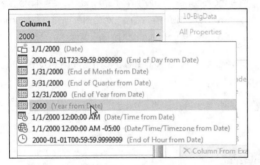

FIGURE 10-22 Type **2000** and Power Query offers all sorts of formulas.

You can keep adding custom column from examples. Check the sample files to see Month Name and Day.

Power Query is like the Macro Recorder but better

As you perform steps in Power Query, a list of steps appears in the Applied Steps panel on the right side. Think of this list as the world's greatest visible undo stack:

- You can click any item in the list and see what the data looked like at that point.

- You can click the Gear icon next to any step and see the dialog box that was used at that step.

- You can remove the last step using the X icon. You can remove other steps as well, but you will likely screw up the query until you edit the Power Query code.

- To see the Power Query code (the language is called the *M* language), go to View, Advanced Editor and you will see the programming code that you created by doing steps in Power Query.

How is this different from the VBA Macro Recorder? The code recorded by Power Query will work the next time. If you get a new text file that has 50,000 new records, the Power Query code will have no problem adapting the code to more or fewer records. In the VBA macro recorder, having more records would almost always make a recorded macro stop working.

See the Applied Steps from this example in Figure 10-23.

FIGURE 10-23 Power Query documents the transformations needed for a file.

Avoiding the Excel grid by loading to the Data Model

In the current example, you have a 1.8 million-row file that is now 1.7 million rows after you deleted the outlet stores. This is too big for the Excel grid. But even if you trimmed the file to 600,000 rows, you should still consider loading the file directly to the Data Model.

The Data Model uses a compression algorithm that frequently trims a 56 MB file to 4 MB in memory. This is a 14:1 compression ratio. If your plan is to create pivot tables from the data, loading straight to the Data Model is the way to save memory.

To skip loading to the Excel grid, go to the Power Query Home tab. Use the drop-down menu at the bottom of Close & Load. Choose Close & Load To..., as shown in Figure 10-24.

FIGURE 10-24 Avoid loading to the Excel grid by choosing Close & Load To....

In the Import Data dialog box, choose Only Create Connection and choose Add This Data To The Data Model (see Figure 10-25) .

FIGURE 10-25 Choose to load the results of Power Query to the Data Model.

When you click OK, Excel will actually load the 1.7 million rows into your workbook. You will watch the row counter in the Queries & Connections panel count up. This will take as long as it will take. Excel doesn't have any magic way to load the data from disk. But as they are loading that data, it is being organized and vertically compressed. From here on, the pivot tables will be very fast.

When the import is finished, the Queries & Connections panel will report how many rows were loaded (see Figure 10-26).

FIGURE 10-26 1.8 million rows loaded to an Excel workbook and are ready for pivoting.

Adding a linked table

The database pros who created your text file are smart. They knew it would take a lot of space to include a 20-character store name on 1.8 million rows of text. Instead, they used a Store ID.

You probably have a small worksheet that maps the store number to the store name and other information. This workbook probably already exists somewhere in your company.

The worksheet shown in Figure 10-27 is a subset of a real StoreInfo workbook that gets a lot of use at a my friend's company. In real life, there are columns for Manager Name, Phone Number, and so on.

Compared to the 1.8 million-row text file, this tiny 175-row worksheet is really small. To add this worksheet to the Data Model, follow these steps:

1. Insert a new worksheet in your workbook that contains the 1.8 million row import.

2. Copy the Store Info to the new worksheet.

3. Select one cell in the data set and press Ctrl+T to define the data as a table.

4. Make sure My Data Has Headers is selected. Click OK.

5. Go to the Table Tools Design tab and replace the name **Table1** with **StoreInfo**.

6. With one cell in the table selected, go to the Power Pivot tab in the Excel ribbon. Choose Add To Data Model.

FIGURE 10-27   Add this lookup table to the Data Model.

Defining a relationship between two tables

To prevent the wrong numbers shown previously in Figure 10-6, you can proactively define a relationship. There are a couple of ways:

1. Use the Relationships icon in the Data Tools group on the Data tab of the Excel ribbon.

2. Use the Diagram view in the Power Pivot grid.

3. To use the Relationships feature, click its icon shown in Figure 10-28.

FIGURE 10-28 Start defining a relationship using the Relationships icon.

In the Manage Relationships dialog box, choose New.... The Create Relationship dialog box appears. You have to fill out four fields to establish a relationship:

- Specify that the main table is **10-BigData** loaded to the Data Model.

- Specify the Column (Foreign) in that table is **StoreID**.

- The Related Table is the Worksheet Table: **StoreInfo**.

- The Related Column (Primary) is **Store**.

The dialog box should appear as shown in Figure 10-29. Click OK to create the relationship.

FIGURE 10-29 Defining a relationship requires four answers.

> **Note** Some lookup tables might require you to map Cost Center and Account from the data and lookup table. While this is not possible using the Create Relationship dialog box in Figure 10-29, you can achieve this in Power Query. Import both tables using Create Connection Only.
>
> Use Data, Get Data, Combine Queries, Merge to define a third query that will join based on multiple fields. In the next dialog box, use the Ctrl key to choose the key fields in both tables.

An alternate way to create the relationship is the Diagram View in the Power Pivot window. Drag an arrow from StoreID to Store (see Figure 10-30).

FIGURE 10-30 Define a relationship in the Power Pivot window.

Adding calculated columns in the Power Pivot grid

In addition to adding calculations with Power Query, you can add calculated columns in the Power Pivot grid. Instead of the Diagram View shown in Figure 10-30, switch back to the Data View shown in Figure 10-31. Click into an empty column and type the correct formula in the formula bar.

The functions in the Power Pivot window are very similar to the functions you already know and love in Excel.

For example, the =YEAR() function in Excel is =YEAR().

The =MONTH() function in Excel is =MONTH.

So far, so good, right? There are two annoying differences:

- The =TEXT() function in Excel is =FORMAT() in Power Pivot. If you wanted to create the Month Name column in Power Pivot, you would use =FORMAT([Date],"MMMM") instead of =TEXT(B2,"MMMM") in Excel. Why did this function change? Remember that Power Pivot was not written by the Excel team. It was written by the SQL Server Analysis Services team. Excel has TEXT. SQL Server has FORMAT. The second argument in FORMAT offers more choices than TEXT, so the team chose to go with FORMAT instead. That was a fine choice.

- The VLOOKUP() function in Excel is =RELATED() in Power Pivot. At this point, you have defined a relationship between the 1.7 million row table and the StoreInfo lookup. If you needed to refer to Selling Square Feet in a calculation in the data table, you would use something like: =[Revenue]/RELATED(StoreInfo[Selling SF]). Related is superior to VLOOKUP in every way. Why should you care that Selling Square Feet is the second column in the lookup table? Why do you have to know the arcane =VLOOKUP(A2,Sheet2!A1:F175,2,False)? When I type RELATED, it says to me, "Hey Excel—just go figure this out. I've given you all the information you need to know what I am talking about."

In Figure 10-31, after you press Enter, the formula is copied down to all 1.7 million rows. That is great. The annoying thing: The new column will be called Column1. You have to right-click the heading, choose Rename, and then type a meaningful name. Or, you can double-click the heading and type the new name.

FIGURE 10-31   Build a formula in the formula bar in the Power Pivot grid.

Sorting one column by another column

The Data Model is better than Excel pivot tables in almost every way. But there is one annoying exception.

Say that your data has a month column with Jan, Feb, Mar, Apr, May, Jun. If you add that to a pivot table in Excel, the data will be sorted Jan, Feb, Mar, and so on.

But in Power Pivot, the resulting pivot table will have the months appear as Apr, Aug, Dec, Feb. Why? That is the alphabetic sequence for the months.

When I wrote *Power Pivot for the Data Analyst* in 2010, I complained about this bug. I suggested that Power Pivot should automatically sort by the Custom Lists just as Excel would do.

In later versions of Power Pivot, the team solved this in a different way. If you choose the Month Name column in the Power Pivot window, and select Home, Sort By Column, you can specify that the Month Name column should be sorted by the data in the Month Number column (see Figure 10-32).

FIGURE 10-32   Specify that Month Name should be sorted by Month Number.

Note that changing the sort sequence using the dialog box in Figure 10-32 will also ensure that any slicers are in the proper sequence. This makes the Sort By Column method better than using More Sort Options in the Pivot Table.

Creating a pivot table from the Data Model

Now that you have two tables loaded to Power Pivot with a relationship, it is time to create your pivot table. Start from any blank cell on a blank worksheet. Choose Insert, PivotTable. In the Create Pivot-Table dialog box, select the choice for Use This Workbook's Data Model (see Figure 10-33).

FIGURE 10-33 Start your pivot table from a blank cell and the dialog box will default to using the Data Model.

The Power Pivot version of the Fields list appears. You have choices at the top for Active and All. The pivot table in Figure 10-34 reports revenue from the data table and region from the lookup table.

FIGURE 10-34 The resulting pivot table combined 1.7 million rows of a text file with an Excel lookup table.

Using advanced Power Pivot techniques

So far, you've seen a simple relationship between a data table and a lookup table. In real life, you might need to join two data tables. This section covers complicated relationships and time intelligence functions.

Handling complicated relationships

Relationships in the Data Model need to be one-to-many. You cannot have a many-to-many relationship in Power Pivot.

Figure 10-35 shows a 54-row budget table and a 2000-row actuals table register. Both tables have Region, Date, and Product in common. You would like to report total budget and actuals for each product or region.

While you can't directly relate Budget to Actuals, you can add three very small tables between the two tables. For example, the Product table contains one row for each product. You define a relationship from Budget to Product. This is a valid one-to-many relationship. Then, define a relationship from Actuals to Product. Again, this is a valid one-to-many relationship.

In your pivot table, the Values area will contain numbers from the budget and actual table. But any time that you need to report Product or Region or Date in your pivot table, use the field from the tiny joiner table.

FIGURE 10-35   Use tiny joiner tables between tables to overcome the many-to-many limitation.

Figure 10-36 shows the two data tables and the three tiny joiner tables.

	A	B	C	D	E	F	G	H	I	J	K	L	M	N	O	P	Q
1	Budget - Top Level					"Joiners"							Invoice Detail				
2																	
3	Product	Region	Date	Budget		Product	Region		Date	Month		Invoice	Date	Region	Product	Revenue
4	Widget	East	1/31/2018	10,300		Gadget	Central		1/2/2018	2018-01		1001	1/2/2018	Central	Gadget	1572
5	Widget	East	2/28/2018	10,600		WhatsIt	East		1/5/2018	2018-01		1002	1/5/2018	Central	Widget	1534
6	Widget	East	3/31/2018	10,900		Widget	West		1/6/2018	2018-01		1003	1/5/2018	Central	WhatsIt	1608
7	Widget	East	4/30/2018	11,200					1/7/2018	2018-01		1004	1/5/2018	Central	Widget	2369
8	Widget	East	5/31/2018	11,500					1/8/2018	2018-01		1005	1/5/2018	East	Widget	1509
9	Widget	East	6/30/2018	11,800					1/9/2018	2018-01		1006	1/5/2018	Central	Widget	2376
10	Widget	Central	1/31/2018	15,450					1/12/2018	2018-01		1007	1/6/2018	East	Gadget	1602
11	Widget	Central	2/28/2018	15,900					1/13/2018	2018-01		1008	1/6/2018	West	Widget	1962

FIGURE 10-36   Use the joiner table fields in your rows and columns of the pivot table.

Using time intelligence

Typically, Excel stores dates as a serial number. When you enter 2/17/2021 in a cell, Excel only knows that this date is 44,244 days after December 31, 1899. Power Pivot adds time intelligence. When you have a date such as 2/17/2021 in Power Pivot, there are time intelligence functions that know that year-to-date means 1/1/2021 through 2/17/2021. The time intelligence functions know that month-to-date from the prior year is 2/1/2020 through 2/17/2020.

Each value cell in a pivot table is a result of filters imposed by the slicers and by the row and column fields. Cell D28 in Figure 10-37 is being filtered to 2001 by the slicer and further filtered to January 25, 2001, by the row field in B28. But that cell needs to break free of the filter in order to add all of the sales from January 1, 2001, through January 25, 2001. The CALCULATE function helps you solve this problem.

In many ways, the DAX CALCULATE function is like a super-charged version of the Excel SUMIFS function. =CALCULATE(Field,Filter,Filter,Filter,Filter) is the syntax. But any *Filter* argument could actually unapply a filter that's being imposed by a slicer or a row field.

DATESMTD([Date]) returns all the dates used to calculate the month-to-date total for the cell. For January 25, 2001, the DATESMTD function will return January 1 through 25, 2001. When you use DATESMTD as the filter in the CALCULATE function, it breaks the chains of the 1/25/2001 filter and reapplies a new filter of January 1–25, 2001. The DAX formula for MTDSales is as follows:

```
=CALCULATE([Sum of Revenue],DATESMTD('10-BigData'[Date]))
```

FIGURE 10-37   Time intelligence lets you calculate MTD or Prior Year sales.

The measure in column E requires two filter arguments. First, you need to tell DAX to ignore the Years filter. Use ALL([Years]) to do this. Then, you need to point to one year ago. Use DATEADD([Date],-1,YEAR) to move backward one year from January 25, 2002 to January 25, 2001. Therefore, this is the formula for LYSales:

```
CALCULATE([Sum of Revenue],
All('10-BigData'[Date (Year)]),
DATEADD('10-BigData'[Date],-1,YEAR))
```

Other time intelligence functions include DATESQTD and DATESYTD.

Overcoming limitations of the Data Model

When you use the Data Model, you transform your regular Excel data into an OLAP model. There are annoying limitations and some benefits available to pivot tables built on OLAP models. The Excel team tried to mitigate some of the limitations for Excel 2019, but some are still present. Here are some of the limitations and the workarounds:

- **Less grouping**—You cannot use the Group feature of pivot tables to create territories or to group numeric values into bins. You will have to add calculated fields to your data with the grouping information.

- **Product is not a built-in calculation**—I've never created a pivot table where I had to multiply all the rows together. That is the calculation that happens when you change Sum to Product. If you need to do this calculation, you can add a new measure using the PRODUCT function in DAX.

- **Pivot tables won't automatically sort by custom lists**—It is eight annoying clicks to force a field to sort by a custom list: Open the field drop-down menu and choose More Sort Options. In the Sort Options dialog box, click More Options. In the More Sort Options dialog box, clear Sort Automatically. Open the First Key Sort Order and choose your Custom List. Click OK to close the More Sort Options dialog box. Click OK to close the Sort dialog box.

- **Strange drill-down**—Usually, you can double-click a cell in a pivot table and see the rows that make up that cell. This does work with the Data Model, but only for the first 1,000 rows.

- **No calculated fields or calculated items**—This is not a big deal, because DAX measures run circles around calculated items.

- **Odd reordering items**—There is a trick in regular Excel pivot tables that you can do instead of dragging field names where you want them. Say that you go to a cell that contains the word *Friday* and type **Monday** there. When you press Enter, the Monday data moves to that new column. This does not work in Power Pivot pivot tables! You can still select Monday, hover over the edge, and drag the item to a new location.

- **No support for arrow keys in formula creation**—In the Excel interface, you might build a formula with =,LeftArrow>*<LeftArrow><LeftArrow><Enter>. This is not supported in Power Pivot. You will have to reach for the mouse to click on the columns that you want to reference.

- **Refresh will be slow**—The Refresh button on the Analyze tab forces Excel to update the data in the pivot table. Think before you do this in Excel 2019. In the current example, this forces Excel to go out and import the 1.7 million-row data set again.

- **February 29 1900 does not exist in power pivot**—There was no February 29 in 1900. Lotus 1-2-3 had a bug: The date algorithms assumed that 1900 was a leap year. As Excel was battling for market share, they had to produce the same results as Lotus, so Excel repeated the February 29, 1900 bug. The SQL Server Analysis Team refused to perpetuate this bug and did not recognize February 29, 1900. In Excel, day 1 is January 1, 1900. In Power Pivot, day 1 is December 31, 1899. None of this matters unless you have sales that happened during January 1, 1900 through

February 28, 1900. In that case, the two pivot tables will be off by a day. No one has data going back that far, right? It will never be an issue, right? Well, in 2018, I met a guy who had a column of quantities. He had values like 30 and 42 and 56. But that column was accidentally imported as a date. All of the quantities were off by one.

- **32-bit Excel is not enough**—I meet people who complain Excel is slow, even though they added more memory to their machine. Unfortunately, the 32-bit version of Excel can only access 3 GB of the memory on your machine. To really use Power Pivot and the Data Model with millions of rows of data, you will need to install 64-bit Excel. This does not cost anything extra. It does likely involve some pleading with the I.T. department. Also, there are some old add-ins that do not run in 64-bit Excel. If you happen to be using that add-in, then you have to choose whether you want faster performance or the old add-in.

Enjoying other benefits of Power Pivot

Nothing in the previous list is a dealbreaker. In the interest of fairness, here are several more benefits that come from using Power Pivot and the Data Model:

- You can hide or rename columns. If your Database Administrator thinks TextSlsRepNbr is a friendly name, you can change it to Sales Rep Number. Or, if your data tables are littered with useless fields, you can hide them from the PivotTable Fields list. In the Power Pivot window, right-click any column heading and choose Hide From Client Tools.

- You can assign categories such as Geography, Image URL, and Web URL to fields. Select the column in the Power Pivot window. Choose a column. On the Advanced tab, choose a Data Category.

- You can define key performance indicators or hierarchies. See "Creating hierarchies" in Chapter 4, "Grouping, sorting, and filtering pivot data."

Learning more

Power Pivot and Power Query are powerful tools that are completely new for most Excellers. These are my favorite books to learn more:

- For Power Query, read *M Is For Data Monkey* by Ken Puls and Miguel Escobar (ISBN 978-1-61547-034-1).

- For DAX formulas in Power Pivot, read *Supercharge Excel* by Matt Allington (ISBN 978-1-61547-053-2).

- For Advanced Power Pivot, read *Power Pivot and Power BI* by Rob Collie (ISBN 978-1-61547-039-6).

Next steps

The 3D Map feature lets you animate your data on a globe. Chapter 11, "Analyzing geographic data with 3D Map," introduces 3D Map.

Analyzing geographic data with 3D Map

In this chapter, you will:

- Prepare data for 3D Map
- Build a column chart in 3D Map
- Explore 3D Map settings
- Animate data over time

Analyzing geographic data with 3D Map

3D Map allows you to build a pivot table on a three-dimensional globe of the Earth. Provided that your data has any geographic field such as Street, City, State, or Zip Code, you can plot the data on a map.

Once the data is on the map, you can fly through the data, zooming in to study a city or zooming back out to a 50,000-foot view. You can either use 3D Map to interactively study the data or build a tour from various scenes and render that tour as a video for distribution to people who do not have 3D Map.

> **Note** The 3D Map feature was known as an add-in called Power Map in Excel 2013 and also formerly known as GeoFlow. If you have previously used Power Map or GeoFlow, you can find that functionality in Excel 2019 as 3D Map.

Preparing data for 3D Map

Although 3D Map uses the Power Pivot Data Model, there is no need to load your data into Power Pivot. You can just select one cell from a data set with a geographic field such as Country, State, County, City, Street, or Zip Code. On the Insert tab, in the Tours group, choose 3D Map, as shown in Figure 11-1.

3D Map converts the current data set to a table and loads it to the Power Pivot Data Model before launching 3D Map. This step might take 10 to 20 seconds as Power Pivot is loaded in the background.

3D Map converts the data to latitude and longitude by using Bing Maps. If your data is outside the United States, you should include a field for country code. Otherwise, Paris will show up in Kentucky, and Melbourne will show up on the east coast of Florida.

There are three special types of geographic data that 3D Map can consume:

- 3D Map can deal with latitude and longitude as two separate fields. Note that west and south values should be negative.

- It is possible to plot the data not on a globe but on a custom map, such as the floor plan for an airport or a store. In this case, you need to provide x and y data, remembering that x runs across the map, starting with 0 at the left edge, and y starts at 0 at the bottom edge.

- 3D Map now allows for custom shapes. You need to have a KML or SHP file describing the shapes. The names in your data set should match values in the KML file.

Although you don't have to preload the data into the Power Pivot Data Model, you can take that extra step if you need to define relationships between tables.

FIGURE 11-1   3D Map appears on the Insert tab.

Geocoding data

The process of locating points on a map is called *geocoding*. When you first launch 3D Map, you have to choose the geographic fields. If you've used meaningful headings such as City or State, 3D Map auto-detects these fields.

In the Choose Geography section, select the check box next to each geographic field. In the Geography and Map Level section, choose a field type for each of the geographic fields (see Figure 11-2).

> **Tip**   Fields such as "123 Main Street" should be marked as Street. Fields such as "123 Main Street, Akron, OH" should be marked as Full Address. Marking "123 Main Street" as an address will lead to most of your data points placed in the wrong state.

Choose one of your geographic fields as the map level. If you choose State, you will get one point per state. If you choose Address, you will get one point for each unique address.

After you've chosen the geographic fields, click Next in the lower-right corner.

FIGURE 11-2 Choose geographic fields.

It takes a short while for 3D Map to complete the geocoding process. When it is finished, a percentage appears in the top of the PivotTable Fields list. Click this percentage to see a list of data points that could not be mapped (see Figure 11-3). Items with a red X are not going to appear on the map. Items with a yellow ! are going to appear at the address shown.

FIGURE 11-3 3D Map indicates which addresses could not be found.

Note When an address is not found, there is currently no tool to place that data point on the map. Other mapping tools such as MapPoint would give you choices such as using a similar address or even adding the point to the center of the zip code. But 3D Map currently simply advises you to add more geographic fields to the original data set.

Building a column chart in 3D Map

3D Map offers five types of layers: Stacked Column, Clustered Column, Bubble, Heat Map, and Region. The processes for building Stacked Column and Clustered Column layers are similar:

1. Choose either the Clustered Column or Stacked Column icon in the bottom half of the Layer pane. Height, Category, and Time areas appear.

2. Drag a numeric field to the Height area. Use the drop-down arrow at the right edge of the field to choose Sum, Average, Count Not Blank, Count Distinct, Max, Min, or No Aggregation.

3. If you want the columns to be different colors, drag a field to the Category area. A large legend covers up the map. Click the legend, and resize handles appear. Right-click the legend and choose Edit to control the font, size, and color.

4. To animate the map over time, drag a date or time field to the Time area. Right-click the large time legend and customize how the dates and times appear.

Figure 11-4 shows an initial map using a clustered column chart.

FIGURE 11-4 One column appears for each street address in the data.

Navigating through the map

Initially, the zoom level is set to show all of your data points. You might discover that a few outliers cause the map to be zoomed out too far. For example, if you are analyzing customer data for an auto repair shop, you might find a few customers who stopped in for a repair while they were driving through on vacation. If 98 percent of your customers are near Charlotte, North Carolina, but three or four customers from New York and California are in the data set, the map will show everything from New York to California.

You can zoom in or out by using the + or – icons in the lower right of the map. You can use the mouse wheel to quickly zoom in or out.

As you start to zoom in, you might realize that you are zooming in on the wrong section of the map. Click and drag the map to re-center it. Or double-click any white space on the map to center the map at that point while zooming in.

Figure 11-5 shows a map zoomed in to show Florida.

FIGURE 11-5   Zoom in to show Florida.

By default, you usually look straight down on the map, but it is easier to see the height of each column if you tip the map. Use the up arrow and down arrow icons on the map to tip the map up or down. Or use the Alt key and the mouse: Hold down Alt and drag the mouse straight up to tip the map so that you are viewing the map from a point closer to the ground.

Hold down Alt and drag the mouse straight down to move the vantage point higher. When you hold down Alt and drag the mouse left or right, you rotate the view left or right. Figure 11-6 shows Miami from a lower vantage point, as you would see the points from the Atlantic Ocean.

FIGURE 11-6   Alt+drag the mouse to tip or rotate the view.

Labeling individual points

In many data sets, you see unusual data points. To see the details about a particular data point, hover over the point's column, and a tooltip appears, with identifiers for the data point. When you move away from the column, the tooltip is hidden.

If you are building a tour, you might want to display an annotation or a text box on a certain point. An annotation includes a custom title and the value of any fields you choose—or it can include a picture. A text box includes just text.

Right-click any point and choose Annotation or Text Box to build the label.

Building pie or bubble charts on a map

A bubble chart plots a single circle for each data point. The size of the circle tells you about the data point. If you add a Category field, the circle changes to a pie chart, with each category appearing as a wedge in the pie chart.

Unlike with column charts, you will likely want your bubble markers to be an aggregate of all points in a state or city. To change the level for a map, click the Pencil icon to the right of Geography at the top of the Layer pane. Then change the level to State and click Next. Drag a numeric field to the size area. Drag a text field to the category area.

You might need to adjust the size of the bubbles or pie charts. There are four symbols across the top of the Layer pane. The fourth symbol is a Settings gear icon. Click it and choose Layer Options. Slicers appear that let you change the opacity, size, thickness, and colors used (see Figure 11-7).

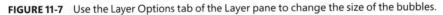

FIGURE 11-7 Use the Layer Options tab of the Layer pane to change the size of the bubbles.

Using heat maps and region maps

3D Maps also offers heat maps and shaded region maps. A heat map is centered on an individual point and shows varying shades of green, yellow, and red to show intensity. A region map fills an outline with the same color and is useful for showing data by country, state, or county.

Figure 11-8 shows a map with two layers: One layer is a region map by state, and the other layer is a heat map by city.

FIGURE 11-8   Region maps and heat maps are combined in a single map.

You might want to create region maps for shapes other than state or country. There are many free SHP or KML files available on the Internet. You can have 3D Map import these custom regions and then shade those areas on the map. To import a custom region, use Import Regions from the 3D Map ribbon.

Exploring 3D Map settings

There are a number of useful settings in 3D Map. Here are some of my favorites:

- **Aerial Photography Map**—If you will be zooming in to the city level, you can show an aerial photograph over the map. Use the Themes drop-down menu in 3D Map and choose the second theme.

- **Add Map Labels**—Click the Map Labels icon in the ribbon to add labels to the map. If you are zoomed completely out, the labels will be country names. As you zoom in, the labels change to states, cities, and even street names. Note that labels are an all-or-nothing proposition. You cannot easily show some labels and not others.

- **Flat Map**—If you want to see the entire Earth at one time, use the Flat Map icon in the 3D Map ribbon.

Figure 11-9 shows a flat map with labels added.

FIGURE 11-9 See the whole Earth with a flat map.

Fine-tuning 3D Map

There are situations where the defaults used by 3D Map are not the best. Here are troubleshooting methods for various situations.

By default, each column in a column chart takes up a fair amount of space on the map. For example, if you plot every house on your street, each column takes up about one city block. You won't be able to make out the detail for each house. Click the Settings gear icon and then Layer Options. Change the Thickness setting to 5% or 10%. 3D Map makes each column very narrow (see Figure 11-10).

3D Map looks great on a huge 1080p monitor. If you are stuck on a tiny laptop, though, you should hide the Tour and Layer panes by using the icons in the 3D Map ribbon.

Most legends start out way too large. You can either resize them or right-click and choose Hide to remove them altogether.

The Funnel icon in the Layer pane allows you to add filters to any field. 3D Map cannot render 5,000 check boxes, so you might have to use the Search utility within the filters to find items to show or hide.

When you hover over a data point, the resulting tooltip is called a data card. You can customize what appears in the card by selecting Layer Options from the gear menu and then clicking the icon below Customize Data Card.

FIGURE 11-10 Change the thickness of individual columns to see more detail.

Combining two data sets

If you want to combine two data sets, you need to do some pre-work. First, convert each data set to a table using Home, Format As Table. Then, from each data set, use Power Pivot, Add To Data Model.

If you are stuck in Excel 2013 or 2016 without the Power Pivot tab, you can create a fake pivot table from each data set and select the check box for Add This Data To The Data Model to load the data to the Data Model. Alternatively, you could use the Power Query tools to edit a table. After viewing the data in the Power Query Editor, use Home, Close And Load To, Add To This Workbook Data Model.

To combine different map types, add a layer using the Add Layer icon. Each layer can be shown at a different geography. You might have a column chart by city on Layer 1 and a region chart by state on Layer 2. The Layer Manager allows you to show and hide various layers.

Animating data over time

You can add a date or time field to any map layer. A time scrubber appears at the bottom of the map. Grab the scrubber and drag it left or right to show the data at any point in time. Use the Play button on the left side of the scrubber to have 3D Map animate the entire time period.

When you add the date or time field to the Time area, a small clock icon appears above the field. There are three choices in this drop-down menu:

- **Data Shows For An Instant**—The data appears when the time scrubber reaches this date, but then the data disappears once the scrubber passes the date.

- **Date Accumulates Over Time**—This option is appropriate for showing how ticket sales happened. If you sold 10 tickets on Monday and then another 5 tickets on Tuesday, you would want the map to show 15 tickets on Tuesday.

- **Data Stays Until It Is Replaced**—Say that you have a list of housing sales for the past 30 years. If a house sold for $200,000 in 2001 and then for $225,000 in 2005, you would want to show $200,000 for all points from 2001 until the end of 2004.

To control the speed of the animation, click the gear icon in the Layer pane and choose Scene Options. The Speed slider in the Time section controls how fast the time will change. Watch the Scene Duration setting at the top of this panel to see how long it will take to animate through the entire period covered by the data set.

You can use the Start Date and End Date drop-down menus to limit the animation to just a portion of the time period.

Building a tour

You can use a tour in 3D Map to tell a story. Each scene in the tour can focus on a section of the map, and 3D Map will automatically fly from one scene to the next.

As you have been experimenting in 3D Map, you have been working on Scene 1 in the Tour pane. If you click the gear icon and then Scene Options, you will see that the default scene duration is 10 seconds, with a default transition duration of 3 seconds. Therefore, when you play a tour, this first scene lasts 10 seconds. The time to fly to the next scene takes 3 seconds.

Once you have the timing correct for the first scene, you can add a second scene by selecting Home, New Scene, Copy Scene 1. Customize the second scene to zoom in on a different section of the country or to show a different view of the map.

Say that you want to have the first scene show the data accumulate over time and then you want the next three scenes to zoom in to three interesting parts of the country. You have to remove the Time field from the Layer pane at the start of Scene 2, or the entire timeline will animate again.

Alternatively, perhaps you want to zoom in to an area at a particular part of the timeline. In this example, you might have these scenes:

- You start with an establishing shot that shows the whole country at the beginning of the time period. Use the Scene Options and set both the start and end date to the earliest date in the data set. By using the same date for start and end, the opening scene will not animate over time.

- You then have a scene that animates over part of the timeline, perhaps 1971 to 1995.

- Next is a scene that zooms in to Florida in 1995. Use Scene Options to set the start and end date to December 31, 1995, to prevent the data from re-animating.

- Finally, you have a scene that is a copy of Scene 2 but with the date range changed from 1996 to 2018.

> **Tip** Note that annotations and text boxes will appear throughout one scene and through the transition to the next scene. If you have a 6-second scene and a 20-second transition, the text box will appear for all 26 seconds. You might want to go to the extra effort to break this up as a 6-second scene with the text box and a 0-second transition, followed by a 1-second scene with no text box and a 20-second transition.

To have the map constantly moving, change the Effect drop-down menu to something other than No Effect. For example, with Circle or Figure 8, the camera flies in an arc above the scene. Depending on how long the scene lasts, you may not get a complete circle. Adjust the Effect speed to increase the chances of finishing the circle.

Click Play Tour to hide all panels and play the tour in full-screen mode. Drag the mouse over the tour to reveal Play and Pause buttons at the bottom of the screen. Press the Esc key to go back to 3D Map.

Creating a video from 3D Map

To share a tour with others, you can use 3D Map to render a video. Build a tour first and then click Create Video. You can choose from three video resolutions and add a sound track.

> **Note** Rendering a several-minute tour in full HD resolution can take more than an hour on a fast PC.

Case study: Using a store map instead of a globe

Say that you have a database of sales in a retail mall. For each day, you have sales for each of several stores in the mall. You would like to animate how sales unfold during the business day in the mall. For example, items located near the coffee bar might sell best in the morning, while high-ticket items might sell best in the evening:

1. Find a drawing or an image of the store map. Figure out the height and width of the image. In this case, say that the image is 800 pixels wide and 366 pixels tall.

2. Build a table in Excel with a unique list of store names. (You could also use a unique list of departments or categories.)

3. Figure out the x and y location for each unique store name. Remember that x measures the number of pixels across the image, starting at the left edge. In Figure 11-11, the image is inserted into Excel. It fills columns E:U. Because the total width is 800, each column represents about 47 pixels. Sears is around 620 pixels from the left edge. For the

y value, remember to start at the bottom. Since the image is 366 pixels tall and fills 29 rows, each row is about 12.62 pixels tall. Cell C15 shows that the word *Sears* falls at about 176 pixels from the bottom edge.

> ⚠️ **Caution** The first time I tried finding x and y locations, I used the cursor location in Photoshop. It was fast and easy. But then I realized that Photoshop is measuring the y location starting at the top edge instead of the bottom edge. This initially seemed like a bad mistake, but since the data was keyed into Excel, a helper column with a formula of =366-F2 was able to quickly correct the Y values.

4. Create a table from your sales data by using Ctrl+T. Add the data to the Data Model.

5. Create a table from your location data by using Ctrl+T. Add the data to the Data Model.

6. In Power Pivot, create a relationship between the two tables.

7. From a blank cell in Excel, choose Insert, 3D Map. 3D Map shows you the fields from the Data Model.

FIGURE 11-11 Locate the X and Y coordinate for each store in the mall map.

8. In the Choose Geography section of the Layer pane, choose X and Y.

9. In the Geography and Map Level section, assign X as X Coordinate. Assign Y as Y Coordinate. 3D Map now asks you a question: Change To A Custom Map? (see Figure 11-12).

FIGURE 11-12 When you choose X and Y, 3D Map asks about using a custom map.

10. Click Yes to choose a custom map. In the Change Map Type dialog box, choose New Custom Map.

11. In the Custom Map Options dialog box, click the Picture icon next to Browse for the Background Picture. Select the same picture used for step 3. As shown in Figure 11-13, the dialog box starts out with Min and Max values for X and Y that represent the data in your data set. Because no data points are falling at the 0,0 coordinate or at the 800,366 coordinate, these estimates will always be incorrect.

FIGURE 11-13 The Min and Max for X and Y will always be incorrect in real life.

12. Change the Min for X and the Min for Y to 0. Change the Max for X to the picture width. Change the Max for Y to the picture height. Click Apply to see your data on the picture. Click Done when everything looks correct.

13. In the 3D Map Layer pane, click Next.

Your data is now plotted on a custom map of the mall, as shown in Figure 11-14. You can use 3D Map navigation to tip, rotate, and zoom the map.

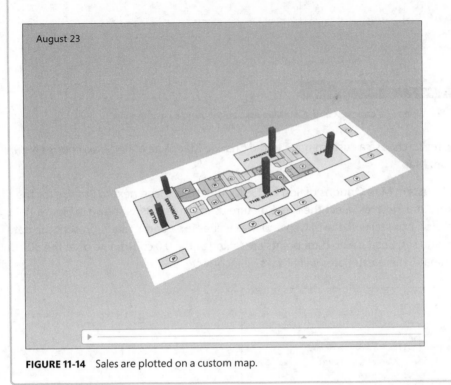

FIGURE 11-14   Sales are plotted on a custom map.

Next steps

Chapter 12, "Enhancing pivot table reports with macros," introduces you to simple macros you can use to enhance your pivot table reports.

Enhancing pivot table reports with macros

In this chapter, you will:

- Use macros with pivot table reports
- Record a macro
- Create a user interface with form controls
- Alter a recorded macro to add functionality

Using macros with pivot table reports

Imagine that you could be in multiple locations at one time, with multiple clients at one time, helping them with their pivot table reports. Suppose you could help multiple clients refresh their data, extract top 20 records, group by months, or sort by revenue—all at the same time. The fact is you can do just that by using Excel macros.

In its broadest sense, a *macro* is a sequence of instructions that automates some aspect of Excel so that you can work more efficiently and with fewer errors. Macros can be created by recording and saving a series of keystrokes. Once saved, a macro can be played back on demand. In other words, you can record your actions in a macro, save the macro, and then allow your clients to play back your actions with the click of a button or press of a keyboard shortcut. It would be as though you were right there with them! This functionality is especially useful when you're distributing pivot table reports.

For example, suppose that you want to give your clients the option of grouping their pivot table report by month, by quarter, or by year. Although the process of grouping can be performed by anyone, some of your clients might not have a clue how to do it. In this case, you could record a macro to group by month, a macro to group by quarter, and a macro to group by year. Then you could create three buttons, one for each macro. In the end, your clients, having little experience with pivot tables, need only to click a button to group their pivot table report.

A major benefit of using macros with your pivot table reports is the power you can give your clients to easily perform pivot table actions that they would not normally be able to perform on their own, empowering them to more effectively analyze the data you provide.

While macros have traditionally been written in VBA using the Excel Macro Recorder, the new Power Query tools also can produce a macro but using the M programming language. When someone refreshes the Power Query results, Excel runs the macro on new data. Given that Power Query gives you the ability to pivot your data, this chapter will include a Power Query example to load all Excel files from a single folder.

Recording a macro

Look at the pivot table in Figure 12-1. You know that you can refresh this pivot table by right-clicking inside the pivot table and selecting Refresh Data. Now, if you were to record your actions with a macro while you refreshed this pivot table, you or anyone else could replicate your actions and refresh this pivot table by running the macro.

FIGURE 12-1   You can easily refresh this basic pivot table by right-clicking and selecting Refresh, but if you recorded your actions with a macro, you could also refresh this pivot table simply by running the macro.

The first step in recording a macro is to initiate the Record Macro dialog box. Select the Developer tab on the ribbon and then select Record Macro.

> **Tip**   Can't find the Developer tab on the ribbon? Right-click the ribbon and choose Customize The Ribbon. In the list box to the far right, select the check box next to Developer. Selecting the check mark next to this option enables the Developer tab.

When the Record Macro dialog box activates, you can fill in a few key pieces of information about the macro:

- **Macro Name**—Enter a name for your macro. You should generally enter a name that describes the action being performed.

- **Shortcut Key**—You can enter any letter into this input box. That letter becomes part of a set of keys on your keyboard that can be pressed to play back the macro. This is optional.

- **Store Macro In**—Specify where you want the macro to be stored. If you are distributing your pivot table report, you should select This Workbook so that the macro is available to your clients.

- **Description**—In this input box, you can enter a few words that give more detail about the macro.

Because this macro refreshes your pivot table when it is played, name your macro **RefreshData**, as shown in Figure 12-2. Also assign the shortcut key **R**. Notice that, based on this, the dialog box gives you the key combination Ctrl+Shift+R. Keep in mind that you use the key combination to play your macro after it is created. Be sure to store the macro in This Workbook. Click OK to continue.

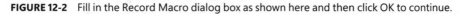

FIGURE 12-2   Fill in the Record Macro dialog box as shown here and then click OK to continue.

When you click OK in the Record Macro dialog box, you initiate the recording process. At this point, any action you perform is recorded by Excel. In this case, you want to record the process of refreshing your pivot table.

Right-click anywhere inside the pivot table and select Refresh Data. After you have refreshed your pivot table, you can stop the recording process by going up to the Developer tab and selecting the Stop Recording button.

Congratulations! You have just recorded a macro. You can now play your macro by pressing Ctrl, Shift, and R on your keyboard at the same time.

A Word on Macro Security

You should be aware that when you record a macro yourself, your macro runs on your PC with no security restrictions. However, when you distribute workbooks that contain macros, your clients have to let Excel know that your workbook is not a security risk in order to allow your macros to run.

Indeed, you will note that the sample file that comes with this chapter does not run unless you tell Excel to enable the macros within.

The best way to do this is to use the workbook in a *trusted location*, a directory that is deemed a safe zone where only trusted workbooks are placed. A trusted location allows you and your clients to run a macro-enabled workbook with no security restrictions, as long as the workbook is in that location.

To set up a trusted location, follow these steps:

1. Select the Macro Security button on the Developer tab. This activates the Trust Center dialog box.

2. Select the Trusted Locations button.

3. Select Add New Location.

4. Click Browse and then specify the directory to be considered a trusted location.

After you specify a trusted location, all workbooks opened from that location are, by default, opened with macros enabled.

> **Note** In Excel 2013, Microsoft enhanced the security model to remember files that you've deemed trustworthy. That is to say, when you open an Excel workbook and click the Enable button, Excel remembers that you trusted that file. Each time you open the workbook after that, Excel automatically trusts it.
>
> For information on macro security in Excel 2019, pick up Microsoft Press's *Excel 2019 In Depth* by Bill Jelen.

Creating a user interface with form controls

Allowing your clients to run your macro with shortcut keys such as Ctrl+Shift+R can be a satisfactory solution if you have only one macro in your pivot table report. However, suppose you want to allow your clients to perform several macro actions. In this case, you should give your clients a clear and easy way to run each macro without having to remember a gaggle of shortcut keys.

A basic user interface provides the perfect solution. A *user interface* is a set of controls such as buttons, scrollbars, and other devices that allow users to run macros with a simple click of the mouse. In fact, Excel offers a set of controls designed specifically for creating user interfaces directly on a spreadsheet. These controls are called *form controls*. The general idea behind form controls is that you can place one on a spreadsheet and then assign a macro to it—meaning a macro you have already recorded. After a macro is assigned to the control, that macro is executed, or played, when the control is clicked.

You can find form controls in the Controls group on the Developer tab. To get to the form controls, simply select the Insert icon in the Controls group, as shown in Figure 12-3.

FIGURE 12-3 To see the available form controls, click Insert in the Controls group on the Developer tab.

> **Note** Notice that there are Form controls and ActiveX controls. Although they look similar, they are quite different. Form controls, with their limited overhead and easy configuration settings, are designed specifically for use on a spreadsheet. Meanwhile, ActiveX controls are typically used on Excel user forms. As a general rule, you should use form controls when working on a spreadsheet.

Here, you can select the control that best suits your needs. In this example, you want your clients to be able to refresh their pivot table with the click of a button. Click the Button control to select it and then drop the control onto your spreadsheet by clicking the location where you would like to place the button.

After you drop the button control onto your spreadsheet, the Assign Macro dialog box, shown in Figure 12-4, opens and asks you to assign a macro to this button. Select the macro you want to assign to the button, in this case RefreshData, and then click OK.

FIGURE 12-4 Select the macro you want to assign to the button, and then click OK. In this case, you want to select RefreshData.

> **Note** Keep in mind that all the controls in the Forms toolbar work in the same way as the command button, in that you assign a macro to run when the control is selected.

As you can see in Figure 12-5, you can assign each macro in your workbook to a different form control and then name the controls to distinguish between them. To edit the text on a button, right-click the button and choose Edit Text. Use any of the eight resize handles on the button to resize the button.

FIGURE 12-5 You can create a different button for each one of your macros.

As you can see in Figure 12-6, when you have all the controls you need for your pivot table report, you can format the controls and surrounding spreadsheet to create a basic interface.

FIGURE 12-6 You can easily create the feeling of an interface by adding a handful of macros, a few form controls, and a little formatting.

Altering a recorded macro to add functionality

When you record a macro, Excel creates a module that stores the recorded steps of your actions. These recorded steps are actually lines of VBA code that make up your macro. You can add some interesting functionality to pivot table reports by tweaking a macro's VBA code to achieve various effects.

To get a better understanding of how this process works, start by creating a new macro that extracts the top five records by customer. Go to the Developer tab and select Record Macro. Set up the Record Macro dialog box, as shown in Figure 12-7. Name your new macro TopNthCusts and specify This Workbook as the place where you want to store the macro. Click OK to start recording.

FIGURE 12-7 Name your new macro and specify where you want to store it.

After you have started recording, right-click the Customer field and select Filter. Then select Top 10. Selecting this option opens the Filter dialog box, where you specify that you want to see the top five customers by sales amount. Enter the settings shown in Figure 12-8 and then click OK.

FIGURE 12-8 Enter the settings you see here to get the top five customers by revenue.

After you record the steps to extract the top five customers by revenue, select Stop Recording from the Developer tab.

You now have a macro that, when played, filters your pivot table to the top five customers by revenue. The plan is to tweak this macro to respond to a scrollbar; that is, you force the macro to base the number used to filter the pivot table on the number represented by a scrollbar in your user interface. In other words, a user can get the top 5, top 8, or top 32 simply by moving a scrollbar up or down.

Inserting a scrollbar form control

To get a scrollbar onto your spreadsheet, select the Insert icon on the Developer tab; then select the scrollbar control from the form controls. Place the scrollbar control onto your spreadsheet. You can change the dimensions of the scrollbar to an appropriate length and width by clicking and dragging the corners.

Right-click the scrollbar and select Format Control. This activates the Format Control dialog box, in which you make the following setting changes: Set Minimum Value to 1 so the scrollbar cannot go below 1, set Maximum Value to 200 so the scrollbar cannot go above 200, and set Cell Link to $M$2 so that the number represented by the scrollbar will output to cell M2. After you have completed these steps, your dialog box should look like the one shown in Figure 12-9.

FIGURE 12-9 After you have placed a scrollbar on your spreadsheet, configure the scrollbar as shown here.

Next, you need to assign the TopNthCusts macro you just recorded to your scrollbar. To do this, right-click the scrollbar and select Assign Macro. Select the TopNthCusts macro from the list shown in Figure 12-10, and then click OK. Assigning this macro ensures that it plays each time the scrollbar is clicked.

FIGURE 12-10 Select the macro from the list.

At this point, test your scrollbar by clicking it. When you click your scrollbar, two things should happen: The TopNthCusts macro should play, and the number in cell M2 should change to reflect your scrollbar's position. The number in cell M2 is important because that is the number you are going to reference in your TopNthCusts macro.

The only thing left to do is tweak your macro to respond to the number in cell M2, effectively tying it to your scrollbar. To do this, you have to get to the VBA code that makes up the macro. You have several ways to get there, but for the purposes of this example, go to the Developer tab and select Macros. Selecting this option opens the Macro dialog box, exposing several options. From here, you can run, delete, step into, or edit a selected macro. To get to the VBA code that makes up your macro, select the macro and then click Edit, as shown in Figure 12-11.

FIGURE 12-11 To get to the VBA code that makes up the `TopNthCusts` macro, select the macro and then select Edit.

The Visual Basic Editor opens, with a detailed view of all the VBA code that makes up this macro (see Figure 12-12). Notice that the number 5 is hard-coded as part of your macro. The reason is that you originally recorded your macro to filter the top five customers by revenue. Your goal here is to replace the hard-coded number 5 with the value in cell M2, which is tied to your scrollbar. Therefore, you need to delete the number 5 and replace it with the following:

```
ActiveSheet.Range("M2").Value
```

Your macro's code should now look like the code shown in Figure 12-13.

FIGURE 12-12 Your goal is to replace the hard-coded number 5, as specified when you originally recorded your macro, with the value in cell M2.

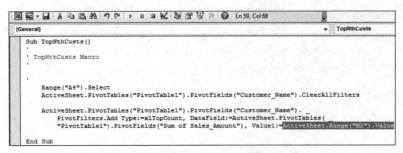

```
Sub TopNthCusts()
'
' TopNthCusts Macro
'

    Range("A4").Select
    ActiveSheet.PivotTables("PivotTable1").PivotFields("Customer_Name").ClearAllFilters

    ActiveSheet.PivotTables("PivotTable1").PivotFields("Customer_Name"). _
        PivotFilters.Add Type:=xlTopCount, DataField:=ActiveSheet.PivotTables( _
        "PivotTable1").PivotFields("Sum of Sales_Amount"), Value1:=ActiveSheet.Range("M2").Value

End Sub
```

FIGURE 12-13   Simply delete the hard-coded number 5 and replace it with a reference to cell M2.

Close the Visual Basic Editor to get back to your pivot table report. Test your scrollbar by setting it to 11. Your macro should play and filter out the top 11 customers by revenue, as shown in Figure 12-14.

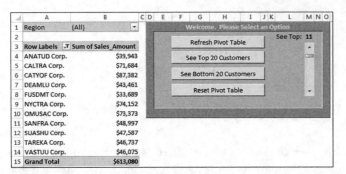

FIGURE 12-14   After a little formatting, you have a clear and easy way for your clients to get the top customers by revenue.

You could improve the buttons shown in Figure 12.14 by creating a formula to change "See Top 20 Customers" to reflect the value selected in the scrollbar.

The formula has to be entered in a cell somewhere on the worksheet. Perhaps use this formula in Z1: ="See Top "&M1&" Customers". Right-click the button to select it. Click in the formula bar and type =Z1 and press Enter.

Repeat in Z2 to create a caption for See Bottom 11 Customers.

Creating a macro using Power Query

In the previous examples, you would record a macro with the VBA Macro Recorder and then had to tweak the VBA code to have it work. That is normal with the VBA Macro Recorder; it is difficult to record a macro that will work with a larger-size data set.

I've written plenty of books on VBA, but here is the secret: Any more, most of my automated tasks are done using Power Query instead of VBA. Power Query is easier, more reliable, and you rarely have to "tweak" any code.

For the example in this chapter, you have a series of similar workbooks. Each workbook has a single worksheet and contains invoice information for one month. Of course, each month's workbook has a different number of rows, but since the file is generated by some enterprise system somewhere, the columns remain constant from month to month.

Your manager would like to see a report showing revenue by product by month. He wants products down the side and months across the top.

You've set up a folder called C:\InvoiceRegisters\ and so far, you have six monthly workbooks in that folder (see Figure 12-15).

FIGURE 12-15 Every month, a new workbook is added to this folder.

All the workbooks look similar to Figure 12-16.

	A	B	C	D	E	F	G	H	I
1	Sector	Region	Product	Date	Customer	Quantity	Revenue	Profit	Cost
2	Training	Midwest	Gizmo	1/1/2022	599CD.com	1000	22810	10220	12590
3	Software	Northeast	Gadget	1/2/2022	F-Keys Ltd.	100	2257	984	1273
4	Associations	South	Gizmo	1/4/2022	Association for Computers	400	9152	4088	5064
5	Consultants	Midwest	Gadget	1/4/2022	Construction Intelligence	800	18552	7872	10680
6	Consultants	West	Gadget	1/7/2022	Data2Impact	1000	21730	9840	11890
7	Software	Midwest	Widget	1/7/2022	Excel4Apps	400	8456	3388	5068
8	Software	Midwest	Widget	1/9/2022	Excel4Apps	800	16416	6776	9640

FIGURE 12-16 Each workbook has the same columns but different number of rows.

Start with a blank workbook with one worksheet. Select Data, Get Data, From File, From Folder, as shown in Figure 12-17.

FIGURE 12-17 Specify that you want data from a folder.

Power Query asks you to browse for your folder. Find `C:\InvoiceRegisters\` and click OK.

Power Query shows you a list of files. Open the Combine drop-down menu and choose Combine & Edit (see Figure 12-18).

FIGURE 12-18 Choose to combine the files.

The next step is a little unusual. A large but blank preview appears. You have to select a sample file and then a worksheet within that file. In Figure 12-19, the default sample file is "First File" and that is fine. When you click on Sheet1 in the left panel, the preview appears. Click OK.

FIGURE 12-19 Power Query shows you a preview of one of the workbooks.

The Power Query editor appears. A new column has been added to the left of your data with a heading of Source.Name (see Figure 12-20). This shows you which column the row came from. That might be nice one day, but it is not needed for today's project.

FIGURE 12-20 A preview shows the first 1,000 records.

The goal today is to produce a report with product, month, and revenue. Click on the heading of Product and then Ctrl+click Date and Revenue to select those three columns (see Figure 12-21).

A^BC Product	Date	A^BC Customer	1²3 Quantity	1²3 Revenue	
Gizmo	4/1/2022	MyOnlineTrainingHub.com	600	14448	
Widget	4/2/2022	MyOnlineTrainingHub.com	300	5370	
Gizmo	4/4/2022	Profology.com	800	20408	
Gadget	4/4/2022	Hartville MarketPlace and Flea Market	400	8632	
Gadget	4/4/2022	Hartville MarketPlace and Flea Market	300	6588	
Gizmo	4/5/2022	F-Keys Ltd.	100	2466	
Widget	4/7/2022	Serving Brevard Realty	700	14686	
Widget	4/7/2022	CPASelfStudy.com	300	5886	
Gadget	4/10/2022	Hartville MarketPlace and Flea Market	500	12095	
Gizmo	4/11/2022	LearnExcelBooks.com	900	19539	

FIGURE 12-21 Select the columns that you want to keep.

In the Power Query Home tab, open the Remove Columns drop-down menu and choose Remove Other Columns (see Figure 12-22). Choosing Remove Other Columns is a better option than removing each individual column. One day, perhaps five years from now, the I.T. department will add an extra column for something. By choosing to Remove Other Columns, you ensure that the new column is deleted.

FIGURE 12-22 Remove the columns that are not selected.

The invoice files had daily dates. You need to convert those to month ending dates. If you are a Power Query wizard, you would not have to look up the fact that this formula is Date.EndOfMonth([Date]). But you don't have to learn that function name or try to type it with the exact upper- and lowercase. Instead, you can use the Power Query analog of Flash Fill, called Column From Examples.

Select the Date column. On the Add Column tab, open the Column From Examples drop-down menu and choose From Selection (see Figure 12-23).

FIGURE 12-23 To transform the date, select that column before invoking Column From Examples.

When you use Column From Examples, the new column appears at the far right of the screen. Since the first record is from 4/1/2022, we'll use 4/30/2022 as the example.

Figure 12-24 is actually more informative. I accidentally typed a 5 instead of a 4 and then back-spaced through the 4. This revealed Power Query's guess of the things that I might want to do in order to transform the Date field. If you are an Excel formula guru, look through all those choices! If you had to create formulas to do all those tasks, it would be a super-quiz of the arcane formulas in Excel. But Column From Examples has them all pre-programmed.

Type **4/30/2022** and click on End Of Month. Click OK. Excel adds a new column.

FIGURE 12-24 Power Query knows all these calculations.

Earlier, I suggested that Column From Examples is similar to Flash Fill in Excel. It actually runs circles around Flash Fill. After you choose how to populate the column, Power Query inserts the correct formula so the calculation can happen again next time.

At this point, you have Product, Date, Revenue, and End Of Month. Right-click Date and Remove Column.

Sort End Of Month ascending. You will notice a few rows that say Null all the way across. These were caused by blank rows in each invoice file. Open the Filter icon for End Of Month and clear the Null option.

Stop and consider what has happened so far. You have combined records from all six workbooks. You've deleted unnecessary columns. You've done a calculation to convert Date to End Of Month.

At this point, you could Close and Load and do the final pivot table in Excel. But you can also do the pivot action right here in Power Query. Select the End Of Month column. On the Transform tab, choose Pivot Column (see Figure 12-25).

FIGURE 12-25 Choose to Pivot End Of Month across the report.

Pivoting in Power Query is a bit different than in regular Excel. Specify the Values column as Revenue. Any other columns in the data set will become Row fields. If you open the Advanced Options, there is a drop-down menu where you can specify how Revenue should be aggregated. The default of Sum works in this case (see Figure 12-26).

FIGURE 12-26 Specify how to create the pivoted report.

The results look great, and you will see those in a moment. But just getting the report from this first day of data is not the important part. Study the Applied Steps on the right side of the screen (see Figure 12-27). This is a list of everything you did to produce the report. Click on any item to see the data as it appears at that step. Click any Gear icon to see the choices you made at that step.

Are these steps the macro? No. Go to the View tab in Power Query and choose Advanced Editor. This is the macro, written in a language called M (see Figure 12-28).

APPLIED STEPS

- Source
- Filtered Hidden Files1
- Invoke Custom Function1
- Renamed Columns1
- Removed Other Columns1
- Expanded Table Column1
- Changed Type
- Removed Other Columns
- Inserted End of Month
- Removed Columns
- Sorted Rows
- Filtered Rows
- Pivoted Column
- ✕ Replaced Value

FIGURE 12-27 Power Query tracks the Applied Steps in a panel.

Advanced Editor   Query Dependencies

Advanced   Dependencies

Advanced Editor

InvoiceRegisters

```
let
    Source = Folder.Files("C:\InvoiceRegisters"),
    #"Filtered Hidden Files1" = Table.SelectRows(Source, each [Attri
    #"Invoke Custom Function1" = Table.AddColumn(#"Filtered Hidden F
    #"Renamed Columns1" = Table.RenameColumns(#"Invoke Custom Functi
    #"Removed Other Columns1" = Table.SelectColumns(#"Renamed Column
    #"Expanded Table Column1" = Table.ExpandTableColumn(#"Removed Ot
    #"Changed Type" = Table.TransformColumnTypes(#"Expanded Table Co
    #"Removed Other Columns" = Table.SelectColumns(#"Changed Type",{
    #"Inserted End of Month" = Table.AddColumn(#"Removed Other Colum
    #"Removed Columns" = Table.RemoveColumns(#"Inserted End of Month
    #"Sorted Rows" = Table.Sort(#"Removed Columns",{{"End of Month",
    #"Filtered Rows" = Table.SelectRows(#"Sorted Rows", each ([End o
    #"Pivoted Column" = Table.Pivot(Table.TransformColumnTypes(#"Fil
    #"Replaced Value" = Table.ReplaceValue(#"Pivoted Column",null,0,
in
    #"Replaced Value"
```

FIGURE 12-28 As you cleaned the data, Excel wrote the macro.

Here is the result of pivoting the data. Somehow, there were some months with no sales of Doodads. Those showed up as Null. You can use Replace Values to change Null to a zero (see Figure 12-29).

Product	1/31/2022	2/28/2022	3/31/2022	4/30/2022	5/31/2022	6/30/2022	
Doodads	17992	0	0	4948	0	0	
Gadget	68445	95259	91438	41207	127128	76250	
Gizmo	55801	98867	103494	164553	83673	27049	
Widget	130984	107494	70861	57058	130611	76256	

FIGURE 12-29 This report is a summary of six workbooks.

You have two choices for running the macro in the future. You can click the Refresh icon at the bottom of the Queries & Connections panel, as shown in Figure 12-30.

FIGURE 12-30   One way to run the macro again is to click Refresh.

But here is the thing: If you are producing this report for your manager, you cannot trust him or her to click the Refresh button. Here is a better way.

Right-click the `InvoiceRegisters` query and choose Properties. In the Query Properties dialog box, choose Refresh Data When Opening The File (see Figure 12-31).

Two months later, your folder of `InvoiceRegisters` now has eight workbooks. When you open the workbook, the Power Query steps will run and your report will be updated to include July and August (see Figure 12-32). This is fairly impressive.

FIGURE 12-31 Choose to run the Power Query macro when the workbook is opened.

⊿	A	B	C	D	E	F	G	H	I
1	Product ▼	1/31/2022 ▼	2/28/2022 ▼	3/31/2022 ▼	4/30/2022 ▼	5/31/2022 ▼	6/30/2022 ▼	7/31/2022 ▼	8/31/2022 ▼
2	Doodads	17992	0	0	4948	0	0		17856
3	Gadget	68445	95259	91438	41207	127128	76250	117410	67859
4	Gizmo	55801	98867	103494	164553	83673	27049	189604	132186
5	Widget	130984	107494	70861	57058	130611	76256	78753	73760
6									
7									

FIGURE 12-32 After adding July and August to your folder, the workbook reflects the new months.

Next steps

In the next chapter, you'll go beyond recording macros. Chapter 13, "Using VBA to create pivot tables," shows how to utilize Visual Basic for Applications to create powerful, behind-the-scenes processes and calculations using pivot tables.

Using VBA to create pivot tables

In this chapter, you will:

- Enable VBA in your copy of Excel
- Use a file format that enables macros
- Use the Visual Basic Editor
- Discover Visual Basic Tools
- Try to use the macro recorder
- Understand object-oriented code
- Learn tricks of the trade
- Understand versions
- Build a pivot table in Excel VBA
- Deal with limitations of pivot tables
- Create a report showing revenue by category
- Calculate with a pivot table
- Use advanced pivot table techniques
- Use the Data Model in Excel 2019

Version 5 of Excel introduced a powerful new macro language called Visual Basic for Applications (VBA). Every copy of Excel shipped since 1993 has had a copy of the powerful VBA language hiding behind the worksheets. VBA enables you to perform steps that you normally perform in Excel quickly and flawlessly. I have seen a VBA program change a process that would take days each month into a single-click operation that now takes a minute of processing time.

Do not be intimidated by VBA. The VBA macro recorder tool gets you 90 percent of the way to a useful macro, and I get you the rest of the way, using examples in this chapter.

Enabling VBA in your copy of Excel

By default, VBA is disabled in Office 2019. Before you can start using VBA, you need to enable macros in the Trust Center. Follow these steps:

1. Click the File menu to show the Backstage view.

2. In the left navigation pane, select Options. The Excel Options dialog box displays.

3. In the left navigation pane of Excel Options, select Customize Ribbon.

4. In the list box on the right, choose the Developer tab from the list of main tabs available in Excel. Click OK to close Excel Options and include the Developer tab in the ribbon.

5. Click the Developer tab in the ribbon. As shown in Figure 13-1, the Code group on the left side of the ribbon includes icons for the Visual Basic Editor, Macros, Macro Recorder, and Macro Security.

FIGURE 13-1 Enable the Developer tab to access the VBA tools.

6. Click the Macro Security icon. Excel opens the Trust Center.

7. In the Trust Center, choose one of the four options:

- **Disable All Macros with Notification**—When you open a workbook that contains macros, a message appears alerting you that macros are in the workbook. If you expect macros to be in the workbook, you can enable the macros. This is the safest setting because it forces you to explicitly enable macros in each workbook.

- **Enable All Macros**—This setting is not recommended because potentially dangerous code can run. Because it can enable rogue macros to run in files that are sent to you by others, Microsoft recommends that you not use this setting.

- **Disable All Macros Without Notification**—Your macros will not be able to run and, as the option says, you will not be notified that they're not running. You don't want to choose this option.

- **Disable All Macros Except Digitally Signed Macros**—You would have to buy a digital code signing certificate from a third party in order to use this option. This is a waste of money if you are building macros for you and your co-workers.

Using a file format that enables macros

The default Excel 2019 file format is initially the Excel workbook (.xlsx). This workbook is defined to disallow macros. You can build a macro in an .xlsx workbook, but it won't be saved with the workbook.

You have several options for saving workbooks that enable macros:

- **Excel Macro-Enabled Workbook (.xlsm)**—This uses the XML-based method for storing workbooks and enables macros. I prefer this file type because it is compact and less prone to becoming corrupt.

- **Excel Binary Workbook (.xlsb)**—This is a binary format and always enables macros.

- **Excel 97-2003 Workbook (.xls)**—Although this legacy file type supports macros, it doesn't support a lot of handy newer features. You lose access to slicers, new filters, rows 65537 through 1048576, columns IW through XFD, and other pivot table improvements.

When you create a new workbook, you can use File, Save As to choose the appropriate file type.

Visual Basic Editor

From Excel, press Alt+F11 or select Developer, Visual Basic to open the Visual Basic Editor, as shown in Figure 13-2. The three main sections of the VBA Editor are described here. If this is your first time using VBA, some of these items might be disabled. Follow the instructions in the following list to make sure that each is enabled:

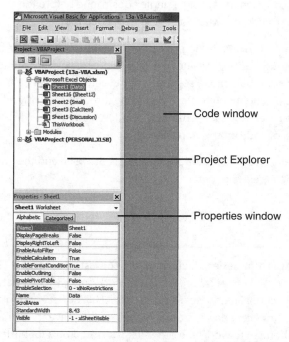

FIGURE 13-2   The Visual Basic Editor window is lurking behind every copy of Excel shipped since 1993.

- **Project Explorer**—This pane displays a hierarchical tree of all open workbooks. Expand the tree to see the worksheets, code modules, user forms, and class modules present in the workbook. If the Project Explorer is not visible, enable it by pressing Ctrl+R.

- **Properties window**—The Properties window is important when you begin to program user forms. It has some use when you are writing normal code, so enable it by pressing F4.

- **Code window**—This is the area where you write your code. Code is stored in one or more code modules attached to your workbook. To add a code module to a workbook, select Insert, Module from the VBA menu.

Visual Basic tools

Visual Basic is a powerful development environment. Although this chapter cannot offer a complete course on VBA, if you are new to VBA, you should take advantage of these important tools:

- **AutoComplete**—As you begin to type code, Excel might offer a drop-down menu with valid choices. This feature, known as AutoComplete, enables you to type code faster and eliminate typing mistakes.

- **Excel Help**—For assistance on any keyword, put the cursor in the keyword and press F1. Excel Help displays a help topic regarding the keyword.

- **Comments**—Excel checks each line of code as you finish it. Lines in error appear in red. Comments appear in green. You can add a comment by typing a single apostrophe before the comment. Use lots of comments so you can remember what each section of code is doing.

- **Debugging**—Despite the aforementioned error checking, Excel might still encounter an error at runtime. If this happens, click the Debug button. The line that caused the error is highlighted in yellow. Hover your mouse cursor over any variable to see the current value of the variable. When you are in Debug mode, use the Debug menu to step line by line through code. If you have a wide monitor, try arranging the Excel window and the VBA window side by side. This way, you can see the effect of running a line of code on the worksheet.

Other great debugging tools are breakpoints, the Watch window, the Object Browser, and the Immediate window. Read about these tools in the Excel Help menu.

The macro recorder

Excel offers a macro recorder that is about 90 percent perfect. Unfortunately, the last 10 percent is frustrating. Code that you record to work with one data set is hard-coded to work only with that data set. This behavior might work fine if your transactional database occupies cells A1:L87601 every single day, but if you are pulling in a new invoice register every day, it is unlikely that you will have the same number of rows each day. Given that you might need to work with other data, it would be a lot better if Excel could record selecting cells using the End key. This is one of the shortcomings of the macro recorder.

In reality, Excel pros use the macro recorder to record code but then expect to have to clean up the recorded code.

Understanding object-oriented code

VBA is an object-oriented language. Most lines of VBA code follow the *Noun.Verb* syntax. However, in VBA, it is called *Object.Method*. Examples of objects are workbooks, worksheets, cells, and ranges of cells. Methods can be typical Excel actions such as `.Copy`, `.Paste`, and `.PasteSpecial`.

Many methods allow adverbs—parameters you use to specify how to perform the method. If you see a construct with a colon and an equal sign (`:=`), you know that the macro recorder is describing how the method should work.

You also might see code in which you assign a value to the adjectives of an object. In VBA, adjectives are called *properties*. If you set `ActiveCell.Value = 3`, you are setting the value of the active cell to 3. Note that when you are dealing with properties, there is only an = (equal sign), not a `:=` (colon and equal sign).

Learning tricks of the trade

This section explains a few simple techniques you need to master in order to write efficient VBA code. These techniques help you make the jump to writing effective code.

Writing code to handle a data range of any size

The macro recorder hard-codes the fact that your data is in a range, such as A1:L87601. Although this hard-coding works for today's data set, it might not work as you get new data sets. You need to write code that can deal with data sets of different sizes.

The macro recorder uses syntax such as `Range("H12")` to refer to a cell. However, it is more flexible to use `Cells(12, 8)` to refer to the cell in row 12, column 8. Similarly, the macro recorder refers to a rectangular range as `Range("A1:L87601")`. However, it is more flexible to use the `Cells` syntax to refer to the upper-left corner of the range and then use the `Resize()` syntax to refer to the number of rows and columns in the range. The equivalent way to describe the preceding range is `Cells(1, 1).Resize(87601,12)`. This approach is more flexible because you can replace any of the numbers with a variable.

In the Excel user interface, you can use Ctrl+any arrow on the keyboard to jump to the edge of a range of data. If you move the cell pointer to the final row on the worksheet and press the Ctrl+up arrow key, the cell pointer jumps to the last row with data. The equivalent of doing this in VBA is to use the following code:

```
Range("A1048576").End(xlUp).Select
```

> **Caution** The arguments for the End property are XLUP, XLDOWN, XLTOLEFT, and XLTORIGHT. Using these properties is equivalent to pressing Ctrl plus the up, down, left, or right arrow keys. Since the VBA Editor shows XLUP as xlUp, many people think the argument contains the number *one* instead of the letter *L*. Think of how "XL" sounds like "Excel." There is also no logical explanation for why Microsoft added the word To in XLToLeft and XLToRight.

You do not need to select this cell; you just need to find the row number that contains the last row. The following code locates this row and saves the row number to a variable named FinalRow:

```
FinalRow = Range("A1048576").End(xlUp).Row
```

There is nothing magical about the variable name FinalRow. You could call this variable x, y, or even your dog's name. However, because VBA enables you to use meaningful variable names, you should use something such as FinalRow to describe the final row:

```
FinalRow = Cells(Rows.Count, 1).End(xlUp).Row
```

> **Note** Excel 2019 offers 1,048,576 rows and 16,384 columns for a regular workbook. If the workbook opens in Compatibility mode, you have only 65,536 rows and 256 columns. To make your code flexible enough to handle either situation, you can use Rows.Count to learn the total number of rows in the current workbook. The preceding code can then be generalized like so:
>
> ```
> FinalRow = Cells(Rows.Count, 1).End(xlUp).Row
> ```

You can also find the final column in a data set. If you are relatively sure that the data set begins in row 1, you can use the End key in combination with the left-arrow key to jump from cell XFD1 to the last column with data. To generalize for the possibility that the code is running in legacy versions of Excel, you can use the following code:

```
FinalCol = Cells(1, Columns.Count).End(xlToLeft).Column
```

> ### End+Down arrow versus End+Up arrow
>
> You might be tempted to find the final row by starting in cell A1 and using the End key in conjunction with the down-arrow key. Avoid this approach. Data coming from another system is imperfect. If your program imports 500,000 rows from a legacy computer system every day for the next five years, a day will come when someone manages to key a null value into the data set. This value will cause a blank cell or even a blank row to appear in the middle of the data set. Using Range("A1").End(xlDown) stops prematurely just above the blank cell instead of including all the data. This blank cell causes that day's report to miss thousands of rows of data, which is a potential disaster that calls into question the credibility of your report. Take the extra step of starting at the last row in the worksheet to greatly reduce the risk of problems.

Using super-variables: Object variables

In typical programming languages, a variable holds a single value. You might use x = 4 to assign the value 4 to the variable x.

Think about a single cell in Excel. Many properties describe a cell. A cell might contain a value such as 4, but the cell also has a font size, a font color, a row, a column, possibly a formula, possibly a comment, a list of precedents, and more. It is possible in VBA to create a super-variable that contains all the information about a cell or about any object. A statement to create a typical variable such as x = Range("A1") assigns the current value of A1 to the variable x.

However, you can use the Set keyword to create an object variable:

```
Set x = Range("A1")
```

You have now created a super-variable that contains all the properties of the cell. Instead of having a variable with only one value, you have a variable in which you can access the values of many properties associated with that variable. You can reference x.Formula to learn the formula in A1 or x.Font.ColorIndex to learn the color of the cell.

> **Note** The examples in this chapter frequently set up an object variable called PT to refer to the entire pivot table. This way, any time the code would generally refer to ActiveSheet.PivotTables("PivotTable1"), you can specify PT to avoid typing the longer text.

Using With and End With to shorten code

You will frequently find that you repeatedly make certain changes to a pivot table. Although the following code is explained later in this chapter, all these lines of code are for changing settings in a pivot table:

```
PT.NullString = 0
PT.RepeatAllLabels xlRepeatLabels
PT.ColumnGrand = False
PT.RowGrand = False
PT.RowAxisLayout xlTabularRow
PT.TableStyle2 = "PivotStyleMedium10"
PT.TableStyleRowStripes = True
```

For all these lines of code, the VBA engine has to figure out what you mean by PT. Your code executes faster if you refer to PT only once. Add the initial line With PT. Then all the remaining lines do not need to start with PT. Any line that starts with a period is assumed to be referring to the object in the With statement. Finish the code block by using an End With statement:

```
With PT
 .NullString = 0
 .RepeatAllLabels xlRepeatLabels
 .ColumnGrand = False
 .RowGrand = False
 .RowAxisLayout xlTabularRow
 .TableStyle2 = "PivotStyleMedium10"
 .TableStyleRowStripes = True
End With
```

Understanding versions

Pivot tables have been evolving. They were introduced in Excel 5 and perfected in Excel 97. In Excel 2000, pivot table creation in VBA was dramatically altered. Some new parameters were added in Excel 2002. A few new properties, such as `PivotFilters` and `TableStyle2`, were added in Excel 2007. Slicers and new choices for Show Values As were added in Excel 2010. Timelines and the Power Pivot Data Model were added in Excel 2013. The `AutoGroup` method was added in Excel 2019. Because of all the changes over the years, you need to be extremely careful when writing code in Excel 2019 that might be run in older versions of Excel.

Each of the last four versions of Excel offered many new features in pivot tables. If you use code for a new feature, the code works in the current version, but it crashes in previous versions of Excel:

- Excel 2016 introduced the AutoGroup functionality for dates in pivot tables. To perform the equivalent action in VBA, use the `AutoGroup` method.

- Excel 2013 introduced the Power Pivot Data Model. You can add tables to the Data Model, create a relationship, and produce a pivot table. This code does not run in Excel 2010 or earlier. The function `xlDistinctCount` was new in Excel 2013, as were timelines.

- Excel 2010 introduced slicers, Repeat All Item Labels, named sets, and several new calculation options: `xlPercentOfParentColumn`, `xlPercentOfParentRow`, `xlPercentRunningTotal`, `xlRankAscending`, and `xlRankDescending`. These do not work in Excel 2007 or earlier.

- Excel 2007 introduced `ConvertToFormulas`, `xlCompactRow` layout, `xlAtTop` for the subtotal location, `TableStyles`, and `SortUsingCustomLists`. Macros that include this code fail in previous versions.

Building a pivot table in Excel VBA

This chapter does not mean to imply that you use VBA to build pivot tables to give to your clients. Instead, the purpose of this chapter is to remind you that you can use pivot tables as a means to an end. You can use a pivot table to extract a summary of data and then use that summary elsewhere.

> **Note** This chapter's code listings are available for download at `microsoftpressstore.com/Excel2019PivotTable/downloads`.

!

Caution Beginning with Excel 2007, the user interface has new names for the various sections of a pivot table. Even so, VBA code continues to refer to the old names. Although the four sections of a pivot table in the Excel user interface are Filters, Columns, Rows, and Values, VBA continues to use the old terms of page fields, column fields, row fields, and data fields. If Microsoft hadn't made this decision, millions of lines of code would have stopped working in Excel 2007 when they referred to a page field instead of a filter field.

In Excel 2000 and newer, you first build a pivot cache object to describe the input area of the data:

```
Dim WSD As Worksheet
Dim PTCache As PivotCache
Dim PT As PivotTable
Dim PRange As Range
Dim FinalRow As Long
Dim FinalCol As Long
Set WSD = Worksheets("Data")

' Delete any prior pivot tables
For Each PT In WSD.PivotTables
 PT.TableRange2.Clear
Next PT

' Define input area and set up a Pivot Cache
FinalRow = WSD.Cells(Rows.Count, 1).End(xlUp).Row
FinalCol = WSD.Cells(1, Columns.Count).End(xlToLeft).Column
Set PRange = WSD.Cells(1, 1).Resize(FinalRow, FinalCol)
Set PTCache = ActiveWorkbook.PivotCaches.Add(SourceType:=xlDatabase, _
 SourceData:=PRange)
```

After defining the pivot cache, use the CreatePivotTable method to create a blank pivot table based on the defined pivot cache:

```
Set PT = PTCache.CreatePivotTable(TableDestination:=WSD.Cells(2, _
 FinalCol + 2), TableName:="PivotTable1")
```

In the CreatePivotTable method, you specify the output location and optionally give the table a name. After running this line of code, you have a strange-looking blank pivot table, like the one shown in Figure 13-3. You now have to use code to drop fields onto the table.

FIGURE 13-3 Immediately after you use the CreatePivotTable method, Excel gives you a four-cell blank pivot table that is not useful.

> **Caution** If you choose the Defer Layout Update setting in the user interface to build the pivot table, Excel does not recalculate the pivot table after you drop each field onto the table. By default, in VBA, Excel calculates the pivot table as you execute each step of building the table. This could require the pivot table to be executed a half-dozen times before you get to the final result.

To speed up your code execution, you can temporarily turn off calculation of the pivot table by using the `ManualUpdate` property:

```
PT.ManualUpdate = True
```

You can now run through the steps needed to lay out the pivot table. In the `AddFields` method, you can specify one or more fields that should be in the row, column, or filter area of the pivot table.

The `RowFields` parameter enables you to define fields that appear in the Rows area of the PivotTable Fields list. The `ColumnFields` parameter corresponds to the Columns layout area. The `PageFields` parameter corresponds to the Filters layout area.

The following line of code populates a pivot table with two fields in the Rows area and one field in the Columns area:

```
' Set up the row & column fields
PT.AddFields RowFields:=Array("Category", "Product"), _
 ColumnFields:="Region"
```

> **Note** If you are adding a single field such as Region to the Columns area, you only need to specify the name of the field in quotes. If you are adding two or more fields, you have to include that list inside the array function.

Although the row, column, and filter fields of the pivot table can be handled with the `AddFields` method, it is best to add fields to the data area using the code described in the next section.

Adding fields to the data area

When you are adding fields to the data area of a pivot table, for many settings it is better for you to have control than to let Excel's IntelliSense decide.

Say that you are building a report with revenue. You likely want to sum the revenue. If you do not explicitly specify the calculation, Excel scans through the values in the underlying data. If 100 percent of the revenue cells are numeric, Excel sums. If one cell is blank or contains text, Excel decides to count the revenue. This produces confusing results.

Because of this possible variability, you should never use the DataFields argument in the AddFields method. Instead, change the property of the field to xlDataField. You can then specify the function to be xlSum.

While you are setting up the data field, you can change several other properties within the same With...End With block.

The Position property is useful when adding multiple fields to the data area. Specify 1 for the first field, 2 for the second field, and so on.

By default, Excel renames a Revenue field to something strange like Sum Of Revenue. You can use the Name property to change that heading back to something normal. Note that you cannot reuse the word Revenue as a name, but you can use "Revenue " (with a trailing space).

You are not required to specify a number format, but doing so can make the resulting pivot table easier to understand and takes only one extra line of code:

```
' Set up the data fields
With PT.PivotFields("Revenue")
 .Orientation = xlDataField
 .Function = xlSum
 .Position = 1
 .NumberFormat = "#,##0"
 .Name = "Revenue "
End With
```

The preceding block of code adds the Revenue field to the Values area of the pivot table with a new name and a number format.

Formatting the pivot table

Microsoft introduced the Compact layout for pivot tables in Excel 2007. This means that three layouts are available in Excel 2019 (Compact, Tabular, and Outline). When a pivot table is created with VBA, Excel usually defaults to using the Tabular layout, which is good because Tabular view is the one that makes the most sense. It cannot hurt, though, to add one line of code to ensure that you get the desired layout:

```
PT.RowAxisLayout xlTabularRow
```

In Tabular layout, each field in the row area is in a different column. Subtotals always appear at the bottom of each group. This is the layout that has been around the longest and is most conducive to reusing a pivot table report for further analysis.

The Excel user interface frequently defaults to Compact layout. In this layout, multiple column fields are stacked up into a single column on the left side of the pivot table. To create this layout, use the following code:

```
PT.RowAxisLayout xlCompactRow
```

> **Tip** The one limitation of Tabular layout is that you cannot show the totals at the top of each group. If you need to do this, you'll want to switch to the Outline layout and show totals at the top of the group:
>
> ```
> PT.RowAxisLayout xlOutlineRow
> PT.SubtotalLocation xlAtTop
> ```

Your pivot table inherits the table style settings selected as the default on whatever computer happens to run the code. If you would like control over the final format, you can explicitly choose a table style. The following code applies banded rows and a medium table style:

```
' Format the pivot table
PT.ShowTableStyleRowStripes = True
PT.TableStyle2 = "PivotStyleMedium10"
```

At this point, you have given VBA all the settings required to correctly generate the pivot table. If you set ManualUpdate to False, Excel calculates and draws the pivot table. Thereafter, you can immediately set this back to True by using this code:

```
' Calc the pivot table
PT.ManualUpdate = False
PT.ManualUpdate = True
```

At this point, you have a complete pivot table, like the one shown in Figure 13-4.

Revenue		Region
Category ▼	Product ▼	Midwest
⊟ Bar Equipment	Bar Cover	1,328
	Cocktail Shaker 28 Oz	4,607
	Commercial Bar Blender	1,704
	Garnish Center	455
	Glass Rimmers Triple Brushes	8,760
	Glass Rimmers Twin Brushes	1,278
	High Power Blender Easy-To-Clean Electronic Membrane	1,500
	High Power Blender With Paddle Switches	1,125
	One Gallon Blender	16,540
	Speed Rail 10 Quart/Liter Bottle Capacity	753
	Speed Rail 5 Quart/Liter Bottle Capacity	989
	Speed Rail 8 Quart/Liter Bottle Capacity	
	Spindle Drink Mixer Single Spindle $ 275.00	1,650
	Spindle Drink Mixers 32 Oz. S/S Containe	1,428
	Spindle Drink Mixers 48 Oz. Poly. Container	21,505
Bar Equipment Total		**63,621**
⊟ Commercial Applianc	2 1/2 Qt. Cap. Batch Bowl	3,520

FIGURE 13-4 Fewer than 50 lines of code create this pivot table in less than a second.

Listing 13-1 shows the complete code used to generate this pivot table.

LISTING 13-1 Code to generate the pivot table shown in Figure 13-4

```
Sub CreatePivot()
'
 Dim WSD As Worksheet
 Dim PTCache As PivotCache
 Dim PT As PivotTable
 Dim PRange As Range
```

```
Dim FinalRow As Long
Set WSD = Worksheets("Data")

' Delete any prior pivot tables
For Each PT In WSD.PivotTables
PT.TableRange2.Clear
Next PT
WSD.Range("N1:AZ1").EntireColumn.Clear

' Define input area and set up a Pivot Cache
FinalRow = WSD.Cells(Application.Rows.Count, 1).End(xlUp).Row
FinalCol = WSD.Cells(1, Application.Columns.Count). _
End(xlToLeft).Column
Set PRange = WSD.Cells(1, 1).Resize(FinalRow, FinalCol)
Set PTCache = ActiveWorkbook.PivotCaches.Add(SourceType:= _
xlDatabase, SourceData:=PRange.Address)

' Create the Pivot Table from the Pivot Cache
Set PT = PTCache.CreatePivotTable(TableDestination:=WSD. _
Cells(2, FinalCol + 2), TableName:="PivotTable1")

' Turn off updating while building the table
PT.ManualUpdate = True

' Set up the row & column fields
PT.AddFields RowFields:=Array("Category", "Product"), _
ColumnFields:="Region"

' Set up the data fields
With PT.PivotFields("Revenue")
.Orientation = xlDataField
.Function = xlSum
.Position = 1
.NumberFormat = "#,##0"
End With

' Format the pivot table
PT.RowAxisLayout xlTabularRow
PT.ShowTableStyleRowStripes = True
PT.TableStyle2 = "PivotStyleMedium10"

' Calc the pivot table
PT.ManualUpdate = False
PT.ManualUpdate = True

WSD.Activate
Cells(2, FinalCol + 2).Select

End Sub
```

Dealing with limitations of pivot tables

As with pivot tables in the user interface, Microsoft maintains tight control over a live pivot table. You need to be aware of these issues as your code is running on a sheet with a live pivot table.

Filling blank cells in the data area

It is a bit annoying that Excel puts blank cells in the data area of a pivot table. For example, in Figure 13-4, the Midwest region had no sales of a Speed Rail 8 Quart/Liter, so that cell (P15) appears blank instead of containing a zero.

You can override this in the Excel interface by using the For Empty Cells Show setting in the Pivot-Table Options dialog box. The equivalent code is shown here:

```
PT.NullString = "0"
```

> **Note** Note that the Excel macro recorder always wraps that zero in quotation marks. No matter whether you specify "0" or just 0, the blank cells in the data area of the pivot table have numeric zeros.

Filling blank cells in the row area

Excel 2010 added a much-needed setting to fill in the blank cells along the left columns of a pivot table. This problem happens any time that you have two or more fields in the row area of a pivot table. Rather than repeat a label such as "Bar Equipment" in cells N5:N18 in the pivot table shown in Figure 13-4, Microsoft traditionally has left those cells blank. To solve this problem in Excel 2019, use the following line of code:

```
PT.RepeatAllLabels xlRepeatLabels
```

Preventing errors from inserting or deleting cells

You cannot use many Excel commands inside a pivot table. Inserting rows, deleting rows, and cutting and pasting parts of a pivot table are all against the rules.

Say that you tried to delete the Grand Total column from column W in a pivot table. If you try to delete or clear column W, the macro comes to a screeching halt with a 1004 error, as shown in Figure 13-5.

FIGURE 13-5 You cannot delete part of a pivot table.

There are two strategies for getting around this limitation. The first strategy is to find if there is already an equivalent command in the pivot table interface. For example, you want to determine whether there is code to perform any of these actions:

- Remove the grand total column.

- Remove the grand total row.

- Add blank rows between each section.

- Suppress subtotals for outer row fields.

The second strategy is to convert the pivot table to values. You can then insert, cut, and clear as necessary.

Both strategies are discussed in the following sections.

Controlling totals

The default pivot table includes a grand total row and a grand total column. You can choose to hide one or both of these elements.

To remove the grand total column from the right side of the pivot table, use this:

```
PT.RowGrand = False
```

To remove the grand total row from the bottom of the pivot table, use this:

```
PT.ColumnGrand = False
```

Turning off the subtotals rows is surprisingly complex. This issue comes up when you have multiple fields in the row area. Excel automatically turns on subtotals for the outermost row fields.

Tip Did you know that you can have a pivot table show multiple subtotal rows? I have never seen anyone actually do this, but you can use the Field Settings dialog box to specify that you want to see Sum, Average, Count, Max, Min, and so on. Figure 13-6 shows the Custom setting where you set this.

FIGURE 13-6 The Custom setting is rarely used, but the fact that you can specify multiple types of subtotals for a single field complicates the VBA code for suppressing subtotals.

To suppress the subtotals for a field, you must set the Subtotals property equal to an array of 12 False values. The first False turns off automatic subtotals, the second False turns off the Sum subtotal, the third False turns off the Count subtotal, and so on. This line of code suppresses the Category subtotal:

```
PT.PivotFields("Category").Subtotals = Array(False, False, False, False, _
 False, False, False, False, False, False, False, False)
```

A different technique is to turn on the first subtotal. This method automatically turns off the other 11 subtotals. You can then turn off the first subtotal to make sure all subtotals are suppressed:

```
PT.PivotFields("Category").Subtotals(1) = True
PT.PivotFields("Category").Subtotals(1) = False
```

> **Note** You might be wondering about the Distinct Count option introduced in Excel 2013. Does it force a twelfth position in the array? No. The Custom subtotals option is grayed out for pivot tables that use the Data Model, so you won't ever be able to choose Sum and Distinct Count together.

See "Using the Data Model in Excel 2019," later in this chapter for an example of using Distinct Count.

Converting a pivot table to values

If you plan on converting a live pivot table to values, you need to copy the entire pivot table. How much space it will take might be tough to predict. If you summarize transactional data every day, you might find that on any given day, you do not have sales from one region. This can cause your table to be perhaps seven columns wide on some days and only six columns wide on other days.

Excel provides two range properties that you can use to refer to a pivot table. The TableRange2 property includes all the rows of the pivot table, including any Filter drop-down menus at the top of the pivot table. The TableRange1 property starts just below the filter fields. It often includes the unnecessary row with Sum Of Revenue at the top of the pivot table.

If your goal is to convert a pivot table to values and not move the pivot table to a new place, you can use this code:

```
PT.TableRange2.Copy
PT.TableRange2.PasteSpecial xlPasteValues
```

If you want to copy only the data section of the pivot table to a new location, you frequently use the Offset property to start one row lower than the top of TableRange2, like so:

```
PT.TableRange2.Offset(1,0).Copy
```

This reference copies the data area plus one row of headings.

Notice in Figure 13-7 that using Offset without .Resize causes one extra row to be copied. However, because that row is always blank, there is no need to use Resize to not copy the extra blank row.

The code copies PT.TableRange2 and uses PasteSpecial on a cell six rows below the current pivot table.

	N	O	P	Q
39	⊟ Southwest	Bar Equipment	73,471	33,408
40	Southwest	Commercial Appliances	289,527	130,744
41	Southwest	Concession Equipment	355,845	159,486
42	Southwest	Fryers	267,408	120,208
43	Southwest	Ovens and Ranges	3,011,743	1,360,228
44	Southwest	Refrigerators and Coolers	3,233,297	1,459,587
45	Southwest	Warmers	1,154,938	522,652
46	⊟ West	Bar Equipment	68,555	31,130
47	West	Commercial Appliances	296,216	133,680
48	West	Concession Equipment	421,420	189,303
49	West	Fryers	275,557	123,535
50	West	Ovens and Ranges	3,633,635	1,642,191
51	West	Refrigerators and Coolers	5,393,086	2,429,377
52	West	Warmers	1,715,528	776,228
53				
54				

Copied range includes extra row

FIGURE 13-7 An intermediate result of the macro. The pivot table plus one blank row has been copied.

You can then eliminate the pivot table by applying the Clear method to the entire table. If your code is then going on to do additional formatting, you should remove the pivot cache from memory by setting PTCache equal to Nothing.

The code in Listing 13-2 uses a pivot table to produce a summary from the underlying data. More than 80,000 rows are reduced to a tight 50-row summary. The resulting data is properly formatted for additional filtering, sorting, and so on. At the end of the code, the pivot table is copied to static values, and the pivot table is cleared.

LISTING 13-2 Code to produce a static summary from a pivot table

```vba
Sub UsePivotToCreateValues()
'
Dim WSD As Worksheet
Dim PTCache As PivotCache
Dim PT As PivotTable
Dim PRange As Range
Dim FinalRow As Long
Set WSD = Worksheets("Data")

' Delete any prior pivot tables
For Each PT In WSD.PivotTables
PT.TableRange2.Clear
Next PT
WSD.Range("N1:AZ1").EntireColumn.Clear

' Define input area and set up a Pivot Cache
FinalRow = WSD.Cells(Application.Rows.Count, 1).End(xlUp).Row
FinalCol = WSD.Cells(1, Application.Columns.Count). _
End(xlToLeft).Column
Set PRange = WSD.Cells(1, 1).Resize(FinalRow, FinalCol)
Set PTCache = ActiveWorkbook.PivotCaches.Add(SourceType:= _
xlDatabase, SourceData:=PRange.Address)

' Create the Pivot Table from the Pivot Cache
Set PT = PTCache.CreatePivotTable(TableDestination:=WSD. _
Cells(2, FinalCol + 2), TableName:="PivotTable1")

' Turn off updating while building the table
PT.ManualUpdate = True

' Set up the row & column fields
PT.AddFields RowFields:=Array("Region", "Category"), _
ColumnFields:="Data"

' Set up the data fields
With PT.PivotFields("Revenue")
.Orientation = xlDataField
.Function = xlSum
.Position = 1
.NumberFormat = "#,##0"
.Name = "Revenue "
End With
With PT.PivotFields("Cost")
.Orientation = xlDataField
.Function = xlSum
.Position = 2
.NumberFormat = "#,##0"
.Name = "COGS"
End With

' Settings to create a solid block of data
With PT
```

```
.NullString = 0
.RepeatAllLabels Repeat:=xlRepeatLabels
.ColumnGrand = False
.RowGrand = 0
.PivotFields("Region").Subtotals(1) = True
.PivotFields("Region").Subtotals(1) = False
End With

' Calc the pivot table
PT.ManualUpdate = False
PT.ManualUpdate = True

' Copy the pivot table as values below the pivot table
PT.TableRange2.Offset(1, 0).Copy
PT.TableRange1.Cells(1, 1).Offset(PT.TableRange1.Rows.Count + 4, 0). _
StartRow = PT.TableRange1.Cells(1, 1).Offset( _
PT.TableRange1.Rows.Count+ 5, 0).Row
' Figure 13.7 at this point

PT.TableRange1.Clear
Set PTCache = Nothing

WSD.Activate
Cells(StartRow, FinalCol + 2).Select

End Sub
```

The code in Listing 13-2 creates the pivot table. It then copies the results as values and pastes them below the original pivot table. In reality, you probably want to copy this report to another worksheet or another workbook. Examples later in this chapter introduce the code necessary for this.

So far, this chapter has walked you through building the simplest of pivot table reports. Pivot tables offer far more flexibility, though. Read on for more complex reporting examples.

Pivot table 201: Creating a report showing revenue by category

A typical report might provide a list of markets by category with revenue by year. This report could be given to product line managers to show them which markets are selling well. The report in Figure 13-8 is not a pivot table, but the macro to create the report used a pivot table to summarize the data. Regular Excel commands such as Subtotal then finish off the report.

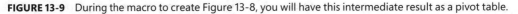

1 2 3		A	B	C	D	E	F	G
	1	Revenue by Category & Region						
	2							
	3	Category	Region	2022	2023	2024	Grand Total	
	4	Ovens and Ranges	South	15,672K	13,796K	8,284K	37,752K	
	5	Ovens and Ranges	Southeast	2,639K	2,745K	1,418K	6,802K	
	6	Ovens and Ranges	West	519K	1,520K	1,594K	3,634K	
	7	Ovens and Ranges	Southwest	572K	1,335K	1,104K	3,012K	
	8	Ovens and Ranges	Northeast	662K	1,146K	801K	2,609K	
	9	Ovens and Ranges	Midwest	290K	1,379K	760K	2,429K	
	10	Ovens and Ranges	North	247K	421K	263K	931K	
	11	Ovens and Ranges Total		20,602K	22,342K	14,225K	57,169K	
	12	Refrigerators and Coolers	South	4,855K	4,659K	12,093K	21,606K	
	13	Refrigerators and Coolers	West	1,957K	348K	3,088K	5,393K	
	14	Refrigerators and Coolers	Southeast	929K	1,311K	2,062K	4,302K	

FIGURE 13-8 This report started as a pivot table but finished as a regular data set.

In this example, you want to show the markets in descending order by revenue, with years going across the columns. A sample pivot table report is shown in Figure 13-9.

N	O	P	Q	R	S
Sum of Rev		Date ▼			
Category ▼	Region ▼	2022	2023	2024	Grand Total
⊟ Ovens ar	South	15,672K	13,796K	8,284K	37,752K
Ovens ar	Southeast	2,639K	2,745K	1,418K	6,802K
Ovens ar	West	519K	1,520K	1,594K	3,634K
Ovens ar	Southwest	572K	1,335K	1,104K	3,012K
Ovens ar	Northeast	662K	1,146K	801K	2,609K
Ovens ar	Midwest	290K	1,379K	760K	2,429K
Ovens ar	North	247K	421K	263K	931K
⊟ Refrigera	South	4,855K	4,659K	12,093K	21,606K
Refrigera	West	1,957K	348K	3,088K	5,393K

FIGURE 13-9 During the macro to create Figure 13-8, you will have this intermediate result as a pivot table.

There are some tricky issues involved in creating this pivot table:

- You have to roll the daily dates in the original data set up to years.

- You want to control the sort order of the row fields.

- You want to fill in blanks throughout the pivot table, use a better number format, and suppress the subtotals for the Category field.

The key to producing this data quickly is to use a pivot table. The default pivot table has a number of quirky problems that you can correct in the macro. To start, use VBA to build a pivot table with Category and Region as the row fields. Add Date as a column field. Add Revenue as a data field. Here's the code to do all this:

```
PT.AddFields RowFields:=Array("Category", _
 "Region"), ColumnFields:="Date"

' Set up the data fields
With PT.PivotFields("Revenue")
```

```
 .Orientation = xlDataField
 .Function = xlSum
 .Position = 1
 .NumberFormat = "#,##0"
End With
```

Figure 13-10 shows the default pivot table created with these settings.

	N	O	P	Q	R	S	T
Sum of Rev			Date	▾				
Category ▾		Region ▾	1/2/2022	1/3/2022	1/4/2022	1/5/2022	1/6/2022
⊟ Bar Equip	West						
	Midwest						
	North						
	Northeast						
	South						
	Southeast						
	Southwest						
Bar Equipment Total							
⊟ Commerc	West		829				829
	Midwest		838				
	North						

FIGURE 13-10 By default, the initial report has many problems.

Here are just a few of the annoyances that most pivot tables present in their default state:

■ The outline view is horrible. In Figure 13-10, the value Bar Equipment appears in the product column only once and is followed by six blank cells. Thankfully, Excel 2019 offers the RepeatAll-Labels method to correct this problem. If you intend to repurpose the data, you need the row labels to be repeated on every row.

■ Because the original data set contains daily dates, the default pivot table has more than 1,000 columns of daily data. No one is able to process this report. You need to roll those daily dates up to years. Pivot tables make this easy.

■ The report contains blank cells instead of zeros. In Figure 13-10, the entire visible range of Bar Equipment is blank. These cells should contain zeros instead of blanks.

■ The title is boring. Most people would agree that Sum Of Revenue is an annoying title.

■ Some captions are extraneous. Date floating in cell P2 of Figure 13-10 does not belong in a report.

■ The default alphabetical sort order is rarely useful. Product line managers are going to want the top markets at the top of the list. It would be helpful to have the report sorted in descending order by revenue.

■ The borders are ugly. Excel draws in myriad borders that make the report look awful.

■ Pivot tables offer no intelligent page break logic. If you want to produce one report for each product line manager, there is no fast method for indicating that each product should be on a new page.

- Because of the page break problem, you might find that it is easier to do away with the pivot table's subtotal rows and have the `Subtotal` method add subtotal rows with page breaks. You need a way to turn off the pivot table subtotal rows offered for Category in Figure 13-10. These rows show up automatically whenever you have two or more row fields. If you had four row fields, you would want to turn off the automatic subtotals for the three outermost row fields.

Even with all these problems in default pivot tables, default pivot tables are still the way to go. You can overcome each complaint either by using special settings within the pivot table or by entering a few lines of code after the pivot table is created and then copied to a regular data set.

Ensuring that Tabular layout is utilized

In legacy versions of Excel, multiple row fields appeared in multiple columns. Three layouts are now available. The Compact layout squeezes all the row fields into a single column. Compact layout is the default when a pivot table is created in the Excel interface. Currently, when you create a pivot table in VBA, the default is the Tabular layout. However, in some future version, Microsoft will correct this discrepancy, so get in the habit of explicitly changing the layout to a Tabular layout with this code:

```
PT.RowAxisLayout xlTabularRow
```

Rolling daily dates up to years

With transactional data, you often find your date-based summaries having one row per day. Although daily data might be useful to a plant manager, many people in the company want to see totals by month or quarter and year.

The great news is that Excel handles the summarization of dates in a pivot table with ease. If you have ever had to use the arcane formula `=A2+1-Day(A2)` to change daily dates into monthly dates, you will appreciate the ease with which you can group transactional data into months or quarters.

> **Tip** Although the Excel 2019 user interface automatically groups daily dates up to months, quarters, and years, pivot tables created with VBA do not automatically group the dates. If you are sure that your code will never have to run in Excel 2013 or earlier, you could use the following code to automatically group dates as in the Excel 2019 interface:
>
> ```
> PT.PivotFields("Date").AutoGroup
> ```
>
> After experiencing the AutoGroup feature for three years, it is quirky enough to avoid. For example, if your data includes January 1 and December 31 of a year, the AutoGroup will include year in the grouping. But if you did not invoice on January 1 or December 31 due to the holiday, then the AutoGroup will exclude years. It is safer to use the following legacy code.

Creating a date group with VBA is a bit quirky. The Group method can be applied to only a single cell in the pivot table, and that cell must contain a date or the Date field label.

In Figure 13-10, you would have to select either the Date heading in cell P2 or one of the dates in cells P3:APM3. Selecting one of these specific cells is risky, particularly if the pivot table later starts being created in a new column. Two other options are more reliable.

First, if you will never use a different number of row fields, then you can assume that the Date heading is in row 1, column 3 of the area known as TableRange2. The following line of code selects this cell:

```
PT.TableRange2.Cells(1, 3).Select
```

You should probably add a comment that you need to edit the 3 in that line to another number any time that you change the number of row fields.

Another solution is to use the LabelRange property for the Date field. The following code always selects the cell containing the Date heading:

```
PT.PivotFields("Date").LabelRange.Select
```

To group the daily dates up to yearly dates, you should define a pivot table with Date in the row field. Turn off ManualUpdate to enable the pivot table to be drawn. You can then use the LabelRange property to locate the date label.

You use the Group method on the date label cell. You specify an array of seven Boolean values for the Periods argument. The seven values correspond to seconds, minutes, hours, days, months, quarters, and years. For example, to group by years, you would use this:

```
PT.PivotFields("Date"),LabelRange.Group _
 Periods:=(False, False, False, False, False, False, True)
```

After you have grouped by years, the field is still called Date. This differs from the results when you group by multiple fields. To group by months, quarters, and years, you would use this:

```
PT.PivotFields("Date"),LabelRange.Group _
 Periods:=(False, False, False, False, True, True, True)
```

After you have grouped up to months, quarters, and years, the Date field starts referring to months. Two new virtual fields are available in the pivot table: Quarters and Years.

To group by weeks, you choose only the Day period and then use the By argument to group into seven-day periods:

```
PT.PivotFields("Date"),LabelRange.Group By:=7_
 Periods:=(False, False, False, True, False, False, False)
```

In Figure 13-10, the goal is to group the daily dates up to years, so the following code is used:

```
PT.PivotFields("Date"),LabelRange.Group _
 Periods:=(False, False, False, False, False, False, True)
```

Figure 13-11 shows the pivot table after grouping daily dates up to years.

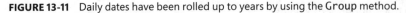

Sum of Rev		Date			
Category ▾	Region ▾	2022	2023	2024	Grand Total
⊟ Bar Equip	West		1,337	67,218	68,555
	Midwest		22,113	41,508	63,621
	North		5,950	14,195	20,145
	Northeast		30,683	37,622	68,305
	South		667,438	523,901	1,191,339
	Southeast		165,241	118,655	283,896
	Southwest		18,652	54,819	73,471
Bar Equipment Total			911,415	857,917	1,769,332
⊟ Commerc	West	9,182	58,739	228,295	296,216
	Midwest	27,017	113,643	58,528	199,188

FIGURE 13-11   Daily dates have been rolled up to years by using the Group method.

Eliminating blank cells

The blank cells in a pivot table are annoying. You will want to fix two kinds of blank cells. Blank cells occur in the Values area when there were no records for a particular combination. For example, in Figure 13-11, the company did not sell bar equipment in 2022, so all of cells P4:P11 are blank. Most people would prefer to have zeros instead of those blank cells.

Blank cells also occur in the Row Labels area when you have multiple row fields. The words Bar Equipment appear in cell N4, but then cells N5:N10 are blank.

To replace blanks in the Values area with zeros, use this:

```
PT.NullString = "0"
```

> **Note**   Although the preceding code appears to use a zero inside of quotation marks, Excel actually puts a numeric zero in the empty cells.

To fill in the blanks in the label area in Excel 2019, use this:

```
PT.RepeatAllLabels xlRepeatLabels
```

The RepeatAllLabels code fails in Excel 2007 and earlier. The only solution in legacy versions of Excel is to convert the pivot table to values and then set the blank cells to a formula that grabs the value from the row above, like this:

```
Dim FillRange As Range
Set PT = ActiveSheet.PivotTables("PivotTable1")
' Locate outer row column
Set FillRange = PT.TableRange1.Resize(, 1)
' Convert entire table to values
PT.TableRange2.Copy
PT.TableRange2.PasteSpecial xlPasteValues
```

```
' Fill Special Cells Blanks with the value from above
FillRange.SpecialCells(xlCellTypeBlanks).FormulaR1C1 = _
  "=R[-1]C"
' Convert those formulas to values
FillRange.Value = FillRange.Value
```

Controlling the sort order with AutoSort

The Excel user interface offers an AutoSort option that enables you to sort a field in descending order based on revenue. The equivalent code in VBA to sort the region and category fields by descending revenue uses the AutoSort method:

```
PT.PivotFields("Region").AutoSort Order:=xlDescending, _
  Field:="Sum of Revenue"
PT.PivotFields("Category").AutoSort Order:=xlDescending, _
  Field:="Sum of Revenue"
```

Changing the default number format

Numbers in the Values area of a pivot table need to have a suitable number format applied. You cannot count on the numeric format of the underlying field carrying over to the pivot table.

To show the Revenue values with zero decimal places and a comma, use this:

```
PT.PivotFields("Sum of Revenue").NumberFormat = "#,##0"
```

Some companies have customers who typically buy thousands or millions of dollars' worth of goods. You can display numbers in thousands by using a single comma after the number format. To do this, you would include a K abbreviation to indicate that the numbers are in thousands:

```
PT.PivotFields("Sum of Revenue").NumberFormat = "#,##0,K"
```

Local custom dictates the thousands abbreviation. If you are working for a relatively young computer company where everyone uses K for the thousands separator, you are in luck because Microsoft makes it easy to use this abbreviation. However, if you work at a more than 100-year-old soap company where you use M for thousands and MM for millions, you have a few more hurdles to jump. You must prefix the M character with a backslash to have it work:

```
PT.PivotFields("Sum of Revenue").NumberFormat = "#,##0,\M"
```

Alternatively, you can surround the M character with double quotation marks. To put double quotation marks inside a quoted string in VBA, you must use two sequential quotation marks. To set up a format in tenths of millions that uses the #,##0.0,,"MM" format, you would use this line of code:

```
PT.PivotFields("Sum of Revenue").NumberFormat = "#,##0.0,,""M"""
```

Here, the format is quotation mark, pound, comma, pound, pound, zero, period, zero, comma, comma, quotation mark, quotation mark, M, quotation mark, quotation mark, quotation mark. The three quotation marks at the end are correct. You use two quotation marks to simulate typing one quotation mark in the custom number format box and a final quotation mark to close the string in VBA.

Figure 13-12 shows the pivot table blanks filled in, numbers shown in thousands, and category and region sorted in descending order.

Sum of Rev	Date			
Category	Region	2022	2023	2024	Grand Total
Ovens ar	South	15,672K	13,796K	8,284K	37,752K
Ovens ar	Southeast	2,639K	2,745K	1,418K	6,802K
Ovens ar	West	519K	1,520K	1,594K	3,634K
Ovens ar	Southwest	572K	1,335K	1,104K	3,012K
Ovens ar	Northeast	662K	1,146K	801K	2,609K
Ovens ar	Midwest	290K	1,379K	760K	2,429K
Ovens ar	North	247K	421K	263K	931K
Ovens and Ranges To		20,602K	22,342K	14,225K	57,169K
Refrigera	South	4,855K	4,659K	12,093K	21,606K

FIGURE 13-12   After filling in blanks and sorting, you have only a few extraneous totals and labels to remove.

Suppressing subtotals for multiple row fields

As soon as you have more than one row field, Excel automatically adds subtotals for all but the innermost row field. That extra row field can get in the way if you plan on reusing the results of the pivot table as a new data set for some other purpose.

In the current example, you have taken 80,000 rows of data and produced a tight 50-row summary of yearly sales by category and region. That new data set would be interesting for sorting, filtering, and charting if you could remove the total row and the category subtotals.

To remove the subtotal, you first set the Subtotals(1) property to True to turn off the other 10 possible subtotals. You can then turn off the first subtotal to make sure that all subtotals are suppressed:

```
PT.PivotFields("Category").Subtotals(1) = True
PT.PivotFields("Category").Subtotals(1) = False
```

To remove the grand total row, use this:

```
PT.ColumnGrand = False
```

Figure 13-13 shows the first section of the pivot table with the subtotals removed.

	N	O	P	Q	R	S
Sum of Rev		Date				
Category	Region	2022	2023	2024	Grand Total	
⊟Ovens ar	South	15,672K	13,796K	8,284K	37,752K	
Ovens ar	Southeast	2,639K	2,745K	1,418K	6,802K	
Ovens ar	West	519K	1,520K	1,594K	3,634K	
Ovens ar	Southwest	572K	1,335K	1,104K	3,012K	
Ovens ar	Northeast	662K	1,146K	801K	2,609K	
Ovens ar	Midwest	290K	1,379K	760K	2,429K	
Ovens ar	North	247K	421K	263K	931K	
⊟Refrigera	South	4,855K	4,659K	12,093K	21,606K	
Refrigera	West	1,957K	348K	3,088K	5,393K	

FIGURE 13-13   Remove the subtotal rows from column A.

Copying a finished pivot table as values to a new workbook

If you plan to repurpose the results of a pivot table, you need to convert the table to values. This section shows you how to copy a pivot table to a brand-new workbook.

To make the code more portable, assign object variables to the original workbook, new workbook, and first worksheet in the new workbook. At the top of the procedure, add these statements:

```
Dim WSR As Worksheet
Dim WSD As Worksheet
Dim WBO As Workbook
Dim WBN As Workbook
Set WBO = ActiveWorkbook
Set WSD = Worksheets("Data")
```

After the pivot table has been successfully created, build a blank report workbook with this code:

```
' Create a New Blank Workbook with one Worksheet
Set WBN = Workbooks.Add(xlWorksheet)
Set WSR = WBN.Worksheets(1)
WSR.Name = "Report"
' Set up Title for Report
With WSR.Range("A1")
 .Value = "Revenue by Category, Region and Year"
 .Style = "Title"
End With
```

There are a few remaining annoyances in the pivot table. The borders are annoying, and there are stray labels such as Sum Of Revenue and Date in the first row of the pivot table. You can solve these problems by excluding the first row(s) of PT.TableRange2 from the Copy method and then using Paste Special(xlPasteValuesAndNumberFormats) to copy the data to the report sheet.

In the current example, the TableRange2 property includes only one row to eliminate, row 2, as shown in Figure 13-13. If you had a more complex pivot table with several column fields and/or one or more page fields, you would have to eliminate more than just the first row of the report. It helps to run your macro to this point, look at the result, and figure out how many rows you need to delete.

You can effectively not copy these rows to the report by using the `Offset` property. Then copy the `TableRange2` property, offset by one row.

Purists will note that this code copies one extra blank row from below the pivot table, but this really does not matter because the row is blank. After copying, you can erase the original pivot table and destroy the pivot cache, like this:

```
' Copy the Pivot Table data to row 3 of the Report sheet
' Use Offset to eliminate the title row of the pivot table
PT.TableRange2.Offset(1, 0).Copy
WSR. Range("A3").PasteSpecial Paste:=xlPasteValuesAndNumberFormats
PT.TableRange1.Clear
Set PTCache = Nothing
```

> **Tip** Note that you use the Paste Special option to paste just values and number formats. This gets rid of both borders and the pivot nature of the table. You might be tempted to use the All Except Borders option under Paste, but that keeps the data in a pivot table, and you will not be able to insert new rows in the middle of the data.

Handling final formatting

The last steps for the report involve some basic formatting tasks and addition of the subtotals. You can bold and right-justify the headings in row 3. Set up rows 1–3 so that the top three rows print on each page:

```
' Do some basic formatting
' Autofit columns, format the headings , right-align
Range("A3").EntireRow.Style = "Heading 4"
Range("A3").CurrentRegion.Columns.AutoFit
Range("A3").EntireRow.HorizontalAlignment = xlRight
Range("A3:B3").HorizontalAlignment = xlLeft
 ' Repeat rows 1-3 at the top of each page
WSR.PageSetup.PrintTitleRows = "$1:$3"
```

Adding subtotals to get page breaks

The Data tab offers a powerful feature: subtotals. Figure 13-14 shows the Subtotal dialog box. Note the option Page Break Between Groups. Rather than looping through records to manually add a page break after each category, you can apply them in one command using the `Subtotal` method.

If you were sure that you would always have three years and a total, you could use the following code to add subtotals for each line of business group:

```
' Add Subtotals by Category.
' Be sure to add a page break at each change in category
Selection.Subtotal GroupBy:=1, Function:=xlSum, _
 TotalList:=Array(3, 4, 5, 6), PageBreaks:=True
```

FIGURE 13-14 Using automatic subtotals enables you to add a page break after each category. Using this feature ensures that each category manager has a clean report with only her data on it.

However, this code fails if you have more or less than three years. The solution is to use the following convoluted code to dynamically build a list of the columns to total, based on the number of columns in the report:

```
Dim TotColumns()
Dim I as Integer
FinalCol = Cells(3, Columns.Count).End(xlToLeft).Column
ReDim Preserve TotColumns(1 To FinalCol - 2)
For i = 3 To FinalCol
 TotColumns(i - 2) = i
Next i
Selection.Subtotal GroupBy:=1, Function:=xlSum, TotalList:=TotColumns,_
 Replace:=True, PageBreaks:=True, SummaryBelowData:=True
```

Finally, with the new totals added to the report, you need to AutoFit the numeric columns again with this code:

```
Dim GrandRow as Long
' Make sure the columns are wide enough for totals
GrandRow = Cells(Rows.Count, 1).End(xlUp).Row
Cells(3, 3).Resize(GrandRow - 2, FinalCol - 2).Columns.AutoFit
Cells(GrandRow, 3).Resize(1, FinalCol - 2).NumberFormat = "#,##0,K"
' Add a page break before the Grand Total row, otherwise
' the manager for the final category will have two totals
WSR.HPageBreaks.Add Before:=Cells(GrandRow, 1)
```

Putting it all together

Listing 13-3 produces the product line manager reports in a few seconds. Figure 13-15 shows the report produced by this code.

LISTING 13-3 Code that produces the category report in Figure 13-15

```
Sub CategoryRegionReport()
' Category and Region as Row
' Years as Column
Dim WSD As Worksheet
Dim PTCache As PivotCache
Dim PT As PivotTable
Dim PRange As Range
Dim FinalRow As Long
Dim TotColumns()

Set WSD = Worksheets("Data")
Dim WSR As Worksheet
Dim WBO As Workbook
Dim WBN As Workbook
Set WBO = ActiveWorkbook

' Delete any prior pivot tables
For Each PT In WSD.PivotTables
PT.TableRange2.Clear
Next PT
WSD.Range("N1:XFD1").EntireColumn.Clear

' Define input area and set up a Pivot Cache
FinalRow = WSD.Cells(Application.Rows.Count, 1).End(xlUp).Row
FinalCol = WSD.Cells(1, Application.Columns.Count). _
End(xlToLeft).Column
Set PRange = WSD.Cells(1, 1).Resize(FinalRow, FinalCol)
Set PTCache = ActiveWorkbook.PivotCaches.Add(SourceType:= _
xlDatabase, SourceData:=PRange.Address)

' Create the Pivot Table from the Pivot Cache
Set PT = PTCache.CreatePivotTable(TableDestination:=WSD. _
Cells(2, FinalCol + 2), TableName:="PivotTable1")

' Turn off updating while building the table
PT.ManualUpdate = True

' Set up the row fields
PT.AddFields RowFields:=Array("Category", _
"Region"), ColumnFields:="Date"

' Set up the data fields
With PT.PivotFields("Revenue")
.Orientation = xlDataField
.Function = xlSum
.Position = 1
.NumberFormat = "#,##0"
```

```
End With

' Ensure tabular layout is used
PT.RowAxisLayout xlTabularRow

' Calc the pivot table before grouping dates
PT.ManualUpdate = False
PT.ManualUpdate = True
PT.PivotFields("Date").LabelRange.Group _
Periods:=Array(False, False, False, False, False, False, True)

' Change number format of Revenue
PT.PivotFields("Sum of Revenue").NumberFormat = "#,##0,K"

' Fill in blank cells
PT.NullString = "0"
PT.RepeatAllLabels xlRepeatLabels

' Sort both label fields by descending revenue
PT.PivotFields("Category").AutoSort Order:=xlDescending, _
field:="Sum of Revenue"
PT.PivotFields("Region").AutoSort Order:=xlDescending, _
field:="Sum of Revenue"

' Suppress Category totals
PT.PivotFields("Category").Subtotals(1) = True
PT.PivotFields("Category").Subtotals(1) = False
PT.ColumnGrand = False

' Calc the pivot table
PT.ManualUpdate = False
PT.ManualUpdate = True

' Create a New Blank Workbook with one Worksheet
Set WBN = Workbooks.Add(xlWBATWorksheet)
Set WSR = WBN.Worksheets(1)
WSR.Name = "Report"
' Set up Title for Report
With WSR.[A1]
.Value = "Revenue by Category & Region"
.Style = "Title"
End With

' Copy the Pivot Table data to row 3 of the Report sheet
' Use Offset to eliminate the title row of the pivot table
PT.TableRange1.Offset(1, 0).Copy
WSR.[A3].PasteSpecial Paste:=xlPasteValuesAndNumberFormats
PT.TableRange2.Clear
Set PTCache = Nothing

' Do some basic formatting
' Autofit columns, bold the headings, right-align
Range("A3").EntireRow.Style = "Heading 4"
Range("A3").CurrentRegion.Columns.AutoFit
```

```vba
Range("A3").EntireRow.HorizontalAlignment = xlRight
Range("A3:B3").HorizontalAlignment = xlLeft

' Repeat rows 1-3 at the top of each page
WSR.PageSetup.PrintTitleRows = "$1:$3"

' Add subtotals
FinalCol = Cells(3, 255).End(xlToLeft).Column
ReDim Preserve TotColumns(1 To FinalCol - 2)
For i = 3 To FinalCol
TotColumns(i - 2) = i
Next i
Range("A3").CurrentRegion.Subtotal GroupBy:=1, Function:=xlSum, _
TotalList:=TotColumns, Replace:=True, _
PageBreaks:=True, SummaryBelowData:=True

' Make sure the columns are wide enough for totals
GrandRow = Cells(Rows.Count, 1).End(xlUp).Row
Cells(3, 3).Resize(GrandRow - 2, FinalCol - 2).Columns.AutoFit
Cells(GrandRow, 3).Resize(1, FinalCol - 2).NumberFormat = "#,##0,K"
' Add a page break before the Grand Total row, otherwise
' the product manager for the final Line will have two totals
WSR.HPageBreaks.Add Before:=Cells(GrandRow, 1)

End Sub
```

1 2 3		A	B	C	D	E	F
	1	Revenue by Category & Region					
	2						
	3	Category	Region	2022	2023	2024	Grand Total
	4	Ovens and Ranges	South	15,672K	13,796K	8,284K	37,752K
	5	Ovens and Ranges	Southeast	2,639K	2,745K	1,418K	6,802K
	6	Ovens and Ranges	West	519K	1,520K	1,594K	3,634K
	7	Ovens and Ranges	Southwest	572K	1,335K	1,104K	3,012K
	8	Ovens and Ranges	Northeast	662K	1,146K	801K	2,609K
	9	Ovens and Ranges	Midwest	290K	1,379K	760K	2,429K
	10	Ovens and Ranges	North	247K	421K	263K	931K
	11	**Ovens and Ranges Total**		20,602K	22,342K	14,225K	57,169K
	12	Refrigerators and Coolers	South	4,855K	4,659K	12,093K	21,606K
	13	Refrigerators and Coolers	West	1,957K	348K	3,088K	5,393K
	14	Refrigerators and Coolers	Southeast	929K	1,311K	2,062K	4,302K
	15	Refrigerators and Coolers	Midwest	882K	544K	1,810K	3,236K
	16	Refrigerators and Coolers	Southwest	1,071K	443K	1,720K	3,233K
	17	Refrigerators and Coolers	Northeast	1,043K	427K	1,591K	3,061K
	18	Refrigerators and Coolers	North	369K	100K	492K	961K
	19	**Refrigerators and Coolers Total**		11,105K	7,833K	22,856K	41,794K
	20	Warmers	South	456K	5,161K	20,044K	25,661K

FIGURE 13-15 Converting 80,000 rows of transactional data to this useful report takes less than two seconds if you use the code that produced this example. Without pivot tables, the code would be far more complex.

You have now seen the VBA code to produce useful summary reports from transactional data. The next section deals with additional features in pivot tables.

Calculating with a pivot table

So far in this chapter, the pivot tables have presented a single field in the Values area, and that field has always shown as a Sum calculation. You can add more fields to the Values area. You can change from Sum to any of 11 functions or alter the Sum calculation to display running totals, percentage of total, and more. You can also add new calculated fields or calculated items to the pivot table.

Addressing issues with two or more data fields

It is possible to have multiple fields in the Values section of a pivot report. For example, you might have Quantity, Revenue, and Cost in the same pivot table.

When you have two or more data fields in an Excel 2019 pivot table that you built in the Excel interface, the value fields go across the columns. However, VBA builds the pivot table with the Values fields going down the innermost row field. This creates a bizarre-looking table like the one shown in Figure 13-16.

	N	O	P
1			
2	State	Data	Total
3	AL	Sum of Revenue	752,789.55
4		Sum of Cost	337,502.00
5		Sum of Quantity	1,890
6	AR	Sum of Revenue	134,244.75
7		Sum of Cost	59,499.00
8		Sum of Quantity	130
9	AZ	Sum of Revenue	3,687,831.25
10		Sum of Cost	1,665,417.00
11		Sum of Quantity	6,950
12	CA	Sum of Revenue	11,322,124.25
13		Sum of Cost	5,108,375.00

FIGURE 13-16 This ugly view was banished in the Excel interface after Excel 2003, but VBA still produces it by default.

To correct this problem, you should specify that a virtual field called Data is one of the column fields.

> **Note** In this instance, note that Data is not a column in your original data; it is a special name used to indicate the orientation of the multiple Values fields.

To have multiple Values fields go across the report, use this code:

```
PT.AddFields RowFields:="State", ColumnFields:="Data"
```

After adding a column field called Data, you then define multiple data fields:

```
' Set up the data fields
With PT.PivotFields("Revenue")
 .Orientation = xlDataField
 .Function = xlSum
 .Position = 1
```

```
 .NumberFormat = "#,##0.00"
End With

With PT.PivotFields("Cost")
 .Orientation = xlDataField
 .Function = xlSum
 .Position = 2
 .NumberFormat = "#,##0.00"
End With

With PT.PivotFields("Quantity")
 .Orientation = xlDataField
 .Function = xlSum
 .Position = 3
 .NumberFormat = "#,##0"
End With
```

This code produces the pivot table shown in Figure 13-17.

	N	O	P	Q
1				
2		Data		
3	State	Sum of Revenue	Sum of Cost	Sum of Quantity
4	AL	752,789.55	337,502.00	1,890
5	AR	134,244.75	59,499.00	130
6	AZ	3,687,831.25	1,665,417.00	6,950
7	CA	11,322,124.25	5,108,375.00	14,585
8	CO	1,280,417.15	580,449.00	1,730
9	FL	65,272,493.30	29,399,753.00	103,763
10	GA	27,955,642.10	12,582,085.00	48,897
11	IA	816,462.00	368,449.00	950

FIGURE 13-17 When you specify the virtual field Data as a column field, multiple values go across the report.

Using calculations other than Sum

So far, all the pivot tables in this chapter have used the Sum function to calculate. There are 11 functions available, including Sum. To specify a different calculation, specify one of these values as the Function property:

- **xlAverage**—Average

- **xlCount**—Count

- **xlCountNums**—Count numeric values only

- **xlMax**—Maximum

- **xlMin**—Minimum

- **xlProduct**—Multiply

- **xlStDev**—Standard deviation, based on a sample

- **xlStDevP**—Standard deviation, based on the whole population

- **xlSum**—Sum

- **xlVar**—Variation, based on a sample

- **xlVarP**—Variation, based on the whole population

Although Count Distinct was added in Excel 2013, you cannot create Count Distinct in a regular pivot-cache pivot table. See "Using the Data Model in Excel 2019" at the end of this chapter.

> **Tip** Note that when you add a field to the Values area of the pivot table, Excel modifies the field name with the function name and the word *of*. For example, "Revenue" becomes "Sum Of Revenue." "Cost" might become "StdDev Of Cost." If you later need to refer to those fields in your code, you need to do so using the new name, such as Average Of Quantity.

You can improve the look of your pivot table by changing the Name property of the field. If you do not want Sum Of Revenue appearing in the pivot table, change the Caption property to something like Total Revenue. This sounds less awkward than Sum Of Revenue. Remember that you cannot have a name that exactly matches an existing field name in the pivot table, so "Revenue" is not suitable as a name. However, "Revenue " (with a trailing space) is fine to use as a name.

For text fields, the only function that makes sense is a count. You will frequently count the number of records by adding a text field to the pivot table and using the Count function.

The following code fragment calculates total revenue, a count of records by counting a text field, and average quantity:

```
With PT.PivotFields("Revenue")
 .Orientation = xlDataField
 .Function = xlSum
 .Position = 1
 .NumberFormat = "$#,##0.00"
 .Name = " Revenue"
End With

With PT.PivotFields("Customer")
 .Orientation = xlDataField
 .Function = xlCount
 .Position = 2
 .NumberFormat = "#,##0"
 .Name = "# of Records"
End With

With PT.PivotFields("Revenue")
 .Orientation = xlDataField
 .Function = xlAverage
 .Position = 3
 .NumberFormat = "#,##0.00"
 .Name = "Average Revenue"
End With
```

```
' Ensure that we get zeros instead of blanks in the data area
PT.NullString = "0"
PT.TableStyle2 = "PivotStyleMedium3"
```

Figure 13-18 shows the pivot table this code creates.

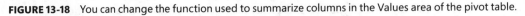

Rep	Data Revenue	# of Records	Average Revenue
Anne Troy	$5,582,120	2,910	1,918.3
Jade Miller	$2,225,244	799	2,785.0
James Tallman	$3,045,306	1,192	2,554.8
Jeffrey P. Coulson	$1,308,212	1,059	1,235.3
John Cockerill	$173,245	182	951.9
John Durran	$331,932	396	838.2
Larry Vance	$575,548	385	1,494.9
Michael Karpfen	$848,890	466	1,821.7
Mike Mann	$282,422	159	1,776.2
Pauline Mccollum	$292,028	262	1,114.6

FIGURE 13-18   You can change the function used to summarize columns in the Values area of the pivot table.

Using calculated data fields

Pivot tables offer two types of formulas. The most useful type defines a formula for a calculated field. This adds a new field to the pivot table. Calculations for calculated fields are always done at the summary level.

To set up a calculated field, use the Add method with the `CalculatedFields` object. You have to specify a field name and a formula, like so:

```
PT.CalculatedFields.Add Name:="GrossProfit", Formula:="=Revenue-Cost"
PT.CalculatedFields.Add "GP_Pct", "=GrossProfit/Revenue"
```

After you define the field, add it as a data field:

```
With PT.PivotFields("GrossProfit")
 .Orientation = xlDataField
 .Function = xlSum
 .Position = 3
 .NumberFormat = "$#,##0"
 .Caption = "Gross Profit"
End With
With PT.PivotFields("GP_Pct")
 .Orientation = xlDataField
 .Function = xlSum
 .Position = 4
 .NumberFormat = "0.0%"
 .Caption = "GP%"
End With
```

Figure 13-19 shows the Gross Profit calculated field.

FIGURE 13-19 A calculated field adds Gross Profit to the pivot table.

A calculated field can be referenced in subsequent calculated fields. The following code uses the Gross Profit field to calculate Gross Profit Percent. Although the Caption property renamed the field to "Gross Profit" (with a space in the middle), the field name in the preceding code is "GrossProfit" (without a space). Use the field name in the following calculation:

```
PT.CalculatedFields.Add "GP_Pct", "=GrossProfit/Revenue", True
With PT.PivotFields("GP_Pct")
 .Orientation = xlDataField
 .Function = xlSum
 .Position = 4
 .NumberFormat = "0.0%"
 .Caption = "GP%"
End With
```

Figure 13-20 shows a report with GP%.

FIGURE 13-20 GP% is based on a field in the data set and another calculated field.

Using calculated items

Calculated items have the potential to produce incorrect results in a pivot table. Say that you have a report of sales by nine states. You want to show a subtotal of four of the states. A calculated item would add a ninth item to the state column. Although the pivot table gladly calculates this new item, it causes the grand total to appear overstated.

Figure 13-21 shows a pivot table with these nine states. The total revenue is $10 million. When a calculated item provides a subtotal of four states (see Figure 13-22), the grand total increases to $15 million. This means that the items that make up the calculated item are included in the total twice. If you like restating numbers to the Securities and Exchange Commission, feel free to use calculated items.

Revenue	
State ▾	Total
Arizona	$550,550
California	$3,165,104
Colorado	$616,097
Louisiana	$814,431
Nevada	$1,170,320
New Mexico	$322,168
Oklahoma	$186,715
Texas	$2,559,021
Utah	$632,897
Grand Total	$10,017,303

FIGURE 13-21 This pivot table adds up to $10 million.

Revenue		
State ▾	Total	
California	$3,165,104	
Nevada	$1,170,320	
Arizona	$550,550	
New Mexico	$322,168	
DesertStates	$5,208,142	← Calculated item
Colorado	$616,097	
Louisiana	$814,431	
Oklahoma	$186,715	
Texas	$2,559,021	
Utah	$632,897	
Grand Total	$15,225,445	← Overstated by $5.2 million

FIGURE 13-22 Add a calculated item, and the total is overstated.

The code to produce the calculated item is shown here. Calculated items are added as the final position along the field, so this code changes the Position property to move the DesertStates item to the proper position:

```
PT.PivotFields("State").CalculatedItems.Add _
 Name:="DesertStates", _
 Formula:="=California +Nevada +Arizona +'New Mexico'"
PT.PivotFields("State").PivotItems("California").Position = 1
PT.PivotFields("State").PivotItems("Nevada").Position = 2
PT.PivotFields("State").PivotItems("Arizona").Position = 3
PT.PivotFields("State").PivotItems("New Mexico").Position = 4
PT.PivotFields("State").PivotItems("DesertStates").Position = 5
```

If you hope to use a calculated item, you should either remove the grand total row or remove the four states that go into the calculated item. This code hides the four states, and the resulting pivot table returns to the correct total, as shown in Figure 13-23:

```
PT.PivotFields("State").CalculatedItems.Add _
 Name:="DesertStates", _
 Formula:="=California +Nevada +Arizona +'New Mexico'"
' Hide the items included in the new subtotal
With PT.PivotFields("State")
 .PivotItems("California").Visible = False
 .PivotItems("Nevada").Visible = False
 .PivotItems("Arizona").Visible = False
 .PivotItems("New Mexico").Visible = False
End With
```

FIGURE 13-23 One way to use a calculated item is to remove any elements that went into it.

A better solution, which is discussed in the next section, is to skip calculated items and use text grouping.

Calculating groups

If you need to calculate subtotals for certain regions, a better solution is to use text grouping to define the groups. If you group the four states, Excel adds a new field to the row area of the pivot table. Although this process requires some special handling, it is worthwhile and creates a nice-looking report.

To group four states in the Excel interface, you select the cells that contain those four states and select Group Selection from the PivotTable Tools Options tab. This immediately does several things:

- The items in the group are moved together in the row area.

- A new field is added to the left of the state field. If the original field was called State, the new field is called State2.

- Annoyingly, the subtotals property for the new State2 field is set to None instead of Automatic.

- A subtotal for the selected items is added with the name of Group1.

- Any items that are not in a group have a new subtotal added to State2 with the state name repeated.

In VBA, it is somewhat tricky to select the cells that contain the proper states. The following code uses the LabelRange property to point to the cells and then uses the Union method to refer to the four noncontiguous cells:

```
Set R1 = PT.PivotFields("State").PivotItems("California").LabelRange
Set R2 = PT.PivotFields("State").PivotItems("Arizona").LabelRange
Set R3 = PT.PivotFields("State").PivotItems("New Mexico").LabelRange
Set R4 = PT.PivotFields("State").PivotItems("Nevada").LabelRange
Union(R1, R2, R3, R4).Group
```

After setting up the first group, rename the newly created States2 field to have a suitable name:

```
PT.PivotFields("State2").Caption = "State Group"
```

Then change the name of this region from Group1 to the desired group name:

```
PT.PivotFields("State Group").PivotItems("Group1").Caption = "Desert States"
```

Change the Subtotals property from None to Automatic:

```
PT.PivotFields("State Group").Subtotals(1) = True
```

After you have set up the first group, you can define the remaining groups with this code:

```
Set R1 = PT.PivotFields("State").PivotItems("Utah").LabelRange
Set R2 = PT.PivotFields("State").PivotItems("Colorado").LabelRange
Union(R1, R2).Group
PT.PivotFields("State Group").PivotItems("Group2").Caption = "Rockies"

Set R1 = PT.PivotFields("State").PivotItems("Texas").LabelRange
Set R2 = PT.PivotFields("State").PivotItems("Louisiana").LabelRange
Set R3 = PT.PivotFields("State").PivotItems("Oklahoma").LabelRange
Union(R1, R2, R3).Group
PT.PivotFields("State Group").PivotItems("Group3").Caption = "Oil States"
```

The result is a pivot table with new virtual groups, as shown in Figure 13-24.

Revenue		
State Group ▼	State ▼	Total
⊟ Desert State	Arizona	$550,550
	California	$3,165,104
	Nevada	$1,170,320
	New Mexico	$322,168
Desert States Total		$5,208,142
⊟ Rockies	Colorado	$616,097
	Utah	$632,897
Rockies Total		$1,248,994
⊟ Oil States	Louisiana	$814,431
	Oklahoma	$186,715
	Texas	$2,559,021
Oil States Total		$3,560,167
Grand Total		$10,017,303

FIGURE 13-24 Grouping text fields allows for reporting by territories that are not in the original data.

Using Show Values As to perform other calculations

The Show Values As tab in the Value Field Settings dialog box offers 15 different calculations. These calculations enable you to change from numbers to percentage of total, running totals, ranks, and more.

You change the calculation by using the Calculation option for the pivot field.

> **Note** The Calculation property works with the BaseField and BaseItem properties. Depending on the selected calculation, you might be required to specify a base field and base item, or sometimes only a base field, or sometimes neither of them.

Some calculations, such as % of Column and % of Row, need no further definition; you do not have to specify a base field. Here is code that shows revenue as a percentage of total revenue:

```
With PT.PivotFields("Revenue")
  .Orientation = xlDataField
```

```
 .Function = xlSum
 .Calculation = xlPercentOfTotal
 .Position = 2
 .NumberFormat = "0.0%"
 .Name = "% of Total"
End With
```

Other calculations need a base field. If you are showing revenue and ask for the descending rank, you can specify that the base field is the State field. In this case, you are asking for this state's rank based on revenue:

```
With PT.PivotFields("Revenue")
 .Orientation = xlDataField
 .Calculation = xlRankDescending
 .BaseField = "State"
 .Position = 3
 .NumberFormat = "0%"
 .Name = "RankD"
End With
```

A few calculations require both a base field and a base item. If you want to show every state's revenue as a percentage of California revenue, you have to specify % Of as the calculation, State as the base field, and California as the base item:

```
With PT.PivotFields("Revenue")
 .Orientation = xlDataField
 .Calculation = xlPercentOf
 .BaseField = "State"
 .BaseItem = "California"
 .Position = 4
 .NumberFormat = "0%"
 .Name = "% of CA"
End With
```

Some of the calculation fields were new in Excel 2010. In Figure 13-25, column I uses the new % of Parent calculation and column H uses the old % of Total calculation. In both columns, Desert States is 52% of the Grand Total (cells H8 and I8). However, cell I5 shows that California is 60.8% of Desert States, whereas cell H5 shows that California is 31.6% of the grand total.

Notice that the Rank field is specified to use State as a base field. The states are ranked within each State Group. There does not appear to be a way to have the states ranked overall unless you remove the State Group column from the pivot table.

Table 13-1 shows the complete list of Calculation options. The second column indicates whether the calculations are compatible with previous versions of Excel. The third column indicates whether you need a base field and base item.

FIGURE 13-25 % of Parent in column I was new in Excel 2010.

TABLE 13-1 Calculation options available in Excel 2019 VBA

Calculation	Version	Base Field/Base Item?
xlDifferenceFrom	All	Both required
xlIndex	All	Neither
xlNoAdditionalCalculation	All	Neither
xlPercentDifferenceFrom	All	Both required
xlPercentOf	All	Both required
xlPercentOfColumn	All	Neither
xlPercentOfParent	2010 and later	Base field only
xlPercentOfParentColumn	2010 and later	Both required
xlPercentOfParentRow	2010 and later	Both required
xlPercentOfRow	All	Neither
xlPercentOfTotal	All	Neither
xlPercentRunningTotal	2010 and later	Base field only
xlRankAscending	2010 and later	Base field only
xlRankDescending	2010 and later	Base field only
xlRunningTotal	All	Base field only

Using advanced pivot table techniques

Even if you are a pivot table pro, you might never have run into some of the really advanced techniques available with pivot tables. The following sections discuss such techniques.

Using AutoShow to produce executive overviews

If you are designing an executive dashboard utility, you might want to spotlight the top five markets. This setting lets you select either the top or bottom *n* records, based on any data field in the report.

The code to use AutoShow in VBA uses the AutoShow method:

```
' Show only the top 5 Markets
PT.PivotFields("Market").AutoShow Top:=xlAutomatic, Range:=xlTop, _
 Count:=5, Field:= "Sum of Revenue"
```

When you create a report using the AutoShow method, it is often helpful to copy the data and then go back to the original pivot report to get the totals for all markets. In the code in Listing 13-4, this is achieved by removing the Market field from the pivot table and copying the grand total to the report. The code in Listing 13-4 produces the report shown in Figure 13-26.

	A	B	C
1	Top 5 Markets		
2			
3	Market	Bar Equipment	Commercial Appliances
4	Florida	1,131,779	5,667,799
5	Charlotte	283,676	1,525,742
6	California	66,233	294,080
7	Dallas	59,560	255,146
8	Buffalo	37,366	237,298
9	Top 5 Total	1,578,614	7,980,064
10			
11	Total Company	1,769,332	8,562,837
12			

FIGURE 13-26 The Top 5 Markets report contains two pivot tables.

LISTING 13-4 Code used to create the Top 5 Markets report

```
Sub Top5Markets()
 ' Produce a report of the top 5 markets
 Dim WSD As Worksheet
 Dim WSR As Worksheet
 Dim WBN As Workbook
 Dim PTCache As PivotCache
 Dim PT As PivotTable
 Dim PRange As Range
 Dim FinalRow As Long
 Set WSD = Worksheets("Data")

 ' Delete any prior pivot tables
```

```
For Each PT In WSD.PivotTables
PT.TableRange2.Clear
Next PT
WSD.Range("M1:Z1").EntireColumn.Clear

' Define input area and set up a Pivot Cache
FinalRow = WSD.Cells(Application.Rows.Count, 1).End(xlUp).Row
FinalCol = WSD.Cells(1, Application.Columns.Count). _
End(xlToLeft).Column
Set PRange = WSD.Cells(1, 1).Resize(FinalRow, FinalCol)
Set PTCache = ActiveWorkbook.PivotCaches.Add(SourceType:= _
xlDatabase, SourceData:=PRange.Address)

' Create the Pivot Table from the Pivot Cache
Set PT = PTCache.CreatePivotTable(TableDestination:=WSD. _
Cells(2, FinalCol + 2), TableName:="PivotTable1")

' Turn off updating while building the table
PT.ManualUpdate = True

' Set up the row fields
PT.AddFields RowFields:="Market", ColumnFields:="Category"

' Set up the data fields
With PT.PivotFields("Revenue")
.Orientation = xlDataField
.Function = xlSum
.Position = 1
.NumberFormat = "#,##0"
.Name = "Total Revenue"
End With

' Ensure that we get zeros instead of blanks in the data area
PT.NullString = "0"

' Sort markets descending by sum of revenue
PT.PivotFields("Market").AutoSort Order:=xlDescending, _
field:="Total Revenue"

' Show only the top 5 markets
PT.PivotFields("Market").AutoShow Type:=xlAutomatic, Range:=xlTop, _
Count:=5, field:="Total Revenue"

' Calc the pivot table to allow the date label to be drawn
PT.ManualUpdate = False
PT.ManualUpdate = True

' Create a new blank workbook with one worksheet
Set WBN = Workbooks.Add(xlWBATWorksheet)
Set WSR = WBN.Worksheets(1)
WSR.Name = "Report"
' Set up title for report
With WSR.[A1]
.Value = "Top 5 Markets"
```

```
.Font.Size = 14
End With


' Copy the pivot table data to row 3 of the report sheet
' Use offset to eliminate the title row of the pivot table
PT.TableRange2.Offset(1, 0).Copy
WSR.[A3].PasteSpecial Paste:=xlPasteValuesAndNumberFormats
LastRow = WSR.Cells(Rows.Count, 1).End(xlUp).Row
WSR.Cells(LastRow, 1).Value = "Top 5 Total"

' Go back to the pivot table to get totals without the AutoShow
PT.PivotFields("Market").Orientation = xlHidden
PT.ManualUpdate = False
PT.ManualUpdate = True
PT.TableRange2.Offset(2, 0).Copy
WSR.Cells(LastRow + 2, 1).PasteSpecial _
Paste:=xlPasteValuesAndNumberFormats

' Clear the pivot table
PT.TableRange2.Clear
Set PTCache = Nothing

' Do some basic formatting
' Autofit columns, bold the headings, right-align
WSR.Range(WSR.Range("A3"), WSR.Cells(LastRow + 2, 9)).Columns.AutoFit
Range("A3").EntireRow.Font.Bold = True
Range("A3").EntireRow.HorizontalAlignment = xlRight
Range("A3").HorizontalAlignment = xlLeft

Range("A2").Select
MsgBox "CEO Report has been Created"
```

End Sub

The Top 5 Markets report actually contains two snapshots of a pivot table. After using the AutoShow feature to grab the top five markets with their totals, the macro goes back to the pivot table, removes the AutoShow option, and grabs the total of all markets to produce the Total Company row.

Using ShowDetail to filter a Recordset

Open any pivot table in the Excel user interface. Double-click any number in the pivot table. Excel inserts a new sheet in the workbook and copies all the source records that represent that number. In the Excel user interface, this is a great way to perform a drill-down query into a data set.

The equivalent VBA property is ShowDetail. By setting this property to True for any cell in a pivot table, you generate a new worksheet with all the records that make up that cell:

```
PT.TableRange1.Offset(2, 1).Resize(1, 1).ShowDetail = True
```

Listing 13-5 produces a pivot table with the total revenue for the top three stores and `ShowDetail` for each of those stores. This is an alternative method to using the Advanced Filter report. The results of this macro are three new sheets. Figure 13-27 shows the first sheet created.

	A	B	C	D	E	F	G
1	Detail for SUASHU Corp. (Store Rank: 1)						
2							
3	Region	Market	State	Customer	Rep	Date	Internet Order
4	South	Florida	GA	SUASHU Corp.	Tory Hanlon	12/30/2019	Yes
5	South	Florida	GA	SUASHU Corp.	Tory Hanlon	12/30/2019	Yes
6	South	Florida	GA	SUASHU Corp.	Tory Hanlon	12/30/2019	Yes
7	South	Florida	GA	SUASHU Corp.	Tory Hanlon	12/30/2019	Yes

FIGURE 13-27 Pivot table applications are incredibly diverse. This macro created a pivot table of the top three stores and then used the `ShowDetail` property to retrieve the records for each of those stores.

LISTING 13-5 Code used to create a report for each of the top three customers

```
Sub RetrieveTop3CustomerDetail()
 ' Retrieve Details from Top 3 Customers
 Dim WSD As Worksheet
 Dim WSR As Worksheet
 Dim WBN As Workbook
 Dim PTCache As PivotCache
 Dim PT As PivotTable
 Dim PRange As Range
 Dim FinalRow As Long
 Set WSD = Worksheets("Data")

 ' Delete any prior pivot tables
 For Each PT In WSD.PivotTables
 PT.TableRange2.Clear
 Next PT
 WSD.Range("M1:Z1").EntireColumn.Clear

 ' Define input area and set up a Pivot Cache
 FinalRow = WSD.Cells(Application.Rows.Count, 1).End(xlUp).Row
 FinalCol = WSD.Cells(1, Application.Columns.Count). _
 End(xlToLeft).Column
 Set PRange = WSD.Cells(1, 1).Resize(FinalRow, FinalCol)
 Set PTCache = ActiveWorkbook.PivotCaches.Add(SourceType:= _
 xlDatabase, SourceData:=PRange.Address)

 ' Create the Pivot Table from the Pivot Cache
 Set PT = PTCache.CreatePivotTable(TableDestination:=WSD. _
 Cells(2, FinalCol + 2), TableName:="PivotTable1")

 ' Turn off updating while building the table
 PT.ManualUpdate = True

 ' Set up the row fields
 PT.AddFields RowFields:="Customer", ColumnFields:="Data"

 ' Set up the data fields
 With PT.PivotFields("Revenue")
 .Orientation = xlDataField
```

```
.Function = xlSum
.Position = 1
.NumberFormat = "#,##0"
.Name = "Total Revenue"
End With

' Sort Stores descending by sum of revenue
PT.PivotFields("Customer").AutoSort Order:=xlDescending, _
field:="Total Revenue"

' Show only the top 3 stores
PT.PivotFields("Customer").AutoShow Type:=xlAutomatic, Range:=xlTop, _
Count:=3, field:="Total Revenue"

' Ensure that we get zeros instead of blanks in the data area
PT.NullString = "0"

' Calc the pivot table to allow the date label to be drawn
PT.ManualUpdate = False
PT.ManualUpdate = True

' Produce summary reports for each customer
For i = 1 To 3
PT.TableRange2.Offset(i + 1, 1).Resize(1, 1).ShowDetail = True
' The active sheet has changed to the new detail report
' Add a title
Range("A1:A2").EntireRow.Insert
Range("A1").Value = "Detail for " & _
PT.TableRange2.Offset(i + 1, 0).Resize(1, 1).Value & _
" (Store Rank: " & i & ")"
Next i

MsgBox "Detail reports for top 3 stores have been created."

End Sub
```

Creating reports for each region or model

A pivot table can have one or more filter fields. A filter field goes in a separate set of rows above the pivot report. It can serve to filter the report to a certain region, certain model, or certain combination of region and model. In VBA, filter fields are called *page fields*.

You might create a pivot table with several filter fields to allow someone to do ad-hoc analyses. However, it is more likely that you will use the filter fields in order to produce reports for each region.

To set up a filter in VBA, add the PageFields parameter to the AddFields method. The following line of code creates a pivot table with Region in the Filters area:

```
PT.AddFields RowFields:= "Product", ColumnFields:= "Data", PageFields:= "Region"
```

The preceding line of code sets up the Region filter with the value (All), which returns all regions. To limit the report to just the North region, use the `CurrentPage` property:

```
PT.PivotFields("Region").CurrentPage = "North"
```

One use of a filter is to build a user form in which someone can select a particular region or particular product. You then use this information to set the `CurrentPage` property and display the results of the user form.

One amazing trick is to use the Show Pages feature to replicate a pivot table for every item in one filter field drop-down menu. After creating and formatting a pivot table, you can run this single line of code. If you have eight regions in the data set, eight new worksheets are inserted in the workbook, one for each region. The pivot table appears on each worksheet, with the appropriate region chosen from the drop-down menu:

```
PT.ShowPages PageField:=Region
```

> **Caution** Be careful with `ShowPages`. If you use `ShowPages` on the Customer field and you have 1,000 customers, Excel attempts to insert 1,000 worksheets in the workbook, each with a pivot table. All of those pivot tables share the same pivot cache in order to minimize memory usage. However, you will eventually run out of memory, and the program will end with a debug error when no additional worksheets will fit in available memory.
>
> The other problem with `ShowPages` is that it creates the individual reports as worksheets in a single workbook. In real life, you probably want separate workbooks for each region so that you can email the reports to the appropriate office. You can loop through all `PivotItems` and display them one at a time in the page field. You can quickly produce top 10 reports for each region using this method.

To determine how many regions are available in the data, use `PT.PivotFields("Region").Pivot-Items.Count`. Either of these loops would work:

```
For i = 1 To PT.PivotFields("Region").PivotItems.Count
 PT.PivotFields("Region").CurrentPage = _
 PT.PivotFields("Region").PivotItems(i).Name
 PT.ManualUpdate = False
 PT.ManualUpdate = True
Next i

For Each PivItem In PT.PivotFields("Region").PivotItems
 PT.PivotFields("Region").CurrentPage = PivItem.Name
 PT.ManualUpdate = False
 PT.ManualUpdate = True
Next PivItem
```

Of course, in both of these loops, the three region reports fly by too quickly to see. In practice, you would want to save each report while it is displayed.

So far in this chapter, you have been using PT.TableRange2 when copying the data from the pivot table. The TableRange2 property includes all rows of the pivot table, including the page fields.

There is also a TableRange1 property, which excludes the page fields. You can use either of these statements to get the detail rows:

```
PT.TableRange2.Offset(3, 0)
PT.TableRange1.Offset(1, 0)
```

> **Caution**   Which statement you use is your preference, but if you use TableRange2, you will not have problems when you try to delete the pivot table with PT.TableRange2.Clear. If you were to accidentally attempt to clear TableRange1 when there are page fields, you would end up with the dreaded "Cannot move or change part of a pivot table" error.

Listing 13-6 produces a new workbook for each region, as shown in Figure 13-28.

FIGURE 13-28   By looping through all items found in the Region page field, the macro produced one worksheet for each regional manager.

LISTING 13-6   Code that creates a new worksheet for each region

```
Sub Top5ByRegionReport()
' Produce a report of top 5 customers for each region
Dim WSD As Worksheet
Dim WSR As Worksheet
Dim WBN As Workbook
Dim PTCache As PivotCache
```

```
Dim PT As PivotTable
Dim PRange As Range
Dim FinalRow As Long

Set WSD = Worksheets("Data")

' Delete any prior pivot tables
For Each PT In WSD.PivotTables
PT.TableRange2.Clear
Next PT
WSD.Range("M1:Z1").EntireColumn.Clear

' Define input area and set up a Pivot Cache
FinalRow = WSD.Cells(Application.Rows.Count, 1).End(xlUp).Row
FinalCol = WSD.Cells(1, Application.Columns.Count). _
End(xlToLeft).Column
Set PRange = WSD.Cells(1, 1).Resize(FinalRow, FinalCol)
Set PTCache = ActiveWorkbook.PivotCaches.Add(SourceType:= _
xlDatabase, SourceData:=PRange.Address)

' Create the Pivot Table from the Pivot Cache
Set PT = PTCache.CreatePivotTable(TableDestination:=WSD. _
Cells(2, FinalCol + 2), TableName:="PivotTable1")

' Turn off updating while building the table
PT.ManualUpdate = True

' Set up the row fields
PT.AddFields RowFields:="Customer", ColumnFields:="Data", _
PageFields:="Region"

' Set up the data fields
With PT.PivotFields("Revenue")
.Orientation = xlDataField
.Function = xlSum
.Position = 1
.NumberFormat = "#,##0,K"
.Name = "Total Revenue"
End With

' Sort stores descending by sum of revenue
PT.PivotFields("Customer").AutoSort Order:=xlDescending, _
field:="Total Revenue"

' Show only the top 5 stores
PT.PivotFields("Customer").AutoShow Type:=xlAutomatic, Range:=xlTop, _
Count:=5, field:="Total Revenue"

' Ensure that we get zeros instead of blanks in the data area
PT.NullString = "0"

' Calc the pivot table
PT.ManualUpdate = False
PT.ManualUpdate = True
```

```
Ctr = 0

' Loop through each region
For Each PivItem In PT.PivotFields("Region").PivotItems
Ctr = Ctr + 1
PT.PivotFields("Region").CurrentPage = PivItem.Name
PT.ManualUpdate = False
PT.ManualUpdate = True

' Create a new blank workbook with one worksheet
Set WBN = Workbooks.Add(xlWBATWorksheet)
Set WSR = WBN.Worksheets(1)
WSR.Name = PivItem.Name
' Set up Title for Report
With WSR.[A1]
.Value = "Top 5 Customers in the " & _
PivItem.Name & " Region"
End With

' Copy the pivot table data to row 3 of the report sheet
' Use offset to drop the page & title rows
PT.TableRange2.Offset(3, 0).Copy
WSR.[A3].PasteSpecial Paste:=xlPasteValuesAndNumberFormats
LastRow = WSR.Cells(65536, 1).End(xlUp).Row
WSR.Cells(LastRow, 1).Value = "Top 5 Total"

' Do some basic formatting
' Autofit columns, bold the headings, right-align
WSR.Range(WSR.Range("A2"), WSR.Cells(LastRow, 3)) _
.Columns.AutoFit
Range("A3").EntireRow.Font.Bold = True
Range("A3").EntireRow.HorizontalAlignment = xlRight
Range("A3").HorizontalAlignment = xlLeft
Range("B3").Value = "Revenue"

Range("A2").Select

Next PivItem

' Clear the pivot table
PT.TableRange2.Clear
Set PTCache = Nothing

MsgBox Ctr & " Region reports have been created"

End Sub
```

Manually filtering two or more items in a pivot field

In addition to setting up a calculated pivot item to display the total of a couple products that make up a dimension, you can manually filter a particular pivot field.

For example, say that you have one client who sells shoes. In the report showing sales of sandals, he wants to see just the stores that are in warm-weather states. This is the code to hide a particular store:

```
PT.PivotFields("Store").PivotItems("Minneapolis").Visible = False
```

> **Caution** You must be very careful never to set all items to `False` because doing so causes the macro to end with an error. This tends to happen more than you would expect. An application may first show products A and B and then on the next loop show products C and D. If you attempt to make A and B not visible before making C and D visible, no products will be visible along the pivot field, which causes an error. To correct this, always loop through all pivot items and make sure to turn them back to visible before the second pass through the loop.

This process is easy in VBA. After building the table with `Product` in the page field, loop through to change the `Visible` property to show only the total of certain products:

```
' Make sure all PivotItems along line are visible
For Each PivItem In _
 PT.PivotFields("Product").PivotItems
 PivItem.Visible = True
Next PivItem

' Now - loop through and keep only certain items visible
For Each PivItem In _
 PT.PivotFields("Product").PivotItems
 Select Case PivItem.Name
 Case "Landscaping/Grounds Care", _
 "Green Plants and Foliage Care"
 PivItem.Visible = True
 Case Else
 PivItem.Visible = False
 End Select
Next PivItem
```

Using the conceptual filters

Beginning with Excel 2007, conceptual filters for date fields, numeric fields, and text fields are provided. In the PivotTable Fields list, hover the mouse cursor over any active field in the field list portion of the pane. In the drop-down menu that appears, you can choose Label Filters, Date Filters, or Value Filters.

To apply a label filter in VBA, use the `PivotFilters.Add` method. The following code filters to the customers that start with 1:

```
PT.PivotFields("Customer").PivotFilters.Add _
 Type:=xlCaptionBeginsWith, Value1:="1"
```

To clear the filter from the Customer field, use the `ClearAllFilters` method:

```
PT.PivotFields("Customer").ClearAllFilters
```

To apply a date filter to the date field to find records from this week, use this code:

```
PT.PivotFields("Date").PivotFilters.Add Type:=xlThisWeek
```

A value filter allows you to filter one field based on the value of another field. For example, to find all the markets where the total revenue is more than $100,000, you would use this code:

```
PT.PivotFields("Market").PivotFilters.Add _
 Type:=xlValueIsGreaterThan, _
 DataField:=PT.PivotFields("Sum of Revenue"), _
 Value1:=100000
```

Other value filters might allow you to specify that you want branches where the revenue is between $50,000 and $100,000. In this case, you would specify one limit as `Value1` and the second limit as `Value2`:

```
PT.PivotFields("Market").PivotFilters.Add _
 Type:=xlValueIsBetween, _
 DataField:=PT.PivotFields("Sum of Revenue"), _
 Value1:=50000, Value2:=100000
```

Table 13-2 lists all the possible filter types.

TABLE 13-2 Filter types in VBA

Filter Type	Description
xlBefore	Filters for all dates before a specified date.
xlBeforeOrEqualTo	Filters for all dates on or before a specified date.
xlAfter	Filters for all dates after a specified date.
xlAfterOrEqualTo	Filters for all dates on or after a specified date.
xlAllDatesInPeriodJanuary	Filters for all dates in January.
xlAllDatesInPeriodFebruary	Filters for all dates in February.
xlAllDatesInPeriodMarch	Filters for all dates in March.
xlAllDatesInPeriodApril	Filters for all dates in April.
xlAllDatesInPeriodMay	Filters for all dates in May.
xlAllDatesInPeriodJune	Filters for all dates in June.
xlAllDatesInPeriodJuly	Filters for all dates in July.
xlAllDatesInPeriodAugust	Filters for all dates in August.
xlAllDatesInPeriodSeptember	Filters for all dates in September.
xlAllDatesInPeriodOctober	Filters for all dates in October.
xlAllDatesInPeriodNovember	Filters for all dates in November.

xlAllDatesInPeriodDecember	Filters for all dates in December.
xlAllDatesInPeriodQuarter1	Filters for all dates in Quarter 1.
xlAllDatesInPeriodQuarter2	Filters for all dates in Quarter 2.
xlAllDatesInPeriodQuarter3	Filters for all dates in Quarter 3.
xlAllDatesInPeriodQuarter4	Filters for all dates in Quarter 4.
xlBottomCount	Filters for the specified number of values from the bottom of a list.
xlBottomPercent	Filters for the specified percentage of values from the bottom of a list.
xlBottomSum	Sums the values from the bottom of the list.
xlCaptionBeginsWith	Filters for all captions beginning with the specified string.
xlCaptionContains	Filters for all captions that contain the specified string.
xlCaptionDoesNotBeginWith	Filters for all captions that do not begin with the specified string.
xlCaptionDoesNotContain	Filters for all captions that do not contain the specified string.
xlCaptionDoesNotEndWith	Filters for all captions that do not end with the specified string.
xlCaptionDoesNotEqual	Filters for all captions that do not match the specified string.
xlCaptionEndsWith	Filters for all captions that end with the specified string.
xlCaptionEquals	Filters for all captions that match the specified string.
xlCaptionIsBetween	Filters for all captions that are between a specified range of values.
xlCaptionIsGreaterThan	Filters for all captions that are greater than the specified value.
xlCaptionIsGreaterThanOrEqualTo	Filters for all captions that are greater than or match the specified value.
xlCaptionIsLessThan	Filters for all captions that are less than the specified value.
xlCaptionIsLessThanOrEqualTo	Filters for all captions that are less than or match the specified value.
xlCaptionIsNotBetween	Filters for all captions that are not between a specified range of values.
xlDateBetween	Filters for all dates that are between a specified range of dates.
xlDateLastMonth	Filters for all dates that apply to the previous month.
xlDateLastQuarter	Filters for all dates that apply to the previous quarter.
xlDateLastWeek	Filters for all dates that apply to the previous week.
xlDateLastYear	Filters for all dates that apply to the previous year.
xlDateNextMonth	Filters for all dates that apply to the next month.
xlDateNextQuarter	Filters for all dates that apply to the next quarter.
xlDateNextWeek	Filters for all dates that apply to the next week.
xlDateNextYear	Filters for all dates that apply to the next year.
xlDateThisMonth	Filters for all dates that apply to the current month.
xlDateThisQuarter	Filters for all dates that apply to the current quarter.
xlDateThisWeek	Filters for all dates that apply to the current week.
xlDateThisYear	Filters for all dates that apply to the current year.

xlDateToday	Filters for all dates that apply to the current date.
xlDateTomorrow	Filters for all dates that apply to the next day.
xlDateYesterday	Filters for all dates that apply to the previous day.
xlNotSpecificDate	Filters for all dates that do not match a specified date.
xlSpecificDate	Filters for all dates that match a specified date.
xlTopCount	Filters for the specified number of values from the top of a list.
xlTopPercent	Sums the values from the top of the list.
xlTopSum	Filters for all values that do not match the specified value.
xlValueDoesNotEqual	Filters for all values that do not match the specified value.
xlValueEquals	Filters for all values that match the specified value.
xlValueIsBetween	Filters for all values that are between a specified range of values.
xlValueIsGreaterThan	Filters for all values that are greater than the specified value.
xlValueIsGreaterThanOrEqualTo	Filters for all values that are greater than or match the specified value.
xlValueIsLessThan	Filters for all values that are less than the specified value.
xlValueIsLessThanOrEqualTo	Filters for all values that are less than or match the specified value.
xlValueIsNotBetween	Filters for all values that are not between a specified range of values.
xlYearToDate	Filters for all values that are within one year of a specified date.

Using the search filter

Excel 2010 added a search box to the filter drop-down menu. Although this is a slick feature in the Excel interface, there is no equivalent magic in VBA. Figure 13-29 shows the (Select All Search Results) check box selected after the search for "be." Using the macro recorder during this process creates a 5,876-line macro that goes through and turns all customers without "be" to invisible:

```
With ActiveSheet.PivotTables("PivotTable3").PivotFields("Customer")
 .PivotItems("ACASCO Corp.").Visible = False
 .PivotItems("ACECUL Corp.").Visible = False
 .PivotItems("ACEHUA Corp.").Visible = False
' snipped 5870_ similar lines
 .PivotItems("ZUQHYR Corp.").Visible = False
 .PivotItems("ZUSOEA Corp.").Visible = False
 .PivotItems("ZYLSTR Corp.").Visible = False
End With
```

There is nothing new in Excel 2019 VBA to emulate the search box. To achieve the same results in VBA, you use the xlCaptionContains filter described in Table 13-2.

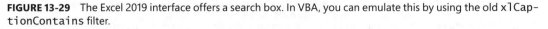

FIGURE 13-29 The Excel 2019 interface offers a search box. In VBA, you can emulate this by using the old `xlCaptionContains` filter.

Setting up slicers to filter a pivot table

Excel 2010 introduced the concept of slicers for filtering pivot tables. A slicer is a visual filter. You can resize and reposition slicers. You can control the color of the slicer and control the number of columns in a slicer. You can also select or clear items from a slicer by using VBA.

Figure 13-30 shows a pivot table with two slicers. The State slicer has been modified to have five columns. The slicer with the caption "Territory" is actually based on the Region field. You can give slicers friendlier captions, which might be helpful when the underlying field is called IDKTxtReg or some other bizarre name invented by the IT department.

FIGURE 13-30 Slicers provide a visual filter for State and Region.

A slicer is composed of `SlicerCache` and `Slicer`. To define a slicer cache, you need to specify a pivot table as the source and a field name as `SourceField`. `SlicerCache` is defined at the workbook level. This enables you to have the slicer on a different worksheet than the actual pivot table. Here's the code to do all this:

```
Dim SCS as SlicerCache
Dim SCR as SlicerCache
Set SCS = ActiveWorkbook.SlicerCaches.Add(Source:=PT, SourceField:="State")
Set SCR = ActiveWorkbook.SlicerCaches.Add(Source:=PT, SourceField:="Region")
```

After you have defined `SlicerCache`, you can add `Slicer`, which is defined as an object of the slicer cache. Specify a worksheet as the destination. The `Name` argument controls the internal name for the slicer. The `Caption` argument is the heading that will be visible in the slicer. Specify the size of the slicer using height and width in points. Specify the location using top and left in points. In the following code, the values for top, left, height, and width are assigned to be equal to the location or size of certain cell ranges:

```
Dim SLS as Slicer
Set SLS = SCS.Slicers.Add(SlicerDestination:=WSD, Name:="State", _
 Caption:="State", _
 Top:=WSD.Range("O2").Top, _
 Left:=WSD.Range("O2").Left, _
 Width:=WSR.Range("O2:U2").Width, _
 Height:=WSD.Range("O2:O17").Height)
' Format the color and number of columns
```

Every slicer starts out as one column. You can change the style and number of columns with this code:

```
With SLS
 .Style = "SlicerStyleLight6"
 .NumberOfColumns = 5
End With
```

> **Note** I find that when I create slicers in the Excel interface, I spend many mouse clicks making adjustments to them. After adding two or three slicers, Excel positions them in an overlapping tile arrangement. I always tweak the location, size, number of columns, and so on. For many years in my seminars, I bragged that I could create a pivot table in six mouse clicks. That was before slicers were introduced. Slicers are admittedly powerful, but they seem to take 20 mouse clicks before they look right. Having a macro make all of these adjustments at once is a timesaver.

After a slicer is defined, you can use VBA to choose which items are activated in the slicer. It seems counterintuitive, but to choose items in the slicer, you have to change `SlicerItem`, which is a member of `SlicerCache`, not a member of `Slicer`:

```
With SCR
 .SlicerItems("Midwest").Selected = True
 .SlicerItems("North").Selected = True
```

```
 .SlicerItems("Northeast").Selected = True
 .SlicerItems("South").Selected = False
 .SlicerItems("Southeast").Selected = False
 .SlicerItems("Southwest").Selected = False
 .SlicerItems("West").Selected = False
End With
```

You might need to deal with slicers that already exist. If a slicer is created for the State field, the slicer cache is named "Slicer_State". The following code is used to format the slicers shown in Figure 13-30:

```
Sub MoveAndFormatSlicer()
 Dim SCS As SlicerCache
 Dim SLS As Slicer
 Dim SCR As SlicerCache
 Dim SLR As Slicer
 Dim WSD As Worksheet
 Set WSD = ActiveSheet

 Set SCS = ActiveWorkbook.SlicerCaches("Slicer_State")
 Set SLS = SCS.Slicers("State")
 With SLS
 .Style = "SlicerStyleLight6"
 .NumberOfColumns = 5
 .Top = WSD.Range("A1").Top + 5
 .Left = WSD.Range("A1").Left + 5
 .Width = WSD.Range("A1:B14").Width - 60
 .Height = WSD.Range("A1:B14").Height
 End With

 Set SCR = ActiveWorkbook.SlicerCaches("Slicer_Region")
 Set SLR = SCR.Slicers("Region")
 With SLR
 .Style = "SlicerStyleLight3"
 .NumberOfColumns = 1
 .Top = WSD.Range("C1").Top + 5
 .Left = WSD.Range("C1").Left - 20
 .Width = WSD.Range("C1").Width
 .Height = WSD.Range("C1:C14").Height
 .Caption = "Territory"
 End With

 ' Choose three regions
 With SCR
 .SlicerItems("Midwest").Selected = True
 .SlicerItems("North").Selected = True
 .SlicerItems("Northeast").Selected = True
 .SlicerItems("South").Selected = False
 .SlicerItems("Southeast").Selected = False
 .SlicerItems("Southwest").Selected = False
 .SlicerItems("West").Selected = False
 End With

End Sub
```

Using the Data Model in Excel 2019

Excel 2019 incorporates Power Pivot into the core Excel product. This means you can add two tables to the Data Model, create a relationship, add a measure, and then build a pivot table from the Data Model.

To follow along with the example in this section, open the 13-BeforeDataModel.xlsm file from the sample download files. This workbook has two tables: Sales and Sector. Sector is a lookup table that is related to the Sales table via a customer field. To build the pivot table, you follow these general steps in the macro:

1. Add the main table to the model.

2. Add the lookup table to the model.

3. Link the two tables with a relationship.

4. Create a pivot cache from ThisWorkbookDataModel.

5. Create a pivot table from the cache.

6. Add row fields.

7. Define a measure. Add the measure to the pivot table.

Adding both tables to the Data Model

You should already have a data set in the workbook that has been converted to a table using the Ctrl+T shortcut. On the Table Tools Design tab, change the table name to Sales. To link this table to the Data Model, use this code:

```
' Build Connection to the main Sales table
Set WBT = ActiveWorkbook
TableName = "Sales"
WBT.Connections.Add2 Name:="LinkedTable_" & TableName, _
 Description:="", _
 ConnectionString:="WORKSHEET;" & WBT.FullName, _
 CommandText:=WBT.Name & "!" & TableName, _
 lCmdType:=7, _
 CreateModelConnection:=True, _
 ImportRelationships:=False
```

Several variables in this code use the table name, the workbook path, and/or the workbook name. By storing the table name in a variable at the top of the code, you can build the connection name, connection string, and command text using the variables.

Adapting the preceding code to link to the lookup table then requires only changing the `TableName` variable:

```
TableName = "Sector"
WBT.Connections.Add2 Name:="LinkedTable_" & TableName, _
 Description:="", _
 ConnectionString:="WORKSHEET;" & WBT.FullName, _
 CommandText:=WBT.Name & "!" & TableName, _
 lCmdType:=7, _
 CreateModelConnection:=True, _
 ImportRelationships:=False
```

Creating a relationship between the two tables

When you create a relationship in the Excel interface, you specify the following four items in the Create Relationship dialog box (see Figure 13-31):

- Table 1 is Sector.

- Columns is Customer.

- Table 2 is Sales.

- Columns is Customer.

The code to create the relationship is more streamlined. There can be only one Data Model per workbook. Set an object variable named MO to refer to the model in this workbook. Use the `ModelRelationships.Add` method and specify the two fields that are linked.

FIGURE 13-31 To create a relationship, specify a field in both tables.

```
' Relate the two tables
Dim MO As Model
Set MO = ActiveWorkbook.Model
MO.ModelRelationships.Add _
 ForeignKeyColumn:=MO.ModelTables("Sales").ModelTableColumns("Customer"),
```

```
PrimaryKeyColumn:= _
 MO.ModelTables("Sector").ModelTableColumns("Customer")
```

Defining the pivot cache and building the pivot table

The code to define the pivot cache specifies that the data is external. Even though the linked tables are in your workbook, and even though the Data Model is stored as a binary large object within the workbook, this is still considered an external data connection. The connection is always called ThisWorkbookDataModel. Here's the code for defining the pivot cache and building the pivot table:

```
' Define the PivotCache
Set PTCache = WBT.PivotCaches.Create(SourceType:=xlExternal, _
 SourceData:=WBT.Connections("ThisWorkbookDataModel"), _
 Version:=xlPivotTableVersion15)

' Create the Pivot Table from the Pivot Cache
Set PT = PTCache.CreatePivotTable(
 TableDestination:=WSD.Cells(1, 1), TableName:="PivotTable1")
```

Adding model fields to the pivot table

You need to add two types of fields to the pivot table. Text fields such as Customer, Sector, and Product are simply fields that can be added to the row or column area of the pivot table. No calculation has to happen for these fields. The code for adding text fields is shown in this section. When you add a numeric field to the Values area in the Excel interface, you are actually implicitly defining a new calculated field. To do this in VBA, you have to explicitly define the field and then add it.

Let's look at the simpler example of adding a text field to the row area. The VBA code generically looks like this:

```
With PT.CubeFields("[TableName].[FieldName]")
 .Orientation = xlRowField
 .Position = 1
End With
```

In the current example, add the Sector field from the Sector table by using this code:

```
With PT.CubeFields("[Sector].[Sector]")
 .Orientation = xlRowField
 .Position = 1
End With
```

Adding numeric fields to the Values area

In Excel 2010, Power Pivot calculated fields were called *measures*. In Excel 2019, the Excel interface calls them *calculations*. However, the underlying VBA code still calls them *measures*.

If you have a Data Model pivot table and you check the Revenue field, you see the Revenue field move to the Values area. Behind the scenes, though, Excel is implicitly defining a new measure called Sum Of Revenue. (You can see the implicit measures in the Power Pivot window if you use Excel 2019 Pro Plus.) In VBA, the first step is to define a new measure for Sum Of Revenue. To make it easier to refer to this measure later, assign the new measure to an object variable:

```
' Before you can add Revenue to the pivot table,
' you have to define the measure.
' This happens using the GetMeasure method.
' Assign the cube field to CFRevenue object
Dim CFRevenue As CubeField
Set CFRevenue = PT.CubeFields.GetMeasure( _
 AttributeHierarchy:="[Sales].[Revenue]", _
 Function:=xlSum, _
 Caption:="Sum of Revenue")
' Add the newly created cube field to the pivot table
PT.AddDataField Field:=CFRevenue, _
 Caption:="Total Revenue"
PT.PivotFields("[Measures].[Sum of Revenue]").NumberFormat = "$#,##0,K"
```

You can use the sample code to create a new measure. The following measure uses the Distinct Count function to count the number of unique customers in each sector:

```
' Add Distinct Count of Customer as a Cube Field
Dim CFCustCount As CubeField
Set CFCustCount = PT.CubeFields.GetMeasure( _
 AttributeHierarchy:="[Sales].[Customer]", _
 Function:=xlDistinctCount, _
 Caption:="Customer Count")
' Add the newly created cube field to the pivot table
PT.AddDataField Field:=CFCustCount, _
 Caption:="Customer Count"
```

Now that Power Pivot ships with every copy of Excel 2019, you can use DAX formulas to create new measures. The following code adds a field for Median Sales:

```
' Add Median Sales using DAX
ActiveWorkbook.Model.ModelMeasures.Add _
  MeasureName:="Median Sales", _
AssociatedTable:=ActiveWorkbook.Model.ModelTables("Sales"), _
Formula:="Median([Revenue])", _
FormatInformation:=ActiveWorkbook.Model.ModelFormatCurrency("Default", 2)
PT.AddDataField PT.CubeFields("[Measures].[Median Sales]")
```

Putting it all together

Figure 13-32 shows the Data Model pivot table created using the code in Listing 13-7.

	A	B	C	D
1	Sector	Total Revenue	Customer Count	Median Sales
2	Apparel	$758K	2	$10,752.50
3	Chemical	$569K	1	$10,137.50
4	Consumer	$2,195K	7	$12,756.00
5	Electronics	$222K	4	$14,554.00
6	Food	$750K	1	$12,743.50
7	Hardware	$2,179K	11	$11,547.50
8	Textiles	$35K	1	$8,908.00
9	Grand Total *	$6,708K	27	$11,858.00
10				

FIGURE 13-32 Two tables linked with a pivot table and two measures, all via a macro.

LISTING 13-7 Code to create the Data Model pivot table in Figure 13-32

```
Sub BuildModelPivotTable()
 Dim WBT As Workbook
 Dim WC As WorkbookConnection
 Dim MO As Model
 Dim PTCache As PivotCache
 Dim PT As PivotTable
 Dim WSD As Worksheet
 Dim CFRevenue As CubeField
 Dim CFCustCount As CubeField

 Set WBT = ActiveWorkbook
 Set WSD = WBT.Worksheets("Report")

 ' Build Connection to the main Sales table
 TableName = "Sales"
 WBT.Connections.Add2 Name:="LinkedTable_" & TableName, _
 Description:="MainTable", _
 ConnectionString:="WORKSHEET;" & WBT.FullName, _
 CommandText:=WBT.Name & "!" & TableName, _
 lCmdType:=7, _
 CreateModelConnection:=True, _
 ImportRelationships:=False

 ' Build Connection to the Sector lookup table
 TableName = "Sector"
 WBT.Connections.Add2 Name:="LinkedTable_" & TableName, _
 Description:="LookupTable", _
 ConnectionString:="WORKSHEET;" & WBT.FullName, _
 CommandText:=WBT.Name & "!" & TableName, _
 lCmdType:=7, _
 CreateModelConnection:=True, _
 ImportRelationships:=False

 ' Relate the two tables
 Set MO = ActiveWorkbook.Model
 MO.ModelRelationships.Add ForeignKeyColumn:= _
 MO.ModelTables("Sales").ModelTableColumns("Customer"), _
 PrimaryKeyColumn:=MO.ModelTables("Sector"). _
 ModelTableColumns("Customer")

 ' Delete any prior pivot tables
 For Each PT In WSD.PivotTables
```

```
PT.TableRange2.Clear
Next PT

' Define the PivotCache
Set PTCache = WBT.PivotCaches.Create(SourceType:=xlExternal, _
SourceData:=WBT.Connections("ThisWorkbookDataModel"), _
Version:=xlPivotTableVersion15)

' Create the Pivot Table from the Pivot Cache
Set PT = PTCache.CreatePivotTable( _
TableDestination:=WSD.Cells(1, 1), TableName:="PivotTable1")

' Add the Sector field from the Sector table to the Row areas
With PT.CubeFields("[Sector].[Sector]")
.Orientation = xlRowField
.Position = 1
End With


' Before you can add Revenue to the pivot table,
' you have to define the measure.
' This happens using the GetMeasure method
' Assign the cube field to CFRevenue object
Set CFRevenue = PT.CubeFields.GetMeasure( _
AttributeHierarchy:="[Sales].[Revenue]", _
Function:=xlSum, _
Caption:="Sum of Revenue")
' Add the newly created cube field to the pivot table
PT.AddDataField Field:=CFRevenue, _
Caption:="Total Revenue"
PT.PivotFields("[Measures].[Sum of Revenue]"). _
NumberFormat = "$#,##0,K"
' Add Distinct Count of Customer as a Cube Field
Set CFCustCount = PT.CubeFields.GetMeasure( _
AttributeHierarchy:="[Sales].[Customer]", _
Function:=xlDistinctCount, _
Caption:="Customer Count")
' Add the newly created cube field to the pivot table
PT.AddDataField Field:=CFCustCount, _
Caption:="Customer Count"

' Add Median Sales using DAX
ActiveWorkbook.Model.ModelMeasures.Add _
  MeasureName:="Median Sales", _
AssociatedTable:=ActiveWorkbook.Model.ModelTables("Sales"), _
Formula:="Median([Revenue])", _
FormatInformation:=ActiveWorkbook.Model.ModelFormatCurrency("Default", 2)
PT.AddDataField PT.CubeFields("[Measures].[Median Sales]")
End Sub
```

Next steps

In Chapter 14, "Advanced pivot table tips and techniques," you'll learn many techniques for handling common questions and issues related to pivot tables.

Advanced pivot table tips and techniques

In this chapter, you will learn 21 pivot table tricks and techniques:

- Tip 1: Force pivot tables to refresh automatically
- Tip 2: Refresh all pivot tables in a workbook at the same time
- Tip 3: Sort data items in a unique order, not ascending or descending
- Tip 4: Use (or prevent using) a custom list for sorting your pivot table
- Tip 5: Use pivot table defaults to change the behavior of all future pivot tables
- Tip 6: Turn pivot tables into hard data
- Tip 7: Fill the empty cells left by row fields
- Tip 8: Add a rank number field to a pivot table
- Tip 9: Reduce the size of pivot table reports
- Tip 10: Create an automatically expanding data range
- Tip 11: Compare tables using a pivot table
- Tip 12: AutoFilter a pivot table
- Tip 13: Force two number formats in a pivot table
- Tip 14: Format individual values in a pivot table
- Tip 15: Format sections of a pivot table
- Tip 16: Create a frequency distribution with a pivot table
- Tip 17: Use a pivot table to explode a data set to different tabs
- Tip 18: Apply restrictions on pivot tables and pivot fields
- Tip 19: Use a pivot table to explode a data set to different workbooks
- Tip 20: Use percentage change from previous for year-over-year
- Tip 21: Do a two-way VLOOKUP with Power Query

In this chapter, you'll discover some techniques that provide unique solutions to some of the most common pivot table problems. Take some time to glance at the topics covered here. Who knows? You might find a few unique tips that can help you tackle some of your pivot table conundrums!

Tip 1: Force pivot tables to refresh automatically

In some situations, you might need to have pivot tables refresh themselves automatically. For instance, suppose you create a pivot table report for your manager. You might not be able to trust that he will refresh the pivot table when needed.

You can force each pivot table to automatically refresh when the workbook opens by following these steps:

1. Right-click the pivot table and select PivotTable Options.

2. In the PivotTable Options dialog box that appears, select the Data tab.

3. Select the check box for Refresh Data When Opening The File Property.

When this property is activated, the pivot table refreshes itself each time the workbook in which it's located is opened.

> **Tip** The Refresh Data When Opening The File Property must be set for each pivot table individually.

Tip 2: Refresh all pivot tables in a workbook at the same time

When you have multiple pivot tables in a workbook, refreshing all of them can be bothersome. There are several ways to avoid the hassle of manually refreshing multiple pivot tables. Here are a few options:

- **Option 1**—You can configure each pivot table in a workbook to automatically refresh when the workbook opens. To do so, right-click the pivot table and select PivotTable Options. This activates the PivotTable Options dialog box. Here, select the Data tab and select the check box for Refresh Data When Opening The File Property. After you have configured all pivot tables in the workbook, they will automatically refresh when the workbook is opened.

- **Option 2**—You can create a macro to refresh each pivot table in the workbook. This option is ideal when you need to refresh pivot tables on demand rather than only when the workbook opens. To do this, start recording a macro, and while the macro is recording, go to each pivot table in your workbook and refresh. After all pivot tables are refreshed, stop recording. The result is a macro that can be fired any time you need to refresh all pivot tables.

> **Note** Revisit Chapter 12, "Enhancing pivot table reports with macros," to get more detail on using macros with pivot tables.

- **Option 3**—Click the Refresh All button on the Data tab, as shown in Figure 14-1. The downside to this method is that it also refreshes an external data connection, which can be a lengthy process. But if you do not have any external data connections, this is an easy way to refresh all of the tables.

FIGURE 14-1 The Refresh All button in the Data tab will refresh all pivot tables and external data connections.

Tip 3: Sort data items in a unique order, not ascending or descending

Figure 14-2 shows the default sequence of regions in a pivot table report. Alphabetically, the regions are shown in the sequence Midwest, North, South, and West. If your company is based in California, company tradition might dictate that the West region be shown first, followed by Midwest, North, and South. Unfortunately, neither an ascending sort order nor a descending sort order can help you with this.

	A	B	C	D	E	F
3	Sum of Sales_Amount	Region				
4	Product_Description	MIDWEST	NORTH	SOUTH	WEST	Grand Total
5	Cleaning & Housekeeping Services	$174,518	$534,282	$283,170	$146,623	$1,138,593
6	Facility Maintenance and Repair	$463,077	$606,747	$846,515	$444,820	$2,361,158
7	Fleet Maintenance	$448,800	$610,791	$1,046,231	$521,976	$2,627,798
8	Green Plants and Foliage Care	$93,562	$155,021	$157,821	$870,379	$1,276,783
9	Landscaping/Grounds Care	$190,003	$299,309	$335,676	$365,928	$1,190,915
10	Predictive Maintenance/Preventative Maintenance	$478,928	$572,860	$472,045	$655,092	$2,178,925
11	Grand Total	$1,848,887	$2,779,009	$3,141,458	$3,004,818	$10,774,172
12						

FIGURE 14-2 Company tradition dictates that the Region field should be in West–Midwest–North–South sequence.

You can rearrange data items in your pivot table manually by simply typing the exact name of the data item where you would like to see its data. You can also drag the data item where you want it.

To solve the problem in this example, you simply type **WEST** in cell B4 and then press Enter. The pivot table responds by resequencing the regions. The $3 million in sales for the West region automatically moves from column E to column B, as shown in Figure 14-3. The remaining regions move over to the next three columns.

	A	B	C	D	E	F
3	**Sum of Sales_Amount**	**Region** ▾				
4	**Product_Description** ▾	**WEST**	**MIDWEST**	**NORTH**	**SOUTH**	**Grand Total**
5	Cleaning & Housekeeping Services	$146,623	$174,518	$534,282	$283,170	$1,138,593
6	Facility Maintenance and Repair	$444,820	$463,077	$606,747	$846,515	$2,361,158
7	Fleet Maintenance	$521,976	$448,800	$610,791	$1,046,231	$2,627,798
8	Green Plants and Foliage Care	$870,379	$93,562	$155,021	$157,821	$1,276,783
9	Landscaping/Grounds Care	$365,928	$190,003	$299,309	$335,676	$1,190,915
10	Predictive Maintenance/Preventative Maintenance	$655,092	$478,928	$572,860	$472,045	$2,178,925
11	**Grand Total**	**$3,004,818**	**$1,848,887**	**$2,779,009**	**$3,141,458**	**$10,774,172**
12						

FIGURE 14-3 After typing WEST in B4, the numbers for West move from column E to column B.

Tip 4: Using (or prevent using) a custom list for sorting your pivot table

The technique of typing **WEST** in cell B4 in the previous tip is a great way to impress your friends at a bar, but it would be tedious to do this over and over. If your source data is stored in a worksheet and not in the data model or external data, you can permanently have all future pivot tables appear in the order of West, Midwest, North, and South by creating a custom list.

Type the regions in consecutive cells in the proper sequence. Select the cells. Go to File, Options, Advanced. Scroll all the way to the bottom and click Edit Custom Lists.

Excel opens the Custom Lists dialog box. This is where Excel stores lists such as January, February, March and Monday, Tuesday, Wednesday.

If you remembered to select your list before opening the dialog box, simply click the Import button to add a new list (see Figure 14-4).

FIGURE 14-4 Add a new custom list with regions in the proper sequence.

Custom lists are specific to one computer and one version of Excel. If you create a custom list in Excel 2013, it will not be available in Excel 2016. But if you are only using one version of Excel, then all future pivot tables will be sequenced using the custom list.

Note: What if you later add a Canada and Mexico region? Items that are in the custom list will appear first, followed by items missing from the custom list in alphabetical sequence. Your report will show West, Midwest, North, South, Canada, and Mexico. The solution in this case is to open the Custom Lists dialog box, edit the list, and click Add to memorize the new list.

Note in Figure 14-4 that two lists contain "West." If there is a tie, the list nearest the bottom of the Custom Lists wins.

Sometimes you might have the opposite problem. Say that your company is really chummy and all the team members are reported by their first name. For some reason, Jan or May or Friday keeps showing up before Andy, Barb, and Chris (see Figure 14-5).

	A	B	C	D	E
1	Team Member	Sales			
2	Andy	87.04			
3	Barb	50.85		Team Member ▾	Sum of Sales
4	Chris	29.99		Jan	67.53
5	Friday	54.88		Friday	171.06
6	Jan	67.53		May	225.31
7	May	80.03		Andy	121.49
8	Diane	69.81		Barb	50.85
9	Ed	14.28		Chris	51.73
10	Gary	86.35		Diane	147.44

FIGURE 14-5   Jan keeps showing up at the top of your pivot table reports.

Notice in Figure 14-4 that the third list already includes Jan and May. You can't see it, but the second list includes Friday. Because those people appear in a custom list, they get sorted before all of the people "missing" from the custom list.

I did ask the Pivot Table team at Microsoft why they split Jan and May with Friday. It is not alphabetical. It is not arranged by list from the bottom of the dialog box to the top. The apparent answer is that no one knows anymore or that they don't have time to research a question that is only of interest to a few people.

One solution: Stop hiring people named May, Jan, or Friday. A less stressful solution: Display the Options dialog box for a pivot table. On the Totals & Filters tab, clear the entry for Use Custom Lists When Sorting (see Figure 14-6).

If Jan or May will permanently be a problem, you can turn this setting off for all future pivot tables. See Tip 5.

FIGURE 14-6 You can stop the sorting by custom lists using this setting.

Tip 5: Use pivot table defaults to change the behavior of all future pivot tables

Do you have a couple of pivot table default behaviors that you always turn off? For me, I always want empty cells to show with 0. I always want to start in Tabular layout with Repeat All Item Labels turned on. Maybe you need to turn off Use Custom Lists When Sorting.

In the summer of 2017, Excel added the Edit Default Layout button for pivot tables. Go to File, Options, Data to find the Edit Default Layout button.

Initially, the Edit Default Layout dialog box only offers a few settings. But if you click the PivotTable Options button, as shown in Figure 14-7, you can permanently change all the settings in PivotTable Options.

FIGURE 14-7 Change defaults for future pivot tables.

Tip 6: Turn pivot tables into hard data

Say that you created a pivot table in order to summarize and shape data. You do not want to keep the source data, nor do you want to keep the pivot table with all its overhead.

Turning a pivot table into hard data enables you to utilize the results of the pivot table without having to deal with the source data or a pivot cache. How you turn the pivot table into hard data depends on how much of the pivot table you are going to copy.

If you are copying just a portion of a pivot table, do the following:

1. Select the data you want to copy from the pivot table, right-click, and select Copy.

2. Right-click anywhere on a spreadsheet and select Paste.

If you are copying an entire pivot table, follow these steps:

1. Select the entire pivot table, right-click, and select Copy. Alternatively, you can choose the Analyze tab, click Select, and then click Entire PivotTable.

2. Right-click anywhere on a spreadsheet and select Paste Special.

3. Select Values and then click OK.

> **Tip** You might want to consider removing any subtotals before turning a pivot table into hard data. Subtotals typically aren't very useful when you are creating a stand-alone data set.
>
> To remove the subtotals from a pivot table, first identify the field for which subtotals are being calculated. Then right-click the field's header (either in the pivot table itself or in the PivotTable Fields list), and select Field Settings. Selecting this option opens the Field Settings dialog box. Here, you change the Subtotals option to None. After you click OK, your subtotals are removed.

Tip 7: Fill the empty cells left by row fields

When you turn a pivot table into hard data, you are left not only with the values created by the pivot table but also the pivot table's data structure. For example, the data in Figure 14-8 came from a pivot table that had a Tabular layout.

	Region	Market	Product_Description	Sum of Sales_Amount
3	Region	Market	Product_Description	Sum of Sales_Amount
4	⊟ MIDWEST	⊟ DENVER	Cleaning & Housekeeping Services	$12,564
5			Facility Maintenance and Repair	$160,324
6			Fleet Maintenance	$170,190
7			Green Plants and Foliage Care	$42,409
8			Landscaping/Grounds Care	$73,622
9			Predictive Maintenance/Preventative Maintenance	$186,475
10		DENVER Total		$645,583
11		⊟ KANSASCITY	Cleaning & Housekeeping Services	$65,439
12			Facility Maintenance and Repair	$132,120
13			Fleet Maintenance	$133,170
14			Green Plants and Foliage Care	$35,315
15			Landscaping/Grounds Care	$52,442
16			Predictive Maintenance/Preventative Maintenance	$156,412
17		KANSASCITY Total		$574,899
18		⊟ TULSA	Cleaning & Housekeeping Services	$96,515
19			Facility Maintenance and Repair	$170,632
20			Fleet Maintenance	$145,440
21			Green Plants and Foliage Care	$15,838
22			Landscaping/Grounds Care	$63,939
23			Predictive Maintenance/Preventative Maintenance	$136,041
24		TULSA Total		$628,405
25	MIDWEST Total			$1,848,887

FIGURE 14-8 It would be impractical to use this data anywhere else without filling in the empty cells left by the row field.

Notice that the Market field kept the same row structure it had when this data was in the row area of the pivot table. It would be unwise to use this table anywhere else without filling in the empty cells left by the row field, but how do you easily fill these empty cells?

The next sections discuss two options provided by Excel 2019 to fix this problem effectively.

Option 1: Implement the Repeat All Item Labels feature

The first option for easily filling the empty cells left by row fields is to apply the Repeat Item Labels functionality. This feature ensures that all item labels are repeated to create a solid block of contiguous cells. To implement this feature, place your cursor anywhere in your pivot table. Then go to the ribbon and select Design, Report Layout, Repeat All Item Labels (see Figure 14-9).

FIGURE 14-9 The Repeat All Item Labels option enables you to show your pivot data in one contiguous block of data.

Figure 14-10 shows what a pivot table with this feature applied looks like.

Now you can turn this pivot table into hard values, and you will end up with a contiguous table of data without gaps.

	A	B	C	D
3	Region ▾	Market ▾	Product_Description ▾	Sum of Sales_Amount ▾
4	⊟ MIDWEST	⊟ DENVER	Cleaning & Housekeeping Services	$12,564
5	MIDWEST	DENVER	Facility Maintenance and Repair	$160,324
6	MIDWEST	DENVER	Fleet Maintenance	$170,190
7	MIDWEST	DENVER	Green Plants and Foliage Care	$42,409
8	MIDWEST	DENVER	Landscaping/Grounds Care	$73,622
9	MIDWEST	DENVER	Predictive Maintenance/Preventative Maintenance	$186,475
10	MIDWEST	DENVER Total		$645,583
11	MIDWEST	⊟ KANSASCITY	Cleaning & Housekeeping Services	$65,439
12	MIDWEST	KANSASCITY	Facility Maintenance and Repair	$132,120
13	MIDWEST	KANSASCITY	Fleet Maintenance	$133,170
14	MIDWEST	KANSASCITY	Green Plants and Foliage Care	$35,315
15	MIDWEST	KANSASCITY	Landscaping/Grounds Care	$52,442
16	MIDWEST	KANSASCITY	Predictive Maintenance/Preventative Maintenance	$156,412
17	MIDWEST	KANSASCITY Total		$574,899
18	MIDWEST	⊟ TULSA	Cleaning & Housekeeping Services	$96,515
19	MIDWEST	TULSA	Facility Maintenance and Repair	$170,632
20	MIDWEST	TULSA	Fleet Maintenance	$145,440
21	MIDWEST	TULSA	Green Plants and Foliage Care	$15,838
22	MIDWEST	TULSA	Landscaping/Grounds Care	$63,939
23	MIDWEST	TULSA	Predictive Maintenance/Preventative Maintenance	$136,041
24	MIDWEST	TULSA Total		$628,405
25	MIDWEST Total			$1,848,887

FIGURE 14-10   The Repeat All Item Labels option fills all cells with data items.

Option 2: Use Excel's Go To Special functionality

The other way to easily fill the empty cells left by row fields involves using Excel's Go To Special functionality.

You start by converting your pivot table into hard data as explained in Tip 4. Next, select the range in columns A and B that extends from the first row with blanks to the row just above the grand total. In the present example, this is A4:B100. Choose Home, Find & Select, Go To Special. (Alternatively, use Ctrl+G or F5 to open the Go To dialog box and then press the Special button.) This activates the Go To Special dialog box, which is a powerful feature that enables you to modify your selection based on various conditions (see Figure 14-11). In this dialog box, choose the Blanks option and click OK. Now only the blank cells in the selection are selected.

FIGURE 14-11   Using the Go To Special dialog box enables you to select all the blank cells to be filled.

Enter a formula to copy the pivot item values from the cell above to the blank cells. You can do this with four keystrokes: Type an equal sign, press the up arrow key, and hold down the Ctrl key while pressing Enter. The equal sign tells Excel that you are entering a formula in the active cell. Pressing the up arrow key points to the cell above the active cell. Pressing Ctrl+Enter tells Excel to enter a similar formula in all the selected cells instead of just the active cell. As Figure 14-12 shows, with these few keystrokes, you enter a formula to fill in all the blank cells at once.

	A	B	C	D
3	Region	Market	Product_Description	Sum of Sales_Amount
4	MIDWEST	DENVER	Cleaning & Housekeeping Services	$12,564
5	MIDWEST	DENVER	Facility Maintenance and Repair	$160,324
6	MIDWEST	DENVER	Fleet Maintenance	$170,190
7	MIDWEST	DENVER	Green Plants and Foliage Care	$42,409
8	MIDWEST	DENVER	Landscaping/Grounds Care	$73,622
9	MIDWEST	DENVER	Predictive Maintenance/Preventative Maintenance	$186,475
10	MIDWEST	DENVER Total		$645,583
11	MIDWEST	KANSASCITY	Cleaning & Housekeeping Services	$65,439
12	MIDWEST	KANSASCITY	Facility Maintenance and Repair	$132,120
13	MIDWEST	KANSASCITY	Fleet Maintenance	$133,170
14	MIDWEST	KANSASCITY	Green Plants and Foliage Care	$35,315
15	MIDWEST	KANSASCITY	Landscaping/Grounds Care	$52,442
16	MIDWEST	KANSASCITY	Predictive Maintenance/Preventative Maintenance	$156,412
17	MIDWEST	KANSASCITY Total		$574,899
18	MIDWEST	TULSA	Cleaning & Housekeeping Services	$96,515
19	MIDWEST	TULSA	Facility Maintenance and Repair	$170,632
20	MIDWEST	TULSA	Fleet Maintenance	$145,440
21	MIDWEST	TULSA	Green Plants and Foliage Care	$15,838
22	MIDWEST	TULSA	Landscaping/Grounds Care	$63,939
23	MIDWEST	TULSA	Predictive Maintenance/Preventative Maintenance	$136,041
24	MIDWEST	TULSA Total		$628,405

FIGURE 14-12   Pressing Ctrl+Enter enters the formula in all selected cells.

At this point, there is no need for the formulas. You will want to convert those formulas to values. Reselect the original range A4:B100. You can then press Ctrl+C to copy and choose Edit, Paste Special, Values to convert the formulas to values. This method provides a quick way to easily fill in the Outline view provided by the pivot table.

Tip 8: Add a rank number field to a pivot table

When you are sorting and ranking a field with a large number of data items, it can be difficult to determine the number ranking of the data item you are currently analyzing. Furthermore, you might want to turn your pivot table into hard values for further analysis. An integer field that contains the actual rank number of each data item could be helpful in analysis outside the pivot table.

Start with a pivot table like the one shown in Figure 14-13. Notice that the same data measure, Sum Of Sales_Amount, is shown twice.

FIGURE 14-13 Start with a pivot table where the data value is listed twice.

Right-click the second instance of the data measure, select Show Values As, and then select Rank Largest To Smallest (see Figure 14-14).

FIGURE 14-14 Adding a rank field is simple with the Show Values As option.

When your ranking is applied, you can adjust the labels and formatting so it looks as shown in Figure 14-15. This gives you a clean-looking ranking report.

	A	B	C
1			
2			
3	**Market** ▼	**Sum of Sales_Amount**	**Rank**
4	BUFFALO	$450,478	12
5	CALIFORNIA	$2,254,735	1
6	CANADA	$776,245	5
7	CHARLOTTE	$890,522	3
8	DALLAS	$467,089	11
9	DENVER	$645,583	7
10	FLORIDA	$1,450,392	2
11	KANSASCITY	$574,899	9
12	MICHIGAN	$678,705	6
13	NEWORLEANS	$333,454	13
14	NEWYORK	$873,581	4
15	PHOENIX	$570,255	10
16	SEATTLE	$179,827	14
17	TULSA	$628,405	8
18	Grand Total	$10,774,172	

FIGURE 14-15   Your final pivot table, with ranking applied.

Tip 9: Reduce the size of pivot table reports

When you initiate the creation of a pivot table report, Excel takes a snapshot of your data set and stores it in a *pivot cache*, which is a special memory subsystem in which your data source is duplicated for quick access. That is to say, Excel literally makes a copy of your data and then stores it in a cache that is attached to your workbook.

Of course, the benefit you get from a pivot cache is optimization. Any changes you make to the pivot table report, such as rearranging fields, adding new fields, and hiding items, are made rapidly and with minimal overhead.

The downside of the pivot cache is that it basically doubles the size of a workbook. So, every time you make a new pivot table from scratch, you essentially add to the file size of your workbook.

Delete the source data worksheet

If your workbooks have both your pivot table and your source data worksheet, you are wasting space. That is, you are essentially distributing two copies of the same data.

You can delete your source data, and your pivot table will function just fine. After you delete the source data, when you save the pivot table, the file shrinks. Your clients can use the pivot table as normal, and your workbook is half as big. The only functionality you lose is the ability to refresh the pivot data because the source data is not there.

What happens if your clients need to see the source data? Well, they can simply double-click the intersection of the row and column grand totals. This tells Excel to output the contents of the pivot table's cache into a new worksheet. So, with one double-click, your clients can re-create the source data that makes up the pivot table!

Tip 10: Create an automatically expanding data range

You will undoubtedly encounter situations in which you have pivot table reports that are updated daily (that is, records are constantly being added to the source data). When records are added to a pivot table's source data set, you must redefine the range that is captured before the new records are brought into the pivot table. Redefining the source range for a pivot table once in a while is no sweat, but when the source data is changed on a daily or weekly basis, it can start to get bothersome.

The solution is to turn your source data table into an Excel table using Ctrl+T. This works even if you convert the table after the pivot table has been built. Again, Excel tables enable you to create a defined range that automatically shrinks or expands with the data. This means that any component, chart, pivot table, or formula tied to that range can keep up with changes in your data.

To implement this trick, simply highlight one cell in your source data and then click the Table icon on the Insert tab (see Figure 14-16). Confirm the range to be included in your table, and then click OK.

After your source data has been converted to an Excel table, any pivot table you build on top of it automatically includes all records when your source data expands or shrinks.

FIGURE 14-16 Convert your source data into an Excel table.

> **Tip** Keep in mind that although you won't have to redefine the source range anymore, you will still need to trigger a Refresh in order to have your pivot table show the current data.

Tip 11: Compare tables using a pivot table

If you've been an analyst for more than a week, you've been asked to compare two separate tables to come up with some brilliant analysis about the differences between them. This is a common scenario where leveraging a pivot table can save you some time.

Say that you have two tables that show customers in 2011 and in 2012. Figure 14-17 shows that these are two separate tables. For this example, the tables were made small for instructional purposes, but imagine that you're working with something bigger here.

	A	B	C	D	E	F	G
1	2021 Customers				2022 Customers		
2	Customer_Name	Fiscal Year	Revenue		Customer_Name	Fiscal Year	Revenue
3	PHALCO Corp.	2021	$456.27		PHALSM Corp.	2022	$1,902.25
4	PHALLA Corp.	2021	$3,974.07		PHALTA Corp.	2022	$2,095.01
5	PHALSE Corp.	2021	$565.34		PHALWH Corp.	2022	$1,740.27
6	PHALSM Corp.	2021	$1,902.25		PHMAN Corp.	2022	$3,228.33
7	POMTRA Corp.	2021	$2,201.90		POPPIT Corp.	2022	$604.18
8	POPAUS Corp.	2021	$1,891.73		POPUSL Corp.	2022	$870.28
9	POPCOA Corp.	2021	$1,284.61		POPUSP Corp.	2022	$2,421.01
10	PORADA Corp.	2021	$10,131.22		PORADA Corp.	2022	$10,131.22
11	PORCFA Corp.	2021	$1,187.71		PORADY Corp.	2022	$1,012.94
12					PORCFA Corp.	2022	$1,187.71

FIGURE 14-17   You need to compare these two tables.

The idea is to create one table you can use to pivot. Be sure you have a way to tag which data comes from which table. In Figure 14-18, a column called Fiscal Year serves this purpose.

Customer	Year	Revenue
PHALCO Corp.	2021	$456.27
PHALLA Corp.	2021	$3,974.07
PHALSE Corp.	2021	$565.34
PHALSM Corp.	2021	$1,902.25
POMTRA Corp.	2021	$2,201.90
POPAUS Corp.	2021	$1,891.73
POPCOA Corp.	2021	$1,284.61
PORADA Corp.	2021	$10,131.22
PORCFA Corp.	2021	$1,187.71
PHALSM Corp.	2022	$1,902.25
PHALTA Corp.	2022	$2,095.01
PHALWH Corp.	2022	$1,740.27
PHMAN Corp.	2022	$3,228.33
POPPIT Corp.	2022	$604.18
POPUSL Corp.	2022	$870.28
POPUSP Corp.	2022	$2,421.01
PORADA Corp.	2022	$10,131.22
PORADY Corp.	2022	$1,012.94
PORCFA Corp.	2022	$1,187.71

FIGURE 14-18   Combine your tables into one table.

After you have combined the tables, use the combined data set to create a new pivot table. Format the pivot table so that the table tag (the identifier that tells which table the data came from) is in the column area of the pivot table. In Figure 14-19, years are in the column area and customers are in the row area. The data area contains the count records for each customer name.

As you can see in Figure 14-19, you instantly get a visual indication of which customers are only in the prior year table, which are in the current year table, and which are in both tables.

Count of Customer	Year		
Customer	2021	2022	Grand Total
PHALCO Corp.	1	0	1
PHALLA Corp.	1	0	1
PHALSE Corp.	1	0	1
PHALSM Corp.	1	1	2
PHALTA Corp.	0	1	1
PHALWH Corp.	0	1	1
PHMAN Corp.	0	1	1
POMTRA Corp.	1	0	1
POPAUS Corp.	1	0	1
POPCOA Corp.	1	0	1
POPPIT Corp.	0	1	1
POPUSL Corp.	0	1	1
POPUSP Corp.	0	1	1
PORADA Corp.	1	1	2
PORADY Corp.	0	1	1
PORCFA Corp.	1	1	2
Grand Total	9	10	19

FIGURE 14-19   Create a pivot table to get an easy-to-read visual comparison of the two data sets.

Instead of Count Of Customer, you could add Revenue to the Values area and see a comparison of this year's revenue to last year's revenue.

Tip 12: AutoFilter a pivot table

The conventional wisdom is that you can't apply the Filter found on the Data tab to a pivot table. Technically, that's true. But there is a way to trick Excel into making it happen.

The trick is to place your cursor directly adjacent to the last title in the pivot table, as shown in Figure 14-20. (You can actually use any empty cell immediately to the right of your pivot table.) Once you have it there, you can go to the ribbon, select Data, and then select Filter.

FIGURE 14-20 Place your cursor just outside your pivot table.

At this point, you have Filter drop-down arrows added to C3 and D3! You can now do cool things like apply a custom filter to find all customers with above-average transaction counts (see Figure 14-21).

FIGURE 14-21 With a Data filter implemented, you can take advantage of custom filtering that's not normally available with pivot tables.

If you have product lines stretching across the top of your report, you might filter to show the top ten customers for one specific product (see Figure 14-22).

Enable filters from this cell

	Landscaping and Area Beautificatio ▼	Maintenance and Repair	Grand Tot ▼	
	$13,844	$20,011	Maintenance and Repair (Busines	
		$50,050	Column: Maintenance and Repair	
		$20,623	$23,363	
		$22,573	$29,241	
		$32,611	$73,373	
		$17,829	$22,952	
		$21,373	$28,818	
		$31,541	$47,587	
	$1,549	$29,402	$30,951	
	$2,467,698	$7,167,881	$10,774,172	

Top 10 AutoFilter

Show

Top ▼ 10 ⬍ Items ▼

OK   Cancel

Use Top 10 from this drop-down arrow

FIGURE 14-22 Choose a Top 10 filter from one column by using the filter trick.

Another use is to create a Top 10 report using the Top 10 filter but ask for the Top 11 values, as shown in Figure 14-23. To the Data filter, the largest "customer" is the Grand Total row. Asking for customers 2 through 11 will show the customers ranked 1 through 10. The advantage of this method is that the Percentage Of Total column will be as a percentage of the Grand Total instead of the percentage of only 10 customers.

Enable filters from this cell

F	G	H	I	J	K
Market	KANSASCITY ▼				
Customer_Name ▼	Revenue ▼	% of Total ▼	Ra ▼		
CATYOF Corp.	$15,511	Revenue (Values)	1		
TSWPRE Corp.	$13,645	Column: Revenue	2		
LUNNOX Corp.	$12,296	2.14%	3		
BUUFPR Corp.	$8,089	1.41%	4		
KANSOS Corp.	$7,849	1.37%	5		
FARUTT Corp.	$7,377	1.28%	6		
OMUSAC Corp.	$6,090	1.06%	7		
SQAORE Corp.	$6,077	1.06%	8		
DUUUUS Corp.	$5,469	0.95%	9		
SAOUSA Corp.	$5,316	0.92%	10		
Grand Total	$574,899	100.00%			

Use Top 10 from this drop-down arrow

Top 10 AutoFilter

Show

Top ▼ 11 ⬍ Items ▼

OK   Cancel

Ask for 11 because Grand Total is number 1

FIGURE 14-23 Using the Filter option and asking for top 11 customers will get you the grand total and 10 customers.

> ⚠ **Caution**   Using the filter from the Data tab is not supported by Microsoft. If you refresh or change the shape of your pivot table, expect to have to reapply any filters created with this method.
>
> Also, to turn off the filters, you have to select a cell immediately to the right of your pivot table.

This is a fantastic way to add an extra layer of analytical capabilities to pivot table reports.

Tip 13: Force two number formats in a pivot table

Every now and then, you have to deal with a situation where a normalized data set makes it difficult to build an appropriate pivot table. For example, the data set shown in Figure 14-24 contains metrics information for each market. Notice that there is a column that identifies the measure, and there is a column that specifies the corresponding value.

	A	B	C	D	E
1	Region	Market	Product_Description	Measure	Value
2	MIDWEST	DENVER	Cleaning & Housekeeping Services	Revenue	12563.91
3	MIDWEST	DENVER	Cleaning & Housekeeping Services	Conversion Rate	0.62
4	MIDWEST	DENVER	Facility Maintenance and Repair	Revenue	160324.22
5	MIDWEST	DENVER	Facility Maintenance and Repair	Conversion Rate	0.64
6	MIDWEST	DENVER	Fleet Maintenance	Revenue	170190.26
7	MIDWEST	DENVER	Fleet Maintenance	Conversion Rate	0.20
8	MIDWEST	DENVER	Green Plants and Foliage Care	Revenue	42408.61
9	MIDWEST	DENVER	Green Plants and Foliage Care	Conversion Rate	0.88
10	MIDWEST	DENVER	Landscaping/Grounds Care	Revenue	73621.62
11	MIDWEST	DENVER	Landscaping/Grounds Care	Conversion Rate	0.92
12	MIDWEST	DENVER	Predictive Maintenance/Preventative	Revenue	186474.67
13	MIDWEST	DENVER	Predictive Maintenance/Preventative	Conversion Rate	0.93
14	MIDWEST	KANSASCITY	Cleaning & Housekeeping Services	Revenue	65439.14
15	MIDWEST	KANSASCITY	Cleaning & Housekeeping Services	Conversion Rate	0.61

FIGURE 14-24   This metric table has many different data types in one Value field.

Although this is generally a nicely formatted table, notice that some of the measures are meant to be number format, whereas others are meant to be percentage. In the database where this data set originated, the Value field is a double data type, so this works.

The problem is that when you create a pivot table out of this data set, you can't assign two different number formats for the Value field. After all, the rule is one field, one number format.

As you can see in Figure 14-25, trying to set the number format for the percentage measures also changes the format for the measures that are supposed to be straight numbers.

	A	B	C
1	Market	BUFFALO	
2			
3	Sum of Value	Measure	
4	Product_Description	Conversion Rate	Revenue
5	Cleaning & Housekeeping Services	27.08%	6684485.00%
6	Facility Maintenance and Repair	99.53%	6956962.00%
7	Fleet Maintenance	75.26%	8646011.00%
8	Green Plants and Foliage Care	0.36%	3483113.00%
9	Landscaping/Grounds Care	5.38%	6546546.00%
10	Predictive Maintenance/Preventative Maintenance	31.58%	12730710.00%

FIGURE 14-25   You can have only one number format assigned to each data measure.

The solution is to apply a custom number format that formats any value greater than 1.5 as a number and any value less than 1.5 as a percentage. In the Format Cells dialog box, click Custom and then enter the following syntax in the Type input box (see Figure 14-26):

```
[>=1.5]$#,##0;[<1.5]0.0%
```

FIGURE 14-26 Apply a custom number format, telling Excel to format any number less than 1.5 as a percentage.

The result, shown in Figure 14-27, is that each measure is now formatted appropriately. Obviously, you have to get a little lucky with the parameters of the situation you're working in. Although this technique doesn't work in all scenarios, it does open up some interesting options.

	A	B	C
1	Market	BUFFALO	
2			
3	Sum of Value	Measure	
4	Product_Description	Conversion Rate	Revenue
5	Cleaning & Housekeeping Services	27.1%	$66,845
6	Facility Maintenance and Repair	99.5%	$69,570
7	Fleet Maintenance	75.3%	$86,460
8	Green Plants and Foliage Care	0.4%	$34,831
9	Landscaping/Grounds Care	5.4%	$65,465
10	Predictive Maintenance/Preventative Maintenance	31.6%	$127,307

FIGURE 14-27 Two formats in one data field. Amazing!

Tip 14: Format individual values in a pivot table

If you have Office 365, a new feature lets you format certain values in a pivot table and that formatting will stick even after pivoting or refreshing the pivot table.

For example, in Figure 14-28, right-click the cell containing East sales of Cherry and choose Format Cells. Apply a red fill to that cell.

FIGURE 14-28 Use Format Cells in the right-click menu to format one or more cells in the Values area of a pivot table.

When you pivot the data, the red formatting sticks with that cell (see Figure 14-29). Move Product from columns to rows. Move Region from rows to columns. After each move, the red cell moves with the $13,036 value.

FIGURE 14-29 After pivoting, the formatting sticks with that value.

Even more amazing: Add a new row field so that the East Cherry values occupy more cells. The red fill expands to include the new cells. I am not sure why the East Total for Cherry is not red in Figure 14-30.

FIGURE 14-30 Even if the pivot table expands, the red formatting stays with East Cherry.

The red formatting will stick if East is removed due to a filter or slicer. But if you completely remove Product or Region out of the pivot table, the formatting will be lost.

This new formatting trick in Office 365 would make the previous solution simpler. Rather than using a custom number format of [>=1.5]$#,##0;[<1.5]0.0%, you can simply select all of the cells in the Revenue column. Right-click. It is tempting to choose Number Format, but that will not work. Instead, choose Format Cells (see Figure 14-31). Apply a currency format.

Format Cells... applies to selected cells

Number Format... applies to entire measure

FIGURE 14-31 To change all of the number formats for Revenue values, select those cells, right-click, and select Format Cells.

Tip 15: Format sections of a pivot table

While the new formatting trick in Tip 14 is great for Office 365, there is another legacy way to format areas of a pivot table available in all versions of Office.

To enable the method, open the Select drop-down menu on the Analyze tab and choose Enable Selection (see Figure 14-32).

FIGURE 14-32 The legacy Selection feature is turned off by default.

Once you have enabled selection, hover the mouse over the left portion of any cell in a pivot table. Watch for the mouse cursor to change to a right-facing black arrow. In Figure 14-33, hovering over the left quarter of cell H5 will select all Rep total rows.

Cursor changes to black arrow
when over left portion of H5

FIGURE 14-33   Hover over the left edge of a cell until you see the black arrow.

Click on the left side of Andy Total and all similar-level rows in the pivot table are selected. Apply a fill color and you've effectively formatted all of the sales rep subtotal rows, as shown in Figure 14-34.

FIGURE 14-34   When you click on the left side of Andy Total, all the cells at a similar level are selected.

There are many ways to select all. If you hover over a Cherry cell in column I of Figure 14-35, all the Cherry cells will be selected.

FIGURE 14-35   Click on the left edge of one Cherry cell to select all the Cherry cells and their associated sales.

Tip 16: Create a frequency distribution with a pivot table

If you've created a frequency distribution with the FREQUENCY function, you know it can quickly devolve into a confusing mess. The fact that it's an array formula doesn't help matters. Then there's the Histogram functionality you find in the Analysis ToolPak, which doesn't make life much better. Each time you have to change your bin ranges, you have to restart the entire process again.

In this tip, you'll learn how to use a pivot table to quickly implement a simple frequency distribution.

First, you need to create a pivot table where the data values are plotted in the Rows area (not the Values area). Notice that in Figure 14-36, the Sales_Amount field is placed in the Rows area.

FIGURE 14-36   Place your data measure in the Rows area.

Next, right-click any value in the Rows area and select Group. In the Grouping dialog box (shown in Figure 14-37), set the start and end values and then set the intervals. This essentially creates the frequency distribution.

FIGURE 14-37   Use the Grouping dialog box to create your frequency intervals.

After you click the OK button, you can leverage the result to create a distribution view of your data.

In Figure 14-38, you can see that Customer_Name has been added to get a frequency distribution of the number of customer transactions by dollar amount.

The obvious benefit of this technique is you can use the pivot table's report filter to interactively filter the data based on other dimensions, such as Region and Market. Also, unlike with the Analysis ToolPak Histogram tool, you can quickly adjust your frequency intervals by simply right-clicking any number in the Rows area and selecting Group.

FIGURE 14-38   The frequency distribution of customer transactions by dollar amount.

Tip 17: Use a pivot table to explode a data set to different tabs

One of the most common requests an analyst gets is to create a separate pivot table report for each region, market, manager, or whatever. These types of requests usually lead to a painful manual process in which you copy a pivot table onto a new worksheet and then change the filter field to the appropriate region or manager. You then repeat this process as many times as you need to get through each selection.

Creating separate pivot table reports is one area where Excel really comes to the rescue. Excel has a function called Show Report Filter Pages that automatically creates a separate pivot table for each item in the filter fields. To use this function, simply create a pivot table with a filter field, as shown in Figure 14-39.

Place your cursor anywhere on the pivot table and then go up to the ribbon to select the Analyze tab. On the Analyze tab, go to the PivotTable group, click the Options drop-down menu, and then select Show Report Filter Pages, as shown in Figure 14-40.

FIGURE 14-39 Start with a pivot table that contains a filter field.

FIGURE 14-40 Click the Show Report Filter Pages button.

A dialog box opens, enabling you to choose the filter field for which you would like to create separate pivot tables. Select the appropriate filter field and click OK.

Your reward is a sheet for each item in the filter field, with each one containing its own pivot table. Figure 14-41 illustrates the result. Note that the newly created tabs are named to correspond with the filter item shown in the pivot table.

FIGURE 14-41 With just a few clicks, you can have a separate pivot table for each market!

> **Note** Be aware that you can use Show Report Filter Pages on only one filter field at a time. This feature will not automatically replicate any pivot charts.

Tip 18: Apply restrictions on pivot tables and pivot fields

I often send pivot tables to clients, coworkers, managers, and other groups of people. In some cases, I'd like to restrict the types of actions users can take on the pivot table reports I send them. The macros outlined in this section demonstrate some of the protection settings available via VBA.

Pivot table restrictions

The PivotTable object exposes several properties that allow you, as a developer, to restrict different features and components of a pivot table:

- **EnableWizard**—Setting this property to False disables the PivotTable Tools context menu that normally activates when you click inside a pivot table.

- **EnableDrilldown**—Setting this property to False prevents users from getting to detailed data by double-clicking a data field.

- **EnableFieldList**—Setting this property to False prevents users from activating the field list or moving pivot fields around.

- **EnableFieldDialog**—Setting this property to False disables the users' ability to alter the pivot field via the Value Field Settings dialog box.

- **PivotCache.EnableRefresh**—Setting this property to False disables the ability to refresh the pivot table.

You can independently set any or all these properties to either True or False. The following macro applies all the restrictions to the target pivot table:

```
Sub ApplyPivotTableRestrictions ()

'Step 1: Declare your Variables
 Dim pt As PivotTable

'Step 2: Point to the PivotTable in the activecell
 On Error Resume Next
 Set pt = ActiveSheet.PivotTables(ActiveCell.PivotTable.Name)

'Step 3: Exit if active cell is not in a PivotTable
 If pt Is Nothing Then
 MsgBox "You must place your cursor inside of a PivotTable."
 Exit Sub
 End If

'Step 4: Apply Pivot Table Restrictions
 With pt
 .EnableWizard = False
 .EnableDrilldown = False
 .EnableFieldList = False
 .EnableFieldDialog = False
```

```
.PivotCache.EnableRefresh = False
End With

End Sub
```

In this macro, step 1 declares the `pt` pivot table object variable that serves as the memory container for the pivot table.

Step 2 sets the `pt` variable to the name of the pivot table on which the active cell is found. It does this by using the `ActiveCell.PivotTable.Name` property to get the name of the target pivot table.

Step 3 checks to see whether the `pt` variable is filled with a pivot table object. If the `pt` variable is set to `Nothing`, the active cell was not on a pivot table, and thus no pivot table could be assigned to the variable. If this is the case, the macro says this to the user in a message box, and then it exits the procedure.

Step 4 applies the pivot table restrictions.

Once your chosen features have been restricted, Excel disables the menu commands for the features you turned off. You can see in Figure 14-42 that the Refresh, Pivot Table Options, and Show Field List commands are grayed out.

FIGURE 14-42   The commands for restricted features will be grayed out in all menus.

Pivot field restrictions

Like pivot table restrictions, pivot field restrictions enable you to restrict the types of actions users can take on the pivot fields in a pivot table. The macro shown in this section demonstrates some of the protection settings available via VBA.

The `PivotField` object exposes several properties that allow you, as a developer, to restrict different features and components of a pivot table:

- **DragToPage**—Setting this property to `False` prevents users from dragging any pivot field into the report filter area of the pivot table.

- **DragToRow**—Setting this property to False prevents users from dragging any pivot field into the row area of the pivot table.

- **DragToColumn**—Setting this property to False prevents users from dragging any pivot field into the column area of the pivot table.

- **DragToData**—Setting this property to False prevents users from dragging any pivot field into the data area of the pivot table.

- **DragToHide**—Setting this property to False prevents users from dragging pivot fields off the pivot table. It also prevents the use of the right-click menu to hide or remove pivot fields.

- **EnableItemSelection**—Setting this property to False disables the drop-down menus on each pivot field.

You can independently set any or all these properties to either True or False. The following macro applies all the restrictions to the target pivot table:

```
Sub ApplyPivotFieldRestrictions()

'Step 1: Declare your Variables
 Dim pt As PivotTable
 Dim pf As PivotField

'Step 2: Point to the PivotTable in the activecell
 On Error Resume Next
 Set pt = ActiveSheet.PivotTables(ActiveCell.PivotTable.Name)

'Step 3: Exit if active cell is not in a PivotTable
 If pt Is Nothing Then
 MsgBox "You must place your cursor inside of a PivotTable."
 Exit Sub
 End If

'Step 4: Apply Pivot Field Restrictions
 For Each pf In pt.PivotFields
 pf.EnableItemSelection = False
 pf.DragToPage = False
 pf.DragToRow = False
 pf.DragToColumn = False
 pf.DragToData = False
 pf.DragToHide = False
 Next pf

End Sub
```

Step 1 declares two object variables, using pt as the memory container for the pivot table and pf as a memory container for the pivot fields. This allows looping through all the pivot fields in the pivot table.

Step 2 sets the pt variable to the name of the pivot table on which the active cell is found. It does this by using the ActiveCell.PivotTable.Name property to get the name of the target pivot.

Step 3 checks whether the pt variable is filled with a `PivotTable` object. If the pt variable is set to `Nothing`, the active cell was not on a pivot table, and thus no pivot table could be assigned to the variable. If this is the case, the macro notifies the user via a message box and then exits the procedure.

Step 4 of the macro uses a For Each statement to iterate through each pivot field and apply all the specified pivot field restrictions.

Once your chosen features have been restricted, Excel disables the menu commands for the features you set to `False`.

Tip 19: Use a pivot table to explode a data set to different workbooks

Imagine that you have a data set with 50,000+ rows of data. You have been asked to create a separate workbook for each market in this data set. In this tip, you'll discover how you can accomplish this task by using a pivot table and a little VBA.

Place the field you need to use as the group dimension (in this case, Market) into the filter field. Place the count of Market into the data field. Your pivot table should look like the one shown in Figure 14-43.

	A	B
1	Market	(All) ▼
2		
3	Sum of Sales_Amount	
4	$10,774,172	

FIGURE 14-43 Create a simple pivot table with one data field and a filter.

As you know, you can manually select a market in the page/filter field and then double-click Sum of Sales_Amount. This gives you a new tab containing all the records that make up the number you double-clicked. Imagine how you could do this for every market in the Market field and save the resulting tabs to their own workbook.

Using this same concept, you can implement the following VBA that goes through each item in the chosen page field and essentially calls the ShowDetail method for you, creating a raw data tab. The procedure then saves that raw data tab to a new workbook:

```
Sub ExplodeTable()
Dim PvtItem As PivotItem
Dim PvtTable As PivotTable
Dim FName as variant

'Change variables to suit your scenario
 Const strFieldName = "Market" '<-Change Field Name
 Const strTriggerRange = "B4" '<-Change Trigger Range

'Set the pivot table name if needed
```

```
Set PvtTable = ActiveSheet.PivotTables("PivotTable1") '<-Change Name if Needed

'Start looping through each item in the selected field
 For Each PvtItem In PvtTable.PivotFields(strFieldName).PivotItems
 PvtTable.PivotFields(strFieldName).CurrentPage = PvtItem.Name
 Range(strTriggerRange).ShowDetail = True

 'Name the temp sheet for easy cleanup later
 ActiveSheet.Name = "TempSheet"

 'copy data to new workbook and delete the temp sheet
 ActiveSheet.Cells.Copy
 Workbooks.Add
 ActiveSheet.Paste
 Cells.EntireColumn.AutoFit

 Application.DisplayAlerts = False
 FName = ThisWorkbook.Path & "\" & PvtItem.Name & ".xlsx"
 ActiveWorkbook.SaveAs Filename:=Fname, FileFormat:=xlOpenXMLWorkbook
 ActiveWorkbook.Close
 Sheets("Tempsheet").Delete
 Application.DisplayAlerts = True

 Next PvtItem

End Sub
```

To implement this technique, enter this code into a new VBA module. Be sure to change the following constants as appropriate for your scenario:

- **Const strFieldName**—This is the name of the field you want to separate the data by (that is, the field you put in the page/filter area of the pivot table).

- **Const strTriggerRange**—This is essentially the range that holds the one number in the pivot table's data area. For example, if you look at Figure 14-44, you see the trigger cell in A4.

Name	Date modified
SEATTLE.xlsx	9/15/2018 1:03 PM
TULSA.xlsx	9/15/2018 1:03 PM
NEWYORK.xlsx	9/15/2018 1:03 PM
PHOENIX.xlsx	9/15/2018 1:03 PM
MICHIGAN.xlsx	9/15/2018 1:03 PM
NEWORLEANS.xlsx	9/15/2018 1:03 PM
KANSASCITY.xlsx	9/15/2018 1:03 PM
DENVER.xlsx	9/15/2018 1:03 PM
FLORIDA.xlsx	9/15/2018 1:03 PM
CHARLOTTE.xlsx	9/15/2018 1:03 PM
DALLAS.xlsx	9/15/2018 1:03 PM
CANADA.xlsx	9/15/2018 1:03 PM
BUFFALO.xlsx	9/15/2018 1:03 PM
CALIFORNIA.xlsx	9/15/2018 1:03 PM

FIGURE 14-44 After running the macro, you will have a separate workbook for each filtered dimension.

As you can see in Figure 14-44, running this macro procedure outputs data for each market into its own separate workbook.

Tip 20: Use percentage change from previous for year-over-year

If you have grouped daily dates to years, you are not allowed to add calculated fields or calculated items. With the pivot table in Figure 14-45, you have revenue from last year and this year in columns B and C. You would like to show a % change in column D.

One hack is to remove the grand total that normally appears in column D and build formulas outside the pivot table, such as =C6/B6-1. This is not the best method, because you have to recopy the formula if the size of your pivot table changes.

Instead, use this method:

1. Drag Revenue to the Values area a second time.

2. In the Columns area, move the new Σ Values tile above the Date tile. This will produce the report shown in Figure 14-45.

	A	B	C	D	E
3		Values	Date		
4		Sum of Revenue		Sum of Revenue2	
5	Sector	2022	2023	2022	2023
6	Associations	34360	51244	34360	51244
7	Consultants	586525	544610	586525	544610
8	Professional	251545	225400	251545	225400
9	Retail	426513	393607	426513	393607
10	Software	623660	652905	623660	652905
11	Training	1484950	1432493	1484950	1432493
12	Grand Total	3407553	3300259	3407553	3300259

PivotTable Fields

Drag fields between areas below:

Filters

Columns
Σ Values
Date

FIGURE 14-45 Build a report with Revenue in the Values area twice.

3. Change the calculation for the second Revenue field. Double-click cell D4 in Figure 14-45 to open the Value Field Settings.

4. In the Value Field Settings, type a new name such as **% Change**.

5. Choose the Show Values As tab.

6. Open the Show Values As drop-down menu and select Choose % Difference From.

7. For the Base Field, choose Date.

8. For the Base Item, choose (previous). The settings from steps 4 through 8 are shown in Figure 14-46.

FIGURE 14-46 Change the calculation for the second Revenue to % Difference From.

9. The results are correct, but column D will be blank. Select one cell in column D and change the column width to 0.1. This will allow the % Change heading from D4 to show up in the pivot table (see Figure 14-47).

FIGURE 14-47 The percentage change column is natively part of the pivot table.

10. Before you swap any fields in the row area, right-click the pivot table and choose PivotTable Options. On the Layout & Format tab, clear the check box for Autofit Column Widths On Update.

11. You can now quickly change the report. Unselect Sector. Choose Product. You can repeat to show year-over-year data for Region, Customer, or Product (see Figure 14-48).

FIGURE 14-48 Change the row field to produce a different year-over-year report.

Tip 21: Do a two-way VLOOKUP with Power Query

A note in Chapter 10, "Unlocking features with the Data Model and Power Pivot," mentioned that you could do a VLOOKUP while importing data with Power Query. This example will show you how to do a two-way VLOOKUP while importing with Power Query.

The source data in Figure 14-49 is a large sales database in columns F through H. For each sale, you have a Region and a Product. You need to report sales by product manager.

The product manager matrix is shown in A1:D6. Sometimes a manager handles one product across all regions (such as Johnny for Apples). But other assignments are not straightforward.

FIGURE 14-49 The table to assign product managers is shown in A1:D6.

The strategy is to process the lookup table first using Power Query and to leave it as a connection-only query.

You will then move the Sales data quickly through Power Query to create a second connection.

Finally, you will use a Merge query to join the two of them:

1. Select A1 and use Data, From Table/Range. The Power Query Editor opens. The Product column is selected by default.

2. In Power Query, choose Transform, Unpivot, Unpivot other columns.

3. Right-click the Attribute column and rename to Region.

4. Go to the Home tab in Power Query. Be very careful to not click Close & Load. Instead, open the drop-down menu at the bottom of Close & Load. Choose Close & Load To... (see Figure 14-50).

FIGURE 14-50 Unpivot the data. Choose Close & Load To....

5. The Import Data dialog box appears. Choose Only Create Connection and click OK (see Figure 14-51). When you return to Excel, the Queries & Connections panel appears. A single query of ProductManagers is listed in the panel.

FIGURE 14-51 Only Create Connection.

Steps 6 and 7 are similar to steps 1 through 5, so there will not be any figures.

6. Select one cell in the Sales table. Select Data, From Table/Range.

7. When Power Query opens, there are no changes needed. Select Home, Close & Load To....

8. In the Import Data dialog box, choose Only Create Connection. Click OK. You should now see two queries in the Queries & Connections panel (see Figure 14-52).

FIGURE 14-52 You've created connections to the data and the lookup table.

9. Select Data, Get Data, Combine Queries, Merge, as shown in Figure 14-53.

FIGURE 14-53 Choose to merge the two queries.

Note A Merge query is used to join two data sets with different fields. An Append query is used to join two data sets with the same fields.

10. The Merge dialog box is confusing. Make sure to follow steps 10 through 17 and then compare to Figure 14-54 before clicking OK. In the top drop-down menu, choose the Sales table.

11. In the bottom drop-down menu, choose the ProductManagers table. The next steps are not obvious, and there are no instructions in the dialog box.

12. In the data preview for Sales, click the Region heading.

13. In the data preview for Sales, Ctrl+click the Product Heading.

14. In the data preview for ProductManagers, click the Region heading (even though it is listed second).

15. In the data preview for ProductManagers, Ctrl+click the Product heading.

16. Note the small "1" and "2" in each heading.

17. For the Join Kind, choose Left Outer Join. The dialog box reports that all 1535 rows have been matched (see Figure 14-54).

FIGURE 14-54 Choose the two tables and the key fields in common between them.

18. Click OK. The Power Query Editor opens. Where you expect to see the product manager, you see a column that says Table over and over (see Figure 14-55).

FIGURE 14-55 The appended query is loaded as a table.

19. Click the Expand icon next to the ProductManagers heading. Clear the fields that are duplicates: Product and Region. Clear the check box for Use Original Column Name As Prefix (see Figure 14-56).

FIGURE 14-56 Choose which fields from the lookup table to show.

20. Rename the Value column to be Product Manager. Drag that column to the left of Revenue (see Figure 14-57).

FIGURE 14-57 The two tables have been joined.

21. Choose Home, Close & Load. Your data will be returned to a new worksheet.

22. Build a pivot table to report sales by product manager (see Figure 14-58).

	A	B	C	D	E	F	G
1	Region	Product	Product Manager	Sales			
2	East	Banana	Mikey	9633			
3	East	Apple	Johnny	8408			
4	East	Apple	Johnny	6790		Product Manager	Sum of Sales
5	Central	Banana	Mikey	6297		Drew	$1,612,795
6	Central	Banana	Mikey	5150		Eve	$544,846
7	Central	Apple	Johnny	9438		Johnny	$1,758,253
8	West	Cherry	Mae	4574		Mae	$1,660,524
9	West	Cherry	Mae	3489		Mikey	$2,944,322
10	East	Cherry	Mikey	5146		Grand Total	$8,520,740
11	West	Fig	Mae	4369			
12	West	Fig	Mae	1867			

FIGURE 14-58 The final pivot table shows sales by product manager. Recall that this data started out in different tables.

It would have been very easy in this example to replace the Sales table with a Data, Get Data, From File, From Workbook. Every time the underlying data changed, a simple Data, Refresh All would refresh all three queries. You will have to refresh the pivot table after the Refresh All. But it will be two steps to update instead of many steps.

Also, it would have been possible in Power Query to group by Product Manager and Sum Of Sales to produce a finished query that had all of the same data as F4:G9 in Figure 14-58.

Power Query is the real game-changer in Excel. This book about pivot tables has made significant use of Power Query in several locations:

- Power Query was used in Chapter 2 while cleaning data before pivoting.

- Power Query was used in Chapter 5 to create a calculated column.

- Power Query was used extensively in Chapter 7.

- Power Query was used in Chapter 10 for dealing with more than 1,048,576 rows of data.

- Power Query was mentioned as a way to get two data sets into 3D Map in Chapter 11.

- Chapter 12 proposed Power Query is an alternative to the VBA Macro Recorder.

- Chapter 14 used Power Query as the lucky twenty-first tip to do a two-way VLOOKUP before pivoting.

Bottom line: You should really take a look at Power Query.

Next steps

In Chapter 15, "Dr. Jekyll and Mr. GetPivotData," you'll learn about one of the most hated pivot table features: the GetPivotData function. However, you'll also learn how to use this function to create refreshable reports month after month.

Dr. Jekyll and Mr. GetPivotData

In this chapter, you will:

- Avoid the aggravating GetPivotData problem
- Use GetPivotData to solve pivot table annoyances

This chapter shows you a technique that solves many annoying pivot table problems. If you have been using pivot tables for a while, you might have run into the following problems:

- Formatting tends to be destroyed when you refresh a pivot table. Numeric formats are lost. Column widths go away.

- There is no easy way to build an asymmetric pivot table. Using named sets is one way, but they are available only in a pivot table model, not in a regular pivot cache pivot table.

- Excel cannot remember a template. If you frequently have to re-create a pivot table, you must redo the groupings, calculated fields, calculated items, and so on.

The technique shown in this chapter solves all these problems. It is not new. In fact, it has been around since Excel 2002. I have taught Power Excel seminars to thousands of accountants who use Excel 40–60 hours a week. Out of those thousands of people, I have had only three people say that they use this technique.

Ironically, far more than 0.3% of people know of this feature. One common question I get at seminars is: "Why did this feature show up in Excel 2002, and how the heck can you turn it off?" This same feature, which is reviled by most Excellers, is the key to creating reusable pivot table templates.

The credit for this chapter must go to Rob Collie, who spent years on the Excel project management team. He spent the Excel 2010 development cycle working on the PowerPivot product. Rob happened to relocate to Cleveland, Ohio. Because Cleveland is not a hotbed of Microsoft developers, Dave Gainer gave me a heads-up that Rob was moving to my area, and we started having lunch.

Rob and I talked about Excel and had some great conversations. During our second lunch, Rob said something that threw me for a loop. He said, "We find that our internal customers use `GetPivotData` all the time to build their reports, and we are not sure they will like the way PowerPivot interacts with `GetPivotData`."

I stopped Rob to ask if he was crazy. I told him that in my experience with about 15,000 accountants, only 3 of them had ever admitted to liking `GetPivotData`. What did he mean that he finds customers actually using `GetPivotData`?

Rob explained the key word in his statement: He was talking about *internal* customers, which are the people inside Microsoft who use Excel to do their jobs. Those people had become incredibly reliant on GetPivotData. He agreed that outside Microsoft, hardly anyone ever uses GetPivotData. In fact, the only question he ever gets outside Microsoft is how to turn off the stupid feature.

I had to know more, so I asked Rob to explain how the irritating GetPivotData could ever be used for good purposes. Rob explained it to me, and I use this chapter to explain it to you. However, I know that 99% of you are reading this chapter because of the following reasons:

- You ran into the unexpected GetPivotData.

- You turned to the index of this book to find information on GetPivotData.

- You are expecting me to tell you how to turn off GetPivotData.

So, let's start there.

Avoiding the evil GetPivotData problem

GetPivotData has been the cause of many headaches since around the time of Excel 2002 when suddenly, without any fanfare, pivot table behavior changed slightly. Any time you build formulas outside a pivot table that point back inside the pivot table, you run into the GetPivotData problem.

For example, say you build the pivot table shown in Figure 15-1. Those years across the top are built by grouping daily dates into years. You would like to compare this year versus last year. Unfortunately, you are not allowed to add calculated items to a grouped field. So, you follow these steps:

1. Add a **% Growth** heading in cell D4.

2. Copy the formatting from C4 over to D4.

3. In cell D5, press Ctrl+1 to open the Format Cells dialog box.

4. In the Format Cells dialog box, choose the Number tab. Click the Custom format and type +0.0%;-0.0%;0.0%. Click OK.

5. In cell D5, type = (an equal sign).

6. Click cell C5.

7. Type **/** (a slash) for division.

8. Click B5.

FIGURE 15-1 You want to add a formula to show the percentage of growth year after year.

9. Type –1 and press Ctrl+Enter to stay in the same cell. Format the result as a percentage. You see that the West region dropped by 43.8% (see Figure 15-2).

D5		f_x	=GETPIVOTDATA("Revenue",$A$3,"Region","West","Y

	A	B	C	D	E	F	G	H
1								
2								
3	Sum of Revenue	Years						
4	Region	2023	2024	% Growth				
5	West	$337,634	$189,723	-43.8%				
6	Midwest	$123,757	$347,509					
7	North	$16,457	$52,767					
8	Northeast	$122,611	$152,341					
9	South	$2,189,994	$3,192,255					
10	Southeast	$359,782	$801,992					
11	Southwest	$141,861	$191,353					
12	Grand Total	$3,292,095	$4,927,939					
13								

FIGURE 15-2 Build the formula in D5 using the mouse or the arrow keys.

> **Note** If you started using spreadsheets back in the days of Lotus 1-2-3, you might like to use this alternative method to build the formula in D5: Type = (an equal sign) and press the left arrow once. Type / (for division). Press the left arrow twice. Press Enter. As you see, the GetPivotData problem strikes no matter which method you use.

10. After entering your first formula, select cell D5.

11. Double-click the tiny square dot in the lower-right corner of the cell. This is the fill handle, and it copies the formula down to the end of the report.

Immediately, you notice that something is wrong because every region happened to fall by 43.8% since last year (see Figure 15-3).

There is no way that this happens in real life. The data must be fabricated.

	A	B	C	D	E
1					
2					
3	Sum of Revenue	Years ▾			
4	Region ▾	2023	2024	% Growth	
5	West	$337,634	$189,723	-43.8%	
6	Midwest	$123,757	$347,509	-43.8%	
7	North	$16,457	$52,767	-43.8%	
8	Northeast	$122,611	$152,341	-43.8%	
9	South	$2,189,994	$3,192,255	-43.8%	
10	Southeast	$359,782	$801,992	-43.8%	
11	Southwest	$141,861	$191,353	-43.8%	
12	Grand Total	$3,292,095	$4,927,939	-43.8%	
13					

FIGURE 15-3   When the formula is copied down, somehow the growth is -43.8% for every region.

Think about the formula you built: 2024 data divided by 2023 data minus 1. You probably could create that formula with your eyes closed (that is, if you use arrow keys to create formulas instead of your mouse).

This is what makes you not notice something completely insidious when you built the formula. When you went through the steps to build the formula, as a rational person, you would expect Excel to create a formula such as =C5/B5-1. However, go back to cell D5 and press the F2 key to look at the formula (see Figure 15-4). Something unanticipated has happened. The simple formula =C5/B5-1 is no longer there. Instead, Excel generated some GetPivotData nonsense. Although the formula works in D5, it does not work when you copy the formula down.

	A	B	C	D	E	F	G	H	I	J
1										
2										
3	Sum of Revenue	Years ▾								
4	Region ▾	2023	2024	% Growth						
5	West	$337,634	$189,723	=GETPIVOTDATA("Revenue",$A$3,"Region","West","Years",2024)/						
6	Midwest	$123,757	$347,509	GETPIVOTDATA("Revenue",$A$3,"Region","West","Years",2023)-1						
7	North	$16,457	$52,767	-43.8%						
8	Northeast	$122,611	$152,341	-43.8%						
9	South	$2,189,994	$3,192,255	-43.8%						
10	Southeast	$359,782	$801,992	-43.8%						
11	Southwest	$141,861	$191,353	-43.8%						
12	Grand Total	$3,292,095	$4,927,939	-43.8%						
13										

FIGURE 15-4   Where did GetPivotData come from?

When this occurs, your reaction is something like, "What is GetPivotData, and why is it messing up my report?" Your next reaction is, "How can I turn it off?" You might even wonder, "Why would Microsoft put this thing in there?"

Excel started inserting GetPivotData in Excel 2002. After being stung by GetPivotData repeatedly, I grew to hate it. I was thrown for a loop in one of the Power Analyst Boot Camps when someone asked me how it could possibly be used. I had never considered that question. In my mind, and in most other people's minds, GetPivotData was no good.

If you are one of those users who would just like to avoid GetPivotData, I've got great news: There are two ways to do so, as presented in the following two sections.

Preventing GetPivotData by typing the formula

The simple method for avoiding GetPivotData is to create your formula without touching the mouse or the arrow keys. To do this, follow these steps:

1. Go to cell D5; type =.

2. Type **C5**.

3. Type **/**.

4. Type **B5**.

5. Type **-1**.

6. Press Enter.

You have now built a regular Excel formula that you can copy to produce real results, as shown in Figure 15-5.

	A	B	C	D
3	Sum of Revenue	Years		
4	Region	2023	2024	% Growth
5	West	$337,634	$189,723	-43.8%
6	Midwest	$123,757	$347,509	+180.8%
7	North	$16,457	$52,767	+220.6%
8	Northeast	$122,611	$152,341	+24.2%
9	South	$2,189,994	$3,192,255	+45.8%
10	Southeast	$359,782	$801,992	+122.9%
11	Southwest	$141,861	$191,353	+34.9%
12	Grand Total	$3,292,095	$4,927,939	+49.7%
13				

FIGURE 15-5 Type **=C5/B5-1**, and the formula works as expected.

It is a relief to see that you can still build formulas outside pivot tables that point into a pivot table. I have run into people who simply thought this could not be done.

You might be a bit annoyed that you have to abandon your normal way of entering formulas. If so, the next section offers an alternative.

Simply turning off GetPivotData

If you do not plan to read the second half of this chapter, you can simply turn off GetPivotData forever. Who needs it? It is bothersome, so just turn it off.

In Excel 2019, follow these steps:

1. Move the cell pointer back inside a pivot table so that the PivotTable Tools tabs appear.

2. Click the Analyze tab.

3. Notice the Options icon on the left side of the ribbon (see Figure 15-6). Do not click the icon; rather, next to the Options icon, click the drop-down arrow.

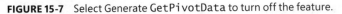

FIGURE 15-6 Don't click the large Options icon. Click the tiny drop-down arrow next to the icon.

4. Inside the Options drop-down menu is the choice Generate GetPivotData (see Figure 15-7). By default, this option is selected. Click that item to clear this check box.

FIGURE 15-7 Select Generate GetPivotData to turn off the feature.

The previous steps assume that you have a pivot table in the workbook that you can select in order to access the PivotTable Tool tabs. If you don't have a pivot table in the current workbook, you can use File, Options. In the Formulas category, clear the check box for Use GetPivotData Functions For Pivot-Table References.

Speculating on why Microsoft forced GetPivotData on us

If GetPivotData is so universally hated, why did the fine people at Microsoft turn on the feature by default? Everyone simply wants to turn it off. Why would they bother to leave it on? Are they trying to make sure that there is a market for my Power Excel seminars?

I have a theory about this that I came up with during the Excel 2007 launch. I had written many books about Excel 2007—somewhere around 1,800 pages of content. When the Office 2007 launch events were happening around the country, I was given an opportunity to work at the event. I watched with interest when the presenter talked about the new features in Excel 2007.

There were at least 15 amazing features in Excel 2007. The presenter took three minutes and glossed over perhaps three of the features.

I was perplexed. How could Microsoft marketing do such a horrible job of showing what was new in Excel? Then I realized that this must always happen. Marketing asks the development team what is new.

The project manager gives them a list of 15 items. The marketing guy says something like, "There is not room for 15 items in the presentation. Can you cut 80% of those items out of the list and give me just the ones with glitz and sizzle?"

The folks who worked on GetPivotData certainly knew that GetPivotData would never have enough sizzle to make it into the marketing news about Excel 2002. So, by making it the default, they hoped someone would notice GetPivotData and try to figure out how it could be used. Instead, most people, including me, just turned it off and thought it was another step in the Microsoft plot to make our lives miserable by making it harder to work in Excel.

Using GetPivotData to solve pivot table annoyances

You would not be reading this book if you hadn't realized that pivot tables are the greatest invention ever. Four clicks can create a pivot table that obsoletes the arcane process of using Advanced Filter, =DSUM, and data tables. Pivot tables enable you to produce one-page summaries of massive data sets. So what if the formatting is ugly? And so what if you usually end up converting most pivot tables to values so you can delete the columns you do not need but cannot turn off?

Figure 15-8 illustrates a typical pivot table experience: You start with raw data. You then produce a pivot table and use all sorts of advanced pivot table tricks to get it close. You conclude by converting the pivot table to values and performing the final formatting in regular Excel.

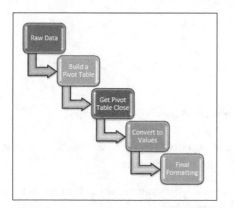

FIGURE 15-8   A typical pivot table process.

Note   I rarely get to refresh a pivot table because I never let pivot tables live long enough to have new data. The next time I get data, I start creating the pivot table all over again. If it is a long process, I write a macro that lets me fly through the five steps in Figure 15-8 in a couple of keystrokes.

The new method introduced by Rob Collie and described in the rest of this chapter puts a different spin on the pivot table experience. In this new method, which people inside Microsoft tend to use, you build an ugly pivot table. You do not care about the formatting of this pivot table. You then go through a one-time, relatively painful process of building a nicely formatted shell to hold your final report. Finally, you use GetPivotData to populate the shell report quickly.

From then on when you get new data, you simply put it on the data sheet, refresh the ugly pivot table, and print the shell report. Figure 15-9 illustrates this process.

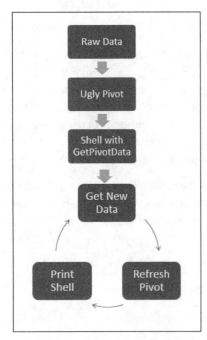

FIGURE 15-9 How people who work in the accounting department at Microsoft use pivot tables.

There are huge advantages to this method. For example, you do not have to worry about formatting the report after the first time. It comes much closer to an automated process.

The rest of this chapter walks you through the steps to build a dynamic report that shows actuals for months that have been completed and a forecast for future months.

Building an ugly pivot table

Say that you have transactional data showing budget and actuals for each region of a company. The budget data is at a monthly level. The actuals data is at a daily level. Budget data exists for the entire year. Actuals exist only for the months that have been completed. Figure 15-10 shows the original data set.

Because you will be updating this report every month, it makes the process easier if you have a pivot table data source that grows as you add new data to the bottom. Whereas legacy versions of

Excel would achieve this through a named dynamic range using the OFFSET function, you can do this in Excel 2019 by selecting one cell in your data and pressing Ctrl+T to make the range a table. Click OK to confirm that your data has headers.

You now have a formatted data set, as shown in Figure 15-10.

	A	B	C	D
1	Region	Date	Measure	Revenue
2	Midwest	1/1/2024	Budget	248000
3	North	1/1/2024	Budget	90000
4	Northeast	1/1/2024	Budget	266000
5	South	1/1/2024	Budget	360000
6	Southeast	1/1/2024	Budget	675000
7	Southwest	1/1/2024	Budget	293000
8	West	1/1/2024	Budget	563000
9	Midwest	2/1/2024	Budget	248000
10	North	2/1/2024	Budget	90000
11	Northeast	2/1/2024	Budget	266000
12	South	2/1/2024	Budget	360000
13	Southeast	2/1/2024	Budget	675000

FIGURE 15-10 The original data includes budget and actuals.

Your next step is to create a pivot table that has every possible value needed in your final report. GetPivotData is powerful, but it can only return values that are visible in the actual pivot table. It cannot reach through to the pivot cache to calculate items that are not in the pivot table.

Create the pivot table by following these steps:

1. Select Insert, PivotTable, OK.

2. In the PivotTable Fields list, select the Date field. You will either see daily dates or years in the first column (see Figure 15-11). If you see years, it's due to the new Excel 2019 AutoGroup functionality, and you should skip Step 3.

FIGURE 15-11 Start with daily dates down the left.

3. Select the first date cell in A4. From the PivotTable Options tab, select Group Field. Select Months and Years, as shown in Figure 15-12. Click OK. You now have actual month names down the left side, as shown in Figure 15-13.

FIGURE 15-12 Group the daily dates up to months and years.

FIGURE 15-13 You have month names instead of dates.

4. Drag the Years and Date fields to the Columns area in the Pivot Table Fields list.

5. Drag Measure to the Columns area.

6. Select Region to have it appear along the left column of the pivot table.

7. Select Revenue to have it appear in the Values area of the pivot table.

As shown in Figure 15-14, you now have one ugly pivot table. Having a total of January Actuals plus January Budget in column D is completely pointless. This is ugly. But for once, you do not care because no one other than you will ever see this pivot table.

	A	B	C	D	E	F	G	H
1								
2								
3	Sum of Revenue	Years ▼	Date ▼	Measure ▼				
4		⊟ 2024	2024	2024	2024	2024	2024	2024
5		⊟ Jan	Jan	Jan Total	⊟ Feb	Feb	Feb Total	⊟ M
6	Region ▼	Actuals	Budget		Actuals	Budget		Actu
7	West	578379	563000	1141379	596267	563000	1159267	53(
8	Midwest	312387	248000	560387	266949	248000	514949	30:
9	North	100742	90000	190742	95197	90000	185197	8!
10	Northeast	277435	266000	543435	336005	266000	602005	33(
11	South	4182773	360000	4542773	4182773	360000	4542773	3979
12	Southeast	926977	675000	1601977	789647	675000	1464647	88/
13	Southwest	361686	293000	654686	329772	293000	622772	36!
14	Grand Total	6740379	2495000	9235379	6596610	2495000	9091610	649!
15								

FIGURE 15-14 The world's ugliest pivot table. Summing Actuals and Budget in column D is completely meaningless.

At this point, the goal is to have a pivot table with every possible data point you could ever need in your final report. It is fine if the pivot table has extra data you will never need in the report.

Building the shell report

Now it's time to put away your pivot table hat and take out your straight Excel hat. You are going to use basic Excel formulas and formatting to create a nicely formatted report suitable for giving to your manager.

Insert a blank worksheet in your workbook and then follow these steps:

1. Put a report title in cell A1.

2. Use the Cell Styles drop-down menu on the Home tab to format cell A1 as a title.

3. Put a date in cell A2 by using the formula =EOMONTH(TODAY(),0). This enters the serial number of the last day of the previous month in cell B1. If you want to see how the formula is working, you can format the cell as a date. If you are reading this on July 14, 2024, the date that appears in cell B1 is June 30, 2024.

4. Select cell A2. Press Ctrl+1 to go to the Format Cells dialog box. On the Number tab, click Custom. Type the custom number format "Actuals Through" mmmm, yyyy. This causes the calculated date to appear as text.

5. Because there is a chance that the text in cell A2 is going to be wider than you want column A to be, select both cells A2 and B2. Press Ctrl+1 to format the cells. On the Alignment tab, select Merge Cells. This allows the formula in cell A2 to spill over into B2 if necessary.

6. Type a Region heading in cell A5.

7. Down the rest of column A, type your region names. These names should match the names in the pivot table.

8. Where appropriate, add labels in column A for Division totals.

9. Add a line for Total Company at the bottom of the report.

10. Month names stretch from cells B4 to M4. Enter this formula in cell B4: `=DATE (YEAR ($A$2),COLUMN(A1),1)`.

11. Select cell B4. Press Ctrl+1 to format the cells. On the Number tab, select Custom and type the custom number format **MMM**.

12. Right-justify cell B4. Use the Cell Styles drop-down menu to select Heading 4.

13. Copy cell B4 to cells C4:M4. You now have true dates across the top that appear as month labels.

14. Enter this formula in cell B5: `=IF(MONTH(B4)<=MONTH($A$2),"Actuals","Budget")`. Right-justify cell B5. Copy across to cells C5:M5. This should provide the word *Actuals* for past months and the word *Budget* for future months.

15. Add a Total column heading in cell N5. Add a Total Budget column in cell O5. Enter 'Var % in cell P5.

16. Fill in the regular Excel formulas needed to provide division totals, the total compa grand total column, and the variance % column. For example:

    - Enter `=SUM(B6:B7)` in cell B8, and copy across.

    - Enter `=SUM(B6:M6)` in cell N6, and copy down.

    - Enter `=IFERROR((N6/O6)-1,0)` in cell P6, and copy down.

    - Enter `=SUM(B10:B12)` in cell B13, and copy across.

    - Enter `=SUM(B15:B16)` in cell B17, and copy across.

    - Enter `=SUM(B6:B18)/2` in cell B19, and copy across.

17. Apply the Heading 4 cell style to the labels in column A and to the headings in rows 4:5.

18. Apply the `#,##0` number format to cells B6:O19.

19. Apply the `0.0%` number format to column P.

> **Note** If the names in the pivot table are region codes, you can hide the codes in a new hidden column A and put friendly region names in column B.

You now have a completed shell report, as shown in Figure 15-15. This report has all the necessary formatting your manager might desire. It has totals that add up the numbers that eventually come from the pivot table.

In the next section, you'll use GetPivotData to complete the report.

FIGURE 15-15 The shell report before the GetPivotData formulas are added.

Using GetPivotData to populate the shell report

At this point, you are ready to take advantage of the thing that has been driving you crazy for years—that crazy Generate GetPivotData setting. If you cleared the setting back in Figure 15-7, go in and select it again. When it is selected, you see a check mark next to Generate GetPivotData.

Go to cell B6 on the shell report (this is the cell for Northeast region, January, Actuals), and then follow these steps:

1. Type = to start a formula (see Figure 15-16).

FIGURE 15-16 Start a formula on the shell report.

2. Move to the pivot table worksheet and click the cell for Northeast, January, Actuals. In Figure 15-17, this is cell B10.

3. Press Enter to return to the shell report and complete the formula. Excel adds a GetPivotData function in cell B6.

The formula says that the Northeast region actuals are $277,435.

Tip Jot down this number because you will want to compare it to the result of the formula that you later edit.

	A	B	C	D	E	F	G	H	I	
1										
2										
3	Sum of Revenue	Years	Date	Measure						
4		⊟ 2024	2024	2024	2024	2024	2024	2024	2024	20
5		⊟ Jan	Jan	Jan Total	⊟ Feb	Feb	Feb Total	⊟ Mar	Mar	M
6	Region	Actuals	Budget		Actuals	Budget		Actuals	Budget	
7	West	578379	563000	1141379	596267	563000	1159267	536640	749000	
8	Midwest	312387	248000	560387	266949	248000	514949	303867	329000	
9	North	100742	90000	190742	95197	90000	185197	85954	120000	
10	Northeast	277435	266000	543435	336005	266000	602005	336005	353000	
11	South	4182773	360000	4542773	4182773	360000	4542773	3979726	480000	
12	Southeast	926977	675000	1601977	789647	675000	1464647	884061	900000	
13	Southwest	361686	293000	654686	329772	293000	622772	368777	389000	
14	Grand Total	6740379	2495000	9235379	6596610	2495000	9091610	6495030	3320000	
15										

FIGURE 15-17 Using the mouse, click the correct cell in the pivot table.

The initial formula is as follows:

```
=GETPIVOTDATA("Revenue",UglyPivotTable!$A$3,"Region","Northeast",
"Date",1,"Measure","Actuals","Years",2018)
```

After years of ignoring the GetPivotData formula, you need to look at this monster formula closely to understand what it is doing. Figure 15-18 shows the formula in the Formula Bar.

B6	▼ : × ✓ *fx*	=GETPIVOTDATA("Revenue",UglyPivotTable!$A$3,"Region","Northeast", "Date",1,"Measure","Actuals","Years",2024)								
	A	B	C	D	E	F	G	H	I	J
1	Actuals & Budget By Region									
2	Actuals Through July, 2024									
3										
4		Jan	Feb	Mar	Apr	May	Jun	Jul	Aug	Sep
5	Region	Actuals	Actuals	Actuals	Actuals	Actuals	Actuals	Actuals	Budget	Budget
6	Northeast	277,435								
7	Southeast									
8	East Division Total	277,435	0	0	0	0	0	0	0	0
9										

FIGURE 15-18 The GetPivotData formula generated by Microsoft.

The syntax for the function is =GetPivotData(*data_field, pivot_table, [field1, item1],*
...). In this case, there are four pairs of field*n*, item*n* arguments. Here are the arguments in the formula:

■ ***Data_field***—This is the field in the Values area of the pivot table. Note that you use Revenue, not Sum Of Revenue.

- **Pivot_table**—This is Microsoft's way of asking, "Which pivot table do you mean?" All you have to do here is point to one single cell within the pivot table. The entry of **UglyPivotTable!$A$3** is the first populated cell in the pivot table. You are free to choose any cell in the pivot table you want. However, because it does not matter which cell you choose, don't worry about getting clever here. Leave the formula pointing to **$A$3**, and you will be fine.

- **Field1, item1**—The formula generated by Microsoft shows Region as the field name and Northeast as the item value. Aha! So this is why the GetPivotData formulas that Microsoft generates cannot be copied. They are essentially hard-coded to point to one specific value. You want your formula to change as you copy it through your report. Edit the formula to change Northeast to $A6. By using only a single dollar sign before A, you are enabling the row portion of the reference to vary as you copy the formula down.

- **Field2, item2**—The next two pairs of arguments specify that the Date field should be 1. When the original pivot table was grouped by month and year, the month field retained the original field name Date. The value for the month is 1, which means January. You probably thought I was insane to build that outrageous formula and custom number format in cell B4. That formula becomes useful now. Instead of hard-coding a 1, use **MONTH(B$4)**. The single dollar sign before row 4 indicates that the formula can get data from other months as it is copied across, but it should always reach back up to row 4 as it is copied down.

- **Field3, item3**—The field name is Measure, and the item is Actuals. This happens to be correct for January, but when you get to future months, you want the measure to switch to Budget. Change the hard-coded Actuals to point to B$5.

- **Field4, item4**—This is Years and 2024. I was almost ready to leave this one alone because it would be months before we have a new year. However, why not change 2024 to **YEAR($A$2)**?

The new formula is shown in Figure 15-19. Rather than a formula that is hard-coded to work with only one value, you have created a formula that can be copied throughout the data set.

	A	B	C	D	E	F	G	H	I	J	K	L	M
1	Actuals & Budget By Region												
2	Actuals Through July, 2024												
3													
4		Jan	Feb	Mar	Apr	May	Jun	Jul	Aug	Sep	Oct	Nov	Dec
5	Region	Actuals	Actuals	Actuals	Actuals	Actuals	Actuals	Actuals	Budget	Budget	Budget	Budget	Budget
6	Northeast	=GETPIVOTDATA("Revenue",UglyPivotTable!$A$3,"Region",$A6,"Date",MONTH(B$4),"Measure",B$5,"Years",YEAR($A$2))											
7	Southeast												
8	East Division Total	277,435	0	0	0	0	0	0	0	0	0	0	0

FIGURE 15-19 After being edited, the GetPivotData formula is ready for copying.

When you press Enter, you have exactly the same answer that you had before editing the formula. Compare this with the number you jotted down earlier to make sure.

The edited formula is as follows:

```
=GETPIVOTDATA("Revenue", UglyPivotTable!$A$3,"Region",$A6,
 "Date", MONTH(B$4),"Measure",B$5,"Years",YEAR($A$2))
```

Copy this formula to all the blank calculation cells in columns B:M. Do not copy the formula to column O yet. Now that you have real numbers in the report, you might have to adjust some column widths.

You can tweak the GetPivotData formula for the months to get the total budget. If you copy one formula to cell O6, you get a #REF! error because the word *Total* in cell O4 does not evaluate to a month. Edit the formula to the pairs of arguments for Month and Years. You still have an error.

> **Caution**   For GetPivotData to work, the number you are looking for must be in the pivot table.

Because the original pivot table had Measure as the third column field, there is no actual column for Budget total. Move the Measure field to be the first Column field, as shown in Figure 15-20.

	V	W	X	Y	Z	AA

Budget Total	Grand Total
3466000	5502194
1260000	1893104
3717000	5868665
5040000	33263565
9450000	15441017
4096000	6574609
7876000	11865026
34905000	80408180

PivotTable Fields

Drag fields between areas below:

FILTERS

COLUMNS
- Measure
- Years
- Date

ROWS
- Region

VALUES
- Sum of Revenue

FIGURE 15-20   Tweak the layout of the Column Labels fields so you have a Budget Total column.

When you return to the shell report, you find that the Total Budget formula in cell O6 is now working fine. Copy that formula down to the other blank data cells in column O (see Figure 15-21). Note with amazement that all the other formulas work, even though everything in the underlying pivot table moved.

	Total	
otal	**Budget**	**Var. %**
665	3,717,000	3.1%
017	3,717,000	176.2%
682	7,434,000	89.7%

FIGURE 15-21   After rearranging the pivot table, you have a working formula for Total Budget.

The formula in O6 is as follows:

```
=GETPIVOTDATA("Revenue",UglyPivotTable!$A$3,"Region",$A6,"Measure",O$5)
```

You now have a nicely formatted shell report that grabs values from a live pivot table. It certainly takes more time to set up this report for the first month that you have to produce it, but it will be a breeze to update the report in future months.

Updating the report in future months

In future months, you can update your report by following these steps:

1. Paste actuals for the new month just below the original data set. Because the original data set is a table, the table formatting automatically extends to the new rows. The pivot table source definition also extends.

2. Go to the pivot table. Click the Refresh button on the Options tab. The shape of the pivot table changes, but you do not care.

3. Go to the shell report. In real life, you are done, but to test it, enter a date in cell B2, such as **8/30/2024**. You will initially see a #REF error, but it will disappear after you add August actuals to the real data and refresh the pivot table.

> **Note** Every month, these three steps are the payoff to this chapter. The first time you update, the data for July changes from Budget to Actuals. Formulas throughout recalculate. You do not have to worry about re-creating formats, formulas, and so on.

This process is so simple that you will probably forget about the pain that you used to endure to create these monthly reports. The one risk is that a company reorganization will add new regions to the pivot table.

To be sure that your formulas are still working, add a small check section outside of the print range of the report. This formula in cell A22 checks to see if the budget total calculated in cell O19 matches the budget total back in the pivot table. Here is the formula:

```
=IF(GETPIVOTDATA("Revenue",UglyPivotTable!$A$3,"Measure","Budget")=$O$19,"", _
 "Caution!!! It appears that new regions have been added to the pivot table.
You might have to add new rows to this report for those regions."
```

In case the new region comes from a misspelling in the actuals, this formula checks the YTD actuals against the pivot table. Enter the following formula in cell A23:

```
=IF(SUMIF(B5:M5,"Actuals",B19:M19)=GETPIVOTDATA("Revenue",UglyPivotTable!$A$3, _
 "Measure","Actuals"),"","Caution!!! It appears that new regions have been _
 added to the pivot table. You might have to add new rows to this report for _
 those regions.")
```

Change the font color of both these cells to red. You do not even notice them down there until something goes wrong.

At one time, I thought that I would never write these words: GetPivotData is the greatest thing ever. How could we ever live without it?

Conclusion

There you have it—everything that we know about pivot tables. You should have all of the tools you need to turn ugly detailed data into beautiful summary reports.

Index

G

J–K

L

M

Q

R

S

Hear about it first.

Since 1984, Microsoft Press has helped IT professionals, developers, and home office users advance their technical skills and knowledge with books and learning resources.

Sign up today to deliver exclusive offers directly to your inbox.

- New products and announcements
- Free sample chapters
- Special promotions and discounts
- ... and more!

microsoftpressstore.com/newsletters

 Pearson

Plug into learning at

microsoftpressstore.com

The Microsoft Press Store by Pearson offers:

- Free U.S. shipping

- Buy an eBook, get three formats – Includes PDF, EPUB, and MOBI to use with your computer, tablet, and mobile devices

- Print & eBook Best Value Packs

- eBook Deal of the Week – Save up to 50% on featured title

- Newsletter – Be the first to hear about new releases, announcements, special offers, and more

- Register your book – Find companion files, errata, and product updates, plus receive a special coupon* to save on your next purchase

Discounts are applied to the list price of a product. Some products are not eligible to receive additional discounts, so your discount code may not be applied to all items in your cart. Discount codes cannot be applied to products that are already discounted, such as eBook Deal of the Week, eBooks that are part of a book + eBook pack, and products with special discounts applied as part of a promotional offering. Only one coupon can be used per order.